THE RISE OF CHRISTIANITY

THE RISE OF CHRISTIANITY

By

ERNEST WILLIAM BARNES

Sc.D. Camb., Hon. D.D. Aber. and Edin.
Hon. LL.D. Glas., F.R.S.
Bishop of Birmingham

LONGMANS, GREEN AND CO.

LONDON ◇ **NEW YORK** ◇ **TORONTO**

LONGMANS, GREEN AND CO. LTD.
6 & 7 CLIFFORD STREET, LONDON, W.1
NICOL ROAD, BOMBAY 1
17 CHITTARANJAN AVENUE, CALCUTTA 13
36A MOUNT ROAD, MADRAS 2

LONGMANS, GREEN AND CO. INC.
55 FIFTH AVENUE, NEW YORK 3

LONGMANS, GREEN AND CO.
215 VICTORIA STREET, TORONTO, 1

First published 1947
Second Impression 1947
Third Impression 1948

CODE NUMBER 42015

THIS BOOK IS PRODUCED IN
COMPLETE CONFORMITY WITH THE
AUTHORIZED ECONOMY STANDARDS

PRINTED IN GREAT BRITAIN
BY WESTERN PRINTING SERVICES LTD., BRISTOL

TO

MY SONS

The Volume, it is hoped, will be received as an attempt to illustrate the advantage derivable to the cause of religious and moral truth, from a free handling, in a becoming spirit, of subjects peculiarly liable to suffer by the repetition of conventional language, and from traditional methods of treatment.

Essays and Reviews, 1860

FOREWORD

MY Gifford Lectures at Aberdeen for the years 1927-9 were published in 1933 by the Cambridge University Press. The book bore the title, *Scientific Theory and Religion: the World described by Science and its Spiritual interpretation.* In the lectures I argued in favour of theism; but, in accordance with the limitations imposed by their founder, I "made no attempt to uphold the distinctive dogmas of Christianity or to subject them to critical analysis."

In the present book I examine the origin of Christianity from the point of view of one who accepts alike the methods of analytical scholarship and the postulate of the large-scale, or finite-scale, uniformity of nature which is fundamental in modern science. (We are ignorant as to whether such uniformities exist in the realm of infinitesimals.)

I have sought with firm impartiality to reach the truth, so far as it can be ascertained. Some, who have been brought up in the belief that there is a deadly opposition between science and scholarship on the one hand and Christianity on the other, may be surprised that the result of the search is not a spiritual desert: there emerges, I submit, a lovely and satisfying faith which contains the essentials of the great Christian tradition. The time has come when mistaken assumptions of the pre-scientific, pre-critical era must be repudiated. Christian doctrine, as shaped by the great masters of theology, gains by such repudiation: when free from crude imaginings it is seen to be worthy of the intellectual homage of religious men. I personally find that the early Christian story as it can now be told explains why men, gaining understanding from prayer and sacraments, have, since the gospel was first proclaimed, worshipped Jesus the Christ as divine. I, too, so worship him: I have been at pains that the fact should not affect my historical inquiry.

The original authorities of primary importance which throw light upon the rise of Christianity are comparatively few: detailed references to them, together with translated extracts of the most important passages, are given in the present work.

But the modern literature based upon ancient evidence is enormous. Had I attempted anything like an adequate bibliography of modern critical enquiries I should have vastly increased the size of my book, and it has seemed better to avoid in the text all mention of individual modern scholars. Those familiar with the subject will readily recognize the groups of scholars to whose work I attach especial importance. At the end of this book, immediately before the Index, I give a short list of modern books, written in English, which may be consulted.

The present volume is intended for those interested in the Christian faith who desire an account of its origin which shall be, so far as is possible, without bias. Many such cannot effectively use any language other than English. This book, in consequence, demands no wider knowledge.

To my wife I am indebted for constant advice and encouragement. With my elder son I have had discussions as to passages in ancient authors; and he has made a number of the translations which are used. My secretary, Miss N. M. V. Owen, has been indefatigable in the help which she has given me: I owe much to her patience and care.

Reading for this book lightened the burden of nearly a decade of diocesan routine: in the writing of it I have found some relief from the anxieties and miseries of war.

E. W. B.

Bishop's Croft
   Birmingham, 17
      April 1945

FOREWORD TO THE THIRD IMPRESSION

IN the second impression of this book a few misprints and mistakes were corrected. But few specific errors had been mentioned even in hostile reviews. A number of these criticized the bibliography as partial to antiquated authors and ideas. My critics failed to notice that the brief list of books cited is for readers, knowing only English, who may wish to extend their knowledge of the subject and, most probably, to contrast my conclusions with an earlier type of apologetic. I make no reference to authorities whose works are only available in French or German, nor do I mention recent English linguistic enquiries which I find unconvincing. Some analytical work produced on the Continent during the last fifteen years seems to me both more sound in its judgment and more free from inhibitions than that which has gained esteem in England.

Complaint has been made that readers can hardly find in the book such words as Trinity, Incarnation, and supernatural. None of these words occurs in the New Testament, and they belong to theology rather than to history.

The postulate of the finite-scale uniformity of nature has been assailed by a number of theologians but, so far as I have observed, by no competent man of science. The theologians have written with a conviction which is not always according to knowledge.

E. W. B.

November 1947

CONTENTS

CHAPTER I

THE REMOTE BACKGROUND OF CHRISTIANITY

PAGE

1. The beginning of man 1
2. Palaeolithic man 1
3. Neolithic man 2
4. The Bronze Age 3
5. Early burials 4
6. The Sumerians 4
7. Egypt 5
8. Progress and decay: Egypt and Babylonia . . 6
9. The religions of Mesopotamia and Egypt . . . 6
10. Egyptian religion 7
11. Sumerian-Semitic religion 8
12. Akhenaten 9
13. Syria in the time of Moses 10
14. Early Hebrew history 11
15. Moses and the Hebrew invasion of Palestine . . 11
16. The kingdoms of Israel and Judah 12
17. Assyria 12
18. Persia 13
19. The Persian empire 14
20. The Jews under Persian rule 15
21. The formation of the Old Testament . . . 15
22. The worship of Jehovah 17
23. The Hebrew prophets 17
24. The background of ethical monotheism . . . 18
25. Zoroaster 18
26. The originality of the Hebrew prophets . . . 19

CHAPTER II

THE MEDITERRANEAN WORLD

I. The Eastern Mediterranean

27. Crete 21
28. Mycenaean civilization 21

PAGE

29. The Greeks 22
30. Greek science and philosophy 22
31. Greek fertility and its exhaustion 24
32. Greek religion and morality 24
33. Alexander the Great 25
34. Hellenistic civilization 25
35. Palestine after Alexander 26
36. The Maccabaean revolt 27
37. Judaea, Rome and Herod 28
38. The influence of Greece on Judaism 29
39. The Apocrypha 30
40. The Septuagint 30
41. The influence of Greece on Christianity . . . 31
42. The *Logos* doctrine 32
43. Christianity and Greek culture 33
44. Judaism in the time of Christ 34
45. The pharisees 35
46. The sadducees 36
47. The pharisees and Christianity 36
48. Judaism and Jewish sects 37

II. *The Western Mediterranean*

49. The Etruscans 38
50. The Etruscan legacy to Rome 39
51. The Carthaginians 39
52. The sources of Carthaginian power 40
53. The struggle with Rome 41
54. Carthaginian culture 41
55. Carthaginian religion 42
56. The Punic stock 42
57. The Romans 43
58. The Roman character 44
59. The winning of world control 44
60. The price of victory 45
61. Augustus and the Julio-Claudians 46
62. Roman religion 47
63. The divine element in man 48
64. Roman religion and Christianity 48

CHAPTER III

THE MYSTERY-RELIGIONS

PAGE

65. The nature of a mystery-religion 50
66. The mysteries were sacramental 52
67. Orphism and its origin 53
68. Its development 54
69. The Eleusinian mysteries 54
70. The religion of the Great Mother: Cybele and Attis . 55
71. The persistence of the Cybele-Attis rites in Rome . 56
72. Isis and Osiris 57
73. Isis worship in the early Christian era . . . 57
74. Mithra 58
75. The Mithra legend 58
76. The progress of Mithraism in the Christian era . . 60

CHAPTER IV

MIRACLES

77. The people among whom Christianity spread . . 62
78. Their government 62
79. Their social condition and new hope . . . 63
80. Their level of education 63
81. Christianity and the new barbarism . . . 64
82. A superstitious world 65
83. The orderly universe of modern science . . . 66
84. The miraculous in the New Testament . . . 67

CHAPTER V

THE BIRTH AND ORIGIN OF JESUS

85. Stories connected with the birth of Jesus . . . 68
86. Features common to *Matthew* and *Luke* . . . 69
87. Contrasts between *Matthew* and *Luke* . . . 71
88. The ancestry of Jesus 72
89. The descent from David 73

PAGE

90. The date of the birth of Jesus 74
91. The census of Quirinius 74
92. Flavius Josephus and his writings 75
93. At what age did Jesus begin his public ministry . . 76
94. His age according to the fourth evangelist . . . 78
95. The birthday of Jesus 79
96. Jesus the Nazarene 80
97. Tiberias 81
98. Nazareth 81
99. Greek culture and the boy Jesus 82

CHAPTER VI

JESUS, SON OF GOD

100. *Mark* not a primitive gospel 84
101. The Son of God in *Mark* 84
102. The centurion's homage 85
103. The family of Jesus in *Mark* 85
104. The virgin birth of Jesus 87
105. The divine and the human in ancient thought . . 88
106. The biological possibility of a virgin birth . . 88
107. The virgin birth as a source of calumny . . 89
108. The growth of early Christian speculation as to Jesus . 89
109. Speculation in the *Epistle to the Hebrews* . . 90
110. A priest after the order of Melchizedek . . 91
111. The Son of God of the *Apocalypse* . . . 92
112. The Son of God as a solar deity . . . 93
113. The Son of God as the *Logos* . . . 94
114. Comparison and conclusion 96

CHAPTER VII

THE GOSPELS

115. The synoptic problem 98
116. The solution of the synoptic problem . . 99
117. The nature of the arguments 100
118. The priority of *Mark* 101

PAGE

119. The Second Source, or Q 101
120. The problem of doublets 102
121. Material peculiar to *Matthew* or *Luke* 103
122. Old Testament quotations 104
123. Authorship and date of the synoptic gospels . . 105
124. The testimony of Papias 105
125. The value of the Papias testimony 106
126. The gospel of *Mark* 107
127. The personality of *Mark* 108
128. The date and place of origin of the second gospel . 109
129. *Luke* 110
130. Editorial changes: the story of the ascension of Jesus . 111
131. The date of the third gospel and *Acts* . . . 111
132. The authorship of the third gospel and *Acts* . . 113
133. *Matthew* 117
134. The fourth gospel 118
135. Symbolic teaching rather than history . . . 119
136. The author's claim to be an eye-witness . . . 122
137. Arguments against the apostolic authorship of the fourth
  gospel 123

CHAPTER VIII

JESUS AND HIS TEACHING

138. The central fact of Christianity 125
139. Jesus no myth 126
140. Apollonius of Tyana 126
141. The village life 126
142. The maturity of Jesus 127
143. The celibacy of Jesus 128
144. Jesus in relation to God 129
145. The attitude of Jesus to children and their elders . 130
146. The exaggerations and the humour of Jesus . . 130
147. The influence of a peasant community . . . 132
148. Jesus and the knowledge of God 133
149. The kingdom of God 134
150. Jewish hopes and their influence 135
151. Jesus and the kingdom 136
152. Evidence that Jesus shared crude popular expectations . 136

PAGE

153. Evidence that Jesus thought of the kingdom as inward
     and spiritual 137
154. The life to come 139
155. The Great Assize 141
156. The communion of Jesus with God 142
157. The length of the ministry of Jesus 144
158. The ministry in Galilee—success or failure? . . 146

CHAPTER IX

PASSION WEEK

159. The journey to Jerusalem 149
160. The date of the Last Supper 150
161. The arrest of Jesus 154
162. The Jewish trial of Jesus 157
163. The trial before Pilate 158
164. The crucifixion of Jesus 160
165. The essentials of the resurrection faith . . . 164
166. The burial of Jesus 166
167. The Marcan story of the empty tomb . . . 167
168. The resurrection according to *Matthew* and *Luke* . . 168
169. The resurrection according to the fourth gospel . . 169
170. The Emmaus story 170
171. The last chapter of the fourth gospel 172
172. The resurrection in the *First Epistle to the Corinthians* . 172
173. The survival of Christianity 173
174. The ascension 175

CHAPTER X

PETER

175. Peter 179
176. Peter and the resurrection of Jesus 180
177. Peter and the early church 180
178. Peter's end 181
179. Peter a married man 182
180. Was Paul married? 182
181. The so-called primacy of Peter 183
182. The death of Peter. Was he ever in Rome? . . 185

CHAPTER XI

THE BOOKS ASCRIBED TO PETER

		PAGE
183.	Authorship and ascription	189
184.	The *First Epistle of Peter*	189
185.	The *Second Epistle of Peter*	190
186.	The transfiguration of Jesus	191
187.	The *Apocalypse of Peter*	192
188.	The *Gospel of Peter*	193
189.	The *Acts of Peter*	194

CHAPTER XII

PAUL

190.	Paul and other pioneers	195
191.	Evidences for Paul's career	195
192.	Paul's origin and circumstances	196
193.	Tarsus	197
194.	Paul's education	198
195.	Paul's civic status	198
196.	Paul's religious changes	199
197.	Paul's physical characteristics	200
198.	The chronology of Paul's early life	201
199.	The conversion of Paul	201
200.	The first Christian years	203
201.	Paul in Asia Minor	204
202.	Paul in Europe	205
203.	The travelling missionary	206
204.	Paul at Athens	206
205.	Corinth and Gallio	208
206.	Ephesus and Apollos	209
207.	The years at Ephesus	209
208.	From Asia Minor to Jerusalem	210
209.	Paul in custody	212
210.	Paul before Felix and Festus	213
211.	The journey to Rome	214
212.	Paul in Rome	214
213.	Paul's end	215

CHAPTER XIII

THE BOOKS ASCRIBED TO PAUL

PAGE

214. The *Epistle to the Hebrews* 217
215. The pastoral epistles 217
216. Their date 218
217. The *Epistle to the Ephesians* 219
218. The witness of the Apostolic Fathers 220
219. The nine "genuine" epistles 222
220. Tests of authorship 222
221. The two *Epistles to the Thessalonians* . . . 223
222. The two *Epistles to the Corinthians* 225
223. The *First Epistle to the Corinthians* 226
224. Is the *First Epistle to the Corinthians* composite? . . 227
225. A tract on the resurrection? 228
226. Other documents included in the epistle . . . 229
227. The *Second Epistle to the Corinthians* 230
228. The *Epistle to the Galatians* 231
229. Paul and Judaism 232
230. The invective against the Law 233
231. Paul and humanism 235
232. The *Epistle to the Romans* 236
233. Christian morality 237
234. Christians and their reputation 237
235. Baptism into the death of Christ 238
236. The two Adams 239
237. Personal information as to Paul in *Romans* . . . 240
238. The epistles of the captivity 241
239. The *Epistle to the Colossians* 241
240. Bondage to "elementals" 241
241. The "pleroma" in Christ 242
242. The *Epistle to the Philippians* 243
243. The *Epistle to Philemon* 244

CHAPTER XIV

EARLY CHRISTIAN WRITINGS OUTSIDE THE NEW TESTAMENT

244. The *Didache* 246
245. The discarding of the *Didache* . . . 247

PAGE

246. The character of the *Didache* 248
247. The *Didache* and the synoptic gospels . . . 249
248. "The Two Ways" 250
249. The eucharist in the *Didache* 250
250. The chief eucharistic prayers of the *Didache* . . 251
251. Primitive church order 253
252. The *First Epistle of Clement* to the Corinthians . . 253
253. The mental background of Clement 255
254. The *Second Epistle of Clement* 256
255. The *Epistle of Barnabas* 256
256. The *Shepherd of Hermas* 258
257. The social position of Christians when Hermas wrote . 259
258. Hermas on sin after baptism 259
259. The date of the *Shepherd of Hermas* 260
260. The letters attributed to Ignatius 260
261. The martyrdom of Ignatius 261
262. The different versions of the Ignatian letters . . 261
263. The shorter version of the Greek letters is the original . 262
264. Arguments in favour of a late date for the Ignatian letters 263
265. Writings relating to Polycarp 264
266. Conclusion 266

CHAPTER XV

BAPTISM

267. John the Baptist in the synoptic gospels . . . 267
268. The synoptic record of the Baptist's preaching . . 268
269. The baptism of Jesus in the fourth gospel . . . 269
270. The implications of John's baptism 269
271. Josephus and John the Baptist 271
272. Jesus and baptism 271
273. The growth of the practice of baptism . . . 272
274. Baptism with the Holy Spirit 273
275. The growth of the theology of baptism . . . 274
276. Baptism, ancient and modern 275
277. Infant baptism 277
278. Baptism in "living" water 277
279. Pauline or pseudo-Pauline theories 278
280. Baptism for the dead 279
281. Sin after baptism 279

CHAPTER XVI

THE EUCHARIST

                                                                    PAGE
282. Modern conclusions as to the eucharist   .   .   . 281
283. The "breaking of bread"   282
284. The institution of the eucharist   283
285. The Last Supper according to the *First Epistle to the
         Corinthians*   284
286. The Last Supper according to *Mark* 285
287. The Last Supper according to *Matthew*   .   .   . 286
288. The Last Supper according to *Luke* 286
289. The Last Supper and a new covenant   .   .   . 288
290. The Last Supper and the fourth gospel   .   .   . 289
291. The general conclusion 290
292. The relative importance of baptism and the eucharist in
         the early church   291
293. Eucharistic theology in the fourth gospel   .   .   . 291
294. Eucharistic teaching in the eleventh chapter of the *First
         Epistle to the Corinthians*   292
295. Eucharistic teaching in the tenth chapter of the *First
         Epistle to the Corinthians*   293
296. Christianity and pagan sacrifices   294
297. The Christian refusal of compromise 295

CHAPTER XVII

THE CHRISTIAN MOVEMENT AND THE ROMAN EMPIRE

298. Christianity, socialist, pacifist, inter-nationalist   .   . 297
299. Christians and taxation 298
300. Christian pacifism 299
301. Christians and the *genius* of the emperor   .   .   . 300
302. Christianity and the rich 301
303. Official Christian teaching as to citizenship   .   . 302
304. Early Christianity in non-Christian writers   .   . 304
305. The witness of Josephus 304
306. Tacitus   305
307. Pliny 307
308. Imperial methods of repression of the Christians .   . 309
309. The Christian movement as Pliny saw it   .   .   . 310

PAGE

310. Pagan and Christian writings contrasted . . . 311
311. Suetonius 311
312. The dearth of second-century historians . . . 312
313. A possible cause 313
314. The *Meditations* of Marcus Aurelius 314
315. Marcus Aurelius and the Christians 314

CHAPTER XVIII

THE EARLY APOLOGISTS

316. The general outlook of the second-century apologists . 316
317. Quadratus 317
318. Aristides 317
319. Justin Martyr 319
320. Justin and Christian history 322
321. Justin and other faiths 322
322. Justin and Christian morality 324
323. Justin's method of argument 324
324. Early Christian worship as described by Justin . . 325
325. Justin and the eucharist 326
326. Justin's eucharistic theology 327
327. Sunday worship 328
328. Justin and the empire: his end 329
329. Athenagoras 330
330. Celsus 331
331. Christians and military service 333
332. Origen's reply to Celsus 333
333. Christianity after Origen 334
334. The strange story and the final questions . . . 336

NOTE

IN quotations from the Bible the revised version has been used unless special circumstances seemed to call for a different translation.

Some dates given are only approximate, though it has not always seemed necessary to state the fact explicitly.

Throughout this book reference is made to each gospel by the name *in italics* of its reputed author: thus *Matthew* stands for the *Gospel according to Matthew*. I also refer to the actual author of the gospel in the same way. Thus *Matthew* may equally refer to the man who wrote the first gospel. I do not assume that he was the apostle Matthew, or that *Luke* was the physician who accompanied Paul at various times during his missionary journeys.

No confusion arises if we thus use the same noun in referring to a gospel and its author; but it is important to distinguish between the actual and the reputed author. Luke the physician is the reputed author of the third gospel: its actual author was *Luke* who, as will be seen, probably wrote at the end of the first century of our era and had never personally known Paul.

CHAPTER I

THE REMOTE BACKGROUND OF CHRISTIANITY

AT the dawn of history we find in the Near East not merely the rudiments but the firm foundations of two great civilizations, which were destined to create, as it were, the cradle of Christianity. One of these developed in the lower reaches of the Tigris and Euphrates rivers, the other in the valley and Delta of the Nile. Our knowledge of these civilizations begins to lose the indefiniteness of pre-history in the fifth millennium before Christ. For many thousands of years before that time men in these fertile areas must have struggled to understand and to conquer nature, to secure safety from wild beasts and human enemies, and to gain the comforts and pleasures of civilized life.

1. The beginning of man

Only during the present century has the immense antiquity of man become an accepted fact in popular thought. It is now generally realized that men of science suggest that the sequence of changes, in some group of higher apes, which gradually led to the production of a group or groups of sub-men may have occurred from one to three million years ago. Changes leading to sub-human forms probably took place repeatedly. Primitive human types will have emerged and flourished and vanished. Crude speech and low human cunning will have given to these early quasi-human stocks a precarious existence, a little higher than that of other mammals. Finally, one type, or set of closely allied types, must have secured a firm foothold on the earth: ancestral forms containing the promise of modern man had arrived.

2. Palaeolithic man

Then an incredibly slow advance began. Men lived in groups: the primitive herd-instinct still remains strong. Customs and rules of group-life sprang up. Palaeolithic man gradually began to use roughly shaped flints as weapons and simple tools. His weapons made him a more successful hunter of animals used as food. He learned—though we know not when—how to make and control fire. Towards the end of the long palaeolithic era the dog was trained. Some races of men, living where the climate was harsh, learned to sew hides. Others tamed the horse. Some made bows and arrows. Highly significant progress showed itself when the hunter became herdsman.

Personal adornment began fairly early: we find at a remote period necklaces and bracelets of teeth and shells. Some later palaeolithic savages have left memorials, as in the Altamira cave in Spain, which show a marvellous feeling for design and a skill as sure as that of Greek vase-painters of two and a half millennia ago. As writing was undiscovered, we know nothing of the religion of these people. But some buried their dead after smearing the body with red iron-oxide, for what reason we cannot say: possibly they intended a suggestion of immortality—the red blood is the life.

How long is it since man began the palaeolithic progress which finally reached such a stage? We do not know: a plausible answer would be that half a million years separate us from that beginning of the early palaeolithic era when man first chipped flints. The creation of the artificial flint industry was as significant as any later industrial revolution.

The progress of man continued, doubtless very unevenly in different parts of the earth. We may assume that from time to time human groups of special mental capacity will have appeared. At intervals advance will have been rapid: then misfortune or adverse circumstances will have wiped it out.

3. Neolithic man

In the end, at an epoch relatively near to our own time, a noteworthy advance somewhat suddenly showed itself. Possibly after a gap caused by adverse climatic conditions, which brought the old culture to an end and allowed the intrusion of a more advanced type, the neolithic age arrived. Flints were finely chipped and polished, so as to make tools with a good cutting edge. From baked clay rough pots were made: the art of glazing earthenware was discovered. We measure progress by these outstanding discoveries because used tools and pottery fragments survive, while other witnesses to primitive civilization have largely perished. But concurrent with the advent of the neolithic age came the making of baskets woven of reeds or of flexible tree-shoots, the weaving of cloth, the breeding of cattle and, above all, agriculture, the sowing and reaping of grain. When the herdsman became a tiller of the soil, another most significant stage of human progress was reached.

All such developments were, of course, prehistoric. We are probably wrong if we think of them as having taken shape but a few thousand years before written records began. The high degree of technical knowledge and practice which meets us at the dawn of history indicates that, at any rate in certain favoured regions, neolithic civilization was of long standing. We may yet discover some part of the world where by a continuous development palaeolithic civilization advanced to neolithic: possibly—though the estimate is an almost pure guess—such a progress took place thirty or forty thousand years ago. But for the present we must be content to say that neolithic civilization showed itself in Egypt somewhat suddenly at a time which experts calculate to have been about 20,000 B.C.: since then Egyptian culture has been continuous, though by no means always progressive. In Crete the coming of neolithic civilization has been put at 14,000 B.C., and in western Europe some five thousand years later.

4. The Bronze Age

Without any sudden break neolithic civilization became in certain areas a metal-using culture. The art of smelting copper was discovered. Metal tools and weapons could for the first time be made. Then it was found that, from an alloy of copper and tin, bronze could be made. Bronze is more useful than copper because it is harder, stronger and more durable. Such developments, of course, could only take place where the necessary ores existed on the surface of the earth. But, even though the materials for smelting were at hand, the production of copper first and then that of bronze were two noteworthy achievements. It need hardly be emphasized that a people whose weapons and tools were of bronze was obviously at a great advantage in the struggle for existence. There is good evidence that in the fifth millennium B.C., before the art of writing was discovered, neolithic civilization had passed into the copper age alike in Egypt and in Mesopotamia. Bronze objects appear about 3500 B.C. Though iron weapons did not apparently come into use before 1500 B.C., necklaces with gold and iron beads have been found in Egyptian tombs which must almost certainly be dated before 4000 B.C.

5. Early burials

In similar tombs, excavated in desert sand, on the edge of the fertile land above the high-water mark of the Nile, we find significant burials. The dead man lies buried knees to chin and hands to face: as he grew in his mother's womb, so he lies in the womb of mother earth. His earthly journey over, he waits to begin another; and around him are placed jars containing the food, together with the tools and weapons, that he may need. With a woman were buried ornaments, bead necklaces and even eye-paint. The certainty of an after-life and the hope of a somewhat mundane immortality had apparently become central in man's religious outlook.

6. The Sumerians

Enough has now been said to show that we cannot point to a definite epoch as the beginning of modern civilization. But possibly the most significant movement occurred when, probably at the end of the fifth millennium before Christ, or even earlier, the Sumerians, coming from somewhere in Central Asia, established themselves in the lower reaches of the Tigris-Euphrates valley. It may well be that they had discovered the art of writing, inasmuch as it shows itself in primitive forms about the time of their advent. Opinions differ as to the spread of this supremely important discovery; but it is at least possible that the linear pictographic writing of the Sumerians was introduced into Egypt before 3500 B.C. By this date Sumerian civilization was already mature: some would say that it was as mature as that of western Europe in the eighteenth century of our era.

The Sumerians were not Semites: they seem to have imposed themselves upon earlier Semitic immigrants from Arabia. They were not Aryans, for they did not speak an Indo-European language. Their language was agglutinative, as we know, because it remained in use, especially in liturgical use, centuries after their political power had passed away. They seem to have been a humane, though forceful, people with imaginative capacity and great powers of organization. Religion occupied a quite astonishingly important place in their lives. Their temples were their great public buildings: their liturgies were more valued than records of secular history. They established a vast irrigation system in Mesopotamia: from the fertility of the soil there arose a numerous people who built splendid cities with luxuriant gardens and magnificent temples, palaces and libraries. The memory of this civilization remained in stories of the garden of Eden and the tower of Babel, stories which were written in the book of *Genesis* some two thousand years after the Sumerians had lost their hold on Mesopotamia.

7. Egypt

When the newly arrived Sumerians were using their knowledge and skill in the Tigris-Euphrates valley, significant parallel developments, the discovery of writing and vast irrigation enterprises, seem to have taken place in Egypt. In fact, the two alluvial civilizations of the Tigris-Euphrates and the Nile were not isolated from one another. Between them trade routes must from time immemorial have gone, as they go to-day, to the north of the Arabian desert, through the coastal area of Palestine, and across the isthmus of Suez.

But, if the first stimulus towards a more advanced culture came with the immigration of the Sumerians into Babylonia, political unity was more rapidly obtained in Egypt. In Mesopotamia, throughout the fourth millennium before Christ, different cities rose to eminence and, after a brief spell of glory, lost their pride of place. In the end Sumerian became subject to Semite; yet his religious influence remained in spite of political subordination. In Egypt the population was more homogeneous; and, in the absence of internal turmoil, the Pharaohs of the early dynasties were able to create a highly organized state. In it were produced works of art, furniture, statues, jewellery, etc., of singular beauty, while the great monuments known as the pyramids remain to-day one of the wonders of the world.

The pyramid-builders and, in particular, Khufu, Khafre and

Menkaure rank among the great rulers of world-history: they lived about 3100–2950 B.C., though dates are doubtful.

8. Progress and decay: Egypt and Babylonia

But among men steady progress is rarely of long duration. After the great era of the pyramids came a period of disorder in Egypt, from which practically no records remain. Then, under the sovereigns of what is called the twelfth dynasty, who flourished before and after 2050 B.C., the most brilliant period of Egyptian civilization began. About 2100 B.C., though possibly several centuries later, the Semitic Babylonian empire reached its zenith under Hammurabi, whose great Code of Laws, found at Susa and now in the Louvre at Paris, shows the high degree of civilization attained many centuries before Moses.

The Babylonian empire finally collapsed about 1750 B.C. under an attack by the Kassites, Aryan invaders from the mountains of western Persia. For some six hundred years they ruled; but apparently under these semi-barbarous conquerors the old civilization persisted: it was submerged but not destroyed. Egypt, after the splendour of the twelfth dynasty, suffered a like disaster. The country was overrun by the Hyksos, probably Semitic invaders who broke through the isthmus of Suez about 1800 B.C. Not until 1580 B.C. were they expelled. But Egyptian civilization had the strength and toughness which enabled it to survive these hated invaders.

Such a brief sketch shows how ancient were the civilizations of Egypt and Mesopotamia. They were splendid in their monuments and in their art, highly developed in their social organization, humane in their laws. In each country the culture of 2000 B.C. was far more advanced than that of the Hebrews a thousand years later in the days of king Solomon. A study of the early books of the Bible leaves us surprised that such culture should have preceded the semi-mythical era of the Hebrew patriarchs. But readers of the Bible must bear in mind that the sojourn of the Hebrews in Egypt and their exodus from that country were, if historical, comparatively late events in the long and splendid, though chequered, history of Egypt.

9. The religions of Mesopotamia and Egypt

In the first half of the nineteenth century of our era, a

number of European scholars succeeded in deciphering Egyptian hieroglyphics. They were aided by the discovery of the Rosetta stone, bearing an inscription three times repeated: one repetition is in hieroglyphic and one in Greek. The record of their success is a wonderful story of enthusiasm and ingenuity. A little later other scholars succeeded in the even more difficult task of deciphering the cuneiform inscriptions of Mesopotamia, where extensive libraries of such inscriptions on baked bricks were excavated by a succession of explorers. In consequence, we have now an extensive knowledge of both Egyptian and Sumerian-Semitic religion. Care has to be taken lest beliefs and practices of later centuries are attributed to early times. But in each area religion was so woven into the texture of living that it changed but little: its hold on each people was probably the main cause of the persistent strength of that people's culture.

Yet the two religions were remarkably different. There were surface similarities. Each was polytheistic. There were nature gods and goddesses, the sun, the moon, a goddess of fertility, and so forth. Each city or region appears to have had its own deity; and with political amalgamations the pantheon increased. In each country a deity's importance grew as his city conquered its neighbours. In each country national and civic life was centred on the temples, built of brick in Mesopotamia and of stone in Egypt. The civilizations resembled one another in that there was the closest association between administrative officials and temple worship. But beneath such similarities there were profound differences of outlook.

10. Egyptian religion

Egyptian religion appears to have been totemistic in origin. Certain animals were sacred in particular regions and the local god was represented in the form of the sacred animal, or in human form with the head of the totem species. In worship men sought to propitiate the god, to secure his good-will and help. He was thought to demand from his servants correct ritual even more than a moral life.

Always the Egyptian's thoughts turned to the life after death; and, from the twelfth dynasty onwards, the attaining of safety and happiness in the world to come was an obsession. Hence came the invocations to Osiris, the great lord of the dead, with whom every dead person was somehow identified. We have also the mummified body, the elaborate tomb furnished with all that the dead man might need, and the texts which everywhere surrounded him. These texts equipped the dead man with replies to any questions that might be asked on his arrival in the next world. They were magical, so powerfully magical that they compelled even the divine judges of that world to give the dead man, whatever his misdeeds on earth, a favourable verdict.

Belief in the power of the right word or phrase, in the might of a great name, recurs throughout ancient religion. It had an important place in Egyptian medicine. We find it not obscurely in early Christianity; but one may doubt if acceptance of this sort of magic was ever so extravagant as in Egyptian religion. With it went a tendency on the part of the Egyptian in worship to boast of his good deeds: in the presence of his gods he was no miserable sinner. Through three thousand years of Egyptian history the faith which we have been describing seems to have maintained in essentials its hold: it lasted, in fact, until Christianity sapped its strength in the third and fourth centuries of our era.

During this long period there were, of course, changes in religious belief and in its expression. But they seem to have been remarkably few and, with one exception, to have been assimilated with supreme ease, for the sufficient reason that the Egyptian was able to hold contradictory beliefs without mental disquiet. In our own era the spectacle is familiar of men maintaining old beliefs while accepting a contradictory outlook created by the development of science and critical scholarship; but they only succeed by using a special technique of evasive statement. The Egyptian apparently felt no such need: religious contradictions did not worry him.

11. Sumerian-Semitic religion

Sumerian-Semitic religion was, speaking generally, of a finer type than Egyptian. Worship was, of course, designed to secure the aid of the gods; and liturgical correctness was deemed important. But in the prayers there were humility and penitence: the need for righteousness was not forgotten. There was little, if any, preoccupation with life after death: religion gave unity, strength and comfort as men made the best of this world with its joys and sorrows and struggles. Egyptian magic was replaced in Mesopotamia by a belief in astrology and divination. The stars in their courses fought for or against men: hence from Babylonia came the first elements of astronomy and, in particular, though not until after the fall of Nineveh, the eighteen-year cycle for eclipses. There was, moreover, a conviction in Babylonia that examination of the liver of a sacrificial victim would reveal the course of events. From Mesopotamia the belief passed to Asia Minor and, carried by the Etruscans, to Italy and Rome.

12. Akhenaten

The most significant event in the long history of Egyptian religion was its attempted reform about the year 1370 B.C. by Amenhotep IV. He repudiated the existing pantheon with its dominant deity Amon-Ra: he moved his court from Thebes, where Amon-Ra's priesthood was all-powerful, to a new capital, Akhetaten, nearly three hundred miles below Thebes; and he changed his own name to Akhenaten (Ikhnaton). These changes were consequent on his development of what was apparently a form of ethical theism. His god was pictured by the sun's disc, from which came rays, all ending in a helping hand. Thus he made it clear that to him God was one, and God was good.

Such changes were, of course, abhorrent to Egyptian religious conservatism. They led to strife at home and to military weakness abroad, especially in Syria. Akhenaten died young; and his capital was forsaken. It is now the village of Tell el-Amarna; and the discovery there of the Foreign Office archives of Akhenaten in the year A.D. 1887 gave us the famous Amarna letters. These letters have thrown a flood of light on conditions in Syria and Palestine in the fourteenth century before Christ, probably at least a hundred years before Moses.

Among the transient successors of Akhenaten was Tutankhamen. He, too, died young; but as the figurehead of religious reaction he was dear to the priests, and they buried him magnificently. His tomb in the Valley of the Kings near Thebes was discovered, almost intact, in A.D. 1922. The

magnificence of the furniture of the tomb, the beauty of design
and the skill in workmanship, reveal to all who see it the high
level of culture reached in Egypt some 3,300 years ago.

13. Syria in the time of Moses

In the century which followed Akhenaten, a new dynasty in
Egypt set out to recover Palestine and Syria. These two lands
were menaced by the Hittite empire, with its capital at Boghaz
Keui in the centre of Asia Minor. Cuneiform clay tablets discovered early in the present century among the ruins on this
site confirm records found in Egypt; and it appears that, about
the year 1272 B.C., Egyptians and Hittites, after severe fighting,
made a treaty of peace. By it Palestine was secured to Egypt;
but the war had clearly ended in a sort of stalemate. The
history of the two empires during the next half-century indicates
that each had spent its strength.

About this time, moreover, great movements were taking
place in the lands to the north of Asia Minor and Greece. The
military value of iron had been discovered; and invaders using
iron swords overwhelmed alike the old Mycenaean civilization
of Greece (see § 28) and the Hittite empire. About the year
1240 B.C. a great horde of invaders from the north swept down
through Palestine, leaving anarchy behind them. They were
repulsed at the gate of Egypt; but a similar horde swept down
about the year 1192 B.C. They, too, seem to have been repulsed;
but evidently the Levant was in a ferment. During this period
of turmoil, apparently, the Trojan war took place: did it
represent an attempt of the Mycenaeans, driven from Greece,
to settle in western Asia Minor?

At this time, also, the Philistines, non-Semitic invaders from
Crete, or more probably from Caria on the mainland of Asia
Minor near Crete, effected a settlement on the sea-coast of
Palestine. There they maintained themselves; and to the land
in which they settled they were destined to give their name.
More important—supremely important in the religious history
of mankind—was the fact that at this time of unrest a group of
Hebrew tribes, Israel, Edom, Moab, Ammon, emerged from
the Arabian desert and passed, probably from the south, into
"the promised land."

14. Early Hebrew history

From the foregoing brief survey it is clear that history, as we can now reconstruct it from the surviving archives (some of them contemporary) of the Egyptian, Hittite and Babylonian empires, differs markedly from that given in the Old Testament. In the Biblical narratives the patriarchs move in a land of spacious quiet, whereas, in fact, Syria and Palestine were restless frontier dependencies of Egypt, seething with political intrigue and sedition. No trace can be found in Egyptian history either of Joseph or of that story of the exodus, which began with the ten plagues of Egypt and ended with the miracle of the crossing of the Red Sea and the destruction of Pharaoh's army.

Moreover, the elaborate narrative of a first repulse, of the forty years' preparation in the desert, and of the final invasion of Palestine, must be legend transmuted into history: it probably assumed its present form in the fifth century before Christ, after the exile of the Jews in Babylonia. The narratives of the books of *Genesis* and *Exodus* doubtless contain much early material; but it had probably been worked over again and again before it assumed its present form. These narratives are written with a simple earnestness which reflects the pride and thankfulness of the final editors. The narratives were, as the New Testament makes clear, an essential part of the national consciousness of the Jews in the time of Christ. But of them little can be retained as exact history.

15. Moses and the Hebrew invasion of Palestine

Moses was certainly believed in later ages to have been a religious leader of outstanding eminence. We have no adequate reason to distrust the tradition. But he may also have been a Semite of the north Arabian desert who, by reason of a supple intelligence coupled with rare spiritual gifts, reached in Egypt an influential administrative position and then, returning to his tribe, organized about the year 1230 B.C. a descent on the settled lands of what was afterwards Judaea. There will have been associated with the invasion, as we have said, a group of tribes, all speaking practically the same language; but, while Edomites remained in the half-desert lands of the south, and Moabites and Ammonites in the half-desert lands to the east of the Dead Sea and the Jordan, the Israelites must gradually have fought their way through the plain of Esdraelon to Galilee. The whole number of invaders will have been small, and their conquests very gradual. The Philistines, simultaneous invaders from the sea, were never conquered; and the rich cities of Phoenicia, in particular Tyre and Sidon, seem to have been regarded with admiring awe as unassailable. After a couple of centuries of gradually lessening anarchy, the conquests were consolidated under David who, beginning as a successful bandit chief in southern Judaea, became king about the year 1010 B.C.

18. The kingdoms of Israel and Judah

It was the weakness of Egypt which allowed David to create his kingdom. That kingdom lasted but a short time. On the death of his son, Solomon, the Aramaeans appear to have made Damascus the centre of a strong confederacy, and the Hebrew groups of Judah and Israel fell apart. In connection with the Aramaean victories, it is worthy of notice that Aramaic had become the speech of Palestine in the time of Jesus. It was the language which Jesus habitually used. But many centuries previously it had been the language of diplomacy in south-western Asia.

We must also bear in mind that the little kingdoms of Judah and Israel were in the no-man's-land, as it were, between Egypt and the Mesopotamian empires. If the Assyrians of the Tigris valley were busy elsewhere, a strong king of Egypt could overrun Palestine: Jerusalem was, in fact, captured by "Shishak," the founder of the twenty-second dynasty of Egypt, shortly after the death of Solomon. But the two little states maintained a precarious existence until, in 722 B.C., Israel fell before Assyria and the flower of the population was transported to Mesopotamia. Judah lasted longer, but in 586 B.C. Nebuchadrezzar, the ruler of the neo-Babylonian empire, captured Jerusalem and took into captivity all that mattered of the people of Judah.

17. Assyria

Assyria rather than Egypt was the dreaded menace of Israel and Judah after the time of Solomon. It was an empire of

which the capital was Nineveh on the Tigris, a city almost due
north of Babylon. The Assyrians were Semites: their features,
portrayed on many monuments revealed by modern excavations, are of a characteristically "Jewish" type. The country
had a chequered history: its power of conquest, and capacity to
rise again after defeat, appear to have been due to the administrative vigour of its ruling class and the military qualities of its
free peasants.

The Assyrian empire seems to have first emerged from
obscurity about 1650 B.C. when the Kassites had overcome
Babylonia. Varying fortune attended successive rulers and
their conquests; but after 1100 B.C. there came a period of
weakness. A new dynasty arose about 950 B.C.; and thenceforth the Assyrians were the scourge of western Asia, until
resurgent Babylonians joined with the Medes to destroy
Nineveh in 612 B.C.

In Biblical history we can feel the terror spread by Assyrian
brutality. More than any other ancient nation of the Near
East, Assyria adopted a policy of deliberate cruelty. She ruled
by fear and was merciless to conquered enemies. Her treatment
of the Israelites was by no means exceptional. By a policy of
deportations she obliterated smaller states throughout south-
western Asia. Naturally, when finally she fell, she received no
mercy: she deserved none.

When Assyria fell, a new Babylonian empire arose. It was
short-lived, but of it splendid monuments remain. It was this
neo-Babylonian empire which, under Nebuchadrezzar, ended
the kingdom of Judah in 586 B.C. In accordance with Assyrian
practice, Semite imitating Semite, the inhabitants were deported
to Babylonia. "By the waters of Babylon we sat down and
wept." In Babylonia, during the period of exile, Judaism was
born.

18. Persia

As we seek to understand the situation of the Jews during
their exile, and during the first two centuries after their return
to Judaea in 538 B.C., we must bear in mind that, in the year
previous to this return, the neo-Babylonian empire had been
brought to an end by Cyrus the Persian.

Cyrus was born heir to the small kingdom of Anshan in the

* Persian highlands to the east of Mesopotamia. He began his career of conquest by uniting under his rule other Iranian peoples, Medes in the north and Persians to the south. From the time when the Medes and Babylonians had united to destroy Assyria, relations between the two peoples were doubtless correct rather than cordial. There was no instinctive sympathy between them: the Medes were Aryans and the Babylonians were Semites. Though Babylonian rule was not stained by the intentional ruthlessness which disgraces the memory of Assyria, it was harsh towards conquered peoples: we have seen that the deportations did not cease and that the Jews, for instance, were deported in 586 B.C.

But the Jews also were Semites; and, though their lamentations may have been loud and their exile resented, their existence by the waters of Babylon was by no means intolerable. Among them were men of shrewd judgment, fully aware that Cyrus and his Iranian peoples were Indo-Europeans, hardy mountaineers for whom Babylonia was a natural prey. These Jewish exiles in Babylon, hearing of the conquests of Cyrus, began to expect an attack on the empire which held them captive. Moreover, it would appear from the writings of a prophet of the exile which find a place in the book of *Isaiah* (xl. *et seq.*), that a certain clemency in the rule of Cyrus was sufficiently well known to warrant the hope that he would allow the Jews to rebuild their cities in Judah and their temple in Jerusalem. Expectations were fulfilled. Cyrus overthrew Babylon in 539 B.C. and apparently in the following years allowed the Jewish exiles to begin to return to Judaea. His action was in accord with the wise and liberal policy which for the most part characterized Persian rule.

19. The Persian empire

After his conquest of Babylon, Cyrus proceeded to incorporate into his empire practically all the great kingdoms and independent cities of the Near East. He died in 529 B.C.; and it was left to his successor to conquer Egypt four years later. On that successor's death in 522 B.C., Darius, after destroying a pretender who had seized the throne, became the Great King. He had to suppress a number of revolts, but gradually consolidated his vast empire. His rule, though firm, was mild.

Obviously he had a genius for organization. He created a magnificent road-system which, though primarily intended for military use, fostered commerce and industry. He divided his empire into twenty satrapies, great provinces under Persian officials. Taxation was carefully planned and, though not light, does not seem to have been oppressive.

We are accustomed to regard the Persians unfavourably, as we know the Greek account of the war between Greece and Persia which took place early in the fifth century before Christ; and we sympathize with the smaller and far more brilliant people in a gallant and successful struggle. But Darius combined with efficient organization the political wisdom of liberal government. The Greeks, on the other hand, were not particularly successful in ruling subject peoples; and their restless intellectual audacity did not lead to routine efficiency in administration.

20. The Jews under Persian rule

No better testimony to the success of the Persian system could be found than the fact that the Jews were apparently content when they lived under it. For two centuries, from their return to Judaea from exile in 538 B.C. until the conquest of the Persian empire by Alexander the Great in about 330 B.C., their history is virtually a blank. Almost our only information as to events in Judaea during this long period is contained in the books of *Ezra* and *Nehemiah*. History in these books is confused: dates are uncertain. But what is certain is that the Jews were at enmity with Semitic neighbours and not with the Persian government under which they lived. There were no fierce revolts; there was no embittered hostility to alien rule.

This contentment contrasts significantly with the passionate hatred felt towards Seleucid kings in the second century before Christ. Equally it contrasts with the murderous dislike of Herod and of the Romans in subsequent years. Discontent under Roman rule, periodically flaming into insurrection, lasted from before the birth of Christ until the emperor Hadrian in A.D. 135 made of Judaea a desert and called it peace.

21. The formation of the Old Testament

The books which are placed at the beginning of the Old

Testament appear to have begun to assume their present form during the exile of the Jews in Babylonia; but probably extensive rewriting took place in the subsequent two centuries which ended with the conquests of Alexander the Great. Though some material in them is certainly ancient, such books as comprise the Pentateuch are not the oldest books of the Bible: of greater antiquity are the prophets. During the time of Persian rule many of the more recent books of the Old Testament will have been written. But some are still later in date: we know that the book of *Daniel* must be dated about 168–165 B.C.; and some of the *Psalms* may belong to the same century.

Doubtless Jewish priests and scholars took with them to Babylon ancient records, containing the troubled history of the· kingdoms of Judah and Israel from the time of Samuel. They will also have preserved with reverent care the writings of the prophets, from *Amos* and *Hosea* early in the eighth century to *Ezekiel* two centuries later. But the history will have been at times romantic, as in stories of David and Solomon, Elijah and Elisha. The prophetic records will have been not seldom confused and fragmentary: thus the book of *Isaiah* probably includes material from a series of teachers spread over at least a century and a half.

But, however inadequate may be the Biblical records of their teaching, the prophets give to the Old Testament its supreme religious value. They created ethical monotheism: there is one God, Lord of the whole earth, and He is good. This message was taken up in the *Psalms*, the hymn-book of later Judaism. It is assumed in the *Wisdom* literature, in such books as *Job*, *Ecclesiastes*, *Ecclesiasticus*, and the *Wisdom of Solomon*. And when the legendary pre-history of Israel was constructed from traditions and myths, its basis was that doctrine of God which had been stamped by the great Hebrew prophets on the consciousness of the later Jews.

Thus the book of *Genesis* opens with the words, "In the beginning God created the· heaven and the earth." This book, and the books of the Bible which immediately follow it, represent, not the writings of a Moses who lived in the thirteenth century before Christ, but the activity of Jewish scholars. Some of these scholarly annalists may have lived before and at the time of the exile in Babylonia, but more probably their main work was done in Palestine during the fifth century before Christ. Whatever their date, the thought of these men was saturated by the lofty monotheism of the pre-exilic prophets.

22. The worship of Jehovah

There is no doubt that, when the Hebrew tribes first moved from the desert into the more fertile lands of Palestine, Jehovah was the god of Israel just as, say, Chemosh was the god of Moab. He was, in fact, a tribal god, "jealous" of rivals whose existence was believed to be as real as his own. When the Israelites settled in the promised land they entered the territory of the gods of that land. Hence came a natural urge towards the worship of Baal and towards the many evils of Syrian polytheism, including even human sacrifice. Apart from such a tendency, early Hebrew religion itself for many centuries preserved religious practices which were primitive rather than admirable.

Curiously little is known of the *provenance* of Yahweh (Jehovah), the national god of the Israelites. The documents of the Old Testament have been so frequently edited that from them it is impossible to say when the name of the god, either singly or in combination, first makes its appearance. Outside the Bible it seems first to occur in the famous Moabite Stone. This block of basalt was discovered at Dibhon (Daibon) in the year A.D. 1869 and is usually dated about 850 B.C. It records the thanks to his god of a king of Moab for victory over the cities of Israel.

23. The Hebrew prophets

From what has been said, it will be seen that the Hebrew prophets had a formidable task in creating, from most unpromising religious beliefs and practices, a worship of Yahweh, supreme and sole God, the righteous and merciful Lord of the whole earth. Their teaching, in fact, made a religious revolution. For instance, when *Hosea* (vi. 6) said, speaking in the name of Yahweh, "I desire mercy and not sacrifice; and the knowledge of God more than burnt offerings," he was breaking away from the sacrificial worship which was central in the nationalist religion of the Hebrews. A possibly late prophet,

C

whose thought is preserved in the book of *Micah*, could say
(vi. 7–8), "Will the Lord be pleased with thousands of rams, or
with ten thousands of rivers of oil? Shall I give my first-born
for my transgression, the fruit of my body for the sin of my soul?
He hath showed thee, O man, what is good; and what doth the
Lord require of thee, but to do justly, and to love mercy, and to
walk humbly with thy God?" There is a vast gulf between such
teaching and the human sacrifices in times of need, which
existed in ancient Canaan, passed from Phoenicia to Carthage,
and there apparently lasted until the first century of our era.

The more the Old Testament is studied in the light of critical
scholarship, and of knowledge of the ancient religions of the
Near East, the more valuable the religious revolution of the
Hebrew prophets is seen to be. Their writings show fine and
profound spiritual understanding. They created a faith of
supreme beauty and value, which is, of course, fundamental to
Christianity. In every generation religious men must use their
deepest experience, their hopes and fears, questionings and
strivings, to decide whether the teaching of the great Hebrew
prophets is true. Here we will only say that, linked to Christ's
teaching, this Semitic faith has satisfied some of the wisest and
best representatives of the leading Aryan races during nearly
two thousand years.

24. The background of ethical monotheism

We cannot meditate upon the ethical monotheism which was
the creation of the Hebrew prophets without reflecting upon
other religious developments in the ancient East which were
similar in tendency.

We have already mentioned the abortive monotheism of the
Egyptian king, Akhenaten, in the fourteenth century before
Christ. His supreme god was typified by the sun's disc, the
source of divine blessings. Such solar monotheism tended to
recur in later centuries: lack of knowledge forbids us to say how
far it was truly ethical. God, the sole lord of the universe, was
good; but how far did He demand justice, mercy, truth and
self-sacrifice from those who served Him?

25. Zoroaster

Another early monotheism, of the origin of which we know

singularly little though it persists to this day, was taught by Zoroaster. Zoroaster, one of the greatest religious leaders in human history, is thought by some to have lived about 1000 B.C., and by others to have been contemporary with the great eighth-century Hebrew prophets. He was not a Semite, but an Aryan. His teaching survives in those hymns of the ancient Persian scriptures which are called the Gathas. The faith which he taught emerges into history with the rise of the Persian empire and notably under Darius, who reigned until 486 B.C. By this time, unhappily, it was already corrupt.

In its pristine form Zoroastrianism appears to have accepted a single God, Ahura-Mazda, the Wise Lord, with whom were goodness, purity, truth and immortality. Opposed to this God was an evil spirit, subsequently called Ahriman, personification of falsehood, or, if we prefer a scriptural term, the father of lies. With this evil spirit Zoroaster associated the old nature gods of the Aryans. He taught that between good and evil there is conflict; and in the spiritual warfare every man is involved. We can, and must, choose whether we will follow Ahura-Mazda or the adversary. In the end right will triumph and men will be judged by their allegiance. The righteous who have served God faithfully will enjoy the happiness of those blessed by Him. For those who have followed the adversary there shall be everlasting torment. Zoroaster's faith is a dualism, inasmuch as he postulates two spiritual principles; but it can rightly be termed monotheistic, as in the end Ahriman shall be destroyed and God will be all in all.

The enduring influence of the Persian dualism which derives from Zoroaster shows itself in the Christian gospels, where Satan is virtually indistinguishable from Ahriman and, as the devil, is the father of lies. When such popular philosophy was given theological shape in later Christian ages it became the Manichaean heresy.

26. The originality of the Hebrew prophets

There is no hint that the earliest Hebrew prophets were in any way influenced by Zoroaster's teaching. He may have been their contemporary, or even earlier in time; but his influence did not penetrate into Mesopotamia until the rise of the

Persian monarchy. If the two developments were parallel, the Hebrew was the more profoundly spiritual.

Some have speculated that the monotheism of Akhenaten influenced Moses a century later and that by him it was transmitted to the eighth-century prophets of Israel. Such an "apostolic succession" is, however, most unlikely. Hebrew religion, in spite of the contiguity of the two peoples, owed nothing to Egypt. For instance, the Egyptian was obsessed by the life beyond the grave; yet, apart from a vague belief in Sheol, there is in the Old Testament no parallel doctrine until, in the second century before Christ, we find in the book of *Daniel* a resurrection of good and bad alike.

Hebrew religion was, in the beginning, Syrian paganism. The Hebrews thought of themselves as Babylonian Semites: according to their legends, their first ancestor, Abraham, came from "Ur of the Chaldees," originally an ancient Sumerian capital. Such culture as they had in the time of David was borrowed from the Phoenicians. We are forced to the conclusion that Hebrew prophecy was a native growth. It owed nothing to outside sources. In fact, the most significant religious development in human history before the Christian era came from the small, none too highly civilized kingdoms of Israel and Judah.

CHAPTER II

THE MEDITERRANEAN WORLD

I. *The Eastern Mediterranean*

27. Crete

DURING the present century we have learned that in distant times there was in Crete, that large island in the eastern Mediterranean which lies nearest to Egypt, a luxurious and long-lasting civilization. It began towards the end of the fourth millennium before Christ. It owed much to Egypt and something to the peoples of the Euphrates valley. It spread its influence far and wide, especially in southern Greece and the islands of the Aegean. The capital of Crete was Cnossos, a city on the north coast of the island, wealthy because it was in its day the great centre of commerce in the Levant. Excavations of Cnossos have revealed, in the palace of Minos, a splendid and surprising luxury. Alike the sanitation and the women's dresses were unexpectedly modern. The frescoes, with their gaiety and with the artist's obvious joy in spring-time flowers, are singularly remote from the heavy and formal art of Egypt. For well-nigh two thousand years Cnossos flourished. Finally, about the year 1400 B.C., sudden destruction came upon it. It passed out of history, leaving among the Greeks legends of the minotaur and the labyrinth, of ugly appetites and cruel power.

28. Mycenaean civilization

The civilization which spread from Crete is often called Mycenaean, because the treasures unearthed, towards the end of the last century, at Mycenae in the Peloponnese indicate the high level of its achievement. This civilization collapsed, apparently somewhat later than the fall of Cnossos, under an attack of Greek-speaking invaders, Aryans who came ultimately from an unknown north. Racially these invaders were probably not greatly different from those whose civilization they overthrew. Relatively uncivilized, they excelled in the art of war, probably because they possessed iron weapons: the

21

culture of Crete and Mycenae was of the bronze age. During the centuries 1200–900 B.C. there will have been in countries bordering on the Aegean a period of much confusion, tribal migrations, infiltration, and then a new adjustment following on intermarriage. When finally the curtain lifts, we find the Greeks, Hellenes as they called themselves, settled in the mainland of Greece, in the islands of the Aegean, and in Ionia, the western coastal area of Asia Minor.

29. The Greeks

As we have indicated, these Greeks were not a pure stock—can such human stocks ever be found?—but, in whatever lands they settled, they showed the same inborn characteristics. In part, this may have been due to the fact that they shared a language which was a gift from the gods, alike for the beauty which it gave to poetry and drama, and for the precision with which it enabled ideas to be expressed. The various Greek communities had, too, the same political instincts. They rejoiced in a quick intelligence, an eager curiosity, and a love of adventure, physical and mental. Their happy pleasure in life moulded their stories of the gods, to whom they attributed with scant reverence human joys and failings. We know too little of their music to pass judgment upon it; but in the arts of painting, sculpture, architecture, poetry and drama they showed unrivalled excellence. Their intellectual triumphs in mathematics, astronomy, medicine, biology and metaphysics disclosed a progressive understanding of nature and man, in rapidity unequalled by any other people. The Greek genius remains supreme in human history.

30. Greek science and philosophy

That genius flowered first in Ionia, because the higher civilization of the Euphrates valley penetrated through Lydia to the Greek settlements. Fundamental to all intellectual progress was, of course, the art of writing. It would appear that about 1000 B.C. an alphabet was derived from the Phoenicians. But it was without vowels. Some Greek of genius created symbols for vowel sounds and thus the Greeks gave to Europe substantially the alphabets now in common use.

In the seventh and sixth centuries before Christ the founda-

tions of modern science were laid in Ionian cities like Miletus
and Ephesus, and in the islands of the Aegean. During the fifth
and fourth centuries in Greece proper, and notably in Athens,
speculations in politics, ethics, sociology and metaphysics were
profound and of lasting value. Conjectures as to the nature of
matter, made by the Ionian philosophers, were shrewd but
inadequate owing to lack of experimental technique: not until
the seventeenth and eighteenth centuries of our era were the
foundations of physics and chemistry laid. But the level of
medical understanding reached by Hippocrates of Cos, who was
probably born about 460 B.C., was astonishingly high. Profoundly ethical, and yet free from the superstitions that
until quite modern times associated diseases with demons or
divine displeasure, Hippocratic medicine still excites the
physician's reverent regard: it foreshadowed modern scientific
humanism.

Greek astronomy was undoubtedly based on Babylonian
knowledge; but the progress shown in the transformation of
empirical facts was astonishing. The Ionian Greeks appear to
have been the first to recognize that the earth is roughly a
sphere: its radius was determined with considerable accuracy
about 200 B.C.; and fifty years earlier Aristarchus, of the island
of Samos, suggested that the earth rotated round the sun, thus
anticipating Copernicus by 1,800 years.

One need hardly add that in philosophy Socrates, Plato and
Aristotle rank among the immortals. Socrates, born about
470 B.C., was put to death at Athens in 399 B.C.: Plato's works
are his great and lasting monument. Plato died in 347 B.C.
The subsequent influence of his writings was, of course, vast.
We see it in the apologists for the Christian faith who wrote
towards the end of the second century of our era: thereafter
the authority of Plato's name was invoked, and what were
asserted to be his ideas were used, to mould Christian theology.

Aristotle (384-322 B.C.) was tutor to Alexander the Great
and outlived him. The modern man of science would probably
claim that he was the greatest thinker of antiquity. Untrammelled by any so-called orthodox opinions, and exceptionally
clear-sighted, he investigated problems ranging from biology to
man's spiritual nature. The spirit of free inquiry by which he
was animated is that of the modern empirical philosopher who,

indifferent to the mere authority of great names, builds upon experimental inquiry and observed fact.

31. Greek fertility and its exhaustion

While the Ionians were laying the foundations of Greek civilization, the fertility of the Greek peoples was amazing. Emigrants swarmed over the seas to create trading stations and colonies. By the middle of the sixth century before Christ, Greeks were settled on the shores of the Black Sea, in southern Italy and eastern Sicily, in Cyrenaica, in southern France and in eastern Spain. They must have seemed ubiquitous. Their seamanship, their trading ability, their energy and initiative, made them between 750 and 550 B.C. the great maritime people of the Mediterranean. Half a millennium later, Greek fertility was at an end. Plutarch, who lived and wrote in Boeotia about A.D. 100, gives a terrible picture of the depopulation of Greece. Possibly malaria, following on centuries of war and infanticide, was the final cause: yet it may be that a spiritual exhaustion, which led to a refusal to beget children, was the ultimate evil.

32. Greek religion and morality

It has often been pointed out that the Greeks were fortunate in that they were largely free from the inhibitions of religious tradition. They had no church claiming divine authority and no sacred book of which the teaching must not be challenged. In Greece, as in all other lands, there were, of course, persistent religious beliefs and superstitions: there were sacred shrines and oracles with their priests and priestesses. In addition to the official pantheon, the gods of mount Olympus, there were quasi-private cults, like the mysteries of Eleusis and the frenzied rites of Dionysus. Moreover, conservative religious sentiment could at times be shocked into intolerance: Socrates was condemned for corrupting the youth by his disquieting opinions. But there was in Greece no wealthy and powerful caste of clergy as in Egypt and Babylonia. The consequent gain to freedom of thought was great. The dry light of reason could illuminate inquiries into the creation of the world and the nature of man. Crude beliefs could be challenged by a gay scepticism.

There was, however, another aspect of this freedom which must not be forgotten. Religious tradition, so long as its teaching can command general assent, gives moral stability to a people; and principles of living, which are the outcome of long, and sometimes bitter, experience, are not easily maintained when religious scepticism shatters old-time certainties. In spite of the wisdom of their great men, the Greeks had grave faults of character. Politics in Greece could be shamefully selfish and opportunist. The Greeks tolerated vices which excite our disgust. They could be passionately jealous. They were callous to human suffering: even Athens in her great days ruthlessly exploited those set to work in the silver mines at Laureion.

33. Alexander the Great

The tragedy of Hellenic civilization is that during its most brilliant period rival cities exhausted alike their best human stocks and their wealth in constant wars. With furious bitterness Greek fought Greek. Dreams of Hellenic unity were associated with centres such as Delos and Delphi; but the dreams proved fruitless. In the end, in 338 B.C., Philip of Macedon, king of a semi-Greek, semi-barbarian land to the north of Thessaly, in a single battle made himself master of Greece. His son, Alexander the Great (356–323 B.C.), succeeded him in 336 B.C., and, after somewhat brutally reasserting his authority in Greece, attacked, conquered and overran the vast Persian empire. In a series of victories, which were literally epoch-making, he first made himself master of Asia Minor; forthwith he destroyed Tyre and brought Phoenician sea-supremacy to an end. He then passed to Egypt, where at Alexandria he founded the first and greatest of his cities; and finally he led his troops as far east as the Indus.

34. Hellenistic civilization

Thus a new era began: what we now call the Near East was hellenized. The change was, of course, largely superficial. A strange race may impose its will on conquered peoples: a new governing class may use its own language and methods in the machinery of government. But the habits of thought, the religious beliefs and practices, and the language of the conquered, persist. None the less, the influence of Greece was great: the Greek language became over a vast area the language of government and commerce. In the university centres, and particularly at Alexandria, Greek science and learning flourished.

But with the rise of Macedon, the great era of Greece came to an end. That era of unrivalled brilliance was followed by what is commonly called the Hellenistic period. In this period the great masters of philosophy, poetry and drama are no more. Sculpture still flourishes. Fine work is done in mathematics and astronomy. Great libraries are formed. Learned professors and competent specialists are many. But there are signs that Hellenic culture has begun to lose its creative *élan*. That culture was to last for many centuries as Latins, Gauls, Spaniards and Africans received, and added their contributions to, the legacy of Hellas. In the end, Graeco-Roman civilization perished by exhaustion from within.

35. Palestine after Alexander

After Alexander's death, his empire was divided between his generals. There was a period of war and confusion, which produced a crop of able and restless adventurers. The Ptolemies ruled Egypt, naturally wealthy and easily defended. Syria fell ultimately to the house of Seleucus with (Syrian) Antioch as its capital. During the third century before Christ, war broke out repeatedly between successive kings of Egypt and Syria; and, as fortune fluctuated, so Jerusalem changed its masters.

About the year 200 B.C. southern Syria and Judaea passed from the Ptolemies to the Seleucids. Soon after that time the cloud of obscurity, which for more than two and a half centuries had covered Palestine, lifted: in the two books of *Maccabees* in the *Apocrypha*, and in the works of Josephus, we find the renewed history of the Jews.

That history begins with quarrels in Jerusalem in which the high-priest and members of a powerful quasi-Jewish family, apparently of Ammonite origin, were involved. These quarrels brought about the intervention of the Seleucid government. This led to an attempt on the part of the Seleucid treasurer, Heliodorus, to enter the treasury of the temple at Jerusalem and

to seize the treasure held there. The attempt failed. The famous
story of the failure after a miraculous intervention by angels,
which has been the subject of many a dramatic picture, is told
in the third chapter of the second book of *Maccabees*.

Apparently shortly after this attempt, Antiochus Epiphanes,
son of Antiochus the Great who reigned from 223 to 187 B.C.,
came to the throne of Syria on the assassination of his brother
in 175 B.C. At once the situation in Jerusalem seems to have
gone from bad to worse. There were two parties in the city,
one fiercely nationalist, the other desirous to accept Greek
culture. At first the Hellenistic party made rapid progress
which scandalized the faithful. The high-priest of the day was
naturally a religious conservative. Fearing that his life was in
jeopardy, owing to the triumph of his opponents, he fled to
Antioch. There he was assassinated. Inevitably Antiochus was
drawn into the quarrel. His sympathies were, of course, against
the Jewish nationalists, who must have seemed, as he surveyed
his kingdom, a troublesome and obstinate minority who could
be fairly easily suppressed.

36. The Maccabaean revolt

In the end a ruthless attempt was made to stamp out Judaism,
especially in Jerusalem. There, as a symbol of the new order,
an altar to Zeus, "the abomination of desolation," was dedi-
cated with the sacrifice of swine and set up in the temple,
probably on December 25, 167 B.C., though possibly a year
earlier. Then, however, Judaea flamed into revolt. The Hasmonaean family, of whom the best soldier was Judas, surnamed
Maccabaeus, led the insurrection; and the book of *Daniel* was
written to encourage those who were committed to what seemed
a desperate adventure. After many vicissitudes of fortune, and
largely owing to the fact that under the later Seleucids royal
authority in Syria crumbled away, the Jews secured their
independence. By the beginning of the first century before
Christ the Hasmonaean princes ruled an area almost as large
as the kingdom of David.

The struggle for Jewish independence with its violent faction-
fights reflects much discredit on many, if not on most, of those
who took part in it. But it preserved Judaism. An effort had
been made to replace Jewish religion by Syrian paganism

veneered by Greek culture; and it had failed. Much that was best in the teaching of the great Hebrew prophets was lost in the bitter strife of the second century before Christ. But ethical monotheism was saved.

37. Judaea, Rome and Herod

During this second century, Rome, having overcome Carthage (see § 53), began for the first time to interfere in the affairs of the countries which had formerly belonged to Alexander's empire. It was by the deliberate policy of Rome that the rule of the later Seleucid kings of Syria became increasingly feeble.

In the first century before Christ Rome was paramount throughout the Levant. Consequently, when in 63 B.C. a dispute arose between two Hasmonaean princes, an elder brother feeble in character and a younger resolute and vigorous, it was submitted to Pompey, who for some years had controlled the Levant as Rome's representative. He decided in favour of the elder brother, who became for practical purposes a puppet in the hands of an Edomite (Idumaean), Antipater by name, and his son Herod. In the end, by the favour of Antony and Octavian at Rome, Herod in 40 B.C. became king of the Jews: his reign is usually said to have begun in 37 B.C. In history he would have been a forgotten adventurer, who by permission of Rome ruled a client-kingdom of little importance, were it not that at the close of his reign Jesus was born.

We probably make a mistake if we think of Herod as a foreigner ruling in Jerusalem. The Edomites were near neighbours of the Jews and racially more closely akin to them than the English to the Welsh. Much evidence goes to show that Herod regarded himself as a Jew; and, if our verdict must be that he was a bad Jew, many others of unimpeachable lineage have deserved that description.

Herod sought to be all things to all men. He was an honoured patron of the Olympic festival in Greece; and in many ways he encouraged Hellenic culture among the non-Jews of his realm. He was in high favour at Rome and his renown added lustre to his Jewish kingdom. But to the Jews he was above all else the man who lavished immense sums on the rebuilding of the temple in Jerusalem. Though this magnificent edifice was not com-

pleted until A.D. 64, the parts of greatest importance were
finished in Herod's reign, and were regarded by Herod's
Jewish subjects with universal admiration. Herod died early
in the year 4 B.C.

38. The influence of Greece on Judaism

Judaea after Alexander's conquests became part of the
Hellenistic world. How far did Hellenic culture affect Judaism?
It is not easy to give an answer. From the seventh century
before Christ onwards different foreign influences affected life
and letters in Jerusalem. Until persecution bred a narrow
exclusiveness, the religious outlook of the Jews seems to have
tended to become more liberal as the centuries passed. Before
the Christian era Judaism may be likened to a stream steadily
becoming broader: it grew spiritually more confident.

In part this movement was due to influences which resulted
from the exile in Babylon. But, before that exile, Jews came
from, and went to, other lands. Jewish mercenaries were fighting in Egypt about 650 B.C. Aramaic papyri were discovered,
in A.D. 1905 and in following years, at Elephantiné, opposite
to Assouan. They show that there was a flourishing Jewish
community, with its own temple of Jehovah, in southern
Egypt in the sixth and fifth centuries before Christ. Jews,
moreover, served in Alexander's army.

Thus, though the later books of the Old Testament have a
different feeling from those written in earlier centuries, we
cannot assume that the change is due to Greek influence. In
fact, of the later books, few clearly reflect the Greek spirit.
Job, a philosophical drama possibly containing some ancient
material, may have been given its present form by an editor who
lived after the conquests of Alexander. But it is in character
essentially Semitic. *Ecclesiastes* is a record, hardly earlier than
the third century before Christ, of the teaching and meditation
of some leader who gave free expression to varying religious
moods. Some have found in it stoic and Epicurean tendencies:
but the resemblances are probably superficial. The book is
definitely Jewish and shows us the religious liberalism which
was possible in an era before Christ. The Book of *Proverbs* contains material of different ages. It is probably a late compilation; and scholars find in it strands of Hebrew and of Hellenized

wisdom. But in actual fact it is difficult to point to any particular proverb and assert that it would not have been written had the Greeks never lived.

39. The Apocrypha

In the *Apocrypha* two books call for mention. *Ecclesiasticus* in style and character resembles *Proverbs*. We know that it was written in Hebrew about 180 B.C., and translated into Greek by the author's grandson some fifty years later. Some passages in it are fine: on the other hand, some of the popular proverbs which it preserves are coarse. Nothing in it is specifically Hellenic.

The book called the *Wisdom of Solomon* differs from all the others which we have mentioned in that in it Greek influence is clear. Probably written in Greek by an Alexandrian Jew about the time of the Christian era, it explicitly uses Greek philosophical terms. The praise of Wisdom to be found in the book has obvious affinities with the Greek doctrine of the *Logos*. It was a man imbued with the Greek spirit who could write (viii. 17), "to be allied unto Wisdom is immortality." Equally he was not far from Christ when, addressing God, he could say (ix. 17), "Thy counsel who hath known, except thou give wisdom, and send thy Holy Spirit from above?"

But we must conclude that the influence of Greek thought on Judaism, even on liberal Judaism, was slight. The ethical monotheism of the Jew was alien from the religious outlook of the Greek: may we not fairly maintain that the Jew had reached a higher religious level?

40. The Septuagint

It remains to be said that the Greek language contributed not a little to spread the Jewish faith after about 150 B.C. During a series of generations, in the third century before Christ and somewhat later, the Old Testament was in Egypt gradually translated into Greek. The Greek was not that of the great era of Athens; but, apart from a slavish use of Hebrew idiom, more like the language spoken in the streets of Alexandria at the time when the translation was made. The version is known as the Septuagint. Jews of the dispersion, to whom Hebrew and Aramaic were alike unfamiliar, read their scriptures in this version. Proselytes to Judaism were numerous at the time of the Christian era: they supplied many of the converts to early Christianity. Such proselytes, knowing no Hebrew, used the Septuagint. Moreover, speaking generally, it is true to say that New Testament writers turned to the same version when they quoted the Jewish scriptures.

41. The influence of Greece on Christianity

Though Jesus spoke in Aramaic when he taught in Galilee, Greek rapidly became the language of the early Christian movement. All our New Testament scriptures were written in Greek; and, if in compiling some of them non-Greek documents were used, these documents have not survived. But the Greek in which they were written was not the language, alike rich and flexible, in which Thucydides wrote history and Plato his dialogues; it was the speech, impoverished and crippled, of shop, home and amusement-hall in the first century of our era.

The Greek language has left an enduring impress on Christianity. Such words as Christ, baptism, eucharist, deacon, priest, bishop, apostle, evangelist, are all Greek. None the less, though early Christians used the Greek language, there are few signs that they had inherited Greek culture. Perhaps, however, we can rightly claim that Greek artistry in words influenced *Luke*, more especially in his gospel, and even *Mark*. *Mark's* account of the crucifixion of Jesus is told with a simplicity, a dignity and a moving reticence which are felt by all readers; and he who tries to re-write the parable of the Prodigal Son (*Luke* xv. 11–32) can learn something of the severe restraint of Greek art.

Again, we must admit that, in so far as Greek religion influenced the early development of Christianity, it was the religion of the Greek underworld. Christianity, as it spread, utilized such redemptive beliefs as were associated with Eleusis and Dionysus, rather than the philosophic faith of great Hellenic teachers. Among the early Christians Greek science counted for nothing. Greek art, expressing itself in pagan temples and statues of the gods, was an offence. Converts to Christianity needed no aid from Greek philosophy to justify their belief in God, as He was revealed by the great prophetic tradition of Israel which culminated in Jesus. The whole world at the time of the Christian era was feeling towards monotheism; and Christian converts knew full certainly that Jesus had revealed the Father: such knowledge was the very basis of their faith.

We can, in fact, only find in the New Testament four clear examples of the influence of classical Greek culture. Two consist of a doubtful quotation from Menander in teaching as to the resurrection (1 *Cor*. xv. 33)—see § 225—and a libel on the Cretans—see § 204—from Epimenides. We find a third appropriately in the speech attributed to Paul at Athens: the fourth is the *Logos* (Word) prologue to the fourth gospel.

Paul's speech at Athens is probably a free composition by *Luke* written, as we shall see in § 204, at the beginning of the second century of our era or, possibly, even later. It has affinities with the writings of the Christian apologists of the middle and second half of the second century.

The *Logos* prologue was probably written at Ephesus about A.D. 110–120 by a Jew who had absorbed not a little of the Greek religious outlook as it was preserved by stoicism. He carried to excess the use of myth in teaching religion; and, as we shall suggest in §§ 113, 114, his *Logos* philosophy as applied to Christ leaves us with grave perplexities. But in using it he continued ancient Greek speculation; and, when Christianity began, about A.D. 160, to make its way into cultured Graeco-Roman homes, apologists who sought to commend it found, at the beginning of the fourth gospel, an Hellenic basis for doctrines of the nature of the person of Jesus, the Christ.

42. The *Logos* doctrine

The fourth gospel came, according to an unvarying tradition, from the Ionian city of Ephesus. In view of this fact, it is interesting to recall that at Ephesus about 500 B.C. a *Logos* doctrine was developed by Heracleitus, one of the most original of Ionian philosophers.

Heracleitus believed that, by exploring his own mind and searching out his own nature, he could discover the *Logos*, the divine truth by which all things come to pass. His belief rested on the assumption that man is, as it were, a small-scale representation of the universe. His *Logos* was the thought which is the divine life of the universe. In this universe all things flow.

Change is perpetual; but the *Logos*, disclosed in wisdom and order, remains. It follows that, to Heracleitus, the *Logos* is nature or God. God, as thus perceived, knows nothing of human standards: good and evil are opposites fundamentally united. It is difficult for the modern man with his enlarged knowledge of the physical universe to entertain with entire sympathy the views of Heracleitus; and to a Christian the divine indifference to morality which he postulates is shocking.

With varying modifications, the assumptions of Heracleitus had a long history and a wide influence in the ancient world. The stoics took much from him. These serious-minded philosophers with a lofty morality traced their descent from Zeno (*c.* 336–264 B.C.), who was probably a Semite. Fundamentally they were, in our terminology, pantheistic materialists or, more accurately, monists. They would have repudiated our own sharp distinction between matter and spirit: they regarded each as a form of the fundamental "stuff" of the universe. Thus emotions, thoughts, intellectual constructs, were all believed by them to have a quasi-material existence, while conversely matter was a mode of spirit. Their whole conception of being was dynamical. For them the total universe was God; and the *Logos* was life-giving spirit, the activity inherent in the world, to be likened to an inward fire giving light and understanding. They recognized the *Logos* in thought and reason, as the source of order and therefore as law and destiny. It follows that, for various stoic philosophers, the *Logos* was alike personal and impersonal, fate and providence, the soul of the world, the creative activity of God, and God Himself.

The author of the fourth gospel held firm to the doctrine of God of the great Hebrew prophets. He repudiated materialism: to him "God is Spirit" (*John* iv. 24). But, with necessary modifications, he took his doctrine of the *Logos*, as we shall see in § 113, from the stoicism which, for some centuries before and after his age, had a profound influence on many of the best minds of paganism.

43. Christianity and Greek culture

The claim has often been put forward that the Christian church combined Hebrew religion with Greek culture. The

D

Jews, who in many ways were singularly fitted to make this combination, ultimately refused the opportunity. After the last wild revolt against the emperor Hadrian in the early part of the second century of our era, the Jews in Palestine were practically exterminated; and Judaism throughout the ancient world withdrew into itself, becoming increasingly rabbinic. In consequence, there were no further successors to such men as Philo who, at Alexandria about the beginning of the Christian era, sought to fuse together Hebrew prophetic monotheism and Greek philosophic religion.

Yet from the survey which we have just made it remains doubtful whether, during the first century and a half of its existence, Christianity did much to create such a fusion. In later centuries Greek modes of thought were used in interminable conflicts concerning the relation of Jesus to the Godhead. But scientific humanism, which can be compounded of Greek science, philosophy, art and medicine, did not enter into the synthesis finally reached. Much that was best in the Greek view of life finds no place in traditional Christianity. On the contrary, the free spirit of inquiry, untrammelled by dead or dying orthodoxies, has been feared by Christian ecclesiastics and teachers, just as Hellenic beauty has often been shunned. Is it possible that a Christian humanism will yet emerge, preserving all that is best in Hebrew religion and Greek culture?

44. Judaism in the time of Christ

We are not very well informed as to the parties within Judaism nor as to the direction of its development when Jesus was teaching in Galilee. There is reason to think that the gospels give too harsh a picture of "scribes and pharisees, hypocrites"—the denunciation occurs no less than seven times in a single chapter (xxiii) of *Matthew*. *Mark* couples pharisees with Herodians, (iii. 6) and (xii. 13), in an alliance hostile to Jesus. The sadducees (*Mark* xii. 16) are described briefly as they "which say there is no resurrection." In *Luke* (vii. 30) "the pharisees and the lawyers" are blamed for having "rejected the counsel of God"; and somewhat later in the gospel "the lawyers" (xi. 46–52) receive a severe condemnation. Doubtless Jesus encountered opposition, both open and secret, from the

recognized leaders of Judaism. But at a somewhat later time
there were bitter conflicts between Christian missionaries of the
first century of our era and official Judaism. It may well be
that these conflicts caused the evangelists to exaggerate the
actual hostility which Jesus experienced.

For our other information as to Judaism and its divisions,
we have to rely on Josephus who, in his *Jewish Antiquities*,
(xiii. 5, 9) and (xviii. 1, 2–6), probably published in A.D. 94,
tells us of Jewish sects as he knew them. In particular he
describes the pharisees, who are not previously mentioned
either in the Old Testament or in the *Apocrypha*.

The Talmud might have been expected to give us a contemporary description of Jewish teachers to set against that of
the gospels; but the writing of the oldest part of it, the Mishnah,
must be dated about A.D. 200. It has little to say of any teacher
before Hillel, who probably died in the lifetime of Jesus; even
what it does tell us apparently rests on oral traditions.

45. The pharisees

According to Josephus, the pharisees must have arisen about
the middle of the second century before Christ. They seem
always to have been a relatively small though most influential
group, characterized by strict observance of the written Law.
This Law they supplemented by a mass of oral tradition, built
up, as is English case-law, from decisions accepted as authoritative.

These decisions were, it would appear, written down by those
whom the gospels call "scribes" or "lawyers." These men
naturally gained the status of acknowledged teachers, especially
when the synagogue became the local chapel, to which all good
Jews went regularly inasmuch as the temple in Jerusalem was
too distant for any but exceptional visits. The priests were
drawn from a privileged class, the sons of Levi. Their influence
declined as the synagogue developed: it practically vanished
with the destruction of the temple. The scribes were not priests,
but accredited teachers; and the pharisees were—shall we say?
—devout laymen who tried to live according to the strict letter
of the Mosaic Law.

46. The sadducees

The pharisees, by the beginning of the first century before Christ, found themselves in strong opposition to the reigning Hasmonaean princes. Such a breach could have been foreseen: worldly rulers and narrowly devout subjects go ill together. On the other hand, the priestly aristocracy was, and continued to be, wealthy and powerful. Its partisans constituted an important group known as sadducees. As upholders of an established system they were naturally conservative. Josephus says that they rejected the additions to the Law which formed "the traditions of the elders" venerated by the pharisees. Probably we shall not be wrong if we say that the sadducees maintained the type of Judaism which had existed before the persecution of Antiochus Epiphanes (168–165 B.C.). We possibly find their creed in *Ecclesiasticus*, while the newer pharisaic Judaism, with its belief in a resurrection and in angels, is preserved in the book of *Daniel*.

47. The pharisees and Christianity

Jewish scholars have insisted that *au fond* Jesus owed much to the local synagogue, and therefore to the pharisees, whose doctrines would have been taught in it. They contend that his piety, and that of the pharisees at its best, were fundamentally akin. The pharisees sought completely to fulfil the Law: Jesus came, as we learn from *Matthew* (v. 17), "not to destroy, but to fulfil." There is much truth in these contentions; and we can only explain the paradox by recalling that piety, when it becomes rancid, is a very horrid thing. If rules impose burdens too grievous to be borne, they who profess to keep such rules insensibly become hypocrites. Religion, if it is to remain wholesome and sweet, must from time to time be challenged by some prophet, audacious and, it may be, almost reckless in his freedom of speech. Otherwise it will be stifled by smooth insincerities or warped by an insidious complacency. Jesus thus challenged the baser pharisaism of his time, even while he owed not a little to the best representatives of the movement.

The influence of the pharisees over popular Judaism in the time of Christ was great. But their type of piety did not apparently create hostility to certain developments within Judaism which Christianity was to absorb. Belief in the coming of a Messiah, "God's anointed," grew steadily. With it went the writing of a series of apocalypses which professed to disclose the future and especially the coming of a "Son of man" who was to be God's agent at the end of the age. Such dreams and hopes seem to have arisen within Judaism. But simultaneously a debased form of Zoroastrianism, coming from Persia, had given to the Jews a belief in evil spirits, and in Satan or Beelzebub, "the prince of the devils." With such developments there appears to have gone a growing belief in magic, which pharisees and Christians alike seem to have allowed to be real, though morally wrong. Jewish and Samaritan magicians had a considerable vogue in the ancient world. Their profession was not reputable; but, doubtless, there was money in it.

48. Judaism and Jewish sects

To the credit of Judaism, at the time of the Christian era, must be set its willingness to tolerate the formation and existence of sects within itself. The Essenes were a small ascetic community, with headquarters near the Dead Sea and apparently with branches elsewhere in Palestine. Some of their rules of physical cleanliness were, to say the least, astonishing; and suggestions that their influence can be traced in the teaching of Jesus cannot be sustained. The movement created by John the Baptist was of a far finer type, emphasizing the need of moral purity and, as we shall see in chapter xv, using baptism as a symbol of moral reformation. Neither of these movements seems to have provoked resentment: there is no evidence that the ecclesiastical authorities of Judaism took hostile action against either.

Moreover, Christianity was for long tolerated in Jerusalem, where James, "the Lord's brother," as head of the sect, seems to have been for many years treated with friendly respect. Early Christians, as we learn from *Acts* (ii. 46), frequented the temple services; and they mainly differed from other pious Jews in that they also "broke bread" at home.

Christians suffered one spasmodic outburst of persecution when Stephen was stoned. But he was spokesman of the Hellenistic Jews and consequently aroused memories of the bitter struggles against Antiochus Epiphanes. He must have seemed to be leader of a movement, not within, but against Judaism. After his death, those who sympathized with him left Jerusalem; and the mission to the gentiles had henceforth the non-Jewish cities of Damascus and Antioch as its centres.

Of other early Christian leaders Paul, of course, broke violently with Judaism; and it is to be also observed that his relations with Jewish Christians in Jerusalem were none too happy. In subsequent ages Jews were often bitterly hostile to Christians. But it is to be feared that the Christians developed a strong anti-Semitic bias. In *Matthew* (xxvii. 25) we read that at the trial of Jesus, the Jews said, "His blood be on us, and on our children." The story is peculiar to *Matthew*; and probably belongs to traditions which grew up towards the end of the first century of our era. Its power for evil is not even yet exhausted.

II. The Western Mediteranean

49. The Etruscans

During the later centuries of the second millennium before Christ there were, as we have seen, extensive movements in the eastern Mediterranean. As a sort of back-wash of these movements, the Phoenicians planted their first trading settlement at Cadiz in Spain about the year 1100 B.C.; and it would seem that almost simultaneously—though possibly a couple of centuries later—pirates from Lydia in western Asia Minor similarly established themselves on the north-west coast of Italy, and founded Etruria.

The Etruscans, as these people were called, finally ceased to have direct political importance in Mediterranean affairs at the beginning of the third century before Christ. But their abiding influence upon Roman religious ideas and moral standards was important and, it should be added, definitely unwholesome.

Arguments may be brought forward for the contention that Rome was founded—the traditional date is 753 B.C.—by Etruscans; and there is no doubt that at an early date Rome was ruled by Etruscan kings. The expulsion of these kings about the year 510 B.C. almost certainly resulted from an uprising of one of those tribal groups, speaking an Indo-

European language and akin to the Gauls, which then covered much of northern and central Italy. Rome grew by conquering and absorbing other such groups; but Etruscan influence within its walls did not cease. The downfall of independent Etruscan power was consequent on the Gallic invasions of Italy in the fifth and fourth centuries before Christ.

50. The Etruscan legacy to Rome

The lictors, with their bundles of rods and axes, which were revived in twentieth-century fascism, came from Etruria; and from Etruscan religion came the devils and horrors of hell familiar in the paintings and frescoes of medieval Christianity. The Roman soothsayer, who professed to foretell the future by inspecting the entrails of a slaughtered animal, was the exponent of an oriental superstition which had flourished in Babylonia and under the Hittites. Homer knew nothing of the practice; but the Etruscans brought it to the west and it became a commonplace of Roman religious practice.

The Etruscans were endowed by nature with great artistic ability. Such ability had apparently lain latent in Tuscany until it showed itself once more at the Renaissance. But with their artistic gifts there went in the pre-Christian era immorality, pride and a love of cruelty and torture. From Etruscan practice came the slaughtering of prisoners led in a Roman triumph. Gladiatorial and similar shows, infamous in connection with early Christian history, were introduced into Rome from Etruria about the middle of the third century before Christ. It is not without significance that Sulla, whose cruelties marked a stage of political demoralization in the faction fights at the close of the Roman republic, bore an Etruscan name.

The Romans, like all other Europeans, were a mixture of races; but Aryan invaders of Italy were probably the late-comers who gave to the Roman stock its dominant characteristics, its domestic virtues and public spirit. Etruscan religion and custom came as corrupting influences, stains from an Oriental underworld.

51. The Carthaginians

The seventh century before Christ was the era of buoyant fertility of the Greek race: the following century probably marked its greatest expansion. There was a time when it seemed as though the whole of the western Mediterranean might fall under Greek control: any such expectation was destroyed when in 535 B.C., at the battle of Alalia off the coast of Corsica, a Greek fleet was destroyed by the combined fleets of the Etruscans and Carthaginians. Thenceforth for several centuries, as Etruscan power decayed, Carthage controlled the western Mediterranean: her rule only ended after an epic struggle with Rome. The bitter fury of this struggle was intensified by the instinctive antipathy between Aryan and Semite.

The Carthaginians were Semites: Carthage—the Semitic name means "new town"—was a Phoenician colony, probably founded from Tyre towards the end of the ninth century B.C. It was not the oldest of the Phoenician settlements in the western Mediterranean: Phoenician maritime enterprise was of long standing; and her traders had passed through the Straits of Gibraltar before 1000 B.C. and therefore before the time of king David. In due course the mother cities of Phoenicia shared the fate of the kingdoms of Israel and Judah in the seventh and sixth centuries before Christ, yielding in turn to Assyrian, Egyptian, neo-Babylonian and, finally, Persian control. Carthage then succeeded to the leadership of the Phoenician world, with its colonies and trading stations along the north coast of Africa and in Spain.

52. The sources of Carthaginian power

The supremacy of Carthage was, in part, due to the natural advantages of its site, a few miles from modern Tunis. It possessed a good harbour situated at the narrowest part of the central Mediterranean, and was thus an admirable centre for commercial enterprise. Carthage in many ways resembled medieval Venice: it was governed by an aristocracy of traders and commercial magnates. Their enterprises were far-reaching: they sought wealth, and therefore needed power to protect the trade that brought them wealth. As has often been true of Semites, their *métier* was to exploit others, whose industry, artistic ability and fighting capacity they used for their own ends. Their troops were largely mercenaries, Berbers from North Africa and Iberians in Spain. These troops proved to be of exceptionally good military quality when well led; and the Carthaginians provided generals of genius, among whom Hannibal is one of the most famous in world history.

53. The struggle with Rome

The prolonged struggle between Rome and Carthage was practically ended in Rome's favour by the battle of Zama in 202 B.C. But, even half a century later, Rome's fear of the revival of an enemy, by whom it had so nearly been destroyed, led to a war of unjustifiable aggression which ended in the total destruction of Carthage in 146 B.C. "Buildings and walls were razed to the ground, the plough passed over the site, and salt was sown in the furrows made."

54. Carthaginian culture

Generations of schoolboys have read the story of the Punic wars, and for the most part Carthage rather than Rome has engaged their sympathies; romance clings to Hannibal rather than to Scipio. Yet undoubtedly the triumph of Rome was the triumph of the better type of civilization. Victory rested with a people whose religious outlook, if uninspiring, was cleaner and more wholesome than that of their rivals. Little has survived from the wreck of Carthage: but there is no reason to suppose that in literature it produced anything to compare with the epics of Semitic Babylonia or with the great writings enshrined in the Old Testament. If it enriched in any way the world's philosophy, poetry or drama, the gain is lost. Though archaeological remains found in the neighbourhood of Carthage are scanty, enough has been discovered to show that its products were of meagre artistic merit. The kingdom of Israel, in the time of David and Solomon, grew wealthy by controlling the transit of goods between Syria and the Red Sea; but its wealth led to no efflorescence of native art. So also Carthage was a great mercantile community, able by reason of its wealth to buy luxuries; but its craftsmen showed little originality and it produced no men of genius to create splendid memorials of their race.

As an instructive instance of the close link between Carthaginian and Jewish Semitism, it may be remarked that Hannibal and John are essentially the same name. John is an abbrevia-

tion of Johannan. Change the Jewish Joh (Yahweh) into the
Phoenician Baal: then invert the order of the two words making
up the name, and the unlikely identity stands revealed.

55. Carthaginian religion

From the denunciations of the Hebrew prophets, we get a
picture of the demoralizing nature of Phoenician religion; and
there are many hints in the Old Testament of the persistence in
Israel and Judah of monstrous religious evils which existed in
Phoenicia, such as human sacrifice and temple prostitution.
Carthage took from Phoenicia such deities as Baal and the
goddess Tanit, supreme in her pantheon. With the fertility
goddess went abominations from which Hebrew religion slowly
purged itself. When the empire of Carthage was but a memory,
human sacrifice lingered on where Punic religion prevailed,
showing itself, according to Tertullian, as late as the first
century of the Christian era. Towards the end of A.D. 1921 there
was excavated near Carthage a site, recently called Salammbô.
Situated just outside the north wall of ancient Carthage, it
was apparently an area sacred to the goddess Tanit; and, in
part, a burial ground, used from at least the fourth century
and until the middle of the second century before Christ
When explored, it was found to contain the calcined bones o
large numbers of very young children who had "passed through
the fire." They were, apparently, victims of the ancient and
horrible Syrian rite of the sacrifice of the first-born.

To this day the peasant in eastern Europe believes that the
Jews kidnap young children for ritual murders: the conviction
adds greatly to the strength of anti-Semitism. Is the belief
founded upon a tradition of horror derived from the religious
practices of other Semites, a tradition still alive centuries after
the practices from which it arose have ceased?

56. The Punic stock

So long as Carthage was unconquered, its people showed
great trading ability and they threw up military leaders of
supreme quality. But the struggle of individuals for wealth and
power was a source of grave dissension within the State. Their
religion sanctioned cruelty and was tolerant of vice. It was
from the Carthaginians that the Romans derived the horrible

practice of crucifixion, though it must be allowed that Cicero ascribes to the Etruscans the introduction into Rome of this infamous form of punishment.

The Carthaginian language and stock endured long after the fall of Carthage. By the irony of fate, Septimius Severus, a north African whose native speech was Punic, became Roman emperor towards the close of the second century of the Christian era. His sister, we are told, spoke Latin imperfectly. His Semitic instincts caused him to make a Syrian marriage. He was an able soldier who, as emperor, showed himself cruel and vindictive. Some of the worst characteristics of the north African Semites emerged in the dynasty which he founded. Though the dynasty lasted but a short time, it proved well-nigh fatal to the Roman empire. The empire, in fact, was with difficulty preserved after desperate struggles by certain great emperors of Balkan origin who preceded Constantine.

We may balance Severus and his dynasty by some great Christian thinkers of north African origin who belonged to his own or later times. Tertullian (c. A.D. 155–c. 230) combined a vivid literary style with passionate religious earnestness. A century later came Lactantius, who expounded Christianity in elegant Latin. Still later Augustine (c. A.D. 354–430) showed himself a master of Christian theology, second only to Paul.

While we have no certain knowledge of the racial origin of any of these Christian teachers, it is possible, and even probable, that all owed an ability, which was not far short of genius, to some Punic strain. Possibly from the same source there came veins of extravagance, and of enthusiasm at times unfairly partisan. In neither Tertullian nor Augustine, men of great distinction though they were, can we find the religious grandeur or the quiet moral beauty of the greatest followers of Christ.

57. The Romans

We have previously, in §§ 29–32, described the Greek temperament and genius. Differences between the Greeks and the Romans were profound; yet we know of no adequate reason for their existence. Each people represented a fusion of invaders from the north, speaking an Indo-European language, with aboriginal people, presumably of the widespread Mediterranean race. In each country the new civilization which the invaders created lay near the sea in not very extensive plains, backed by difficult mountainous areas. Differences of climate were not great. Each country seems to have been originally free from the malaria by which it was afterwards cursed. Yet, notwithstanding all these likenesses, the two races showed striking contrasts in temperament and innate aptitudes.

Perhaps Greek quickness of mind was stimulated by love of the sea, to which the Romans took with reluctance but ultimately with characteristic thoroughness. As opposed to the Greeks, the Romans lacked intellectual brilliance. They had no native artistic gifts: such art as they had in early times came from the Etruscans. In the realm of ideas they were unadventurous. There are few inventions for which they deserve credit. Their literature owes more to Greek models than to native capacity.

58. The Roman character

Before they were corrupted by the wealth which poured in after the final destruction of Carthage in 146 B.C., the Romans had a tradition of simplicity, trustworthiness and honest work. Family life was patriarchal and stern. Romans of the best type had massive integrity and ardent patriotism. In demeanour and in spirit they were grave. In public and private life they showed tenacity and the wisdom of moderation. Firmness of character was coupled with a strong sense of the value of law: the Roman legal system survived the disappearance of the Roman empire.

The Romans had naturally the defects of their good qualities. Towards dependants they tended to be cold and harsh. As conquerors their thoroughness made them ruthless. Slaves were at times treated with a shocking lack of feeling. From the Etruscans, as we have said, there came a taint of cruelty.

59. The winning of world control

Originally the Romans must have consisted of a few thousand people, landowners, herdsmen and agriculturists, whose centre was a large village on the Tiber. From this village a small city-state arose by the conquest of Latin neighbours. This conquest ended in the first of a series of alliances, which erased from memory the bitterness of strife and gave new strength to the

victor. Within the city the same capacity for wise conciliation
was shown. During the fifth and fourth centuries before Christ,
there was a long and hard struggle between patricians and
plebeians. Gradually the plebeians wrested power from its
holders. The political and social tension must have been often
severe: but civil war was avoided. Plebeians could at length
reach the Senate: but, though Rome could thus make full use
of her most able citizens, the Senate remained a body in which
the great families took their full share of government.

The Romans, notwithstanding the Roman virtues, had no
smooth passage to the control of Italy. At a date usually given
as 390 B.C., the Gauls sacked Rome. Though the overrunning
of Etruria by these northern barbarians was its death-blow, the
harm done to Rome was soon made good: the tenacity of her
citizens stood her in good stead. Fifty years later there began
a prolonged war with the Samnites, hardy mountaineers of
central Italy; but, shortly after 300 B.C., Rome was supreme
in Italy south of the valley of the Po. During the first half of the
third century before Christ, there were further struggles, always
successful in the end, with the Gauls in the north and the
Greeks in the south. Then came the war with Carthage which,
in all, lasted more than a century (264–146 B.C.). That war
ended, Rome was obviously in a position to be master of the
then known world.

60. The price of victory

After the downfall of Carthage, wealth poured into Rome
and slaves into Italy. The price of victory had been heavy. Few
of the peasants who were the mainstay of the Roman armies
returned. The small holdings on which they had lived disappeared, their place taken by greater landed estates tilled by
slaves. The demoralization of the great Roman families
accompanied this economic disaster. Soon the republic was
torn by fights between wealthy and ambitious generals. The
names of Marius, Sulla, Pompey, Caesar, Antony, Octavian
remind us of dreadful civil wars which preceded the end of the
Roman republic.

Finally, in 29 B.C., Octavian, Julius Caesar's great-nephew,
on his father's side of sound middle-class origin, emerged
supreme. Two years later he elected to be styled Augustus:

thereupon, while carefully preserving the appearance of republican citizenship, he became virtually the first Roman emperor. He held supreme power until his death in A.D. 14. *Luke* begins his story of the birth of Jesus with the words (ii. 1), "Now it came to pass in those days, there went out a decree from Caesar Augustus, that all the world should be enrolled." *Luke's* history, as we shall see, is probably erroneous; but in the reign of Augustus, and possibly in 6 B.C., Jesus was born.

61. Augustus and the Julio-Claudians

Augustus was not a great military leader; but he was a statesman of extraordinary sagacity. Shrewd in his choice of lieutenants, whether for civil or military service, he set himself to organize the vast possessions of Rome. Internal peace was established. Order was brought into the financial administration, which had been amateurish and often corrupt. Perfection was not attained; for the Senate was naturally jealous of its rights, which included the appointment of the governors of certain provinces. But after the uncertainties, the bloodshed and confiscations of a century of civil war, a new era of good government began.

Augustus gave to the Graeco-Roman world the Augustan peace. That peace may be said to have lasted for more than two centuries, until the death in A.D. 180 of the emperor Marcus Aurelius. There was one terrible interruption, "the year of the four emperors," on the murder of the unspeakable Nero in A.D. 68. Then the fierce civil wars, which broke out between ambitious generals, awakened fear throughout the empire and deluged the streets of Rome itself with blood.

Christian writers have argued that the Augustan peace was designed by Divine providence as a preparation for the coming of Christ and the spread of the gospel. Alternatively, it may be claimed that Christianity owed its initial success to the relatively happy and suitable conditions, political stability and religious chaos of the world into which it was born. As we read of the origin and progress of the then new faith, it is an aid to understanding to bear in mind that the government established by Augustus sought to be strong and paternal, to preserve order and to allow freedom. Standards deteriorated under Tiberius and his three immediate successors, Gaius,

Claudius and Nero. These men ruled by virtue of their kinship to Augustus; and unfortunately Tiberius (A.D. 14–37) became moody and suspicious, Gaius (Caligula) (A.D. 37–41) was mad, Claudius (A.D. 41–54) was a learned recluse physically repellent, and Nero (A.D. 54–68) a disgrace to mankind.

Jesus began his ministry in Galilee, according to *Luke* (iii. 1), "in the fifteenth year of the reign of Tiberius Caesar": Paul was martyred in Rome in the reign of Nero. Thus, though most of the books of the New Testament were written later, the whole of New Testament history belongs to an era in which each emperor lacked some of the qualities needed in a position of absolute, lonely and demoralizing power.

62. Roman religion

Although Rome dominated the world in which Christianity arose and spread, the influence upon Christianity of the religious ideas of the Roman people was slight. Probably in its origin Roman religion was that of Aryan invaders from the north, though it was modified by beliefs and practices both of the Etruscans and of primitive stocks of the so-called Mediterranean race. The notion of taboo remained strong: certain persons and animals must be excluded from certain ceremonies and places, or they would bring disaster. Allied beliefs that extraordinary, and even certain ordinary, happenings were portents of ill-fortune were associated with acceptance of magic. Certain acts were supposed to constrain nature: certain practices had in themselves a super-natural efficiency. Such an outlook is even to-day widespread in so-called civilized lands. It is independent of a belief in a god or gods though, when it enters into religious practice, it is sometimes defended by theological arguments.

Worship of the deified powers of nature or of the heavenly bodies does not seem to have played an important part in early Roman religion. What was fundamental appears to have been the belief in spirits or powers associated with particular places or objects. Some of these *numina*, according to such belief, were to be found guarding the door of a house; others protected its hearth. Others again watched over the boundary-stones of a farm. Even more important were the spirits who presided over different activities of man, such as the sowing of grain, or over such functions as childbirth. The worshipper gave to the spirits their due, whatever it might be; and, in return, they were expected to bestow upon him the good things which he sought.

Religion, as thus conceived, is primarily of practical value; and Roman worship was essentially of this nature. The Lares and Penates were the guardian spirits of the household; and the head of the house sought their blessing by prayer with an offering on the family altar. Vesta was the spirit of the hearth-flame; and the Vestal Virgins tended the hearth of the City of Rome.

63. The divine element in man

Just as *numina*, or attendant spirits, were associated with places or activities, so each person was supposed to have his *genius*, somewhat analogous to an indwelling *numen*. The *genius* does not seem to have been an attendant spirit, a "familiar" or guardian angel, but was rather the man himself in his essential nature. A family would worship the *genius* of the father, while he was still alive, at a celebration on his birthday. The *genius* came to be thought of as the divine element in a man; and, naturally, in great or important men the notion of divinity was emphasized. In this way, when the Roman republic ended, the worship of the *genius* of the emperor grew up. His *genius* and that of the City of Rome were twin spirits, jointly presiding over the destinies of the Roman empire. A great emperor, when dead, became *divus* by decree of the Senate and thus took his place among the gods. Julius, Augustus and Claudius were all deified. The gulf between man and God was absolute in Jewish thought. It hardly existed for a populace which offered sacrifice to the *genius* of the emperor, just as an Englishman takes the oath of allegiance to his sovereign or sings his national anthem.

64. Roman religion and Christianity

So vast was the difference between Roman religion and the Jewish monotheism in which Christianity took its rise that no sympathy between the two faiths was to be expected. But there was also a profound ethical divergence between the Roman outlook on life and Christianity. The virtues admired by the Roman were courage, strength, self-reliance, disciplined firmness, patriotism. He sought wealth and power, happiness and success, as things good in themselves. Though he could not be classed as vicious or cruel, his attitude towards sins of the flesh was by no means stern—the gallantries of Julius Caesar, though notorious, did no harm to his reputation—and pity on occasion could be surprisingly absent. The Christian, on the other hand, strongly condemned sexual impurity: at the same time he extolled friendliness, peace, long-suffering, kindness, goodness, meekness, the slave virtues as they have been scornfully called.

The Roman of the first century of our era, if he knew anything of Christianity, must have thought it a proletarian religion, not unsuited to his slaves, yet in itself absurd in its pretensions and contemptible in its ideals. But the narrow realm of civilized society was, when Christianity began to spread, rapidly shrinking, depopulated by the luxury and immorality which the existence of slavery fosters. The future lay with the children of the proletariat, with the common people to whom the gospel gave new hope in a harsh world.

E

CHAPTER III

THE MYSTERY-RELIGIONS

WHENEVER a people is converted to a new form of faith, that faith is modified by the previous religion of those among whom it spreads. As Christianity made its way over the Mediterranean area in the century following the death of its Lord, it did not escape the process of change.

Remaining firmly monotheistic, it refused any recognition of the numerous deities of the different official cults of the cities and states of the Roman empire. But these cults had largely exhausted their vitality. They served as the formal expression of a politico-religious unity in which, on suitable occasions, all loyal citizens would join; but ardent faith found a natural home in the so-called mystery-religions.

These religions were influential in Greece as early as the sixth century before Christ. They were associated with, and modified by, analogous forms of faith rising from the Orient. They lasted until after the triumph of Christianity in the fourth century of our era. During the third century of our era, when the Roman empire was barely saved from collapse by the emperors from Illyricum and adjacent lands, Christianity and the mystery-religion of Mithra ran a neck-and-neck race, of which the outcome was long in doubt. It has often been said that Christianity ultimately triumphed in the ancient world as a mystery-religion; and undoubtedly the influence of ideas from these faiths is to be found in the New Testament, and especially in the writings attributed to Paul.

65. The nature of a mystery-religion

A mystery-religion differed from an official State religion in that the latter was associated with public worship, while the rites of a mystery-religion were, as its name indicates, secret. Participation in these rites, and even the privilege of seeing them, was limited to those who had been initiated by some process of ritual purification. Because of this element of secrecy we are ill-informed as to the beliefs and practices of the various mystery-faiths. We know that they had a general likeness to one another: apart from sex-differentiation—women, for instance, were not admitted to Mithraic fraternities—they were open to all, slave or free. They had, more often than not, come up from a barbarous underworld. They were singularly persistent. The mysteries at Eleusis, near Athens, lasted for a thousand years; and there is reason to believe that they changed little during that long period.

At the basis of the mystery-faiths is the idea of renewal of life. We see such apparent renewal each springtime: roots and branches, which seemed dead, burst into life. Can man similarly live after death? The question has probably intrigued men for tens of thousands of years.

Again, is there any religious rite by means of which the peasant in his family, his crops and herds, can have life more abundantly? New life and sex are intimately associated: hence come many disgusting features of primitive religion. Some rites of some of the mystery-faiths had their origin in fertility magic. As these faiths developed, old symbols and practices, repulsive, immoral or obscene, were either changed or, more commonly, were reinterpreted.

Primarily, then, the primitive worshipper seeks the bounty of nature: plenteous harvests, the increase of flocks and herds, and the birth of children. His mysteries are designed to gain aid from the divine powers that govern nature. But, as he meditates upon the objects of his worship or wonders at the annual miracle of spring, he is led further to seek for divine aid to intensify his own life. The gods are active around him: an intimate approach to them may give him the thrill of divine communion. If he can gain the help of their creative activity, he may even be born again.

What man, when age or sickness oppresses him, has not desired to awake with a confident sense of well-being and power? Such a sense of well-being comes in the early stages of intoxication. Though we are shocked by the idea of comparing spiritual ecstasy with alcoholic excess, the primitive worshipper regarded all types of frenzy as manifestations of the divine. Bacchic orgies were not merely drunken revels: they showed that the worshipper was under the influence of the god.

66. The mysteries were sacramental

He who took part in the mysteries was assured that they were sacramental: the rites were outward and visible signs of the grace which he was conscious of having received. He had won communion with the Lord of his cult, Dionysus, or Mithra, or whoever it might be. Often enough the rites were thought to be effective because they appealed to man's instinctive belief in sympathetic magic. To go through an experience similar to that which was crucial in the life of the Lord of one's faith, was to gain a mystical identification with him. Alternatively, his blood could save. To be drenched in the blood of the Creator-Lord's sacred animal, as in the *taurobolium*, was to be purified by him, cleansed and made ready for eternal life, reborn for eternity.

Animals were thought to be sacred to the god either in their essential nature or through sacrificial offering: when their flesh was eaten, the worshipper believed that he became united to, or even identified with, the god, partaking of his substance and qualities. Ordinary food, by consecration, that is, by giving it the right associations, could when eaten ensure such union or identification. Hence a votary could secure the spiritual indwelling of the divine Lord by symbolically eating his flesh and drinking his blood. Through such indwelling, life after death was supposed to be ensured. Equally, in Egyptian religion, immortality was gained by an identification with Osiris, reached by other rites. Thus the various Lords of the different cults in many ways gave salvation to eternal life. Each was a Saviour-God.

Enough has been said to show that the mystery-faiths embraced a wide range of religious ideas and emotions: one could pass from the coarse instincts of the primitive savage to the highest—or nearly the highest—levels of spiritual understanding. But common to all these faiths was the fact that they were independent of the social structure of the community. Worshippers came from every class, though all who were admitted had to undergo some preliminary rite of initiation or purification.

During the early Christian era it was possible for the same individual to have the experience of admission, after due purification in each case, to different mystery-ceremonies. Thus the various cults were not mutually exclusive rivals. In so far as Christianity was a mystery-religion, it refused all such friendliness. To the Saviour-Lords of the mystery cults it was as implacably hostile as to the gods and goddesses of official paganism. It retained—should we not say rightly retained?— an intolerance inherited from Jewish monotheism.

67. Orphism and its origin

The heights to which the mystery-religions could rise from sordid depths are well seen in Orphism. This faith spread in Greece as early as the sixth century before Christ; and, in association with the teaching of Pythagoras, was a creative factor in what may be termed the mystical tradition of Greek philosophy. Orpheus, a shadowy figure, the music of whose lyre enchanted even the beasts, gave his name as a revealer to rites which had their roots in the cult of Dionysus.

This cult appears to have been of Thracian origin; and the name Dionysus is said to mean "god's son." He was associated with Zagreus, who appears to have had his origin in the mountainous country east of Assyria and to have reached Greece through Phoenicia, or perhaps Egypt, and Crete. The fusion created Dionysus-Zagreus, who was asserted to have been born of the marriage of Zeus with his own daughter. Dionysus-Zagreus was, in the form of an ox, torn to pieces by the Titans. They, after boiling his limbs, devoured them. But his heart was preserved and became the basis of his resurrection. Zeus, moreover, slew the Titans and from their blasted ashes made man. Man is thus, like the Titans, prone to evil; but within him, because of their food, is a divine element.

This grotesque story, which has many variants and developments, well shows how unpromising was the material out of which a mystery-faith could evolve. Dionysus was originally a god of fruitfulness. The ivy-leaf wreath, with which he was crowned, shows him as god of vegetation. In the spring he appeared on the mountains; and his frenzied worshippers, mainly women, sought him to the sound of wild music. Professing to find him in some ox or goat, they tore his flesh to pieces and devoured it raw. The whole *mise en scène* is dreadfully and horribly barbarous.

68. Its development

But gradually from the welter of absurdity and savagery emerged the higher mysteries. The twofold origin of man necessitates war within his members. The god, in whose divinity men have a share, had proved immortal. He had become Lord of life and, as such, guaranteed immortality to those who gave him service. Religious teachers, using the story, taught that we must condemn the Titan-born world of sense and by purification escape "the sorrowful weary wheel" of successive incarnations. So came Orphic theology teaching the salvation, by rites of purification, of the individual soul. Communion with the god in frenzied orgies was replaced by less barbarous rites, as in the mysteries at Eleusis, near Athens.

69. The Eleusinian mysteries

These mysteries—their secret was well kept—consisted, apparently, of the sight of sacred scenes and the handling of certain holy things. But their effect was not merely that of an impressive ritual: it was in some way associated with the assurance of immortality, the triumph of life over death. Those truly initiated at Eleusis passed through an experience so charged with intense feeling that they were, to use a modern religious term, "changed." Their outlook on life became different: their moral standards were higher. They had been "converted." Doubtless many of the initiated, perhaps the majority, were not so moved; they merely saw forms and ceremonies, external to themselves. But the mysteries at Eleusis would not have lasted for a thousand years had they, for all who partook of them, been empty of religious inspiration.

The Eleusinian mysteries were quasi-official. They had an assured place in Greek civilization. Orphism was not a phase of national life of which the best Greek thinkers were ashamed. We have already mentioned Pythagoras, who lived in the latter half of the sixth century before Christ. He in a most exceptional way combined intellectual power with spiritual distinction; and, in part at any rate, built his way of life upon Orphic mysticism.

But practically all the mystery cults which ran their course through the Graeco-Roman world after the third century before Christ met at first with official disapproval. In essentials they were alien from Graeco-Roman civilization. Some were demoralizing: some repellently barbarous. Some openly pandered to the baser instincts of mankind. But all offered religious excitements which the cold State-faith failed to give. All ultimately disappeared as Christianity grew in strength. None the less, certain ideas or modes of feeling common to all had their influence within the victorious faith.

70. The religion of the Great Mother: Cybele and Attis

The first of the oriental religions to invade Rome seems to have been the cult of Cybele, the Great Mother of Ida, from Phrygia in Asia Minor.

In 205 B.C. Hannibal was still in Italy. The struggle against him had been exhausting and terrible. The *morale* of the Roman people was shaken: there were widely believed rumours of disquieting portents; for example, what were described as repeated torrents of stones caused grave apprehension. When the books of the Sibylline oracles were consulted, it was learned that Hannibal might be driven from Italy if the Great Mother came from Phrygia to Rome. So from Pessinus, presented by the king of the land, came a black aerolite, supposed to be the abode of the goddess. The stone was reverently received by a Roman citizen bearing the great and honoured name of Scipio. It was carried in splendid state to the Palatine hill, overlooking the Forum, at Rome. There a temple to the goddess was built; and annually the dedication of the sanctuary was celebrated. The Great Mother had delivered Rome from the Carthaginians and must henceforth be honoured.

But her worship had a crudity suited to half-savage peoples. She was "mistress of the wild beasts," and with her the lion especially was associated. Her husband was the god Attis, the spirit of vegetation. His sacred trees were the pines of the forest and the prolific almond-trees, with their early blossom. Every year Attis died and came to life again. In the spring-time were festivals commemorating Cybele's discovery of Attis, his death and resurrection. Attis was symbolized by a pine-tree wrapped like a corpse in woollen bands and decked with violets. All the rites of the cult were carried out by Phrygian priests, who in frenzied ecstasy had mutilated themselves. In fact, the religion of the Great Mother, as the Romans received it, was a superstitious fetichism, its rites sensual and disgusting.

71. The persistence of the Cybele-Attis rites in Rome

The grave Romans of the republic and of the time of Augustus naturally regarded with aversion an orgiastic religion which dangerously excited the masses. Hence for two centuries it was virtually isolated on the Palatine, save that its priests, during the holidays celebrated in honour of Cybele, patrolled the streets, eunuchs adorned with discreditable finery. In the time of the emperor Claudius (A.D. 41–54), apparently because the rival cult of Isis had been authorized a few years earlier, the restrictions were withdrawn. At almost exactly the same time, Christianity must have first reached Rome. After Claudius had ended the repression, respectable Romans seem to have acted as chief priests of the mysteries and probably exercised some much-needed restraint over Phrygian frenzy.

One is tempted to ask why a form of religion with associations so foul and degraded should have persistently maintained its influence in Rome. Nothing more unlike the sober gravity of the Roman temperament can well be imagined. As we attempt an answer, we have to remember that there was an increasingly large Asiatic population in Italy, inasmuch as the importation of slaves was continuous. But, also, in native Italian stocks there was probably a growing desire for warmth and colour and excitement in religion. Above all, men craved the immortality that the mysteries of the Great Mother professed to give. Attis died and rose again: those mystically joined to him would likewise after death rise to newness of life. As the years passed, the cult changed somewhat; and by the fourth century of our era it developed a surprising similarity to Christianity. The feasts of the Great Mother were likened by her votaries to the Christian eucharist. The blood of the frenzied priests was symbolically the blood of Attis, which was alleged to save men more potently than the blood of the Christian Lamb of God. Finally, however, the more wholesome religion triumphed; the mysteries of Cybele and Attis decayed and disappeared.

72. Isis and Osiris

A similar fate awaited the other mystery-religions, two of which we may describe.

Superficially the religion of Isis and Serapis differs profoundly from that of Cybele and Attis. The latter had emerged, and in many ways was not remote, from primitive barbarism: the former came from the splendid and ancient civilization of Egypt, of which the Romans always stood somewhat in awe. Egypt, more than any other province, was under the emperor's personal control. It was largely staffed by a highly competent native bureaucracy: in the practice of accountancy, for example, its servants were without a rival. Before the Egyptian noble or priest, the heir of age-long traditions, the Roman had the uncomfortable feeling of the *parvenu*.

Now, according to Tacitus (*Histories* iv. 83), the old cult of Osiris, the Lord of the dead, had, early in the third century before Christ, been modified by the reigning Ptolemy. With the aid of a Greek, hereditarily connected with the Eleusinian mysteries, he evolved the cult of Serapis. It would appear that in popular thought Serapis was quickly identified with Osiris; and the Egyptians readily accepted the new worship, although the liturgy was Greek. In fact, the monarch's attempt to make a religious synthesis met with a somewhat surprising success. The headquarters of the cult were in a famous sanctuary, known as the serapeum, which was erected at Alexandria.

Gradually the new-old cult spread over the Graeco-Roman world. For more than five centuries it persisted, maintaining itself in Rome even though, five different times in the first century before Christ, the Senate ordered its altars and statues to be demolished. At length, by A.D. 391, a Christian patriarch at Alexandria destroyed the serapeum there, together with the world-famous statue of Serapis which it enshrined. Perhaps his religious zeal justified his iconoclasm; but the statue seems to have been a noble work of art.

73. Isis worship in the early Christian era

The Isis cult emphasized originally the passion and resurrection of Osiris: in later centuries the worship of Isis, "mother of tenderness," "goddess of a thousand names," was largely developed. Apart from the annual festivals at the beginning of

March and the end of October, there were daily services, morning and evening, conducted by tonsured priests clad in linen vestments. The morning service began with the withdrawal of curtains, revealing Isis richly attired for adoration— a veritable Egyptian Madonna. Hymns and prayers, a morning sacrifice with litany and holy water, to say nothing of a temple choir, completed the likeness to later developments within Christianity. Isis was worshipped as the mother of sorrows, who had sought the dead Osiris and had found him restored to life. The god was himself giver of life and Lord of eternity. At the heart of the Isis cult the old Egyptian belief persisted that, as an initiate was identified with Osiris, immortality could be gained. "As truly as Osiris lives, he also shall live: as truly as Osiris is not dead, he shall not die."

74. Mithra

Among the different Oriental mystery-religions which invaded Roman paganism before, or at the time of, the Christian era, that of the Persian god Mithra proved the most formidable rival to Christianity. In primitive Aryan religion Mithra had had his place. When the Persians first emerge into history, he is the genius of light. He drives away darkness. From him comes the warmth which "causes grass to grow for the cattle, and herb for the service of man: that he may bring forth food out of the earth." Thus he is "Lord of wide pastures." He is the source of the good things that make glad the heart of man.

By an obvious transition Mithra brings spiritual no less than material blessings. As the god of light Mithra was naturally thought of in close alliance with the sun: he was therefore the enemy of the powers of darkness. Thus he was the defender of truth and justice, the guardian of righteousness, the leader in the conflict with evil. Not only was he the soldiers' protector, helping them in their struggle with the barbarians, but in the moral realm he gave his followers victory over temptation. In essentials he became the *Logos* who brought salvation: he was the mediator between Ahura-Mazda (see § 25) and man.

75. The Mithra legend

The legend of Mithra has to be recovered from the Mithraic

monuments which have survived. They are many; and, though the liturgy has perished, the reconstruction is tolerably certain.

The birth-story comes first. As light proceeds from the supposedly solid vault of heaven, so Mithra was born from the rock. He emerged with the characteristic Phrygian cap on his head, a knife in his right hand and a torch in his left. His first "labour" was a struggle with the Sun, which rendered him homage as a preliminary to lasting friendship. Then came the struggle with the bull, the first living creature created by Ahura-Mazda.

This struggle became the symbol of man's striving against evil. Mithra overcame the strong animal and carried it to his cave. But it escaped and he was bidden to slay it. Mithra hated his task; and as he plunged his knife into the victim turned his head away. The pathos of this supreme moment was admirably depicted, probably in the second century before Christ, by a sculptor of Pergamon. He created the type which became invariable; and some copy, perhaps not very exact, of his slaying of the bull was an altar-piece in every mithraeum.

Mithra's reluctant obedience was astonishingly justified, for from the body of the dying bull came all the useful grasses and plants that cover the earth. From death came life. There followed other "labours" against famine and flood; but, in the end, his earthly mission fulfilled, Mithra after a Last Supper ascended into heaven, whence he has never ceased to succour his own.

The legend of the bull-slaying, of the god who in suffering created civilization, was obviously shaped in an agricultural community. In every altar-piece Mithra wore the Phrygian cap and the barbarian trousers, thus emphasizing his Persian origin. We never find him in the dress of a Roman soldier, though he became *par excellence* the soldiers' god. His worship recalled its wild origin, for the initiates met, not in a house, but in a cave, natural or, more commonly, artificial. Mithra had his sacraments of purification and communion, and seven orders of initiates. But, whereas women added greatly to the strength of the Christian movement, they were, as we have previously said, excluded from the worship of Mithra.

76. The progress of Mithraism in the Christian era

Though Mithraism was of great antiquity, it did not apparently begin to make headway in the Roman world until the first century of our era. In that world at that time political security, as we have said, combined with religious anarchy to give it, like Christianity, its chance. An era of rapid progress alike for it and for Christianity set in towards the close of the first century after Christ. By the end of the second century, if we may judge by the number of monuments which remain, its progress had been considerably more rapid than that of Christianity. By the end of the third century Christianity had virtually triumphed. Doubtless the adherents of Mithra had a brief hour of glorious hope when the emperor Julian, "the apostate," in A.D. 361 tried to make it the religion of the empire; but, on his speedy death, its final overthrow was rapid.

Many questions can be asked. Why should an Asiatic faith, whose god retained the barbarous dress of the hereditary Persian enemy, have become the creed of the Roman soldier? It made no intellectual appeal, for its theology was a naive mixture of solar pantheism with fragments of the teaching of Zoroaster, to which were added astrology and primitive fables. Oriental ideas of the inferiority of women were perpetuated by its ostracism of them. Yet, when all that is to its disfavour has been said, we must remember that it encouraged brave and resolute action alike on the field of battle and in the struggle against evil. Furthermore, like Christianity, it satisfied man's desire for immortality and promised final justice for the unfortunate and oppressed.

The likenesses between Mithraism and Christianity, as each had developed by the end of the second century of our era, were many. Each faith had borrowed from the other, and the borrowings of Christianity were perhaps the more extensive. As we proceed with our inquiry, reasons for the ultimate triumph of Christianity may become evident. But it was a miracle that a pacifist creed should have proved stronger than the soldiers' faith: that men should have acclaimed as Saviour-Lord, not the god of light with his venerable antiquity, but a peasant-artisan comparatively recently born in a Jewish district to the south of Syria. The pretensions advanced for Jesus the Christ must have seemed to followers of the rival mystery-faiths a colossal impertinence. Is there a hint of mockery in the Christian reply: "He hath put down the mighty from their seat and hath exalted the humble and meek"?

CHAPTER IV

MIRACLES

THE books of the New Testament were, with little doubt, all written within about a century, from A.D. 50 to A.D. 150. There may be in them some earlier written material: equally, editorial corrections and modifications may have been made later. The main statement, however, stands.

Probably nothing in the New Testament of primary importance should be dated later than A.D. 120. We should expect that during the years A.D. 50–120 pagan writers would have had much to say of the Christian movement. There is, however, in classical literature written before A.D. 110, a practically complete silence as regards the new religion. It was ignored, contemptuously or angrily or from mere lack of interest.

77. The people among whom Christianity spread

Putting together all the information, Christian and non-Christian, that can be obtained, we get the impression that at first Christianity was primarily a movement among the lower-middle and upper artisan classes. It did not affect the scum of great cities like Rome, Corinth, or Ephesus, though, once planted in these centres, it grew vigorously. The slaves attracted to the movement were relatively few; and we may surmise that they, for the most part, were household servants.

The movement spread only exceptionally and sporadically among the governing classes: there is no reason to doubt that members of Caesar's household were drawn to it some thirty years after the crucifixion of Jesus, but they may well have been petty clerks. For the most part, the early converts to Christianity were pious, kindly people, ill-educated and, as we should deem them, superstitious. To a large extent they were, as their numbers increased, town-dwellers.

78. Their government

Under the Roman empire in the first century of our era there was a marked improvement in the administration of the provinces: the worst abuses of the later years of the Roman republic had been brought to an end. But taxation was heavy: the alien rule of provincial governors was often hard. Conquest had led to a unified economy, within which large landowners and great corporations exploited the common people. The existence of slavery meant that the free worker was exposed to a form of competition ruinous to his economic status.

At the head of a province there might be a governor with high stoic ideals, and the men in close contact with him might share his standards; but the petty officials were probably grasping, mean and tyrannical. Moreover, some of the legates and procurators, sent from Rome during the first century of our era while the Julio-Claudians and Flavians were ruling, were far from satisfactory.

79. Their social condition and new hope

Speaking generally, Christianity spread through an unhappy proletariat which found life hard. The converts lived meanly in squalid quarters in the cities: around them was the moral filth of paganism.

To those of this population who were "called," Christianity came as a great hope. It replaced uncertainty as to fundamentals by a confident faith. It gave the strength born of unity to men and women who were striving for better things. The hardships of the harsh social system were mitigated by the friendly help forthcoming within the Christian brotherhood. To those carried away by Christian enthusiasm, the kingdom of God on earth seemed a not impossible dream: Christianity, in fact, brought the impulse to create a new social order. With the movement there went naturally aloofness from, or even hostility to, the existing order which Rome imposed and maintained. The new religion vehemently repudiated paganism: in its enmity it was uncompromising.

80. Their level of education

Christianity began, of course, in Palestine. There slavery was comparatively rare: and among the Jews it appears to have been true that artisans, small shopkeepers and peasants had, speaking generally, some education. But, in spreading, Christianity seems quickly to have lost touch with Palestine;

and all the books of the New Testament are coloured by the outlook which prevailed in the Hellenistic East, not among the intellectuals, but among the semi-educated or illiterate populace.

We cannot understand the New Testament unless we constantly keep in mind the level of education and the types of aspiration of those who left the impress of their thought and emotion on its pages. In particular, we cannot account for the presence of the miracles which pervade the *Gospels* and *Acts*, save by imaginatively entering into the mental processes of those from whom and through whom miraculous stories came.

The ancient world, as we have said, had its science, largely developed under Greek leadership subsequent to the great intellectual movement in Ionia in the seventh and sixth centuries before Christ. At the time when Christianity began to spread, certain branches of science, such as medicine, mathematics and astronomy, were still maintained at a high level. In the great university of Alexandria, as in lesser intellectual centres like Gadara, men would have smiled at a primitive belief in a heaven above, the flat earth and a hell beneath it— a belief assumed in the so-called Apostles' Creed. But even in the time of Christ the decay of Graeco-Roman civilization had begun. A century and a half later, as we shall mention in § 313, the intellectuals were dying out: the finer types of mental creative activity were disappearing: a new barbarism was submerging the cultural achievements of the past. In the second half of the second century medical science still had a distinguished leader in Galen, physician to the emperor Marcus Aurelius; but by the year A.D. 400 the great Hippocratic tradition in medicine had entirely disappeared.

81. Christianity and the new barbarism

Now Christianity was a redeeming leaven in the new barbarism. It gave, to groups within the upthrusting populace, cohesion and moral strength. While it ultimately with its pacifism weakened the empire as a fighting machine, it lessened tendencies to social disorder. But because Christianity, as it spread, was associated with an ill-educated proletariat, and because the thought, even of its leaders, was shaped by the growing intellectual deterioration of the time, the books of the New Testament are a strange mixture of spiritual insight, religious beauty and moral strength, combined with incredible stories and bizarre beliefs.

It is sometimes said that, if we repudiate the miracles of the New Testament, we impugn the honesty of the writers. We do nothing of the sort: we impugn their critical acumen. Amid a population such as that in which Christianity was shaped, illustrations, allegories and fanciful possibilities rapidly change into plain narratives and are accepted as historical facts. . Unless a writer is so balanced by his intellectual training that he almost instinctively sifts fact from fancy, he will give us legend instead of prosaic truth when he tries to write religious history as shaped by groups of enthusiastic and superstitious people. We cannot ignore the fact that man is naturally superstitious. Even in a modern scientifically educated population beliefs and practices, alike primitive and irrational, persist. Credulity in the ancient world was amazing.

82. A superstitious world

Only in quite modern times has belief in the large-scale (finite as contrasted with infinitesimal) uniformities of nature become an authoritative dogma. To most thinkers, when Rome ruled the ancient world, the affairs of men appeared to be capriciously ordered: why then should a like caprice not be possible in nature? Who knew the limitations of the powers of the gods? Strange and unpredictable events were constantly happening. Ancient legends preserved stories of signs and wonders which only the impious could doubt. It was officially maintained that unlikely and inexplicable connections existed between facts: for instance, the specks on a sacrificial victim's liver were used to predict the course of human affairs. There was some scepticism, of course; but it tended to be half-hearted. Well-educated historians of the first century of our era accepted miraculous stories with untroubled credulity.

The Jewish populace, especially in Palestine, escaped the evil influences of polytheism and divination; but Persian beliefs as to angels and demons corrupted the fine monotheism of the great Hebrew prophets. To the Jew, God was the all-powerful Creator. He had made the world. It was subject to His guidance. Moreover, the sacred books of the Jewish race recorded miracles wrought by the prophets to whom Jehovah

F

had given his aid : the Elijah-Elisha cycle of stories, once heard, could never be forgotten. And, if the later wisdom-literature contained no such records, it was over-intellectualized, and at times sceptical. Popular feeling found natural expression, when national passions were greatly stirred, in such fictitious history as the book of *Daniel* with its flamboyant miracles. Widely, with the belief that Jehovah was the Lord, there went the conviction that natural phenomena obeyed His will. Hence among the Jews miracles existed to declare the power of God. Among the pagans, myth, magic and superstition had even fuller sway.

83. The orderly universe of modern science

During the last three centuries of our modern era, a wholly new understanding has gradually, and of late rapidly, grown strong. Science has been built upon "the uniform repetition of likenesses." Observed sequences are formulated as invariable laws of nature. The triumphant discoveries which have resulted from scientific research based upon these principles, bid fair to transform human life. Hence the principles of science and, in particular, the large-scale, or finite-scale, uniformity of nature are now understood and accepted, not merely by a restricted group of learned men, but by practically the whole community.

It remains possible, and even most probable, that creative activity, which the Christian would ascribe to God, may be taking place continuously; but such activity must be in the realm of extremely small particles, such as the genes in the living cell. It is also possible that exceptional cases of the influence of mind over body may occur at periods of extreme religious emotion, or when the influence of a man of exceptional quality has free play : in such cases normal laws, ill-understood, may have surprising consequences.

But modern man, with his thought shaped by scientific investigation, is certain that miracles, in the sense of finite-scale activities contrary to the normal ordering of nature, do not happen. Only figuratively can the blind receive their sight, or the lame be made to walk, or the lepers be cleansed, or the deaf be made to hear, or the dead be raised up. It is useless to say that hysterical conditions may simulate physical disorder, or that faulty diagnosis may have led to apparent marvels : the dispute between the world of modern science and some of the beliefs which the early Christians accepted does not relate to miracles that can be explained away.

84. The miraculous in the New Testament

It is, moreover, useless to try to put the miracles attributed to Jesus into a special category. They are on a par with those stated to have been performed by his apostles. The tradition is that the disciples, like their Master, were wonder-workers; and that they, like him, were able to expel the evil spirits then thought to cause epilepsy and madness. Of recent years we have witnessed a willingness to surrender all other New Testament miracles on condition that the virgin birth and the physical resurrection of Jesus are retained. But no sound defence for such a position is possible. The tendency is the outcome of deep-seated desire: it cannot be supported by critical inquiry.

Without a doubt the need to jettison the miraculous element in the New Testament has been, and still is, profoundly disturbing to most of those who accept the Christian faith. It weakens the reliability of the gospel narratives; and, in so far as Christian teaching has been built upon the power of Jesus to perform miracles and upon the miracles associated with his birth and death, it calls for a drastic refashioning of such teaching.

We do well, however, to remember that a miracle proves nothing but itself. Ignore the miracles of the New Testament and Christianity remains that same way of life, lived in accordance with Christ's revelation of God, which through the centuries men have been drawn to follow: Jesus remains the one of whom it was said (2 *Corinthians* v. 19), "God was in Christ reconciling the world to himself." Such indwelling was a spiritual, not a physical, fact. It must be established by spiritual evidence. In the discussion of alleged miracles, much nonsense would be avoided by ardent controversialists if they remembered the first rule of experimental religious psychology, "spiritual truths must be spiritually discerned."

CHAPTER V

THE BIRTH AND ORIGIN OF JESUS

IN previous chapters we have tried briefly to describe the shaping of the world into which Jesus was born. We will now write of him and of the faith which arose out of his teaching. The rise of Christianity shows the growth of his well-nigh incredible influence. That influence was from time to time twisted and contorted: it has been combined with strange and bizarre theories and beliefs. But the inherent greatness of Jesus has repeatedly emerged through perversions and corruptions. His teaching lives; and men's reverence for him "fails not but increases."

85. Stories connected with the birth of Jesus

At the beginning of the gospel according to *Matthew* and also of the gospel according to *Luke*, there are collections of stories relating to the birth and early infancy of Jesus. In the opinion of analytical scholars who accept modern scientific postulates, these stories are not history: they are edifying legend. Nothing corresponding to them is to be found in the earlier gospel according to *Mark*, or in the later gospel according to *John*, or, indeed, elsewhere in the New Testament. They represent developments of the Christian tradition: other such developments finally ended in the fantastic puerilities of some of the so-called apocryphal gospels.

At the beginning, Christianity seems to have been a way of life centred on the person and teaching of Jesus. Christian preaching emphasized particularly the death of Jesus, "whom ye crucified"; and laid stress also on his resurrection, which was held to prove that he was "a Prince and a Saviour," "he who should come," God's anointed, the Christ. But, simultaneously, with a profound and reverent interest in the teaching of Jesus, there must have been a desire to hear of the details of his mission, his acts and manner of life, from his baptism by John to his crucifixion.

At a later stage, there grew up a desire to know of his parents and of the circumstances of his birth. Surely—one can imagine the play of fancy—he who was so exceptional in spiritual power was not born normally, the child of Galilean peasants: surely his birth must have been surrounded by marvels. To meet such expectations the birth stories of the first and third gospels grew up, apparently rather more than half a century after the crucifixion of Jesus, and thus about the year A.D. 90. The examination of details to which we proceed shows that the development of these stories must have taken shape independently before they were incorporated in *Matthew* and *Luke*: apart from certain dominant features, they are irreconcilable.

86. Features common to *Matthew* and *Luke*

The dominant features show that the stories were not mere inventions of pious fancy. By the time they took shape it was believed that Jesus was the Messiah of Jewish expectation, and that therefore he fulfilled Old Testament prophecy. The Jewish scriptures, usually in the Greek translation known as the Septuagint (see § 40), were searched; and collections of significant texts were made. From these texts as a basis, the birth stories were apparently built up. It may be added that there also seems little doubt that some other stories in the first three gospels owe their form, if not their substance, to texts in the Old Testament which were deemed prophetic.

The birth stories in the first and third gospels have in common four dominant features. They agree that Jesus was born in the reign of Herod the Great (37–4 B.C.): his birthplace was the small town of Bethlehem in Judaea, the city of David: his mother's husband was Joseph, a descendant of David: and Jesus was "conceived by the Holy Spirit, born of the Virgin Mary." There is, further, no dispute that in early childhood Jesus was taken by his parents to Nazareth in Galilee, and that there he grew to manhood. In this place, in fact, he lived until he was baptized by John and began to preach. But whereas *Matthew* implies that the parents belonged to Bethlehem, *Luke* says that a Roman census forced them to go to this home of Joseph's ancestors, at the time when the birth of Jesus was imminent.

The story of the birth in David's city, Bethlehem of Judah,

was derived from the prophet *Micah* (v. 2), as *Matthew* says (ii. 6):

> And thou, Bethlehem, land of Judah,
> Art in no wise least among the princes of Judah:
> For out of thee shall come forth a governor,
> Which shall be shepherd of my people Israel.

Belief in the virgin birth of Jesus arose from a mistranslation, in the Greek version of the scriptures, of a passage in *Isaiah* (vii. 14). *Matthew* gives the mistranslation in the form (i. 23):

> Behold, the virgin shall be with child, and shall bring forth a son,
> And they shall call his name Immanuel.

In the original Hebrew, however, the word translated "virgin" means "young woman." The prophet, in the book of *Isaiah*, is reassuring Ahaz, king of Judah, who fears a joint attack by the kings of Israel and Syria. He says that the king need only wait for a time in which a child might be conceived, born, and show signs of moral intelligence, before the hostile allies will be crushed by Assyria. The prophecy, in fact, had no Messianic significance: and there is no evidence that it was regarded as having such significance by Jewish rabbis at the beginning of the Christian era.

The birth stories in *Matthew*, taken as a whole, were built up conscientiously on texts of the Old Testament which could be regarded as prophetic.

The flight into Egypt to avoid the ill-will of Herod the Great was supposed to have been foretold by *Hosea* (xi. 1). The words, "When Israel was a child, then I loved him, and called my son out of Egypt," are quoted by *Matthew* (ii. 15) in the form "out of Egypt did I call my son."

The "slaughter of the innocents" is based by *Matthew* (ii. 18) on a text of *Jeremiah* (xxxi. 15): "A voice is heard in Ramah, lamentation, and bitter weeping, Rachel weeping for her children; she refuseth to be comforted for her children, because they are not."

The return of Jesus and his parents, not to Bethlehem but to Nazareth, is asserted by *Matthew* (ii. 23) to be in accordance with an unidentified text prophesying that "he should be called a Nazarene."

87. Contrasts between *Matthew* and *Luke*

Luke uses none of these texts; and, instead, weaves into his narrative early Christian hymns. He gives us, in particular, the *magnificat* (i. 46–55), which is probably the most triumphant welcome in religious literature to the uprising of the common man. No other primitive document shows so plainly that Christianity made headway as a movement among the proletariat.

Apart from the dominant features to which we have alluded, the narratives of *Matthew* and *Luke* are in somewhat marked contrast with one another. In *Matthew* wise men from the east are led by a star. They visit Herod the Great who, apprehensive, asks that, if they find the child born to be king, they will inform him. They find the child in a house, give their gifts and adoration; and, warned by a dream, return without seeing Herod. Joseph, also warned in a dream, takes the child and his mother to Egypt, whereupon Herod slays all male children in Bethlehem under two years old. The story is told with dramatic force: through it run anxiety and gloom. Herod, though an able king, was not a good man; but even he did not deserve the infamous reputation which he owes to the author of the first gospel.

In *Luke* the whole atmosphere is different. The angel Gabriel announces to the aged Zacharias and to his barren wife, Elisabeth, that to them a son shall be born: the child is the future John the Baptist. The same angel is sent to Mary, a kinswoman of Elisabeth, living in "a city of Galilee, named Nazareth." She, according to the story, is a virgin betrothed to a man named Joseph, of the house of David: by the overshadowing of the Most High she is to conceive a son who shall be called holy, the son of God. Mary and Joseph go to Bethlehem, because of a census which required every man to be registered in his ancestral home. At Bethlehem the child is born and laid in a manger, because there was no room for them in the inn. An angel announces the glorious birth of "a Saviour, which is Christ the Lord," to shepherds keeping watch by night in the field; and a multitude of the heavenly host praise God, saying,

Glory to God in the highest,
And on earth peace among men in whom he is well pleased.

Luke's story is told with rare art. There is in it a tender beauty and delicacy of feeling, an atmosphere of quiet happy joy that has made it loved wherever Christianity has spread. Careful examination, as we shall see, has shown conclusively that the story is not history, but legend. Yet, though pure fancy, it is also pure gold, conveying with supreme skill the spirit of the Christian message.

That the stories of *Matthew* and *Luke* differ so profoundly in character and detail is proof that they were written independently. The fact that the contrasts between them are not more glaring suggests that some process of harmonization may have taken place before they were accepted as authoritative Christian writings. Such skilful removals of contradictions may often be suspected in New Testament writings: they probably were effected during the second century of our era, while the New Testament was being formed, and possibly within the years A.D. 140–175.

88. The ancestry of Jesus

Two genealogies of Jesus are given in the first and third gospels respectively. That in *Matthew* (i. 1–16) traces the descent of Jesus from Abraham through David and Joseph by means of three groups of fourteen generations each. The pedigree in *Luke* (iii. 23–38) starts with Jesus and traces the ascent through David to Adam, "which was the son of God." The two pedigrees contradict one another: it is now generally agreed that they are valueless.

The discrepancy between the genealogies was from early times a cause of concern to those defenders of Christianity who were not willing to allow the presence of mistakes in its authoritative books. In his *Ecclesiastical History* (i. 7) Eusebius (see § 123) quotes a most ingenious explanation—we might almost term it a reconciliation of contradictions—taken from a letter by Julius Africanus, a learned Christian writer of the beginning of the third century of our era. The argument is obscure; and perhaps even Africanus did not find it wholly convincing, for he ends, "in any case the gospel speaks the truth."

It is, however, of interest that in each genealogy the descent goes through Joseph: both pedigrees must have been invented before the rise of belief in the virgin birth of Jesus. According to *Luke*, Mary was a kinswoman of Elisabeth, who was of the daughters of Aaron. There is no suggestion that Mary herself was a descendant of David.

89. The descent from David

Belief that Jesus was of the house of David appears early in Christian teaching. It must have been firmly established when the two genealogies were made. Paul expressed such belief when probably just before A.D. 57 he wrote, in his epistle to the *Romans* (i. 3), that Jesus was "of the seed of David according to the flesh." *Mark*, moreover, records (x. 47) that the blind beggar at Jericho appealed to Jesus with the words, "Jesus, thou son of David, have mercy on me." A little later, when Jesus made his triumphant entry into Jerusalem, *Mark* says (xi. 9–10) that the crowd acclaimed him with the words, "Blessed is he that cometh in the name of the Lord. Blessed is the kingdom that cometh, of our father David."

Such evidence of early belief in the royal descent of Jesus from David seems at first sight decisive, though strictly the welcome at Jerusalem is a greeting to the one who should come and not to the son of David. But there is in *Mark* (xii. 35–37) an argument, attributed to Jesus himself, to show that the Christ would not be the son of David. Such teaching takes the form, "David himself calleth him Lord; and whence is he his son?" To us the argument is strange and unconvincing; but it would hardly have survived had it not belonged to an early and genuine tradition.

There is, further, the important fact that the author of the fourth gospel, who could not have been ignorant of the belief that Jesus was a descendant of David, did not apparently accept it. He records (vii. 40–42) the taunt, "What, doth the Christ come out of Galilee? Hath not the scripture said that the Christ cometh of the seed of David, and from Bethlehem, the village where David was?" But he does not give any reply of Jesus, affirming either his descent from David or his birth in Bethlehem. In fact, nowhere in the gospels does Jesus claim descent from David. Almost certainly Christians in the first place believed that Jesus was the anointed of God, the Christ: they were later led to infer that he was descended from David.

They did not defend their belief that he was the Christ by argument from his royal descent.

90. The date of the birth of Jesus

It is a curious fact that we have no certain knowledge either of the year in which Jesus was born or of the year when he died. The data by which the two years must be determined are scanty and confused.

Mark says nothing by which the year of the birth of Jesus can be inferred. The early Christians for whom he wrote apparently regarded with little interest the life of Jesus before his baptism.

Matthew (ii. 1) states simply that "Jesus was born in Bethlehem of Judaea in the days of Herod the king." He was plainly of opinion that Herod died not long afterwards, for on Herod's death Joseph (ii. 19–20) was advised to return from Egypt to Israel, that is to say, to Galilee, with "the young child and his mother." The Herod to whom *Matthew* refers was Herod the Great, for the evangelist records that he was succeeded as ruler of Judaea by his son, Archelaus. It is a known fact that Herod the Great died in the spring of 4 B.C.: on his death Archelaus reigned over Judaea until he was banished from his little kingdom by the Roman government in A.D. 6.

Luke appears to give more exact information. We learn (i. 5) that in the days of "Herod, king of Judaea," Elisabeth conceived. In the sixth month of her pregnancy there came to Mary (i. 26–38) the annunciation that she, though a virgin, should have a son. Before Mary's pregnancy was completed (ii. 1–2) "there went out a decree from Caesar Augustus that all the world should be enrolled. This was the first enrolment made when Quirinius was governor of Syria." These statements in the third gospel seem conclusively to assign the birth of Jesus to a particular time in the history of the Roman empire and of the satellite kingdom of Judaea. Unfortunately, the statements occur in the birth narratives of *Luke*, which we have reason to regard as legend rather than history; and their accuracy cannot be accepted.

91. The census of Quirinius

There is, elsewhere than in the third gospel, no record that a census of the whole world was ordered by Augustus. The order, according to *Luke*, demanded that, to be enrolled, each man should go to his ancestral city: Joseph went up from Galilee to the city of David, because he was of the house and family of David: and this journey was undertaken although his ancestors had left Bethlehem a thousand years before! The Romans were a practical race, skilled in the art of government: it is incredible that they should have taken a census according to such a fantastic system. If any such census had been taken, the dislocation to which it would have led would have been world-wide: Roman historians would not have failed to record it.

92. Flavius Josephus and his writings

By singular good fortune two works of Flavius Josephus (A.D. 37–*c.* 100) have survived which give in considerable detail the history of the Jews from the revolt of the Maccabees to A.D. 70. The first is the *Jewish War*, originally written in Aramaic and translated into Greek between A.D. 75 and 79. In this book the account of the war of A.D. 66–70, which ended in the destruction of Jerusalem by Titus, is preceded by a long introduction beginning with the rise of the Maccabees. The second work of Josephus is the *Jewish Antiquities*, which was completed in A.D. 93–94 and ranges from the Creation to A.D. 66. Josephus gives us valuable knowledge as to events in Rome: he is also for all practical purposes our sole surviving source of information for the reign of Herod the Great and for the history of his descendants. Two other works of his have survived: of them his *Life* is an autobiography which reveals him as clever and none too scrupulous. A detailed examination of his writings, however, shows him to have been, when his personal reputation was not in question, a careful historian who used his authorities with critical care. He ended his days after high favour with the Flavian dynasty at Rome.

Josephus says nothing of a census taken by Roman direction under Herod the Great. Any such census is highly improbable, inasmuch as it would be made for purposes of taxation; and Herod managed, and showed great skill in managing, his own finances: he was a most competent ruffian. But we learn from the *Jewish Antiquities* (XVIII. i. 1) that, after the deposition of Archelaus in A.D. 6, Quirinius, the legate of Syria, ordered a census for the purpose of imposing a Roman tax. Josephus implies that this action was a new measure, much resented in Judaea. Had a census been taken ten or a dozen years earlier, it is difficult to understand its repetition.

Quirinius was a man of character and capacity who played a considerable part in Roman civil and military administration under Augustus. He did not belong to one of the old Roman families; but he was an important consul in 12 B.C. He is known to have been legate of Syria between A.D. 6 and A.D. 12; and it is practically certain that he only once held this office and that there was no earlier tenure during the lifetime of Herod the Great. We must conclude that the author of the gospel according to *Luke* was mistaken in associating the birth of Jesus with the census. If Jesus was born before the death of Herod the Great, the date of his birth must be put before, or very early in, 4 B.C.: the census which *Luke* wrongly believed to have been taken at the same time was, in point of fact, at least ten years later.

93. At what age did Jesus begin his public ministry?

Luke tells us (iii. 23) that "Jesus, when he began, was about thirty years of age." This statement follows immediately after a brief record of the baptism of Jesus by John the Baptist. There is no similar indication of the age of Jesus in either *Mark* or *Matthew*. At the beginning of the account in *Luke* of John the Baptist and his preaching, there is (iii. 1–2) a remarkably detailed description of the year in which "the word of God came unto John the son of Zacharias in the wilderness." We are told that it was "in the fifteenth year of the reign of Tiberius Caesar, Pontius Pilate being governor of Judaea, and Herod being tetrarch of Galilee, and his brother Philip tetrarch of the region of Ituraea and Trachonitis, and Lysanias tetrarch of Abilene, in the high-priesthood of Annas and Caiaphas."

It is probable—for our knowledge of the Roman calendar is not adequate—that the fifteenth year of the emperor Tiberius (A.D. 14–37) fell between August of A.D. 28 and August of A.D. 29. But doubt is cast on the accuracy of *Luke's* dating by the fact that there is no evidence, save a broken inscription carrying little weight, that Lysanias was at the time "tetrarch" of Abilene. We reach this conclusion by combining scanty information given by two men, Strabo and Josephus. Strabo (c. 64 B.C.–c. A.D. 21) was of mixed Greek and Anatolian descent, a Greek by education and a Roman in sympathy. From internal evidence we conclude that he probably wrote his valuable and discursive historical *Geography* in about 6 B.C. and revised it in his old age about A.D. 18. He states (xvi. 2, 10) that a certain Ptolemy, son of Mennaeus, had possessed the hill country of the Ituraeans, a district which seems to have included Abila. Now according to Josephus (*Jewish Antiquities*, xv. iv. 1) Lysanias, the son of this Ptolemy, was executed by Mark Antony about 36 B.C. Apparently the territory, over which he had ruled since about 40 B.C., continued to bear his name. We have, at any rate, no information of any other younger Lysanias ruling in this region. Moreover, Josephus in his *Jewish War* (II. xi. 5) speaks of "that kingdom which was called the kingdom of Lysanias"; and the same writer in his *Jewish Antiquities* (xx. vii. 1) says that, when the emperor Claudius (A.D. 41–54) had completed his twelfth year, that is apparently in the year A.D. 53, (Herod) Agrippa II, a great-grandson of Herod the Great, received from the emperor "the tetrarchy of Philip, and Batanaea, together with Trachonitis and Abila"; and he adds that Abila "had been the tetrarchy of Lysanias." *Luke* seems to have hastily read this passage in Josephus and to have concluded wrongly that Abila about A.D. 29 belonged to Lysanias, whereas he had died more than sixty years earlier.

Even if we set aside this mistake, our difficulties are not at an end. According to *Luke*, Annas and Caiaphas were joint high-priests. But Annas, or Ananus, who was appointed by Quirinius, was deposed in A.D. 15, having held the office for some nine years. Joseph, called Caiaphas, probably became high-priest in A.D. 18 and held office for some eighteen years. *Luke* is in error in thinking that there could be two high-priests at the same time. For the rest, it is practically undisputed that Pontius Pilate was procurator of Judaea during the years A.D. 26–36: for this fact the evidence of Josephus in his *Jewish Antiquities* (XVIII. iv. 2) is clear and decisive.

Luke's elaborate statement, when analysed, thus leaves us in much uncertainty. So far as we can trust his chronology, Jesus *may* have begun his teaching, shortly after his baptism by John, in A.D. 29. If he was born just before the death of Herod the Great in the spring of 4 B.C., he must have been at least thirty-three years of age when his ministry began; and thus his actual age might be described as "about thirty."

Unfortunately, even this conclusion must be accepted with caution. The age of thirty had an especial significance in Jewish history: it was (*Genesis* xli. 46) the age of Joseph when he became prime minister of Egypt and (2 *Samuel* v. 4) of David when he became king. It was also the age at which, according to one regulation (*Numbers* iv. 3), Levites became eligible for service in the tent of meeting. If then, when *Luke* wrote, there was no accurate knowledge of the age at which Jesus began his ministry, thirty years would be naturally accepted.

94. His age according to the fourth evangelist

It seems, moreover, that the author of the fourth gospel accepted another tradition. Careful study of this gospel shows that its author does not formally correct elements in the Christian tradition with which he disagrees, but insinuates obliquely his divergence.

There are two passages in which he hints that Jesus was considerably older than *Luke* suggests. In controversy with the Jews (viii. 57), when there was no occasion for them to exaggerate his age, they are reported to have said to him, "Thou art not yet fifty years old." Earlier in the record of his ministry (ii. 19–21) occurs the passage,

> Jesus answered and said unto them, Destroy this temple, and in three days I will raise it up. The Jews therefore said, Forty and six years was this temple in building, and wilt thou raise it up in three days? But he spake of the temple of his body.

There will always remain some doubt as to the implication of the latter passage; but, combined with the former, the probability that *John* thought of Jesus as nearly fifty years old is fairly strong.

The upshot, then, of such inquiries as we can make is that Jesus *may* have been born in 6–5 B.C., and that he *may* have begun his ministry in A.D. 29. To neither date can any certainty be attached. The traditional date of the birth of Christ, com-

monly said to be due to a Scythian monk living at Rome in the
sixth century of our era, is valueless.

95. The birthday of Jesus

There is, moreover, no authority for the belief that December 25 was the actual birthday of Jesus. If we can give any
credence to the birth-story of *Luke*, with the shepherds keeping
watch by night in the fields near Bethlehem, the birth of Jesus
did not take place in winter, when the night temperature is so
low in the hill country of Judaea that snow is not uncommon.
After much argument our Christmas Day seems to have been
accepted about A.D. 300. The decision was reached when
Christianity, after a long and severe struggle during the third
century of our era, was finally triumphing over the religion of
Mithra, the Persian cult which proved so markedly attractive
to soldiers of the cosmopolitan Roman army. As we have said
in §§ 74–76, Mithra was god of the invincible sun; and his festal
day was suitably that on which, after the winter solstice, the
sun again began clearly to show his strength. It was natural
that, in a process of incorporation of the defeated faith, Christians should give to Christ Mithra's day.

The assignment was the more easy as from early times there
was close metaphorical association between Christ and the sun.
Sunday—the day of the sun—was the weekly reminder of the
resurrection of Christ. To early Christians Christ was the sun
of righteousness of the prophet *Malachi* (iv. 2), who had arisen
"with healing in his wings." The writer of the *Apocalypse*
(*Rev.* xix. 11–16) describes his Lord as though he were a solar
deity, a god of the mystery-faiths. Doubtless Christians argued
that Jesus must have had a birthday, and that December 25
had a symbolic significance not wholly unworthy.

As the day of the renewal of the sun's strength, December 25
was chosen to be the day in 167 B.C. (or possibly a year earlier)
when a Greek altar was consecrated in the temple at Jerusalem
in connection with the attempt of the Syrian king, Antiochus
Epiphanes, to extirpate Judaism. It was this attempt which
gave rise to the book of *Daniel*. It also, as we previously narrated in § 36, produced the revolt, ultimately successful, led
by the Hasmonaean family. One of the first signs of the success
of the national uprising was the cleansing and re-dedication of

the temple exactly three years after the profanation, that is on December 25, 164 (165) B.C. From that day the feast of the Dedication of the House has been annually observed as a festival by the Jews. In the fourth gospel (x. 22) we read,

> And it was the feast of the dedication at Jerusalem: it was winter; and Jesus was walking in the temple in Solomon's porch.

If the evangelist had known that the day was the birthday of Jesus, would he not probably have said so?

96. Jesus the Nazarene

At the beginning of the gospel according to *Mark* it is stated (i. 9) that "Jesus came from Nazareth of Galilee, and was baptized of John in the Jordan." *Luke* (i. 26) gives "a city of Galilee, named Nazareth" as the home of Joseph and Mary. Somewhat later he records that "they returned into Galilee, to their own city Nazareth." *Matthew* (ii. 22–23) states that, after the sojourn in Egypt, Joseph "withdrew into the parts of Galilee, and came and dwelt in a city called Nazareth: that it might be fulfilled which was spoken by the prophets, that he should be called a Nazarene."

We have seen that the birth stories of *Matthew* and *Luke* are late developments built up, at any rate in part, on Old Testament texts: the birth at Bethlehem cannot be regarded as historical. It would thus appear that, almost certainly, Jesus was born at Nazareth, and that from his place of birth he was called Jesus of Nazareth, or Jesus the Nazarene.

But there has of late been much dispute as to whether "the Nazarene" can mean "of Nazareth." It appears to be certain that an affirmative answer would have been given by the gospel writers. There is, moreover, no doubt that early Christians in Aramaic-speaking parts of the Near East were called Nazarenes. But some modern scholars maintain that the term Nazarene is derived either from a word meaning "observer of the law," and so would correspond to "methodist"; or from a word meaning "holy," "one separated from others." The argument rests upon obscure and complicated questions of philology. In favour of the second interpretation is the fact that there is no Old Testament text "he shall be called a Nazarene"; and that possibly *Matthew* had in mind a passage in *Deuteronomy* (xxxiii. 16)

containing a philologically possible word, "Let the blessing
come upon the head of Joseph, and upon the crown of the head
of him that was separate from (*or*, that is prince among) his
brethren."

Scholars who claim that the word Nazarene had such an
origin suggest that its meaning was forgotten as Christianity
spread in Greek-speaking communities. Then Christians
remembered that Jesus came from rural Galilee, his native
place lying in the hill country west or south-west of the city of
Tiberias on the lake of Galilee. Learning that there was a place
called Nazareth in this area, Christ's followers accordingly
assumed that Jesus the Nazarene meant Jesus of Nazareth.

97. Tiberias

Not twenty miles from Nazareth lay the capital of Galilee.
Herod Antipas, son of Herod the Great and own brother of
Archelaus, on his father's death in 4 B.C. became tetrarch of
Galilee and Peraea. He built a new capital for his province on
the south-western shore of the lake of Galilee; and called it
Tiberias. It was named after the emperor Tiberius, who was
his friendly patron at Rome. Antipas was finally banished in
A.D. 39–40, shortly after Tiberius died. His capital must have
been partly Jewish but, in all probability, was largely pagan.
There is, surprisingly, no record that Jesus ever visited it.

98. Nazareth

Nazareth must have been a small, obscure place. It is never
mentioned in the Old Testament, or in Jewish writings before
the time of Christ, or even in Josephus, who in the years
A.D. 66–7 had fought in Galilee and knew intimately the
countryside.

The Greek word translated "city" could be applied to a
relatively small town; but it is doubtful whether Nazareth
merited even this description. Quite possibly none of the gospel
writers had ever seen the place. Jerome (*c.* A.D. 340–420)
lived for the last thirty years of his life in Palestine and had, at
an earlier time, spent some years at Antioch and in the Syrian
desert. He terms Nazareth a *viculus*, or small hamlet. At the
beginning of the present century there was in the town only
one well, with a none too copious water-supply. There were

G

never any aqueducts—the absence of ruins is conclusive—so that, even though there may have been rain-water cisterns, it is improbable that the population could ever have been large. Forty years ago, with all the prestige of its association with the Christian story, the inhabitants numbered some 7,500: in the census of A.D. 1940 the population had risen to 10,700.

Luke states (iv. 16–30) that Jesus, after a time in Galilee, came to Nazareth and that its people were so angry with his words that "they rose up, and cast him forth out of the city, and led him unto the brow of the hill whereon their city was built, that they might throw him down headlong." Nazareth is set in the hill country of Galilee; but there is now no obvious precipice to correspond to the Lukan story.

In ancient times no great roads ran through Nazareth, though from the hills above the village a young man might have seen caravans passing along important highways. The village lay, as the crow flies, some fifteen miles from the cosmopolitan government centre of Tiberias: and, again as the crow flies, some twenty-five miles from Gadara on the other side of the Jordan.

99. Greek culture and the boy Jesus

We speculate in vain as to how far influences radiating from these cities could have reached a peasant-artisan child in Nazareth. In Tiberias the common people must have been bilingual, speaking both Greek and Aramaic: the rabbis will have been familiar with Hebrew, and the governing class with Latin. Gadara was one of the important cities of a prosperous and populous region, east of the Jordan, known as Decapolis. The ruins of Gadara are impressive: among them is a great aqueduct which brought water some twenty-five miles. It was an important intellectual centre from the first century before Christ, though its zenith appears to have been reached in the second century of our era. Among the famous men it produced was Meleager (*c.* 60 B.C.), who wrote elegiac poetry and made an early collection of Greek epigrams. Ultimately the civilization of Decapolis disappeared: the desert with its Bedouin obliterated "the sown."

To estimate the chance of Hellenistic influences penetrating to Nazareth we should need to have greater knowledge than we possess of the character of the population of central Galilee. Was the population purely Jewish, or was there in it a considerable gentile admixture?

The term "Galilee of the Gentiles" used by *Matthew* (iv. 15), and the mention of Galilee in connection with deportation of the people by Tiglath-pileser (2 *Kings* xv. 29), suggest an admixture of non-Jewish blood. But in a hill country old stocks survive: in Wales to-day there are, in mountainous districts near to English or bilingual towns, many purely Welsh people who know only the language of their race. It may have been that Joseph and Mary were of purely Jewish stock, and that their home was untouched by Greek or by any other non-Jewish influences. On the other hand, it is an interesting speculation that the teaching of Jesus, with its appeal so much wider than that of Jewish religious leaders of his time, owed its character to the fact that he was of mixed ancestry and was brought up in a home in which Greek influences, so strong in Decapolis thirty miles away, were not wholly lacking.

There has been much speculation as to whether Jesus knew Greek. *Mark* makes it clear by an occasional reference to an Aramaic saying that Jesus normally spoke Aramaic. We are given the actual words used in the raising of the daughter of Jairus (v. 41), in the healing of "one that was deaf, and had an impediment in his speech" (vii. 34), and in the last despairing words from the cross (xv. 34). The ministry of Jesus was spent among the presumably Aramaic-speaking fishermen at the north end of the Lake of Galilee: as we have said, he seems to have avoided Tiberias. He may, none the less, as we shall suggest in § 147, have had some knowledge of Greek, though no arguments to this end carry conviction.

CHAPTER VI

JESUS, SON OF GOD

100. *Mark* not a primitive gospel

MARK, our earliest gospel, was, as we shall see in chapter vii, not written until Christianity had spread widely. During the forty years or more which separated the crucifixion of Jesus from the period when the gospel assumed substantially its present form, there were many developments of Christian thought and belief. What finally became the authoritative Christian tradition shaped itself gradually. It was, in part, built up of texts in the Old Testament which were regarded as Messianic. Then, too, illustrations and exaggerations of popular preaching were hardened into what were asserted to be historical facts. Religious influences potent in Greek-speaking communities of the Levant contributed to the development of worship and belief. The intellectual atmosphere of the era began to make its contribution to the framing of an explanation of the relation to God of His anointed, the Christ.

We must not, then, expect to find in *Mark* a primitive record uncoloured by later developments. In reading the gospel we must remember that the influence of Paul and his theories lies in the background: other forgotten teachers—the name of Apollos was remembered—doubtless left traces of their enthusiasm for the Lord whose followers they had joined.

101. The Son of God in *Mark*

The keynote of the gospel according to *Mark* is struck in the opening sentence. It is the "gospel of Jesus Christ, the Son of God." The words, "the Son of God" are omitted in some ancient manuscripts of authority; and, as we cannot imagine a mistaken omission of such importance, we must assume that these words were not in the original text. None the less they strike the keynote of the gospel, for they are the comment of the representative of Rome, ruler of the world, at the supreme moment when Jesus died. We read (xv. 39), "And when the centurion, which stood by over against him, saw that he so cried out, and gave up the ghost, he said, Truly this man was the Son of God." In the original Greek there is, in the last words of this passage, no definite article, so that accurately the words run, "Truly this man was son of God." There is thus no necessary implication that Jesus, when the story was first told, was regarded as the only son of God: it may be that he was thought of as God's son in a sense in which other men might also be sons of the Father in heaven. *Luke* gives the centurion's words in the form (xxiii. 47), "Certainly this was a righteous (*or, possibly*, innocent) man." *Matthew* follows *Mark*.

102. The centurion's homage

The centurion's homage to the crucified Jesus, as we have it in *Mark*, is a beautiful and fitting climax to the story of the death of Christ. But quite possibly it is theology under the guise of history.

A Roman legion in the first century of our era generally consisted of six thousand men, divided into ten cohorts and into sixty "centuries." The latter were each in charge of a centurion; and it was on the sixty centurions that the discipline and the efficiency of a legion chiefly depended. Thus a centurion might be a man, not only trustworthy and capable of leadership, but also of some education and width of understanding. Yet it is hardly likely that a centurion, detailed for execution duty about the year A.D. 30 in an outlying Roman province, would be a monotheist. A century and a half later he might well have been a Mithraist, and then his praise would have been that Jesus was worthy to rank in the highest order of the Mithraic hierarchy. But, at the time of the crucifixion of Jesus, a religious centurion would probably have spoken piously of the gods; the term "son of God" would not have come naturally to the lips of one who would have offered incense with patriotic devotion to the *genius* of the City (Rome) and to the *genius* of the emperor.

We are left with the feeling that in *Mark* a Christian writer has told the story in order to show that the disciplined strength of Rome gave instinctive homage to Jesus the Christ.

103. The family of Jesus in *Mark*

Though the belief that Jesus was the Christ, "son of God," is a dominant *motif* of the gospel according to *Mark*, there is, throughout the record, no hint that he was not born in the usual way. Quite naturally the names of his brothers are given (vi. 3), "Is not this the carpenter, the son of Mary, and brother of James, and Joses, and Judas, and Simon? and are not his sisters here with us?" Such, we are told, was the attitude of the people of Nazareth after they had heard him teach in the synagogue. Earlier in the gospel (iii. 31) we hear of "his mother and his brethren" coming to him.

It is to be observed that *Mark* says nothing of Joseph—he does not even mention his name—neither does he say that Jesus was the first-born of the family. *Luke*, on the contrary, describes him as Mary's "first-born son" (ii. 7), thus suggesting that other children were subsequently born to her. In his version of the story of the visit to Nazareth, which was adapted from *Mark*, *Luke* says (iv. 22) that the people asked, "Is not this Joseph's son?" The corresponding passage in *Matthew* runs (xiii. 55–56), "Is not this the carpenter's son? is not his mother called Mary? and his brethren, James and Joseph, and Simon, and Judas? And his sisters, are they not all with us?"

Members of the family of Jesus are thus spoken of in the most natural way. There is no hint that his brothers were half-brothers or cousins; and no attempt would ever have been made to prove that they were not brothers in the fullest sense, but for the growth of the story of the virgin birth of Jesus and a consequent desire to claim the perpetual virginity of Mary.

Had the birth narratives of *Matthew* and *Luke* never come into existence, the writings of the New Testament would have left us with the knowledge that Jesus was one of a family of five sons and at least two daughters. The father of the family was, it would seem, a village craftsman, who no doubt combined with his trade of carpenter the care of a piece of land. Jesus was probably the eldest child who, when he grew to manhood, followed his father's occupation. There is little in his teaching to suggest the carpenter's shop; but he was, as we shall show in chapter viii, plainly familiar with the poverty of a village home and with the daily life of a peasant farmer.

Syria and Palestine appear to have differed from the rest of the Levant in that the normal villager was neither slave nor serf: he was a free man holding a small piece of land, a typical peasant. This independent status must never be forgotten when we think of the background of Jesus. Though poor he was free, dependent on no man's smile or frown; and his teaching shows it.

104. The virgin birth of Jesus

We have, in § 86, seen reason to believe that the story of the virgin birth, which only occurs in the picturesque introductions to *Matthew* and *Luke*, arose from a mistranslation in the Greek version of the book of the prophet *Isaiah*. The story can hardly have had its beginning on Jewish soil. The whole background, and the analogues cited in defence of it by Christian apologists of the second century of our era, are pagan. To an orthodox Jew the story would have seemed blasphemous. Though it was probably not current when Paul was still living, it must have been known to the author of the fourth gospel. He pointedly ignores it, and twice over refers to Jesus as the son of Joseph (i. 45 and vi. 42).

Notwithstanding its late origin, and the distaste for it which many must have shared with the author of the fourth gospel, belief in the virgin birth of Jesus rapidly won favour and became the orthodox proof and explanation of the divinity of Christ. Jesus was deemed to be the son of God, because in a physical sense God was his father just as "the Virgin Mary" was his mother. To a pagan who knew of similar stories in classical mythology, and who was aware that an analogous divine paternity was ascribed to Plato and Augustus among others, the belief was not unreasonable.

The story of the birth of Plato is preserved by Diogenes Laertius in a book sometimes called *Lives of eminent philosophers* (III. i. 1), a work of the early third century of our era: the author rests his statements on three earlier authorities whom he names. In the narrative of Diogenes the paternity of Plato is ascribed to Apollo: the narrative itself somewhat resembles that of *Matthew*. Suetonius in his *Lives of the Caesars* (ii. 94), published about A.D. 120, names an earlier writer for his story of the conception of Octavian (Augustus) during a midnight visit of his mother to a temple of Apollo. Such stories are, of course, valueless save as showing that, in the first century of our era, popular thought was prepared to accept the statement that

Jesus was son of God, because he was conceived by that divine manifestation which Christians called the Holy Spirit.

105. The divine and the human in ancient thought

It should be recalled that neither the philosophy nor the religion of the ancient world drew a sharp distinction between the divine and the human. The worship, throughout the East, of such deified men as Alexander and his successors seemed, save in Judaea, natural. In Roman thought the gods protected the domestic hearth. The *genius* of the home, as we saw in discussing Roman religion in § 63, could reside in the householder. A divine *genius* was especially to be seen in great men. Augustus, quite apart from legends as to his paternity, was regarded throughout the East as an incarnation of divinity. In Roman tradition, the Julian house had a divine origin; and Julius Caesar, after his death, was formally proclaimed *divus*, divine. Augustus called himself *Imperator Caesar Divi filius*: he was son (by adoption) of the deified Julius. When such ideas were pervasive, it would not have been deemed beyond reason to say that a man was son of God; and, outside strict Jewish circles, the statement would not have seemed blasphemous. It must always be remembered that Christianity was formulated in a non-Jewish environment.

106. The biological possibility of a virgin birth

Biological research seems to indicate that a human virgin birth may be proved to be possible. Among the insects reproduction from unfertilized egg-cells is common. The artificial growth of a frog from an unfertilized frog's egg has been achieved: and a frog is relatively high in the evolutionary scale. If, however, biological research should show that in humanity a virgin birth could take place, and that therefore the "miracle" of the virgin birth of Jesus was not impossible, those who now regard the miracle as essential to the Christian faith would feel disquieted. It would be asked why the son of God should be born in a manner common among the insects rather than by a normal human process. The answer, doubtless, would be that God's direct intervention was established either, as *Matthew* says, by an angel appearing to Joseph in a dream; or, according to *Luke*, by the visit of the angel Gabriel to Mary. The divergence between these statements, coupled with widespread modern doubt as to the intervention of angels in human affairs, would weaken such a defence of the traditionalist position. It remains to be added that, in the earliest tradition preserved by *Mark*, Mary seems throughout unconscious of her son's divine origin and destiny.

107. The virgin birth as a source of calumny

When the story of the virgin birth was accepted as part of the Christian tradition—and acceptance seems to have been widespread by the middle of the second century of our era—those hostile to Christianity made it the basis of calumny. Stories attacking the chastity of Mary were common. One such story is preserved by Origen (*c.* A.D. 185–254) in his treatise, *Against Celsus* (i. 33). It is to the effect that Mary, having been guilty of adultery, bore a child to a certain soldier named Panthera. Origen, of course, knew nothing of the principles and possibilities of Mendelian inheritance. So, in repudiating the libel, he urged that the high character of Jesus implied honourable parents. "Why, from such unhallowed inter-course there must rather have been brought forth some fool to do injury to mankind, a teacher of licentiousness and wickedness and other evils; and not of temperance and righteousness and the other virtues." But the argument was not as sound or as scientific as the teaching of Jesus when he said that one does not gather grapes of thorns, or figs of thistles.

The artificial nature of the calumny recorded by Celsus is apparent from the name Panthera. Those familiar with the way in which, in certain circles, the ancients took pleasure in playing with words, will recognize in Panthera a transformation of *parthenos*, the Greek word for virgin. The malice of the story is singularly childish.

108. The growth of early Christian speculation as to Jesus

If, as we saw in § 93, there seems good reason to believe —further evidence is set forth in § 131—*Luke* had read hastily the *Jewish Antiquities* of Josephus, a book which was not pub-lished until about A.D. 94, the third gospel must have first seen the light near the end of the first century of our era. The gospel according to *Matthew*, with its divergent birth-stories, must have been written about the same time: it could not have been produced when *Luke* was in wide circulation. We may doubt whether, before these two gospels began to spread, *Mark* was generally known and accepted as authoritative. The story of the life and teaching of Jesus was still in a state of development some sixty or seventy years after his crucifixion: it could hardly have become definite before the fourth gospel was written.

During this period of uncertainty, which lasted until after the close of the first century of our era, various attempts were made to explain how Jesus was son of God. The subject lent itself to fanciful speculation; and, by the middle of the second century of our era, a riot of fantastic theology characterized what is known as the gnostic movement. The comparative sobriety of the books of the New Testament, as compared with works of early Christian speculation which were excluded from it, witnesses to the sound judgment of the church of the second century. But there was, in the nature of things, no absolute dividing line; and two attempts to create a background for the belief that Jesus was, in an especial sense, son of God show the ease with which strange fancies could arise and have a vogue in an unscientific age and among people whose philosophico-religious ideas were almost completely fluid.

109. Speculation in the *Epistle to the Hebrews*

The first of these attempts is to be found in a short theological treatise known as the *Epistle of Paul the Apostle to the Hebrews*. This treatise is at times perplexingly obscure: it was certainly not written by Paul, as its title suggests: its origin is unknown. The writer bases his theological speculations on the Greek version of the Old Testament known as the Septuagint (see § 40), drawing especially on the book of *Psalms*.

He begins by asserting (i. 2) that God had recently spoken by "a Son," "who being the effulgence of his glory, and the very image of his substance, and upholding all things by the word of his power, when he had made purification of sins, sat down on the right hand of the Majesty on high."

Such an exaltation of the Son prepares us for that identification of him with the *Logos* or Word of God which we find in the fourth gospel. Though the identification is not explicitly made in *Hebrews*, it is possibly adumbrated (iv. 12–13):

> the *Logos* of God is living, and active, and sharper than any two-edged sword, and piercing even to the dividing of soul and spirit . . . and quick to discern the thoughts and intents of the heart. And there is no creature that is not manifest in his sight: but all things are naked and laid open before the eyes of him with whom we have to reckon.

The chief aim of the writer, however, is to emphasize that Jesus is unique priest and victim. He explicitly (vi. 1–2) passes beyond "the first principles of Christ" to show Jesus (vi. 20) as "a high-priest for ever after the order of Melchizedek."

110. A priest after the order of Melchizedek

A fragment of a story in the book of *Genesis* (xiv. 18–20) and a verse in one of the *Psalms* (cx. 4) form the basis of speculations so fanciful that we find it hard to take them seriously. Melchizedek is described (*Hebrews* vii. 2–3) as King of righteousness and King of peace, "without father, without mother, without genealogy, having neither beginning of days nor end of life, but made like unto the Son of God." Jesus, who is termed "our Lord," has been made after the likeness of Melchizedek. He is stated (vii. 14) to have arisen out of Judah: apparently the thought is that he has come forth as a star, the reference being to a prophecy of Balaam (*Numbers* xxiv. 17), "There shall come forth a star out of Jacob, and a sceptre shall rise out of Israel." We rub our eyes and ask whether the writer actually wishes to maintain that his Lord was without father, or mother, with neither beginning of days nor end of life. The answer seems to be that such a theory is seriously maintained.

The writer of *Hebrews* is silent as to the earthly parents of Jesus. In fact, he says almost nothing as to his personal history. He lets us know (vi. 6 and xii. 2) that Jesus was crucified and that he "suffered without the gate" (xiii. 12). By his sufferings he was the supreme and final sacrificial victim. There was no intellectual difficulty in the ancient world in regarding the same Lord as both priest and victim. But it was difficult for the writer of *Hebrews* to think of God's Son as a man with human parents and a human birth in time. Whether the resolution of this difficulty in the fourth gospel was finally satisfactory remains to be seen.

When *Hebrews* was written, persecution of the Christians was rife. They are encouraged to persevere in their faith. They are also exhorted to maintain the moral purity, the high standards of conduct, that gave them their strength and cohesion. We are, in fact, made aware of groups of serious-minded believers, living dangerously under the pressure of the surrounding paganism, but slowly being consolidated into the Christian church.

III. The Son of God of the *Apocalypse*

An alternative attempt, or attempts, to exhibit Jesus as son of God is to be found in that strange and seductive book, *The Revelation of St. John the Divine*, or *The Apocalypse*, as it is for brevity called. As all know, it comes last in the New Testament.

Written, in its final form, probably towards the end of the first century of our era, it was a disclosure of what the writer believed to have been revealed to him as to the future. This writer tells us that his name was John and that (i. 9) he "was in the isle that is called Patmos, for the word of God and the testimony of Jesus." His background was the region of western Asia Minor, which was then as prosperous as ever in its history. His *Apocalypse* was probably, in part, built up of similar Jewish writings, suitably modified. It is a perplexing work, often enough non-Christian in its temper. Its author, or editor, seems to have experienced the ill-will of the Roman authorities who, from the time of the emperor Nero onwards, regarded the Christians with marked disfavour; and his de-nunciation of Rome, under the name of Babylon, is extravagantly bitter. He expressed his thoughts and feelings in a barbarous Greek, disfigured by Semitic uses. His style is conclusive against his having been the John who wrote the fourth gospel.

John of the *Apocalypse* resembles the author of *Hebrews* in that he seems to know little of the personal history of Jesus. He tells us (xi. 8) that Jesus "our Lord" was crucified in "the great city, which spiritually is called Sodom and Egypt," that is to say, in Jerusalem. Jesus, moreover, is (i. 5) "the first-born of

he dead" and Sunday, the day of the resurrection, is already
he Lord's day.

12. The Son of God as a solar deity

But the writer thinks of the son of God in terms of a solar
deity such as Mithra. He "hath eyes like a flame of fire, and his
feet are like unto burnished brass" (ii. 18). Elsewhere
(xix. 11–16) the *Logos* of God rides on a white horse: on his
head are many diadems: "out of his mouth proceedeth a sharp
sword, that with it he should smite the nations: and he shall
rule them with a rod of iron." We find the feet glowing like
burnished brass and the sharp sword with a double edge issuing
from the mouth at the beginning of the book (i. 15–18) where
"the living one" has seven stars in his right hand: he was dead
and is alive for evermore with the keys of death and of Hades.

The birth of the *Logos* is actually ascribed to a star goddess
(xii. 1–6), "a woman arrayed with the sun, and the moon under
her feet, and upon her head a crown of twelve stars." "She was
delivered of a son, a man child, who is to rule all the nations
with a rod of iron." Her child escaped the great red dragon
with seven heads and ten horns, whose tail swept away to the
earth a third part of the stars of heaven. The dragon sought to
devour the child who, however, "was caught up unto God, and
unto his throne." Such a bizarre equivalent of the virgin birth
has distressed many a commentator; and the suggestion has
gained favour that the child is not Christ, but the church.
But the *Logos*, the son of God, is identified by the phrase, "he is
to rule the nations with a rod of iron," which we have just
quoted (xix. 15).

There was in the early church much hesitation, which lasted
long, as to whether the *Apocalypse* should find a place in the
New Testament. There are fine passages in it: the picture
(xxi. 1–7) of the new Jerusalem, "made ready as a bride
adorned for her husband," is sublime. But too often the writer's
imagery gets out of control. In dreaming of the son of God his
fancies become exotic: in his exuberance he forgets the actual
world. The Master who taught in Galilee becomes the rider on
a white horse, clad in a robe dipped in blood: on his robe is
written and on his thigh is tattooed (xix. 16) his title, "King of
Kings, and Lord of Lords."

From the *Apocalypse* we can learn of extravagant developments of Christianity which might have ended in riotous
confusion had not the steadying force of the four gospels, and
of the great epistles ascribed to Paul, given to the movement, in
the first half of the second century of our era, a sane guidance
obviously much needed.

113. The Son of God as the *Logos*

It was left for the writer of the fourth gospel, by his doctrine
of the *Logos*, to reach the highest level of early Christian
speculation as to the nature of Jesus as son of God. The concept
of the *Logos* had had, as we have seen in § 42, a long history
since the speculations of Heracleitus about the year 500 B.C.
As has been said, these speculations were modified by the stoics
under the influence of Zeno, a native of Cyprus, of Phoenician
origin, who taught at Athens some two hundred years later.
We recall that the stoics were philosophically monists: hence in
religion they were pantheists, for whom God was in all. The
Logos was, for them, His creative activity in the world, the
source of the order which we perceive. When Christianity
began to spread, stoicism, as an ethical system rather than
as a creed, was preached with immense intellectual authority
—the influence of Cicero, Seneca and Tacitus may be mentioned: it was the strongest moral force among the leaders of the
Roman world. Some of its concepts appear in the Alexandrian
Judaism of Philo.

John of Ephesus, if we may so term the writer of the fourth
gospel, took and modified ideas associated with the *Logos*,
setting out his own view in the introduction to his gospel.
After this introduction the term *Logos* is never used again; but
the belief that Jesus was the *Logos*, the Christ, son of God, runs
through his book. It is perhaps unfortunate that, in the English
Bible, *Logos* is translated by "Word," for the term entirely fails
to convey to the uninstructed reader the meaning and associations which belong to it.

The gospel opens with sentences familiar to, and beloved by,
every Christian. "In the beginning was the Word, and the
Word was with God, and the Word was God." More accurately,
as the definite article is absent from the Greek, the last phrase
should read "and the Word was divine." The Word was with

God and partook of His nature without being identical with Him. By the Word all things were made: he is God's creative activity. In the Word was life, the life which is the light of men. Thus the Word is the source of life: all that lives, lives in him. But the Word also is the source of light, the light which gives man understanding. This light, says the writer, shines in the darkness of this world: and "the darkness apprehended it not." The belief that Jesus, as the *Logos*, is the source of light and life runs as a recurrent theme through the fourth gospel. The writer's supreme message is that in Jesus "the *Logos* became flesh and dwelt among us (and we beheld his glory, glory as of an only-begotten from a father), full of grace and truth" (i. 14).

Jesus was "the true light, which lighteth every man coming into the world." Though the world knew him not, it was made by, or through, him. From his light shining in the darkness came spiritual understanding. "He that heareth my word, and believeth him that sent me, hath eternal life, and cometh not into judgment, but hath passed out of death into life" (v. 24).

Thus the writer of the fourth gospel in a few brief sentences, by adapting ideas which had much vogue among intellectuals of his time, claimed for Jesus a complete supremacy. It is possible to contend that this writer, a supreme artist in the use of words, did not completely identify the *Logos* with Jesus: but, if the *Logos* became flesh and, in Jesus, dwelt among us, the approach to identity is well-nigh complete.

Symbolical miracles point this teaching. Jesus (ix. 1–12) cures the man who was blind from his birth; but before the miracle, he gives its explanation, "When I am in the world, I am the light of the world." Jesus, the *Logos* become flesh, is thus source of light.

Similarly (xi. 1–44) Jesus raises Lazarus from the dead; but only after he has said of himself, "I am the resurrection, and the life: he that believeth on me, though he die, yet shall he live: and whosoever liveth and believeth on me shall never die." Jesus, the *Logos* become flesh, is thus source of life.

The religious symbolism of the fourth gospel has a spiritual beauty unsurpassed in Christian literature. The writer's use or the concept of the *Logos* leads to a profound and emotionally satisfying mysticism. His language with its studied simplicity is perfectly adapted to his theme. When we compare his presentation of Jesus, son of God, as the *Logos*-Christ with the crude semi-pagan story of the virgin birth, we can well understand why the latter is silently ignored.

But we have to confess that the *Logos* doctrine sets us insoluble intellectual puzzles. In particular, how precisely—and when exactly—did the incarnation of the *Logos* take place? There is a hint that John of Ephesus thought of it as having taken place at "the beginning of his signs" in Cana of Galilee (ii. 1–11). The behaviour of Jesus to his mother, at the outset of the story of the miracle at Cana, shocks the reader who comes to it for the first time. The mother of Jesus says, "They have no wine." He replies, "Woman, what have I to do with thee? mine hour is not yet come." The rudeness is unthinkable unless one understands that the *Logos* replies to Mary. The *Logos* is not born of the flesh and has neither father nor mother. His arrival has to be signalized by a formal dissociation from Mary. This severance made, there follows at once the miracle by which water is turned into wine: Jesus, as the *Logos*-Christ, "manifested his glory."

The writer of the fourth gospel is so elusive, alike in thought and word, that it is not always easy to seize his implications. But probably he intends that Jesus can transform the water of daily life into the wine of spiritual exaltation: the ideas of Dionysiac ritual—we may refer to what we have said in §§ 65–67—were not wholly absent from his allegory.

114. Comparison and conclusion

We have now passed under rapid review five different attempts in the New Testament to present Jesus as son of God. That in the *Apocalypse* is fantastic; and the speculations of the writer of *Hebrews* are hardly less extravagant. The legend of the virgin birth proved widely popular: unfortunately, if analytical scholars are right, it depends upon dubious history. There remain the story preserved by *Mark* and the theory of the philosophical mystic who wrote the gospel according to *John*. In *Mark* we read of the Galilean peasant-craftsman who, by his quality of spirit, his rare perfection of character, his profound wisdom and brave loyalty to his Father in heaven, showed himself to be God's son. In *John* we meditate upon the man in whom the divine *Logos* came to dwell. The mysticism of *John* is sublime: but, when from its heights we come down to earth, we ask whether it is actually true of Jesus that all things were made by, or through, him. Had he the knowledge of One who from the beginning was with God? Was the future not hid from him as from us? *John*, if we apprehend him aright, claims too much. His Christ has ceased to have the limitations of humanity.

Essentially, the *Logos* theory and the story of the virgin birth are incompatible. The virgin birth of traditional dogma ought to have produced a semi-divine being, half God and half man. For this reason *John* rightly ignored the story: his *Logos*-Christ is wholly divine, really present with and in Jesus. But such thought was too rarefied for popular acceptance. In the defensive Christian literature of the second century of our era, the virgin birth of Jesus is robustly affirmed and ingeniously defended. Ultimately, Christian apologists, assuming the virtual inerrancy of scripture, claimed to find no difficulty in combining the virgin birth of Jesus with the *Logos* doctrine. Even so, intellectual discomfort was not at an end. There were centuries of argument during which men sought to explain the relation of the Son to the Father, of Jesus to God. We pass no harsh verdict on the protagonists in these protracted disputes if we say that the intellectual difficulties which arose were never satisfactorily overcome.

H

CHAPTER VII

THE GOSPELS

AMONG the sacred books of Christianity, the four gospels are of unique importance: they tell us practically all that we can know of the earthly life of Jesus and contain the most authoritative record of his teaching.

The first three gospels give an account of events in the life of Jesus, if not from the same point of view, at any rate under the same general aspect: they are therefore called the synoptic gospels. They are thus distinguished from the gospel according to *John*, which has profound differences from them, the significance of which is enhanced by close study.

115. The synoptic problem

The relation between the synoptic gospels constitutes what is called the synoptic problem. The ancient church gave first place to the gospel according to *Matthew*: that is why it is still placed before the other gospels in our New Testament. It was thought to have been the earliest gospel: such an opinion was held by, say, Augustine (c. A.D. 354–430) and lasted until the nineteenth century. In fact, it was undisputed until the rise of modern critical investigation.

Matthew was accepted as being a first-hand record by Matthew the apostle. The gospel according to *Mark* was regarded as containing the reminiscences of Peter the apostle, transcribed by Mark, the kinsman of Barnabas and at times in attendance on Paul. The gospel according to *Luke* was believed to be from the pen of "Luke, the beloved physician" (*Colossians* iv. 14) and travelling companion of Paul. The substantial agreement of these independent authorities, with especial opportunities of acquiring intimate knowledge, was deemed to be a providential guarantee of the exact truth of the main gospel story; and an old Jewish proverb (*Ecclesiastes* iv. 12), "a threefold cord is not quickly broken," was often quoted.

116. The solution of the synoptic problem

An entirely different estimate of the authorship of the gospels, and of their relation to one another, has now been reached. By the end of the nineteenth century, exact scholarship had definitely established that *Mark*, either as we know it or in a form which was a first edition of our present gospel, was used by *Matthew* and *Luke*. The two latter evangelists wrote with a copy of *Mark* before them; and they also relied on another document, now lost, sometimes called Q and sometimes termed the *Second Source*. The *Second Source* contained most of the Sermon on the Mount; and, so far as we can say, was mainly a record of the teaching of Jesus. These conclusions of nineteenth-century scholarship are of outstanding importance. They imply that *Mark* is, in effect, our sole authority for most incidents in the ministry of Jesus.

Synoptic scholarship since the beginning of the present century has given much attention to the authorship and date of the gospels, and especially of *Mark*. There is now fairly general agreement that the author of *Matthew* was an unknown Palestinian Jewish-Christian, whose gospel was composed towards the end of the first century of our era. *Mark* may have been written in Rome and, much more doubtfully, by the cousin of Barnabas; but the tradition that he acted as little more than an amanuensis of Peter is hardly credible. The date of the gospel is singularly difficult to determine. On the other hand, we may regard it as settled that *Luke* was written after the publication in A.D. 93–94 of the *Jewish Antiquities* of Josephus. Its author also wrote *Acts* and, in doing so, used a travel-diary which had been kept by Paul's physician; but he was almost certainly not that physician and, in fact, had probably not known Paul personally.

After this short summary of conclusions relating to the synoptic gospels, we will give briefly the arguments by which they were reached. The reader should obtain one of the many harmonies of the gospels which exist. In them the different accounts of the same incident or teaching are placed in parallel columns, so that we see at a glance how far these accounts agree in detail, and to what extent they are divergent.

117. The nature of the arguments

From the study of such a harmony we notice, in the first place, that there is very little in *Mark* which does not find a place in either *Matthew* or *Luke*.

In the second place, it is clear that the order of the incidents recorded is the order of *Mark*. *Luke* sometimes takes a different order: *Matthew* often takes an order that is not that of *Mark*. But *Matthew* and *Luke* never agree in the way in which they desert *Mark's* order.

In the third place, we notice, when the same incident is recorded in all three gospels, that the detailed development of the story is often so exactly the same that the story could not have been derived from a floating oral tradition. Stories belonging to what has been called the triple tradition must have their origin in a single document.

Take, for instance, the story of the healing of the man sick of the palsy. It is told in *Mark* (ii. 3–12). It appears in a very similar form in *Luke* (v. 18–26) and, more briefly, in *Matthew* (ix. 2–8). In each case Jesus at first says to the sick man that his sins are forgiven. Then scribes who were present murmur. Jesus asks whether it is easier to forgive sins or to say, "Arise and walk." He then turns to the sick man and bids him arise. The man arises; and the onlookers "glorified God." An oral tradition would never have preserved such exact resemblance between the three narratives.

We can easily pick out a score of similar likenesses. As we shall see at the beginning of chapter xv, when we come to consider the baptism of Jesus by John, our records of the incident show plainly how, in sequence of sentences and turns of phrase, *Matthew*, *Luke* and *Mark* are closely associated with one another: linking them is some common document.

Again and again there is such detailed similarity between parallel records in the synoptic gospels that we are forced to admit that they depend, so far as these triple parallels are concerned, on a single literary source. It becomes clear, however, that this source was used with considerable freedom. It was by no means slavishly copied: variations are numerous and sometimes, to the historian, difficult to defend.

118. The priority of *Mark*

From what has already been said at the beginning of § 117, it is clear that, if one of the synoptic gospels is the source from which the common triple record is derived, that source must be *Mark*. This conclusion is confirmed by the fact that *Mark* represents a more primitive stage in the development of the Christian tradition than either *Matthew* or *Luke*.

But, it may be asked, may not the fundamental source be, not our present *Mark*, but an earlier document, a sort of first edition of *Mark*? To answer this question we observe that, if there were such an earlier document, we should expect that at times *Matthew* and *Luke* would have copied it *verbatim*, word for word, while *Mark* would have used altered words: we should thus get verbal agreement in the first and third gospels as against the second. A harmony of the gospels (made, of course, in the original Greek) shows that such agreements against *Mark* are very rare. They have been tabulated and examined with laborious care; and the conclusion reached is that *Matthew* and *Luke* used *Mark* substantially as we have it now. In fact, whenever stories are told substantially in the same way in all three gospels, they come to us on the authority of a single man, the author of the gospel according to *Mark*.

It must, however, be carefully noticed that there are some narratives to be found in all the synoptic gospels which rest on wider testimony. As regards the Last Supper, for instance, *Matthew* has virtually (see § 287) nothing to add to what *Mark* tells us; but *Luke* is not based on *Mark*. So, also, in the account of the trial and crucifixion of Jesus, *Matthew* follows *Mark*, though he adds certain stories, such as the earthquake at the time of the crucifixion and the placing of the guard at the tomb; but *Luke* only inserts some statements of *Mark* in another record which was his main authority. It is, of course, not surprising that there should have been more than one authority for events naturally regarded as particularly important by the early Christians.

119. The Second Source, or Q

Suppose that we have before us a harmony of the first three gospels arranged in parallel columns: and that we cut out from all three columns all material which *Matthew* and *Luke*, or either of them, used after taking it from *Mark*. In the process *Mark* will practically have disappeared: the other two gospels will have become much abbreviated. But there will be left, common to both of them, a mass of material, mainly the teaching of Jesus, which is obviously of great importance and value.

As regards this material, there are in the two gospels so many exact resemblances that the two evangelists must have obtained it from the same written source. We must, however, observe that the discrepancies in the two groups of Infancy narratives, to say nothing of the divergent Passion stories, show clearly that neither the third nor the first of the evangelists copied from the other. Thus the material that is plainly duplicated forces us to the conclusion that *Matthew* and *Luke*, when they wrote their gospels, had before them, not only our *Mark*, but also another document. This document, as we said in § 116, is usually termed either the *Second Source*, or Q.

Q has been lost. We do not know, save in part, what it contained: all that we can reconstruct is such part of Q as was taken from it by both *Matthew* and *Luke*. Such a reconstruction has been made and is naturally of much interest. It proves to be primarily a record of the teaching of Jesus: in particular it contained much of the material in the Sermon on the Mount.

120. The problem of doublets

We have now reached the firm conclusion of modern New Testament scholarship: *Mark* and Q are the two main documents that lie behind our synoptic gospels.

It is natural to ask whether these booklets were entirely independent of one another. There is no reason to think that Q knew and used *Mark*: what we know of it differs too much in content and in character. But the question as to whether *Mark* had seen Q is less easily answered. An approach to an answer can be obtained by considering the doublets, or doubly attested sayings, in which the same teaching seems to have been preserved twice over in the synoptic gospels.

For instance, there are in *Mark* (xiii. 11) the words of Jesus, "And when they lead you and deliver you up, be not anxious beforehand what ye shall speak: but whatsoever shall be given you in that hour, that speak ye: for it is not ye that speak, but the Holy Spirit." This passage occurs in teaching with regard to the "end of the age" which is reproduced, by no means exactly, in *Luke* xxi. *Luke* writes (xxi. 12–15), "They shall lay their hands on you, and shall persecute you . . . Settle it therefore in your hearts, not to meditate beforehand how to answer: for I will give you a mouth and wisdom, which all your adversaries shall not be able to withstand or to gainsay."

Clearly these words, especially when we bear in mind their context in the two gospels, have their origin in a free modification of *Mark*. But we also have in *Luke* (xii. 11–12), "And when they bring you before the synagogues, and the rulers, and the authorities, be not anxious how or what ye shall answer, or what ye shall say: for the Holy Spirit shall teach you in that very hour what ye ought to say."

We thus have in *Luke* the same teaching doubly preserved, the first passage having been taken from *Mark*. As we ask where the second passage came from, we notice that in *Matthew* (x. 19–20) we read, "But when they deliver you up, be not anxious how or what ye shall speak: for it shall be given you in that hour what ye shall speak. For it is not ye that speak, but the Spirit of your Father that speaketh in you." The context of this passage recalls the context alike of the passage in *Mark* and of each of the two passages in *Luke*. In fact, the second Lukan passage must have come from Q; and *Matthew* has combined the two sayings which he found in his authorities, *Mark* and Q. This is *Matthew's* general practice, as becomes clear from an examination of the doublets which exist: they are about thirty in number. Their existence is held by some scholars to suggest that *Mark* knew Q and took the doublets from Q as a source. But it may well be that the doublets were sayings so well known in the Christian tradition that *Mark* and Q independently found them in the material, oral or written, which they used.

121. Material peculiar to *Matthew* or *Luke*

After all the material which *Matthew* and *Luke* derived from *Mark* and Q has been removed, there remain fragments of their gospels, as to the origin of which we can say nothing. Among such fragments are the birth-narratives, which most analytical scholars, as we have seen, now class as *midrash*, religious teaching conveyed by poetic fancy and allegory, not sober history. In *Matthew* there are also embellishments of narratives, such as the part assigned to Pilate's wife in the story of the trial of Jesus. Most of such additions seem to have won credit because of their popular appeal: they may be regarded as romantic embroidery made to adorn the story.

The material peculiar to *Luke* is, speaking generally, of far greater value. Besides numerous short sections, it comprises nearly six chapters (xiii. 1–xviii. 14) of the gospel. In the special Lukan material are to be found no less than twelve parables. Among them are three of the greatest parables of Jesus, the Good Samaritan (x. 25–37), the Prodigal Son (xv. 11–32), and the Pharisee and the Publican (xviii. 9–14). There is no good reason to think that these parables are not genuine records of the teaching of Jesus. There is, on the contrary, every internal indication that they come from the great Teacher to whom are due the other parables which give such a distinctive character to the story of the ministry in Galilee. Possibly the brilliant brevity with which they are told owes something to the art of the author of the third gospel; but in essence they must be from Jesus. The parable of the Prodigal Son has been called the finest story in the world.

It is *Luke* alone who records the ascension of the risen Jesus, alike at the end of the third gospel and at the beginning of the *Acts of the Apostles*: the questions which arise in connection with his differing narratives are, of course, highly important. They will be discussed at the end of chapter ix.

122. Old Testament quotations

Both *Matthew* and *Luke* have many quotations from the Jewish scriptures, our Old Testament. These are intended to show that Jesus was the fulfilment of Jewish prophecy: they have well been called proof-texts. It is an interesting fact that *Luke* seems always to have used the Septuagint, the standard Greek version of the Old Testament: in his style the influence of Semitic uses can be seen. *Matthew*, on the other hand, if he made his own quotations, sometimes went to the Septuagint but sometimes independently translated the original Hebrew into Greek: each fact becomes certain when a careful examination of mistranslations is made. In one, or possibly two, instances *Matthew* assigns a quotation to the wrong source. We may deduce that the author of our first gospel did not quote directly either from the Hebrew Bible or from the Septuagint, but used a collection of proof-texts which had been made by some Christian at an earlier time. It is highly probable that the making of such collections was an early task of Christian piety.

123. Authorship and date of the synoptic gospels

As the gospels tell us practically all that we know of the life and teaching of Jesus, it is obviously of great importance to know when, and by whom, they were written. Such external evidence as we have is meagre. In fact, the old tradition accepted by the church until quite recent times may be said to rest on a passage (iii. 39) in the *Ecclesiastical History* of Eusebius (*c*. A.D. 260–*c*. A.D. 339). Eusebius was Bishop of Caesarea in Palestine, and probably wrote his history during the period A.D. 311–324. He was a careful historian, his quotations apparently accurate and his opinions worthy of respect. Unfortunately he was separated from the early years of Christianity by nearly three centuries. He gives the testimony of Papias, who was bishop of Hierapolis, near Ephesus, about the middle of the second century of our era.

124. The testimony of Papias

The passage needs to be quoted at some length, in spite of its prolixity, for we are thus enabled to realize the mental limitations and credulity of Papias. It runs:

> This same Papias whom we are now considering admits that he accepted the sayings of the apostles as told him by their own followers; but claims to have himself heard what was said by Aristion and John the Presbyter. At least he mentioned them often by name in reporting their version of events in his own writings. These words of his should then be of value to us. But we can usefully associate with the remarks of Papias quoted above other sayings of his, where among other things he recounts certain strange happenings which would appear to have come to him from traditional sources. We have already seen how Philip the apostle lived with his daughters at Hierapolis; but this is the place to describe the amazing story which Papias says he heard from

Philip's daughters when he was with them there. For he records how in his own time a dead body came to life; and he tells another strange tale of Justus, known as Barsabas, who drank a dangerous drug but through the Lord's grace suffered no ill effects. . . . The same author sets beside these stories others, apparently derived from verbal tradition, including some unknown parables and doctrines of the Saviour, with other even more fanciful tales.

Among these tales he declares that there will be after the resurrection of the dead, some sort of millennium, in which the kingdom of Christ will be established in physical fact on this earth. I imagine he misunderstood the versions he heard of apostolic sayings, without realizing the pictorial and imaginative nature of what was said. For, as his writings testify, he was a man of very limited intelligence. But he must be held responsible for the prevalence of ideas like his own among so many church writers (who were impressed by the date at which the man lived) such as Irenaeus or anyone else who obviously shares the same opinions.

In the same work he also quotes other versions of the Lord's words, as given by this Aristion previously mentioned, and other sayings of John the Presbyter. Leaving these to the studious, we must now add to the statements we have already quoted from him a tradition which he repeats about Mark, the author of the gospel, in these words: "The Presbyter used to tell this story: Mark became Peter's interpreter and wrote down accurately, but certainly not in order, all that he remembered of the sayings or actions of the Lord. For he had never heard the Lord himself nor had he been a disciple of his, but of Peter's, as I said, later. For Peter used to teach as occasion required without marshalling the Lord's sayings in any order; so that there was nothing wrong in Mark writing down any points he remembered in this way. For he kept one aim in view, to omit nothing of what he heard and to include nothing that was false." This then is Papias's record of Mark; and of Matthew he says, "Matthew put together the 'sayings' (*or*, 'oracles') in the Hebrew language and everyone interpreted them as best he could."

125. The value of the Papias testimony

It is clear from this passage that Eusebius was dubious as to some of the statements of Papias; yet, of course, a man may write foolish things but at the same time remember valuable information. Papias wrote, let us say, in A.D. 140–160. He

quoted John the Presbyter who, according to the late witness
of Epiphanius (c. A.D. 320–403), died in A.D. 117 and whom
Papias might have known in his youth. Assuming, as is by no
means obvious, that the recollection of Papias was accurate, we
desire to know how far John the Presbyter was in a position to
have the knowledge attributed to him. There exists a fairly
early tradition that John the Presbyter was the apostle John,
the son of Zebedee; but in the time of Papias's youth, about
A.D. 110, it is hardly likely that any apostle would still be living.
Many modern scholars, in fact, as we shall see later in § 137,
incline to the opinion that the apostle John died at the same
time as his brother James, a martyr slain by (Herod) Agrippa I
about the year A.D. 44: the story of his death at a hoary old age
in Ephesus is probably legendary.

At the time when Papias wrote his *Exposition of the Oracles of
the Lord*, from which Eusebius quoted, the gospels of *Matthew*
and *Mark* were certainly in existence much as we now have
them: small editorial corrections might subsequently have been
made; but by A.D. 175 the two books were regarded as authoritative, and therefore unalterable, scripture. We may take it,
then, that Papias regarded the evidence of John the Presbyter
as referring to our gospels. Papias wrote, in fact, with the
object of confirming or enhancing the prestige of two books
which had already acquired great esteem. On the authority
of John the Presbyter one gospel is associated by Papias with
the apostle Matthew, and the other with the apostle Peter.
An apostolic origin for the two gospels was highly desirable—to
say the least—if they were to be successfully used in the conflict,
on the one hand, with Jews and pagans and, on the other hand,
with heretical Christians seduced by the crude speculative
theology termed gnosticism.

126. The gospel of *Mark*

It is now agreed, as we have seen, that our *Matthew* is based
on *Mark* and Q, and therefore was never a collection of
"sayings" or "oracles" written in Hebrew: most scholars
would admit that it is almost equally certain that our *Mark*
is not a transcript of reminiscences of Peter. *Mark*, in fact,
is not a single source embodying in the main the recollections
of a follower of Jesus. It is rather to be likened to a pool into

which many rivulets have flowed. It is not an historica
biography, but a collection of anecdotes from many sources
strung together. These anecdotes have been collected from
rough popular preaching. Teaching and preaching materia
which proved especially effective as Christianity made headway
was gradually standardized. Finally, it was gathered together
and possibly edited more than once before it assumed its present
form. Such an origin of our *Mark* explains the extent to which
Jesus appears in his record as a wonder-worker, and also as an
exorcist, one who drove out evil spirits.

There is no reason to doubt that the chief author of *Mark*
believed profoundly in the truth of the story which he tells
From many different sources he had gathered material
Mark xiii, for example, incorporates a fly-sheet dealing with the
shape of things to come. Some material in *Mark* had a long
tradition behind it. For instance, the story of the Last Supper
had been often told; and, as we have it, shows signs (see § 286)
of having been altered from its original form. *Mark* is, in short
an honest compilation made by an earnest and credulous man
He was credulous inasmuch as the miracles, as they are
narrated, cannot, in the light of our modern knowledge of the
uniformity of nature, be accepted as historical facts. But his
credulity was not exceptional, even for an educated man of the
age in which he lived.

127. The personality of *Mark*

Who was *Mark*? We do not know: he can hardly have been
the cousin of Barnabas: his story is too far removed from actual
history. None the less, a careful examination of the gospel as
we have it shows that, beneath popular legend, there are
numerous genuine reminiscences of the ministry of Jesus in
Galilee, such as might have come from Peter. Stories told by
Peter were used, possibly after they had filtered through the
recollection of several persons, one after another. But we must
reiterate that it is impossible to believe that all the material
comes from the apostle.

There are, for instance, in *Mark* two stories of the miraculous
feeding of the multitude. The earlier (vi. 30–44) is "the
feeding of the five thousand," with a number of dramatic
touches: in the later narrative (viii. 1–9) four thousand are

aid to have been filled, and the story is more pedestrian. Such a general likeness exists between the two narratives that they are plainly doublets, varying accounts of the same symbolic story which *Mark* received from two different sources. The story, of course, cannot be literal fact: the creation, out of nothing, of food or of any other material substance is contrary to established physical law. It is practically certain that the story is a eucharistic myth, implying that the bread and wine of the eucharist, though small in amount, give spiritual food to large numbers who partake of the Lord's Supper.

We are thus left with the conclusion that the author of *Mark* was a Christian; and, inasmuch as Aramaic appears to have been his mother-tongue, a Jew. He was near the centre of the Christian movement, as it had developed during at least a generation and a half since the crucifixion: legend could not in a less time have taken such a firm place in popular preaching. He probably was familiar with Christian missionary activity: he most certainly shared to the full the enthusiastic regard for Jesus of his "brethren in the faith." He believed that Jesus was son of God; in other words, that the Spirit in Jesus was the eternal redeeming Spirit of the divine Wisdom, and that from the indwelling Spirit Jesus drew the moral strength and spiritual certainty which revealed him as the Christ.

28. The date and place of origin of the second gospel

When did *Mark* write? Unfortunately, we cannot say. There is no way of discovering when the gospel assumed substantially its present form. We can at most claim that it was earlier than *Matthew* and *Luke*, while, because miraculous stories are so firmly rooted in it, at least a generation and a half must have separated it from the crucifixion of Jesus. As will be seen later, we can date *Luke* about A.D. 100, so that *Mark* must have been written during the first Christian century. Such a date as A.D. 75 is often assigned to it; but there is little reason to regard it as more than possible: the gospel might have been written ten years later.

Where was *Mark* written? Of the answer to this question we are equally ignorant. But there are arguments, by no means cogent, for the view that it was written in Rome. Certain it is that *Mark* uses a few transliterated Latin words. For instance, in the story of the demand of Herodias for the head of John the Baptist, we learn (vi. 27) that the king "sent forth a *speculator*," which is a Latin word for one of the bodyguard employed in conveying messages. We have similarly Greek forms of Latin words such as may have been used in Palestine, *praetorium*, *denarius*, *legio* and *centurio*. When the narrator writes that Pilate wished to "content the multitude," he uses a phrase which is said to be a literal rendering in Greek of the Latin idiom *satis facere*. Stronger than these verbal niceties is the fact that, in giving what he believed to be the teaching of Jesus as to divorce, *Mark* writes (x. 11–12), "Whosoever shall put away his wife, and marry another, committeth adultery against her: and if she herself shall put away her husband, and marry another, she committeth adultery." Under Roman law a woman could thus divorce her husband: she had no such right in Palestine. *Matthew* and *Luke* both quote the first part of the command recorded by *Mark*: the second part, which assumed the existence of Roman custom in Galilee or Judaea, they omit.

129. *Luke*

The author of the third gospel also wrote the *Acts of the Apostles*: the two books are, as it were, two volumes of the same work. This author, though his Greek style shows Semitic influences, is the most brilliant writer in the New Testament in many ways, notably in his regard for the poor and in his respect for women, he is the most "modern." He used his sources with considerable care: thus the passages which he takes from *Mark* are usually in the same relative order. He abbreviates at times; but, speaking generally, he does not insert, as does *Matthew*, fresh incidents into *Mark's* stories. From the Last Supper onwards *Luke* does not follow *Mark*: apparently he had another source which he deemed more trustworthy. We get the impression that *Luke* tried to write history: he does not invent in order to edify. His history, however, is in the fashion of his age: he concocts, especially in *Acts*, speeches suited to the occasion, thus following the example of many historians of antiquity. At times he makes a use of his material which we tend to criticize: for instance, he places many sayings and stories in the last journey of Jesus to Jerusalem, though they must have belonged to an earlier period of the ministry of Jesus.

130. Editorial changes: the story of the ascension of Jesus

It is almost certain that *Luke* and *Acts*, after they were originally written, were edited, perhaps more severely than we can now discover. The most conspicuous example of such editing is to be seen by comparing the last chapter of *Luke* with the beginning of *Acts*. The conclusion of *Luke* implies that, on the Sunday of his resurrection, Jesus led his disciples from Jerusalem "over against Bethany," and that there "he parted from them and was carried up into heaven." At the beginning of *Acts*, however, we are told (i. 3) that he "showed himself alive after his passion by many proofs, appearing unto them by the space of forty days." Then (i. 9) "as they were looking, he was taken up: and a cloud received him out of their sight." Whereupon "two men stood by them in white apparel"; and these angelic visitors prophesied Christ's return "in like manner as ye beheld him going into heaven." The evidence of ancient manuscripts for certain parts of verses at the end of *Luke* is unsatisfactory; but almost certainly at the beginning of *Acts* an editor has interpolated later developments into the original story. The insertion, as we shall argue in § 174, was probably made towards the middle of the second century of our era.

131. The date of the third gospel and *Acts*

When we inquire as to authorship and date, we can take *Luke* and *Acts* together. The opinion universally held in antiquity, and still maintained by a majority of scholars, is that the author of the two booklets was Luke, "the beloved physician" and for some time the travelling companion of Paul. Some scholars further maintain that, inasmuch as *Acts* brings Paul to Rome and then merely says that "he abode two whole years in his own hired dwelling," the book must have been finished before the time of the trial for which Paul had been taken to Rome. This trial probably ended in Paul's condemnation and was followed by his death. Certainly, if one can trust a very strong Christian tradition, Paul was martyred during or before the persecution of the Christians by Nero after the fire of Rome in A.D. 64.

The argument, thus based on the fact that Paul's death is not made the natural end of *Acts*, seems strong until we recollect that the author of *Luke* and *Acts* had no wish to antagonize the

Roman authorities. His first volume ended with the death of Jesus by order of a Roman procurator: to end the second by an account of the death of the greatest Christian missionary by order of the emperor's tribunal, in theory the emperor himself, would, to say the least, have been most tactless. When *Luke* wrote, every Christian presumably knew Paul's fate. It was better to end the story with a suggestion that Paul, during his imprisonment while waiting for his trial, received kindly treatment, rather than to have as a climax his martyrdom.

Fortunately we are not left in doubt as to the approximate time when *Acts* was written. As we have already been led to suspect in § 93, there is fairly good evidence that *Luke* dates from at least thirty years after Nero's persecution. Moreover, in *Acts*, as in the third gospel, there are plain indications that the author of these books had read, hastily and incorrectly, the *Jewish Antiquities* of Flavius Josephus, a work of which, as we have said in § 92, we know the date of publication.

We recapitulate that, in the gospel (iii. 1–2), *Luke* attempts to give an accurate date for the beginning of the ministry of Jesus. He describes the regions over which Herod Antipas and his half-brother Philip were ruling, and adds that Lysanias was tetrarch of Abilene. But, if the argument which we set out in § 93 be accepted, Lysanias had been dead for more than sixty years when Jesus began his ministry. The reader will remember that Josephus writes in his *Jewish Antiquities* (xx. vii. 1) that, after A.D. 53, (Herod) Agrippa II had possession of the tetrarchy of Philip together with Trachonitis, and also of Abila that had been the tetrarchy of Lysanias. It would seem that *Luke* wrongly assumed from this passage that, in the fifteenth year of Tiberius (A.D. 28–29), not only was Philip tetrarch of Ituraea and Trachonitis, but that Lysanias was lord of Abila. He had, in fact, read—too hastily—a statement made by Josephus in a book which was, according to evidence that is indisputable, not published before A.D. 93.

From *Acts* comes precisely similar evidence. Gamaliel is represented (v. 34–40) as having made a telling speech to the sanhedrin, in which he urged that there should be no official Jewish interference with the apostles, who were then beginning to make converts in Jerusalem. The speech is not, of course, a verbatim report; but, in the fashion of ancient historians, a free composition in which *Luke* states what he imagined Gamaliel to have said. The gist of the speech is that previous quasi-Messianic leaders had come to grief. Theudas, "giving himself out to be somebody" was slain. And "after this man rose up Judas of Galilee in the days of the enrolment": he also perished.

Now in Josephus we read—again in the *Jewish Antiquities* (xx. v. 1)—that, in the period A.D. 44–45, Theudas was slain; and the movement associated with him is described in almost the same terms by Josephus as by *Luke*. Gamaliel must have made his speech before A.D. 35, unless the crucifixion of Jesus took place much later than is usually supposed. *Luke* is therefore in error, for he makes Gamaliel refer to an unsuccessful popular movement which did not take place until at least ten years after the date of his supposed speech.

Luke, moreover, makes another serious error, for he puts Theudas before the uprising of Judas of Galilee in the time of the census. To find the reason for this further mistake, we read a little further in Josephus and find that he records that Tiberius Alexander, procurator of Judaea about A.D. 46–48, put to death *two of the sons* of Judas of Galilee, who himself had led a protest against the census, and the consequent paying of taxes to the Romans, in the time of Quirinius. As the census under Quirinius took place in A.D. 6–7, the uprising of Judas of Galilee preceded Theudas by nearly forty years. Obviously *Luke* had hastily read Josephus and had omitted to notice that the sons of Judas were mentioned, and not Judas himself. This oversight is plainly the source of his inaccurate history.

We thus reach the conclusion that *Luke* and *Acts* were both written after A.D. 93. We can with fair safety date them about A.D. 100, with the proviso that editorial corrections and additions were made until the two books received quasi-official recognition in the period A.D. 150–175.

132. The authorship of the third gospel and *Acts*

The authorship of *Luke* and *Acts* is not so easily settled. We have already mentioned the common opinion that their author was Luke the physician, Paul's some-time travelling companion. Undoubtedly the author of *Acts* used a travel-diary kept by a companion of Paul. In four places in the latter part of *Acts*, excerpts from this diary (the famous "we-passages")

I

retain the first person plural. They begin at Troas (xvi. 10), where Paul had a vision of a man saying, "Come over into Macedonia, and help us." "Straightway," the narrative goes on, "we sought to go forth into Macedonia." The chronology of Paul's travels—and, indeed, of his whole life—is obscure: it rests mainly on the fact that he was at Corinth when Gallio was proconsul, probably during a period covering A.D. 51–52. Now, if Paul arrived at Corinth during the course of the year A.D. 50, he may well have left Troas for Salonica during the year A.D. 48; and this will be the date—we discuss the question in §§ 203, 205—when we first know for certain that the writer of the travel-diary was with him.

There are further "we-passages" in *Acts* (xx. 5–15 and xxi. 1–18), the first of these recording the circumstances under which Paul left Philippi for Troas on his way to Jerusalem, and the second the later stages of the same journey, *via* Rhodes and Tyre, ending with the meeting at Jerusalem with James. The final excerpt from the diary (*Acts* xxvii. 1–xxviii. 16) describes the journey of Paul, as a prisoner from Palestine remitted to Rome. It contains the graphic narrative of the shipwreck at Malta and practically forms the conclusion of the book of *Acts*.

We may take it that there is no good reason to doubt the ancient tradition that the author of the travel-diary was Luke, "the beloved physician." Was he also the author of the book of *Acts*; or had that author, among other authorities which he consulted, used the travel-diary? Scholars have made careful examination of the literary characteristics of the "we-passages" and of the rest of the *Acts*; and they assert that they are from the same hand. But, if Luke was merely thirty years old when we first hear of him at Troas in A.D. 48, he must have been nearly or quite eighty years old when he wrote the third gospel and *Acts*. Such an age is not quite impossible; but human life was shorter then than now, and neither book shows any sign of the weaknesses of age.

We have also to remember that our author, whoever he may have been, was a great literary artist, who may well have been too easy-going to make a change from "we" to "they," while to the style of the narrative he gave characteristic touches. When in his gospel he used *Mark*, he dexterously put the imprint of his own style upon the passages which he quoted.

These arguments make it highly probable that *Luke*, the actual author of the third gospel and of *Acts*, was not Luke the physician. He will have been a well-educated Christian of the second generation, who had laboriously acquired such information as he could of the early Christian movement, and who wrote nearly forty years after Paul perished at Rome. The speech at Athens (*Acts* xvii. 22–31) which he ascribes to Paul, shows him to have been, for his time, well educated. There are in it a suggestion of philosophy and two classical quotations—mentioned later in § 204—one from the poet Epimenides and one from Aratus, a Greek writer of Cilician origin much esteemed by Romans of the first century before Christ.

Our conclusions are confirmed by other significant facts. The first dozen chapters of *Acts* contain no little legendary history. Peter, the central figure of a number of miraculous tales, drops out of the story when (*Acts* xii. 17) he leaves Jerusalem for another place, probably Antioch, about the year A.D. 44. This is but five years before the "we-passages" begin; and we should have expected Luke the physician to have been better informed as to events than most scholars, after a study alike of the miraculous narratives and of the letter to the *Galatians*, can allow.

We have, for instance, accounts, at the end of *Acts* xi and in *Acts* xv, of two visits, in the first place of "Barnabas and Saul," and in the second place of "Paul and Barnabas," from Antioch to Jerusalem. It is highly probable that these accounts are two records of the same event which is also described in *Galatians* (ii. 1–10). *Luke* had before him different memoranda; and he did not realize that in these documents the same occasion was described from different standpoints. In the first, because of the famine "in the days of Claudius," Barnabas and Saul take monetary help to the poverty-stricken converts in Jerusalem: in the second, the extremely tendentious narrative, as it has been termed, is concerned with the demands to be made of gentile Christians.

There is also the most unexpected fact that *Luke*, recounting so much of Paul's missionary life, never once refers to his *Epistles*. Much of Paul's time when his travelling companion was with him must have been taken up either in discussing the issues mentioned in the letters written before his captivity, or in actually writing these letters; but the whole record in *Acts* is of Paul's external activity. It is a most surprising fact that, as we shall see later, references to the *Epistles* during the first century do not exist. The *Apocalypse*, moreover, though Asia Minor, the scene of Paul's main missionary work, was its background, has no apparent knowledge of him. There is a reference, both to Paul and to his letters, in the short *Second Epistle General of Peter* (iii. 15–16); but, as we shall see later in § 185, it is now generally agreed that this document must be dated about A.D. 150, and that the reference to Paul's epistles is a warning against the use made of them by Marcion and his followers.

Among early Christian writings outside the New Testament there occurs, in the *First Epistle of Clement*, a quotation from the *First Epistle to the Corinthians*, which is explicitly ascribed to Paul; but Clement, if an argument put forward later in § 182 is sound, cannot well be dated before A.D. 120. There is, in fact, as again we shall see later in §§ 217–20, much to be said for the view that Paul's letters were not collected, edited and put into general circulation before the second century. The author of *Acts* in all probability never heard of them. We can thus account for his silence as to their existence: had the physician Luke written *Acts*, the silence that we find would have been inexplicable.

We conclude, then, that the third gospel and *Acts* were written about A.D. 100 by a well-educated man, otherwise unknown, who collected such records of the early Christian movement as he could acquire. He wrote with brilliance and skill, though at times he used his material with undue freedom, and though he was occasionally careless in quoting from the information to which he had access. He belonged to an age of intellectual decline and was credulous, though not more credulous than other men of his time. Miracles were recorded with unquestioning faith by his contemporaries, learned historians such as Tacitus and Suetonius. But *Luke*, whatever his faults, had an artist's sense of words, and of his earnestness and sincerity there can be no doubt. To him Christianity was a way of life (*Acts* ix. 2) in which he profoundly believed.

133. *Matthew*

The Gospel according to Matthew, as we have seen, is based, like *Luke*, on *Mark* and Q. While *Luke* was most probably written for gentile Christians, *Matthew* appears to have been used at first by Greek-speaking communities in Palestine and Syria. *Matthew* must have been written about the same time as *Luke*; otherwise we should not have such marked divergence in the birth-stories. We, therefore, date its production about A.D. 95–100. In assigning this date we do not imply that there are in it no late editorial changes.

There are in *Matthew* few trustworthy records of the life of Jesus that do not come from *Mark*: from Q we have mainly sayings, not doings, of Jesus. If it be true that *Mark* was written in Rome, while *Matthew* was a Syrian gospel, we are forced to the conclusion that, by the end of the first century, information as to the life and ministry of Jesus was decidedly meagre. The gospel of the early Christian missionaries was fundamentally threefold—a body of teaching, a way of life, and a mode of worship. Interest was primarily in Christ the Lord, not in Jesus of Nazareth. Only gradually does the desire to have the full story of the earthly life of Jesus appear to have spread, and then accurate remembrance of him had largely disappeared. The historic Jesus is a figure seen in the New Testament amid swirling mists. We get, mainly in *Mark*, tantalizing glimpses of him; but the materials for a biography of Jesus are lacking.

Matthew did what was possible. He produced a gospel which, from the time when it was written until the nineteenth century, was valued more highly than any other. It was more complete than *Mark*, for it gave the birth and infancy narratives which the second gospel lacked. Its resurrection story accorded better with the later tradition than did the lost ending of *Mark*, which must have put the resurrection appearances in Galilee and not in Jerusalem. Moreover, in the excerpt from Q which forms the basis of the Sermon on the Mount, and in other excerpts, it preserved teaching which was characteristic and supremely valuable. Doubtless, also, its display of proof-texts from the Old Testament, more lavish than in any other gospel, made a strong appeal, which lasted until the rise of modern estimates of the Old Testament writings. Add to all these considerations the fact that it was permeated by religious earnestness, and one understands the esteem in which it has been, and still is, held.

Originally anonymous, the first gospel was, before the middle of the second century, associated with the name of Matthew, the customs officer who, according to one tradition, had been among the immediate followers of Jesus during his ministry in Galilee. In *Mark* (ii. 14) this officer is called Levi, the son of Alphaeus; in *Luke* (v. 27) he is called Levi and his father is not named. Why he should be called Matthew in the first gospel (ix. 9), and why the gospel should be called after him, are questions which no one can answer. There is doubtless weight in the general consideration that books, accepted as authoritative during the second century of our era, were given added prestige if it were said that they were written by an apostle.

134. The fourth gospel

The *Gospel according to John* is the chief enigma of the New Testament. It is supreme in its religious appeal; and its thought has dominated Christian speculation, especially as to the person of Christ, throughout the Christian ages. But the book is singularly uneven: the argumentative Christ of certain chapters —they are happily few in number—in which Jesus is represented as an anti-Jewish controversialist, is not an attractive figure; while, in the great discourses which are placed after Jesus has washed the feet of his disciples at the Last Supper, we have teaching which by its superb quality is naturally thought of as coming from the son of God.

The language of the book seems to have been specially created for its sublime use. It is unlike that of any other work in the New Testament: as we have already suggested in § 111, it is ludicrous to imagine that the fourth gospel could have been written by the author of the barbarous Semitic Greek of the *Apocalypse*. The style, in the greatest passages, is deceptively simple. The vocabulary is small: the same key-words occur again and again. Sometimes one is inclined to think that the masterly beauty of the English translation is the source of the peculiar appeal of the gospel: but a Frenchman, for instance, feels the appeal equally in his own tongue. Sheer religious genius has shaped both thought and expression. The symbolism has a rare perfection: it is developed with the rhythm of fine poetry. Though the great discourses rise to far-off spiritual heights, they never lose touch with human feelings and needs: countless followers of Christ, as the end of life has come, have asked that "the fourteenth chapter of St. John" should be read to them.

135. Symbolic teaching rather than history

We know nothing of the author of the fourth gospel, and the book itself is of such a character that speculation as to its origin is indecisive. Early tradition is unanimous in associating its author with Ephesus, the great city in western Asia Minor which was an important centre of Paul's activity. Probably the fourth gospel and the three *Epistles General of John* come from the same writer, though ingenuity can make a somewhat surprisingly strong case for divergence of outlook between gospel and first epistle.

We may venture the theory that, at some time before the beginning of the second century of our era, there was at Ephesus a religious teacher who, having a Christian background, was a speculative theologian to whom *Mark* and, if he knew them, *Luke* and *Matthew* were new presentations of Christianity. This teacher was to no small extent engaged in anti-Jewish controversy: he was also noteworthy for his addresses at Christian gatherings. These addresses were largely symbolic, having as little relation to history as, say, Bunyan's *Pilgrim's Progress*. Semi-historical persons like Nicodemus, the Woman of Samaria and Lazarus were introduced into these symbolic narratives, to which colour was given by miraculous stories. In due course, either by their original author or by a disciple, these addresses were combined into a life of Jesus which bore some resemblance to the tradition formulated in the synoptic gospels.

At times the synoptic narrative was set aside, either because it was in conflict with the teaching preserved in the local Christian congregation, or because the writer wished to heighten his appeal. Thus, on the one hand, the Pauline or pseudo-Pauline story of the Last Supper, which with variations appears in all the synoptists, was omitted; and, on the other hand, Mary, the mother of Jesus, was put at the foot of the Cross. The author was far from attempting crudely to deceive. He felt, as we emphasized in § 113 and as it is important to reiterate, that religious truth was sometimes best reached by symbols and allegories. We do not know what he had in mind when he brought Mary to the crucifixion of her son; but, speaking generally, he makes his miracles so symbolic and, we may add, so extreme, that his immediate readers would not have imagined them to be fact.

Take, for instance, the symbolic story (ix. 1–12) which teaches that the Christ is the spiritual light of the world: it is the cure of a blind man. But we notice that it was not the cure of a man who had become blind: his blindness was from birth. Many, it is true, are spiritually blind from birth; but, while this birth-blindness in no way detracts from the symbolism of the miracle, it also emphasizes its improbability.

The manner of the cure of this blind man differs from that of a somewhat similar story in *Mark* (viii. 22–26) and possibly gives some indication of the date of the fourth gospel. Jesus, we are told in the fourth gospel, "spat on the ground, and made clay of the spittle, and anointed the eyes [of the blind man] with the clay." Compare such action with that of Vespasian, according to a story in the *Histories* (iv. 81) of Tacitus, a work of the reign of Trajan, probably published shortly after A.D. 100. We abbreviate somewhat drastically: "A certain man of the people of Alexandria, well-known for his loss of sight, kneeled down and begged of Vespasian the cure of his blindness. He desired that the emperor would be pleased to put some of his spittle on his cheeks and eyes. Vespasian at first began to laugh: then he ordered the physicians to give their opinion. They said that the power of sight had not been completely eaten away. If the cure succeeded, Caesar would have the glory: if not, the poor miserable object would only be laughed at. Vespasian did what was desired and the blind man saw immediately. *The tale is told by eye-witnesses, even now when falsehood brings no reward.*"

As a second instance of the way in which, obliquely, the author of the fourth gospel insists that his miracles are symbols and not facts, we may take the raising of Lazarus (xi. 1–44). Here Jesus affirms himself to be "the resurrection and the life." But it must not be overlooked that Lazarus is not just dead: there is no possibility of a swoon or of the resuscitation of a man in whom life still lingers: he has been dead four days and decomposition has presumably set in. The miracle, while a fitting tribute to the spiritual power of Jesus to lead men to eternal life, cannot, in fact, be taken literally.

In the miracle at Cana (ii. 1–11), of which we have previously written in § 113, we have the same warning conveyed by a sly touch of humour. The *Logos* makes his appearance—possibly there is a recollection of the worship of Dionysus—by turning water into wine. But at a village wedding, when merely a little more wine was needed because supplies had run short, the water in six great stone vessels, each containing two or three firkins—in all more than a hundred gallons—is turned into wine. Symbolically, the supply of divine refreshment brought by the *Logos* is overwhelming. Regarded literally, the story is fantastic.

Yet one more illustration may be given of our author's skill in indirect statement. Originally, as is evident to all who read carefully, the gospel ended with what is now the twentieth chapter: the present last chapter is a subsequent addition. When the book was in its original form, the final incident was the conclusive revelation of the risen Christ to "doubting Thomas." The apostle touches the wounds of Christ and exclaims (xx. 28), "My Lord and my God."

John of Ephesus thus, in the mouth of Thomas, claims for the Christ at the close of his gospel precisely the titles which the emperor Domitian had wished to receive. Domitian, who was Vespasian's son, was emperor during the years A.D. 81–96; and there seems little doubt that, towards the end of his reign and at his instigation, there was some persecution of Christians because of their "atheism." The historians, Suetonius and Cassius Dio, relate that Domitian sorely offended the Roman nobility by his desire to be styled *Dominus et Deus*. He was not satisfied to be merely *divus*, divine, an honour accorded after death to Julius Caesar and to Augustus among other emperors: he wished in his lifetime to receive homage as "Lord and God." The author of the fourth gospel quietly hints at such much-resented imperial pretensions; and ends his work with the suggestion that his Christ should rightly be given the honour of which even the emperor, a few years before he wrote, was deemed unworthy.

136. The author's claim to be an eye-witness

When the question of the authorship of the fourth gospel is discussed, great stress is usually placed on two statements in it which purport to claim that the author was a first-hand witness of what he narrates. The first statement (xix. 34–35) describes how, when Jesus was on the cross, one of the soldiers "pierced his side, and straightway there came out blood and water. And he that hath seen hath borne witness, and his witness is true : and he knoweth that he saith true, that ye also may believe." This claim to be an eye-witness is taken up again in the editorial addition which now forms the last chapter of the gospel. Peter, we are told (xxi. 20–24), "seeth the disciple whom Jesus loved following; which also leaned back on his breast at the supper. . . . This is the disciple which beareth witness of these things, and wrote these things : and we know that his witness is true."

In view of the emphasis throughout the gospel on truth— Jesus (xiv. 6) is "the way, and the truth, and the life"—it has been widely held that the author must have been the beloved disciple who lived to write the gospel at a ripe old age in Ephesus. Internal evidence, as we have indicated, is decisive against any such view. Nor need it be maintained. The last chapter is, by general agreement, an editorial addition; and the same editor will have inserted the verse just quoted from chapter xix with the object, which he no doubt deemed laudable, of giving to the gospel the authority of an apostle or, at least, of an eye-witness.

We cannot too often remind ourselves that the gospels were circulated in manuscript: editorial insertions and additions were easy: those which commended themselves gave credit to manuscripts which served as the originals of future copies : and it must never be forgotten that, though earlier fragments have been found, none of our existing manuscripts of the New Testament goes back beyond the fourth century of our era.

By a most unlikely chance, minute portions of the fourth gospel have been found in a torn bit of manuscript which is very early indeed. In the year A.D. 1935 there was published the facsimile of a fragment of an ancient manuscript written on papyrus: it had come from Egypt, and was discovered among the large collection of such scraps now in the John Rylands library of Manchester. There is writing on both sides of the fragment: it has come from a codex, a book not a roll. Obviously the book was a copy of the fourth gospel, for on one side there is what is left of verses 31–33 of chapter xviii of the gospel, and on the other side a fragment (verses 37–38) of the same chapter.

Experts judge by the style of the writing that it was written in the first half of the second century of our era, and possibly as early as the middle of that period. If they are right, it must have been written shortly after the gospel was composed, and possibly before the appendix (chapter xxi) was added. "It is the earliest known fragment of any part of the New Testament and probably the earliest witness to the existence of the gospel according to *John*."

137. Arguments against the apostolic authorship of the fourth gospel

Against the opinion that the fourth gospel was composed by the apostle John, the son of Zebedee and brother of James, there can be set a number of indications, each slight in itself but cumulatively somewhat impressive.

In *Mark* (x. 39) Jesus is reported as saying to the two brothers, "The cup that I drink ye shall drink; and with the baptism that I am baptized withal shall ye be baptized." This verse suggests that the two brothers perished together before the date, say A.D. 75, when *Mark* was written.

Eusebius, the Christian historian who wrote towards the beginning of the fourth century of our era (see § 123), in his *Ecclesiastical History* (iii. 31), quotes from a letter of Polycrates, bishop of Ephesus. In the course of this letter the bishop says, "John also, who leaned on the Lord's breast, who had been a priest and had worn the *petalon* [probably the mitre or breast-plate of the high-priest], both a martyr and a teacher, sleeps in Ephesus." Here there is no hint that the author of the fourth gospel, who obviously was the John in question, was a fisherman from the lake of Galilee: it is rather suggested that this author originally belonged to a sadducean high-priestly family.

Two other scraps of evidence, similar in tendency, can be adduced. A late manuscript fragment was discovered half a century ago which stated that Papias (about A.D. 150) said that "John the divine and James his brother were slain by the

Jews." Once again, our church calendar commemorates, on December 27, "St. John, Apostle and Evangelist": an ancient Syrian calendar is known in which John and James, the apostles, are said to have been martyred at Jerusalem on this day.

Finally we would observe that in *Acts* (xii, 1–2) we read "About that time (the time of famine under Claudius) Herod the king put forth his hands to afflict certain of the church. And he killed James the brother of John with the sword." One would have expected that James would have been described as "the son of Zebedee"; and some scholars find here an editorial correction, the passage having originally read, "killed James and John with the sword." The correction, if accepted, would bring the statement into line with the evidence just brought forward. Claudius became emperor in A.D. 41. (Herod) Agrippa I, a grandson of Herod the Great by an Hasmonaean princess, died in A.D. 44; and the execution of James is said to have taken place shortly before Herod's death. We conclude that in all probability John the apostle, the son of Zebedee, was martyred with his brother James in A.D. 44.

CHAPTER VIII

JESUS AND HIS TEACHING

138. The central fact of Christianity

A Christian writing of Jesus must exercise restraint lest enthusiasm for one whose life and thought permeate all that he holds sacred should lead to what others might deem extravagant statement. On the other hand, he should be able without irritation to weigh cold or even hostile appraisal. He must not forget that the test of his faith in his Lord is to be found in his own experience of life. The memory of the peasant-artisan of Galilee would have perished long ago but for the greatness of his character and the truth of his insight.

The central fact of Christianity is, and has always been, Jesus. Upon him, upon men's belief in the truth of his teaching and the divine beauty of his character, the Christian movement was, and continues to be, based. Some Christian moralists, as their faith disintegrates, are led to regard him, or his teaching, as of little account: they pass to ethical monotheism, or to some variant of ancient stoicism, fine creeds but not Christianity. Religious enthusiasts, whose emotions are veneered by Christianity, pass, when they find his moral teaching too exacting, to some form of mystery-religion, rich in sound and colour but of slight value to a world in distress.

The teaching of Jesus as to God's nature and as to man's duty and destiny, the loyalty of Jesus to his teaching, the example of Jesus as he went to the cross and, above all, the certainty of his knowledge of God—these facts are fundamental in Christianity. They give, to an amalgam that is by no means all pure gold, its proved excellence. They were fundamental to its initial success. They remain the elements of the Christian faith to which men return after every period of its decay. The Christian faith continues to exist because men still feel that of Jesus it was truly said that "never man spake like this man." To him they continue to come, saying, "Thou hast the words of eternal life"; and, coming, they worship him with the old words, "Thou art the Christ, the Son of God."

139. Jesus no myth

In modern times a number of scholars have advanced, and defended, the thesis that Jesus never lived. Much ingenuity has been vainly spent in supporting this paradox. Our present study of the gospels should have made it clear that Jesus is no myth, however mythical be some of the stories told in connection with him. Considering the obscurity of his origin and of his mission, he is, behind a somewhat blurred portrait, surprisingly definite. His personality is not vague and shadowy, but real and powerful. In the first three evangelists we do not get the play of imagination that has created an artificial figure of religious romance. Analysis of their writings does not dissolve Jesus into myth and fancy: it reveals him more clearly in his simplicity and his greatness.

140. Apollonius of Tyana

Those who are tempted to doubt the historicity of Jesus may with advantage compare with the gospel narrative the *Life of Apollonius of Tyana*, which was written by Philostratus on the basis of earlier documents and published about A.D. 220. Apollonius was born at Tyana in Cappadocia, of wealthy parents, about the time of the birth of Jesus. He was an ascetic, who lived long and travelled far, meeting some of the great ones of the earth. The *Life*, which is elaborate and by no means brief, obviously comes from a practised writer. Pagans early maintained that its hero was as great a sage, as remarkable a worker of miracles and as potent an exorcist as Jesus. Notwithstanding miracles and exorcisms Apollonius obviously was no myth. But an air of languor pervades the pages of Philostratus: they lack the freshness, the naïve charm, the passionate earnestness of the synoptic gospels.

141. The village life

When an analysis of the gospels is made, we become aware that the synoptists, especially when they rely upon Q, preserve many obviously faithful memories. It might have been expected that the small touches which link Jesus to the peasant's fields and the village cottage would not have been retained. But they abound in the records of his Galilean ministry. Illustrations natural to one who spent his time at the carpenter's bench are lacking. But the lack only makes it the more probable that Jesus was countryman rather than craftsman.

Again and again in the teaching of Jesus there come hints that he was familiar with the poverty, the duties, the contents and the insecurity of a cottage. In all the first three gospels we have his inquiry (*Mark* iv. 21), as to whether a lamp is brought to be "put under the bushel, or under the bed." The form of the question shows that the home which came naturally to the mind of Jesus had not several corn measures and a number of beds. From Q (*Matthew* vi. 20 and *Luke* xii. 33) comes the familiar passage as to moth and rust, thieves breaking in and stealing. Q also (*Luke* xi. 25 and *Matthew* xii. 44) tells us of the house swept and tidied. In *Luke* (xv. 8) we have the story of the woman losing a coin, lighting a lamp and making careful search until she finds it. Jesus knew full well how serious the loss of a single silver coin could be to one who lived in a working-class home in a Galilean village.

All three synoptists (*Mark* ii. 21-2) recall the teaching as to the patching of old clothes and the mending of old leather wine-bottles: there comes a stage when the old material is so frail that new stuff is worse than useless. From Q (*Matthew* vii. 9-10 and *Luke* xi. 11) comes the picture of a hungry boy asking his father for a piece of bread and a bit of fish, the cheap food of a cottage home near the lake of Galilee. Jesus also used naturally —the passage comes from Q (*Matthew* xiii. 33 and *Luke* xiii. 21)— an illustration of the effect of yeast in dough. He had obviously, as a boy, sat in a corner of the living-room, watching his mother make the family bread. It is unnecessary to add to this series of illustrations. They rose so naturally to the lips of Jesus and entered so easily into his teaching that, had we been entirely ignorant of the circumstances of his youth, we could have been certain that he had known, and had been happy in, the poverty of a cottage.

142. The maturity of Jesus

Whether Jesus was some thirty-four years of age, or a dozen years older, when he began his mission, he must have previously had many years of relative maturity during which, while he did his daily work, he thought of the ultimate problems of human life. His teaching, as it has come to us, bears no trace of immaturity. It is clear, coherent, unhesitating, the expression of the mind of one who has pondered long and deeply.

Jesus speaks, of course, in the idiom of the Galilean villager— demons, for instance, cause mental disease. But he is serene with the confidence of one who has felt God's protecting care during the years. He has no doubts as to the presence of God in his life, or as to the value of prayer to God. The love of nature, strangely absent from most early Christians, if one may judge by the writings they have left, had grown strong within him. A kindly regard for children was part of his nature : they were to him symbols of the kingdom of heaven. Like many another religious and social reformer, he had grown critical of the official religious teachers of his time : professional piety left him not merely cold, but often indignant. But his alienation was not that of the clever boy on the threshold of manhood : it grew out of prolonged disappointment and grave causes of distrust. They who should have been trusted leaders had too often proved themselves mean and greedy seekers after power.

143. The celibacy of Jesus

As we reflect that Jesus, when he began his ministry, was a mature man, we are led to remember that he had never married. In a different civilization, this fact might not call for special comment. But among the Jews, especially perhaps at that epoch, the celibacy of an ordinary villager was so exceptional as to call for explanation. Though the Talmud is of later date, its teaching will have faithfully preserved the outlook of the kinsfolk of Jesus. "A man without a wife is not a man." "At eighteen the bridal." "The Holy One sits and watches a man till he is twenty years old, to see if he will marry. If he comes to twenty and is not married, He says, Let the spirit of his bones be breathed out."

The young villager must have been strangely different from his fellows to remain unmarried, against the pressure of the public opinion surrounding him. We cannot argue in explanation that he was an ascetic, always intending to join some group in the desert. He deliberately rejected asceticism, saying of himself, as Q records, "The Son of man is come eating and drinking; and ye say, Behold, a gluttonous man, and a winebibber, a friend of publicans and sinners!" (*Luke* vii. 34 and *Matthew* xi. 19). Evidently, in that early life which is almost entirely hidden from us, Jesus felt himself different from his fellows. Outwardly carpenter and peasant, he was inwardly a dreamer and thinker, feeling sensitively towards an ever-deepening understanding of God and an ever-closer union with Him.

144. Jesus in relation to God

Attempts to explain the relation betweer Jesus and God have in the past given rise—strangely enough—to fierce arguments and violent quarrels. The orthodox solution of an impossibly difficult problem has been expressed in quasi-physical terms, such as by saying that Jesus was of one "substance" with God. But essentially the Christian position is the assertion not only of a realization by Jesus of God's being and an understanding of His purpose, but also of a union between him and God, as complete as was compatible with his humanity. We must think of the boy, as his intelligence unfolded, realizing God's character by observing His creation, feeling after God in all the experiences which came to him, growing nearer to God in trying to serve Him, strengthening his understanding through those flashes of insight which are given, though perhaps rarely and in less measure, to many men. So there was fashioned—should we say, revealed?—so complete a union that it could be termed a unity of Jesus and God.

We can imagine the boy sitting in some corner of a corn-field, watching and wondering at the miracle of growth, "first the blade, then the ear, after that the full corn in the ear." The sense of God's bounty, of God as a loving Father, grew to be a part of himself. The lad must also have thrilled sensitively to the beauty with which God revealed Himself, when, for a few days in springtime, the hillsides were great stretches of glorious colour, as the anemones flowered. To Jesus, it is God who doth so "clothe the grass in the field." The passage which records his remembrance comes from Q (*Matthew* vi. 28 and *Luke* xii. 27): it is, of course, known to all. "Consider the lilies, how they grow: they toil not, neither do they spin; yet I say unto you, Even Solomon in all his glory was not arrayed like one of these."

K

There must have been many hours, and even days, of silent meditation when Jesus was in charge of sheep on the hills. Allusions to sheep and shepherds are numerous in his teaching. The separation of the sheep from the goats, the sheep that is lost on the hills or fallen into a pit, the danger from wolves, all come easily into his speech. Possibly the fourth gospel, with its allusions to the thief and to the careless hired watchman, equally preserves genuine recollections of the teaching of Jesus. The night solitudes had gone to the fashioning of his trust in God.

145. The attitude of Jesus to children and their elders

We may doubt if Jesus was ever quite happy in the world of adult men and women. Children, as we have seen, were a delight to him: in spirit he would enter with zest into their games. Obviously, he had many a time watched them at play in the village street. There comes from Q (*Matthew* xi. 16-17 and *Luke* vii. 32) the picture of "children that sit in the market place, and call one to another; which say, We piped unto you and ye did not dance; we wailed, and ye did not weep." We have in *Mark* (x. 13-16) the episode when "they brought unto him little children, that he should touch them." The way in which he put out his hands was so significant, and so revealing, that the story naturally and inevitably found a place also in *Matthew* and *Luke*. So long as Christianity endures, mothers will remember that Jesus said, "Suffer the little children to come unto me; forbid them not: for of such is the kingdom of God."

But, though Jesus had this moving love for children, he viewed their elders with none of the hearty satisfaction of the man who can rejoice in the *joie de vivre* of his fellow-men. Primarily he is the reformer, disappointed at the lack of response in those around him. He was burdened by the sense of the hardness of men, the unfairness of human life; and yet he remained convinced that in all men, if only it could be kindled into flame, is a spark of divinely given goodness. Because of this conviction he held aloof from none, not even from the outcast of the little world in which he moved.

146. The exaggerations and the humour of Jesus

Profound misunderstanding of the teaching of Jesus has repeatedly arisen from his deliberate use of exaggeration to give emphasis to his statements. Sometimes this exaggeration is designedly grotesque, as with the famous maxim, "It is easier for a camel to go through a needle's eye, than for a rich man to enter into the kingdom of God" (*Mark* x. 25). This saying occurs in each of the first three gospels. All the hearers of Jesus would be familiar from childhood with the camel, an ungainly beast, which takes up all the space in a narrow lane. Jesus made them think of the animal trying to get through the eye of a needle, and of a rich man with equal difficulty trying to enter the kingdom of God. Once heard, the jest with its bitter taste was not easily forgotten. Though now largely ignored, the early church learned the lesson which it taught.

The camel is, even to-day, a common sight in Palestine; and Jesus drew from the beast's awkward and sprawling gait yet another grotesque exaggeration. It comes in a denunciation of the pharisees: "Ye blind guides, which strain at the gnat, and swallow the camel." *Matthew* (xxiii. 24) alone gives the saying; but it is so characteristic of Jesus that there is no need to doubt its authenticity. No one, of course, could imagine that Jesus thought that even a pharisee would literally try to swallow a camel. Equally he is deliberately using exaggerated language to raise a laugh when he says—the passage comes from Q (*Matthew* vii. 3–5 and *Luke* vi. 41–2)—that the average man sees a speck in his brother's eye, but is unaware of a log in his own.

In view of this use of exaggeration, often with a touch of humour in the background, it is strange that critics of Christianity should so often assume that, in his economic teaching, Jesus expected extravagant statements to be taken literally. For instance, in a passage partly from Q, he lays stress on generosity, "Give to him that asketh thee, and from him that would borrow of thee turn not thou away" (*Matthew* v. 42). But, when such a saying is made the basis of a solemn disquisition as to the ignorance of Jesus of the evils resulting from indiscriminate charity, the critic merits a smile of pity.

So, also, Jesus emphasized by exaggeration the duty of non-resistance in a court of law, an attitude which his followers maintained for many generations. He is reported as saying, again in Q, "If any man would go to law with thee, and take away thy coat, let him have thy cloke also" (*Matthew* v. 40 and *Luke* vi. 29). No sensible man will believe that Jesus held the

opinion that if, by sharp practice under an appearance of
legality, a man had been defrauded, he ought deliberately to
increase his loss. Yet Jesus has often been thus misunderstood,
because the method of his teaching is strange to us. It suffices,
without piling up illustrations, to state that Jesus taught by
picturesque imagery, by deliberate over-emphasis, by ludicrous
exaggeration. He laid down principles of conduct, not rules of
action. On the surface there was a rippling play of fancy:
underneath there was profound seriousness. Only a man
completely sure of himself could thus have been at once grave
and gay, jester and prophet of righteousness.

147. The influence of a peasant community

The picture of a Jesus, meek and mild, easily hurt by life's
roughness, remote from its sordid realities, is singularly
mistaken. Jesus surely had no illusions as regards human
nature. He had lived in a peasant community, where life was
hard. The Galilean hills near Nazareth, mainly of bare and
dusty limestone, can never have been fertile. Corn-growing
must always have been hampered by lack of water; and supplies of grass for sheep and goats will, except after the rains,
have been scanty. Moreover, the tax-gatherer, as the gospels
make clear, was always at hand. A peasant community,
struggling hard with poverty, is not a school where a man can
grow soft. The toughness and tenacity of the peasant must, for
all the formative years of his life, have impinged on Jesus. One
is, in fact, amazed that he could, in such surroundings, have
grown to such buoyancy of spirit, that there could have arisen
within him the serene trust in God's goodness which his sayings
reveal.

But life's experience had matured a moral strength and
courage which never failed. His indignation could be fierce, his
rebuke stern and telling. He was ready in speech, never apparently at a loss when men sought to trap him in conversation.
At times a certain grim humour, akin to the irony of the
common man, seems to have shown itself. As his speech, before
being recorded in writing, was translated from Aramaic into
Greek many a telling turn of phrase, possibly many a pun,
would be lost. *Luke* (xxii. 25), however, in a passage from *Mark*,
inserts the saying, "The kings of the Gentiles have lordship

over them; and they that have authority over them are called
Benefactors"; and he quotes it in a way that brings out its
scornful implications. The word for "benefactor" is the title
euergetes, given to a number of Hellenistic monarchs. If the
passage in *Luke* preserves an original form of words, Jesus must
have had at least a smattering of Greek, to say nothing of a
contemptuously critical regard for Levantine sovereigns.

148. Jesus and the knowledge of God

Jesus taught by clear and direct statement, seldom using
argument. His knowledge of God was not the outcome of chains
of reasoning, or the crown of a philosophy. The strength of his
teaching lay in its simplicity and certainty. Jesus knew, he was
sure beyond any possibility of doubt, that God is good; and the
problem of evil he set aside. He was sure that man could turn
from past sins, that he could "arise and go to his father"; and
the baffling complexities of determinism did not trouble him.
Similarly Jesus was sure that God answers prayer; and he
expressed his certainty with characteristic exaggeration. For
instance (*Matthew* xxi. 22), Jesus is reported as saying, "All
things, whatsoever ye shall ask in prayer, believing, ye shall
receive." Such teaching is in line with his emphasis on the
power of faith. From Q (*Matthew* xvii. 20 and *Luke* xvii. 6)
there comes emphatic overstatement, "If ye have faith as a
grain of mustard seed, ye shall say unto this mountain, Remove
hence to yonder place; and it shall remove; and nothing shall
be impossible unto you." The differences in the way in which
the two evangelists record this saying point either to a mistranslation from Aramaic into Greek or to the fact that the
teaching was given more than once.

As we reflect upon the somewhat blurred portrait of Jesus
given in the first three gospels, and as we get rid of what seem
to be later touches, we find superb beauty of character and spiritual power, a constant consciousness of the indwelling presence of
God. Because he feels that he can at any time go to God and
enjoy His goodness, because he is, as it were, a child expecting
and gaining his Father's love and care, his teaching as to God
is simple and certain. From his trust in God came his profound
faith in his own mission, his conviction that the kingdom of God
would come on earth. This faith went naturally with the loveli-

ness of his character, the breadth of his humanity. If God was so good, there were surely wells of unseen goodness in His children. A God, distant and unapproachable, coldly revealed by Wisdom, was entirely outside his experience. Because he knew God, he knew also that he must love God. Loving God, he must love his neighbour. So Jesus taught forgiveness of wrongs, mercy and pity towards all men. Because God will forgive us, we must forgive those who trespass against us.

The piety of Jesus is thus simple and very strong. It has been described as childish in its intensity, because there are so many sides of human thought and achievement that it ignores. But, if Jesus correctly apprehended the ultimate Power of the universe, the Purpose within the creative activity to which we all belong, what he ignored was of relatively minor importance. The abiding influence of his teaching rests on the belief, which sways successive generations of men, that Jesus truly knew God, that no misunderstanding marred his certainty, that he was blessed with a purity of heart which enabled him to see God. We may confidently prophesy that, so long as men hold to this belief, Christianity will maintain its authority among them.

149. The kingdom of God

From the certainty of Jesus that he knew God truly, came his hope of the kingdom of God on earth. All are agreed that Jesus put the idea of the kingdom of God in the centre of his teaching. *Mark* (i. 15) attributes to Jesus at the outset of his preaching the message, "The time is fulfilled, and the kingdom of God is at hand: repent ye, and believe in the gospel." In the Lord's prayer we have, as the opening petition, "Thy kingdom come," with, as it were, the consequence, "Thy will be done on earth as it is in heaven." Parables relating to the kingdom abound, especially in what seem to be the earlier strata of the synoptic gospels. Jesus himself, speaking of God as "your heavenly Father" in a passage which comes from Q (*Matthew* vi. 33 and *Luke* xii. 31), says, "Seek ye first his kingdom, and his righteousness; and all these things shall be added unto you." Sometimes, owing to a reluctance to use the divine name, the term "the kingdom of God" becomes "the kingdom of heaven": no difference of meaning is intended. The good news of the gospel is that the kingdom is at hand.

Unfortunately, Jesus does not, in any saying which has been preserved, explain or analyse what he means by the kingdom, whether it is present or future, an inward spiritual change or an outward manifestation of the power of God. Moreover, when an analysis is made of the gospel texts, we find such confusion that different scholars reach diametrically opposite conclusions; and these conclusions seem to be determined mainly by personal bias. We can, in fact, discover no clear or consistent evidence either as to the nature of the kingdom or as to the manner of its coming.

150. Jewish hopes and their influence

Such inability ought not perhaps to surprise us. Jesus took and modified Jewish hopes, common among his contemporaries. Their Messianic dreams involved the setting up of a new order, an ideal kingdom ruled by God. With its coming the whole social and political order under which they lived would be changed. The new order was, in general expectation, to follow upon a period of catastrophic disturbance. It would result from Divine intervention and would rest upon a profound spiritual change; but it would have the brilliant glory of an earthly kingdom. These Messianic hopes, of course, changed from time to time, and from writer to writer, in a way somewhat similar to that in which the bits of coloured glass rearrange themselves in a kaleidoscope. They were generally associated with the advent of a national leader, a Messiah, God's anointed. It was commonly expected that, when the kingdom was being established, those still alive would come to judgment at a great assize, and also that the righteous dead would arise to enjoy the kingdom. There would thus be a vast transformation, sudden and splendid. "Take ye heed, watch and pray: for ye know not when the time is": such is the warning (*Mark* xiii. 33) in what seems to have been a Jewish tract modified by a Christian writer.

Now when such beliefs and dreams were widespread among those drawn to Jesus, his teaching, as it was received and remembered, would take on their colour. The stronger the convictions of his hearers, the more likely were those convictions to become part of memories of his teaching. Thus only in so far as what purports to be his teaching differed from generally held expectations, can we be fairly certain that it is actually his. We can, for instance, be sure that he rejected all Jewish nationalist hopes as he pictured the kingdom. When in the fourth gospel (xviii. 36) Jesus is made to say, "My kingdom is not of this world," there is attributed to him, although the words are those of the fourth evangelist, an attitude which was undoubtedly his.

151. Jesus and the kingdom

Apart, however, from such a certainty we find it impossible, if we attach equal weight to all relevant texts in the first three gospels, to see clearly what Jesus thought as to the kingdom. Such a fact ought not to surprise those who accept the account of the origin of the gospels which was reached in chapter vii. From the beginning, the ideas of Jesus will have been blended by his hearers with their own expectations. Memories of his words, thus blended, will have been further modified by tradition. In the end statements, difficult if not impossible to reconcile with one another, were allowed to stand side by side in the authoritative gospels.

152. Evidence that Jesus shared crude popular expectations

In favour of the view that Jesus shared the common belief of his contemporaries that the kingdom would be a sudden and speedy external manifestation of the power of God, and not a gradual change, inward and spiritual, in the hearts of men, a number of texts can be quoted. We will set aside the earlier part of *Mark* xiii as being, not the teaching of Jesus, but a Jewish tract. But some contend that in the concluding verses of this same chapter we have ideas based on actual words of Jesus. Thus they argue that there is a genuine reminiscence in the words (*Mark* xiii. 30–2), "Verily I say unto you, This generation shall not pass away, until all these things be accomplished. Heaven and earth shall pass away: but my words shall not pass away. But of that day or that hour knoweth no one, not even the angels in heaven, neither the Son, but the Father." Each reader must judge for himself as to how far in these sentences we have the actual words of Jesus. Most of our critical scholars doubt their authenticity. The egoism of the statement that, though heaven and earth shall pass away, his words shall endure, is not like Jesus. Moreover that he should describe himself as the Son, in a way that implies an especial association with God the Father, seems to be an invention resulting from the theology of a later age. If two of the three sentences which make up the passage which we have quoted are thus suspect, we can hardly place much confidence in the third.

However, even though we reject this passage, we must certainly not ignore an address said to have been made by Jesus to the twelve disciples when he sent them on their mission. It comes in part from *Mark* and in part from Q, and contains the verse (*Matthew* x. 23), "When they persecute you in this city, flee into the next: for verily I say unto you, Ye shall not have gone through the cities of Israel, till the Son of man be come." With such a prophecy we may conjoin a passage in the second gospel (ix. 1), "Verily I say unto you, There be some here of them that stand by, which shall in no wise taste of death, till they see the kingdom of God come with power."

153. Evidence that Jesus thought of the kingdom as inward and spiritual

If there were no contradictory evidence, the passages just quoted would establish beyond a doubt that Jesus expected a sudden and almost immediate manifestation of the power of God, whereby the hopes associated with the kingdom of God would be fulfilled. But there is most weighty evidence for the view that Jesus thought of the kingdom as an already existing spiritual reality, established in the hearts and minds of those who had "repented," had changed their outlook and way of life, and had turned to God. Take, for instance, the beatitude (*Matthew* v. 3 and *Luke* vi. 20), "Blessed are ye poor: for yours is the kingdom of God." We give the words as they occur in *Luke*: their source is Q, and they are as likely to be a genuine utterance of Jesus as any we can quote. The sentence most clearly implies that the kingdom is already in existence and that the poor or, as Matthew describes them, the "poor in spirit" are members of it.

An even more definite witness to the belief of Jesus that the kingdom was already in existence is afforded by another text from Q. It is a story of how Jesus was "casting out a devil," and the pharisees said that he had the aid of Beelzebub, the prince of the devils. Jesus replied (*Matthew* xii. 28 and *Luke* xi. 20), "If I by the Spirit of God cast out devils, then is the kingdom of God come upon you." The words used by Jesus can only mean that the kingdom is already present, and that its existence has been revealed by the activity of the Spirit of God.

But most conclusive of all the texts that can be quoted is a passage which occurs solely in the third gospel. It runs (*Luke* xvii. 20–21), "And being asked by the Pharisees, when the kingdom of God cometh, he answered them and said, The kingdom of God cometh not with observation : neither shall they say, Lo, here! or, There! for lo, the kingdom of God is within you." This passage, naturally, has been a battle-ground where the conflict has raged furiously between, on the one hand, those who contend that Jesus shared the crude apocalyptic hopes of his contemporaries and, on the other hand, those who maintain that he looked forward to a gradual spiritual transformation within the hearts of men. It has been asserted that the word *entos*, translated "within," has rather the meaning "among." Against this view is the fact that the word occurs in *Matthew* (xxiii. 26), where Jesus exhorts the pharisees to "cleanse first the *inside* of the cup."

A still more cogent argument comes from an Egyptian rubbish-mound. In the years A.D. 1897 and A.D. 1903 respectively, there were found at Oxyrhynchus in Egypt two papyrus fragments containing sayings in Greek ascribed to Jesus. The collections in both fragments are thought to have been formed before A.D. 140. The second discovery contains a saying (II) a sentence of which, when the faulty text is reconstructed, can be translated, "And the kingdom of Heaven is within you; and whosoever shall know himself shall find it."

Obviously the Lukan saying was familiar to the writer : equally obviously to him *entos* meant "within," for he thinks of a man finding verification of the words of Jesus by looking within his own heart. Thus, if the passage of *Luke* correctly records a saying of Jesus, it is conclusive that he thought of the kingdom as a spiritual reality growing within the hearts of men. Not a little teaching to be found solely in *Luke*, such as certain great parables, has a quality that makes us think it genuine. It may well be that the passage just considered should be placed in this category.

We must, however, allow that our gospels give us a greatly confused tradition, from which no complete certainty can be drawn as to the thought of Jesus with regard to the coming of the kingdom of God. Without a doubt he taught that for entrance to the kingdom a change of heart and life was needed. He also held that, when such a change took place, a man had, in some sense, entered the kingdom. But we cannot say definitely that Jesus thought of the kingdom as entirely an inward spiritual realm for which men could fit themselves by change of heart. He may also have pictured it as an external manifestation of the power and glory of God which, within a few years of his mission, would appear upon earth. If he made for himself such a picture, he was in error, misled by the beliefs of his contemporaries; but it may well be that such beliefs have in the gospels been wrongly attributed to him.

Belief in the coming of a kingdom of God which shall be the reign of the saints on earth, a belief associated with the second coming of Christ, has never quite vanished from Christian thought; and it tends to revive in every period of acute distress. We can only say, with regard to the expectation, that it is out of harmony with all that we know of the mode of God's activity through nature or among men.

154. The life to come

There can be no doubt whatever that Jesus shared the belief in human immortality held, apparently, by all his Jewish contemporaries save the sadducees. Jesus was certain that man's life did not end with the grave, and that every man took into the next world responsibility for his doings on earth. After death would come judgment. Of these facts in the belief of Jesus our knowledge is sure. But such brief statements comprise, in effect, all that is certain as to his thought and teaching with regard to survival after death.

We have no means of ascertaining whether Jesus expected a physical "resurrection of the body." This belief, as enshrined in the so-called Apostles' Creed, originally meant the resuscitation of this present flesh of ours. The clause in the creed was probably derived, not from any certain knowledge as to the teaching of Jesus, but from reflection upon stories of his post-resurrection appearances. Jesus seems to have held that the soul of man was a potentially immortal principle of his being, distinct from his body. With regard to the dead, he would have endorsed the teaching of the contemporary author of the *Wisdom of Solomon* (iii. 1), "The souls of the righteous are in the hands of God, and there shall no torment touch them."

We cannot safely assume that Jesus expected the eternal punishment of the wicked. Such a belief would be out of harmony alike with his own character and with his teaching as to God's nature. In *Mark* (ix. 47–48) there is ascribed to Jesus the teaching that "it is good for thee to enter into the kingdom of God with one eye, rather than having two eyes to be cast into hell; where their worm dieth not, and the fire is not quenched." It may be regarded as certain, however, that the last clause reflects later Christian opinion rather than the thought of Jesus.

The most explicit teaching of Jesus, as to the life to come, occurs in a passage in *Luke* (xx. 27–40) in which he is reported to have answered an objection of the sadducees, "which say that there is no resurrection." Unfortunately, the passage occurs solely in the third gospel. In it Jesus speaks of those "that are accounted worthy to attain to that world [*or* age], and the resurrection from the dead." The implication of the words ascribed to him would appear to be that some persons were unworthy of the resurrection. The passage also gives as the opinion of Jesus that those who are worthy to attain to the world to come, "neither marry, nor are given in marriage: for neither can they die any more: for they are equal unto the angels: and are sons of God, being sons of the resurrection." If, as seems probable, such teaching is genuine, the normal Jewish belief in a bodily resurrection cannot have been shared by Jesus. The words imply a clear breach with any theory of an idealized renewal of earthly activities in the world to come: it suggests an "entirely other" mode of being in the after-life.

Perhaps in the nature of things we cannot expect that Jesus should have given clear teaching as to heaven and hell or as to the last judgment, the great assize at which, in the light of the knowledge of a man's deeds on earth, his status is to be determined in the world to come. The parable of the Rich Man and Lazarus (*Luke* xvi. 19–31) depicts the beggar being carried by angels to Abraham's bosom, and the rich man as being in torment in Hades. Though the rich man can speak to Abraham, there is between him and Lazarus a great gulf fixed, that none may cross over. The story, apart from its moral teaching, is fanciful, even fantastic. Nothing can be determined from it as to what Jesus thought of conditions in the life after death.

155. The Great Assize

Much the same must be our verdict on the brilliantly told story of the Great Assize, which *Matthew* (xxv. 31–46) alone gives. Here there is a picture of the Son of man coming in all his glory and his angels with him. He takes his seat on his throne and all the nations appear before him. From among them he separates individuals, on his right hand or on his left, as a shepherd separates his sheep from his goats. Then follows the dramatic verdict. Those on the king's right hand are told to "inherit the kingdom prepared for you from the foundation of the world," for "I was an hungred and ye gave me meat: I was thirsty, and ye gave me drink. . . ." The surprised reply comes, "Lord, when saw we thee an hungred, and fed thee? or athirst, and gave thee drink? . . ." And the king answers, "Inasmuch as ye did it unto one of these my brethren, even these least, ye did it unto me."

The story is told with exquisite simplicity and in its essentials may well have come from Jesus. But, while the point of the story is brought out with rare skill, the accessories merely give colour. We cannot argue as to the thought of Jesus from the fact that the Son of man, possibly by an addition to the original parable, is identified with the king who acts as judge, enthroned in royal state. What we must take from the allegory is the conclusion that, as we show kindness and pity to all, even to those of least account, so shall we enjoy God's love in the world to come.

While it cannot be finally concluded, from the teaching of Jesus as to life after death, that he did not expect the immediate coming of an external and visible kingdom of God on earth, yet it would appear that the whole direction of his thought was towards a purely spiritual kingdom reached through obedience to the will of God. As men sought to create such a kingdom on earth, they would fit themselves for its membership after death.

156. The communion of Jesus with God

Before we bring to an end our brief, and necessarily inadequate, attempt to understand the personality and thought of
Jesus we will, at the risk of some repetition, write anew of him
in relation to God.

All our authorities are at one in testifying that the communion of Jesus with God was continuous and tranquil. There
were no visions, no trances; there were no ecstatic occasions
when the normal and wholesome working of his mind was
violently disturbed. It would appear to be certain that the
revelation of God which he received was never so sudden and
exceptional as to produce physical disorder: it was never
associated with marked mental agitation. God's presence
with Jesus seems rather to have been a quiet and steady process,
the abiding splendour in a character of rare beauty and purity.

We have reason to feel surprise that testimony of this kind
should be so undeviating. One would have expected that, as
accretions to early history were shaped by myth and legend,
there would have been assigned to Jesus such an experience as
that of Paul before Damascus. Even more probably he might
have been represented as coming from communion with God
to give his message with the emphatic and traditional opening,
"Thus saith the Lord." But there is a significant lack of similarity in this respect between him and the Old Testament
prophets; and there is no likeness between his tranquil communion with his Father and the visions and trances, the "mystic
rapture," of later Christian saints.

To this statement three incidents offer possible exceptions:
they are the baptism, the temptation, and the transfiguration of
Jesus. We will briefly consider each in turn. We shall discuss
the baptism of Jesus by John at some length in chapter xv. It
suffices now to say that the details of the story are plainly
legendary; but, even so, they indicate no mental agitation on
the part of Jesus, no catastrophic change of outlook or understanding as the result of his baptism. According to the narrative in *Mark*, which *Matthew* and *Luke* copied, Jesus saw the
heavens opened, and the Spirit descending as a dove, and "a
voice came out of heaven"; but *John* silently corrects this
story, and ascribes, not to Jesus but to John the Baptist, the
vision of the dove.

Some would claim that the story of the temptation of Jesus arose from a hypernormal trance or ecstasy which he experienced; but surely the story is a pure allegory, recorded by Q as an illuminating comment on the teaching of Jesus. In it the Master is made to set forth the principles by which he was guided throughout life: he sought neither the power to make stones into bread, nor the glory of the kingdoms of the world, nor exceptional divine protection.

The story of the transfiguration is, as we shall argue in §§ 186–187, misplaced in *Mark*: it arose, as is evident from the *Apocalypse of Peter*, as a post-resurrection myth. Moreover, it is not stated to be a vision seen by Jesus: it is represented as a joint experience of Peter, James and John when they were with their Master on the "high mountain."

Obviously the calm and unruffled communion of Jesus with God was so characteristic of him that the memory of it endured as the story of his ministry was told to, and by, successive groups of Christians. It was remembered that God did not, as it were, speak to him from without. His Father was intimately with him or, if we may use a spatial metaphor, within him. Jesus seems always to have felt God's presence: the unity was to him so natural and complete that he never suggested that it was something exceptional or abnormal. As we have repeatedly stated, we find in the fourth gospel words ascribed to Jesus which are, in fact, the teaching of *John* the evangelist himself. But we cannot deny that, when he describes the relation between Jesus and God in the words (xiv. 11), "Believe me that I am in the Father, and the Father in me," he interprets correctly the relationship which the synoptic gospels reveal. In things of the spirit, the words of Jesus show the wisdom of God. His life was that which God would have lived under human limitations.

The fearlessness and freedom from care which Jesus manifested will have been derived from his constant sense of the presence of God. A quiet courage showed itself throughout his life; and he never seems to have been anxious, either as to his personal safety or as to his material needs. With good bodily health there went an unobtrusive self-confidence. For him, moreover, nature was not hostile, inasmuch as he knew that God in nature not only revealed beauty but also lavished His bounty on the world. Hence came a buoyancy of spirit which could draw increase from rest in silent spaces. *Mark* (vi. 31) ascribes to him the illuminating saying, "Come ye yourselves apart into a desert place, and rest a while."

But though Jesus almost of necessity found solitude a blessing, because he could thus feel God's nearness the more intensely, he was not remote from, or indifferent to, the needs of others. He showed, on the contrary, great tenderness and profound compassion. He was especially sensitive lest others should suffer hunger. At the close of the story of the raising of the daughter of Jairus which we find in *Mark* (v. 21–43), "he commanded that something should be given her to eat." And it is significant that among the few petitions in the Lord's Prayer we have, "Give us this day our daily bread." In fact, what Jesus knew as God's pitying love for His children was reflected in his own thought for those weaker or less spiritually confident than himself. Alike in the nearness of Jesus to God, and in the manifestation in Jesus of God's nature, we see why Paul could write (2 *Corinthians* v. 19) that "God was in Christ reconciling the world unto himself."

157. The length of the ministry of Jesus

The influence upon humanity of the teaching of Jesus has been so vast and, it may be added, so surprising because of its "other-worldliness," that we naturally wish to know how long his ministry in Galilee lasted. All his recorded sayings could easily have been spoken in a few days; and though the varied incidents which called them forth could not be thus crowded together without an entire absence of probability, they might well be fitted into a scheme covering but a few months. Such a length for the ministry in Galilee is, in fact, sometimes advocated. On the other hand, a tradition, going back to the fourth gospel, makes its duration approximately three years.

There is, however, no clear evidence by which a conclusion can be reached. The only satisfactory source for such evidence would be *Mark*; but his gospel, as we have seen, is not an orderly narrative. It is a series of recollections and stories from many sources, loosely strung together. We recall the testimony of Papias, quoted in § 124, that "Mark became Peter's interpreter and wrote down accurately, but certainly not in order, all that he remembered of the sayings or actions of the Lord." While we are unable to agree with Papias that the substance of the second gospel came from Peter, we can see that it is, as he stated, a disordered narrative, a collection of fragments of teaching in no proper sequence.

For instance, chapter vii of *Mark* begins vaguely, "And there are gathered together unto him the Pharisees, and certain of the scribes." There follows teaching of Jesus as to defilement, and at its end we read (vii. 24), "And from thence he arose, and went away into the borders of Tyre and Sidon." There he is said to have cured the hysterical daughter of a Syrophoenician woman. But, the story of the cure ended, we read (vii. 31), "And again he went out from the borders of Tyre, and came through Sidon unto the sea of Galilee, through the midst of the borders of Decapolis." No hint is given of the time spent at Tyre and Sidon; and observation of the map makes one wonder whether there is not some error in the journey described.

As another example of the lack of coherence of the Marcan narratives we notice that, near Caesarea Philippi, Peter in answer to a question says (viii. 29), "Thou art the Christ." There follows a discourse by Jesus, which has probably been gathered from several sources; and then, quite unexpectedly, we have the story of the transfiguration of Jesus, introduced by the words (ix. 2), "And after six days Jesus taketh with him Peter and James, and John." From such material we cannot construct ordered history. Moreover, apart from the discourses derived from Q, *Matthew* and *Luke* depend, as regards the Galilean ministry, almost wholly on *Mark*: we cannot therefore hope to get from either gospel independent information as to the length of the ministry.

Unfortunately, such information as we can derive from the fourth gospel is of doubtful value. When we discussed this gospel in § 135, we pointed out that it gives us religious symbolism rather than history. It is a sustained allegory rather than a record of fact. Thus, though it mentions three passovers as occurring during the ministry of Jesus, and so suggests that the length of the ministry may have been as much as three years, there is always the possibility that the writer has created the longer period for some symbolic reason which we do not now perceive.

Of the three passovers in the fourth gospel, the first arouses

L

grave doubts. Mention of it occurs in the sentence (ii. 13), "And the passover of the Jews was at hand, and Jesus went up to Jerusalem." But the occasion of the alleged visit was the cleansing of the temple at Jerusalem, an incident described by *Mark* (xi. 15–18) as having taken place at the beginning of the last visit to Jerusalem, and within a week of the death of Jesus. That such a challenge to established practice could have taken place two whole years before the arrest of Jesus is most improbable.

The second passover is mentioned by *John* in the words (vi. 4), "Now the passover, the feast of the Jews, was at hand." The sentence serves as an introduction to the story of the feeding of the five thousand, a eucharistic myth described in *Mark* (vi. 30–44) without any indication as to time, though with a suggestion that the place was, as *John* indicates, a desert region on the other side of the lake of Galilee from Bethsaida.

Finally, we learn in the fourth gospel that, after the raising of Lazarus, Jesus withdrew into hiding. Then we are told (xi. 55), "the passover of the Jews was at hand"; and Jesus made his Palm Sunday entrance into Jerusalem.

Our brief survey of the circumstances associated with the three passovers mentioned by *John* is sufficient to warn us that they cannot provide the framework of an historical scheme. In default of adequate information we may perhaps assume that the public life of Jesus extended to about a year; and that during this time, save for a journey to Phoenicia, he taught continuously in Galilee, only visiting Jerusalem for the passover when he was crucified.

158. The ministry in Galilee—success or failure?

It proves singularly difficult to make a satisfactory picture of the Galilean ministry. Had the teaching of Jesus an immediate success? Did he almost at once achieve such a reputation as a healer and exorcist that crowds gathered whenever he appeared? Was his teaching the talk of the countryside? Was Herod Antipas, the tetrarch of Galilee, disturbed by his popularity; and did Jesus visit Tyre and Sidon that he might escape the unwelcome surveillance of Herod's police? To none of these questions can we return answers which convince us of their truth.

Legend has undoubtedly transformed the nature, and magnified the number, of the miracles of healing. Though, in the synoptic gospels, Jesus is an exorcist—he drives out evil spirits—there is no record of such activity in the fourth gospel.

The story of the beheading of John the Baptist makes clear that Herod had no love for prophets, who might easily be disturbing elements in an excitable populace. Prophetic religion would hardly appeal to the Herodian dynasty. But there is no indication in *Mark* that Herod regarded Jesus with hostility: *Luke* alone records (xiii. 31–3) that certain pharisees warned Jesus that Herod sought his life. Jesus is reported to have referred contemptuously to the tetrarch as "that fox," and to have added, "it cannot be that a prophet perish out of Jerusalem." Occasionally the information which *Luke* alone supplies is of high value; but we may doubt whether Jesus spoke thus slightingly of Herod—it is unlike him, in spite of "the leaven of Herod" in *Mark* (viii. 15)—or that he with such definiteness thus prophesied his own end in Jerusalem.

Probably the ministry in Galilee was successful in the sense that the fame of Jesus was "noised abroad." The populace thronged round him in the belief that he could cure all manner of diseases, just as to-day in Syria a medical missionary is besieged by crowds of sick folk with their relatives. Doubtless, also, a few disciples, men and women, were strongly attracted by his grave beauty of character even more than by his religious teaching, so that they made a small band of followers who were constantly with him. A larger number of devout people will have felt his innate spiritual power and will have welcomed his presence, though they did not follow him on his journeys. We must add the important fact that his appeal to outcasts was unexpected and surprisingly successful.

But, on the whole, the call to such a change of heart as would bring the kingdom of God into being met with little response. Some will feel satisfied to say that Jesus was driven to realize that he must break fresh ground, make a wider and more dramatic appeal, whatever its dangers; and that therefore he set his face to go to Jerusalem. But this verdict cannot be unhesitating. There is nothing to indicate clearly that Jesus felt that in Galilee he was sowing seed on barren soil. We must not forget that his ministry was the result of an inward urge which he knew to be the will of God : it is highly probable that, because he obeyed the voice of God, he had no sense of failure. But, also, if he felt that God commanded him to preach in the temple at Jerusalem, the religious centre of his race, he would obey without anxiety or misgiving.

There are in the gospels many indications that Jesus was well aware that death might be the end of the attempt to preach the kingdom of God in Jerusalem, though we may doubt if his anticipation was so definite as to make him expect the certainty of crucifixion. There is, of course, in *Mark* (viii. 34) the saying, "If any man would come after me, let him deny himself, and take up his cross, and follow me"; but the form of words will have arisen in later years, when to think of Jesus was to remember his crucifixion. We may rightly assume that Jesus had the profound foresight of a leader of men : but we have no reason to deny his complete humanity by claiming for him supernatural foreknowledge. It belonged to his greatness that, though for him, as for all of us, the future was hidden in obscurity, his courage never failed. To his tragic end he went forward with simple dignity.

CHAPTER IX

PASSION WEEK

159. The journey to Jerusalem

ACCORDING to *Mark's* narrative (x. 1), as Jesus began
his journey to Jerusalem, he came "into the borders of
Judaea and beyond Jordan." Later in the same chapter
(x. 32) we learn that "they were in the way, going up to
Jerusalem; and Jesus was going before them: and they were
amazed; and they that followed were afraid." Then, we are
told, Jesus took "the twelve" aside and spoke in detail of the
end that awaited him. Subsequently (x. 46) we are informed
that "they come to Jericho," where Jesus is reported to have
healed blind Bartimaeus. The journey ends with the statement (xi. 1), "And when they draw nigh unto Jerusalem, unto
Bethphage and Bethany, at the mount of Olives, he sendeth
two of his disciples." The disciples are to go "into the village
that is over against you," and there to find a colt tied and to
bring it. On this colt Jesus entered Jerusalem to the hosannas
of Palm Sunday. In the evening he returned to Bethany with
the twelve.

In this brief sketch we have extracted from the second gospel
practically all that we can learn as to the final journey to
Jerusalem and as to the circumstances of the arrival there of
Jesus. It makes a singularly vague and unsatisfactory narrative.
We are forced to conclude that *Mark*, writing nearly half a
century after the events which he describes, was ignorant of all
but the broad outlines.

Bethany appears to have been about a mile and a half from
Jerusalem on the road to Jericho; and Jesus must have had
friends there. But plainly *Mark* did not know who they were.
Similarly he could not tell us whose was the house where the
Last Supper took place: the disciples (xiv. 13) were to "go into
the city, and there shall meet you a man bearing a pitcher of
water: follow him." We can well understand that there were
many Galileans in or near Jerusalem, just as there are many
Welsh in London; and, as now so of old, clannishness will have

149

been strong. With some kinsfolk living in Jerusalem Jesus or, more probably, some of his disciples will have had close ties.

The fourth gospel (xii. 1–2) puts Lazarus and his sisters at Bethany; but the evangelist is probably using *Mark's* vagueness as a background for symbolical persons needed in his story. *John*, in fact, states that "they made him a supper" and that "Lazarus was one of them that sat at meat with him," while Martha served. But *Mark* (xiv. 3) puts the same supper "in the house of Simon the leper." In the face of apparent discrepancies, none too skilfully harmonized, no certainty is possible. There seems, however, to be a definite recollection that Jesus, from the time of his arrival in Jerusalem until his arrest, stayed each night outside the city in this particular village of Bethany. It lay less than a mile from the summit of the mount of Olives; and, on the other side of the mount, above the Kidron valley which separated it from the temple quarter of Jerusalem, lay the garden of Gethsemane. Some reasonable doubt, of course, attaches to the exact site of the garden. At the presumed site olive trees still grow. There or thereabouts Jesus, if we can trust the gospel tradition, prayed that the cup of suffering might pass from him; and no Christian visits Gethsemane unmoved.

160. The date of the Last Supper

When did Jesus die? All our authorities agree that the crucifixion took place about the time of the passover. Some critical scholars have doubted whether it can have been so early in the spring as the time of the passover, inasmuch as at Gethsemane Jesus and his disciples do not seem to have felt the cold, which after nightfall can at this season be unpleasant in the hills near Jerusalem. We have previously said (§ 90) that the year of the death of Jesus cannot be determined, apart from the fact that Pontius Pilate was then procurator of Judaea; and we know that he governed the province from A.D. 26 to A.D. 36. But, setting aside the question of the year and assuming the truth of the passover tradition, we ask whether the crucifixion took place a few hours before, or rather more than twelve hours after, the passover meal. The question is difficult to answer, inasmuch as the gospels retain contradictory traditions.

The Jewish passover meal began in the evening of the fourteenth day of the month Nisan: this was for the Jews the beginning of the fifteenth day. The passover lamb was slain towards evening: it was eaten during the night. The passover meal consisted of the lamb, together with herbs and unleavened bread. Wine was drunk with the meal.

The earliest Christian tradition, of which traces remain in the synoptic gospels, is preserved in the fourth gospel. According to this tradition, the Last Supper took place in the evening of the thirteenth day of Nisan, twenty-four hours before the passover. Jesus was crucified on the following day; and died at the hour at which the passover lamb was killed. He was thus (*John* i. 29) "the Lamb of God, which taketh away the sin of the world." So also Paul could write (1 *Corinthians* v. 7), "For our passover also hath been sacrificed, even Christ: wherefore let us keep the feast, not with old leaven, neither with the leaven of malice and wickedness, but with the unleavened bread of sincerity and truth." The parallel between Jesus and the passover lamb is pressed by *John*. He tells us that the soldiers did not break the legs of the crucified Jesus (xix. 36) "that the scripture might be fulfilled, A bone of him shall not be broken." The reference is to the passover regulations of *Exodus* (xii. 46), "neither shall ye break a bone thereof."

This Johannine tradition is consistently maintained throughout the narrative of the fourth gospel. For instance, when Jesus was led from his examination by the high-priest Caiaphas to his trial before Pilate in the palace, his accusers (xviii. 28) "entered not into the palace, that they might not be defiled, but might eat the passover." The final end of the crucifixion was hastened that it might be over before the passover began.

For a long time the tradition of the fourth gospel was so strong that certain Asiatic Christians, known as Quarto-decimans, or "Fourteenth-ers," kept Easter on the fourteenth of Nisan, so that it coincided with the Jewish passover. Easter was thus, for them, the festival—or memorial—of redemption, of the slaying of Jesus, the Christ, the Lamb of God. Their Easter Day could thus occur on any day of the week: it was not necessarily a Sunday. At the close of the second century of our era there' was vigorous controversy between the Quarto-decimans and Western churches. According to the *Ecclesiastical History* of Eusebius (v. 23), Western synods declared, "On the Lord's Day only the mystery of the resurrection of the Lord from the dead was fulfilled, and on that day only we keep the close of the paschal fast." But the Johannine usage was maintained by some Asiatic churches until after it was condemned by the Council of Nicaea in A.D. 325.

The other Christian tradition which, probably as a result of editorial revision, is now that of the synoptic gospels, put the Last Supper in the evening of the fourteenth day of Nisan. According to this tradition, the Last Supper was the actual passover meal. Jesus will thus have been arrested, tried and executed on the day of the passover, for the sacred period extended until the evening of the fifteenth of Nisan.

Mark, according to the present text, is definite in his narrative. In his record (xiv. 12–16), preparations for the passover are described; and at the end of the paragraph we read, "and they made ready the passover." Then at the beginning of the next paragraph we read (xiv. 17), "and when it was evening, he cometh with the twelve": the account of the Last Supper follows. *Matthew* bases his record on that of *Mark*. *Luke* seems to have used another source; but he is equally definite that the Last Supper was the passover meal. He tells (xxii. 8) how Jesus "sent Peter and John, saying, Go and make ready for us the passover, that we may eat." Then, after they had (xxii. 13) "made ready the passover and when the hour was come, he sat down, and the apostles with him." The account of the Last Supper follows forthwith.

Yet, if the Last Supper was actually the passover meal, we are bewildered by many inconsistencies. There is, in the first place, no mention of any lamb at the meal. In the second place, the term used to describe the bread which Jesus broke at the meal describes ordinary leavened bread and not the ritual unleavened bread of the passover. In the third place, we may recall that the ritual prescribed for the passover meal is well known from Jewish sources. Four cups were drunk at stated intervals; and certain psalms chosen from a particular group were sung before and after the meal. But at the Last Supper there is no suggestion of this ritual. We cannot explain such perplexing divergencies unless we assume that the account of what took place at the Last Supper was firmly established in the tradition before the Supper was believed to be the passover meal.

But even graver difficulties are caused by the synoptic record as we now have it. The passover, as we have said, lasted from the meal in the evening of the fourteenth of Nisan until the evening of the following day. During this solemn period all business was suspended; and during the night, in accordance with the command in *Exodus* (xii. 22), no one left the house in which he partook of the meal. Yet immediately after the Supper the disciples, according to the synoptic story, went out with Jesus to Gethsemane. Moreover, during the early morning after the passover meal Jesus was arrested (*Mark* xiv. 43), not by Romans, but by "a multitude" "from the chief priests and the scribes and the elders." In addition, there was a more or less formal meeting of the sanhedrin, after which Jesus was sent to Pilate. Thus on the actual passover day business was transacted by the high-priest and his officers, notwithstanding the explicit prohibitions of rabbinical law and custom.

We thus seem forced to believe that *John* preserves the more probable tradition, and that Jesus died at the very hour at which the passover lamb was slain. The coincidence is remarkable, so remarkable that a number of scholars contend that the actual circumstances of the crucifixion were forgotten and that the Johannine hour for the death of Jesus is purely symbolic: it is, they say, theology, not history. Early Christians thought of Jesus as the Lamb of God. In the book of *Revelation* (v. 6) he is "a Lamb standing, as though it had been slain." What more natural than that he should have been thought to be slain, that he might take away the sins of the world, at the very hour when the passover lamb was killed. It may be that those analytical scholars are right who maintain that accurate knowledge of the arrest, trial and death of Jesus had perished when the gospels were written; and that the stories which have come down to us were shaped for use at worship.

In itself the question as to whether Jesus was crucified before or after the passover meal is of little importance. What matters in our inquiry is that from it we realize that we can have little certainty as to circumstances surrounding the death of Jesus. Early Christians supplemented their ignorance by allowing religious imagination to clothe the bare stark fact of the death of their Lord. Such a suggestion is repugnant to many; but, if the crucifixion story as it stands is drama and not history, it is, at least, drama shaped by the great art that can result from love reverence and tears.

According to the synoptic tradition, the fifteenth day of Nisan in the year of the crucifixion of Jesus, fell on a Friday. It migh be thought that this fact—if it be a fact—would furnish a clue to the year in which his crucifixion took place. Experts, how ever, seem to be agreed that there are too many uncertaintie connected with the Jewish calendar to allow of a satisfying argument.

The Quartodeciman Easter, as we have said, coincided with the Jewish passover. The synoptic Easter, on the other hand commemorated the resurrection which took place, according both to the synoptic story and to the Johannine, on the Sunday following the Friday of the crucifixion. Sunday rapidly became the Lord's day; and the great Sunday of the year was Easter Day. The fact that it did not normally coincide with the pass over made it not less but more acceptable to Christian since, with the passage of time, hostility to the Jews grew in strength.

161. The arrest of Jesus

There is no reason to doubt that Jesus, after his arrival a Jerusalem, began to teach in the temple. To that end he had come to the city. Excerpts from his teaching are given in *Mark* and they may well be based on fairly accurate recollection Inevitably his teaching aroused opposition. His obviou spiritual distinction and his religious certainty would quickly have made him a marked man. He had that quality of per sonality which is easy to recognize, if hard to define. Chal lenged by quasi-official religious teachers he showed himself— and we need not doubt the tradition—ready in speech but also impressively sincere.

The climax of his offence was probably "the cleansing of the temple." The Marcan narrative (xi. 15) suggests the use of force: he "overthrew the tables of the money-changers, and the seats of them that sold the doves; and he would not suffer that any man should carry a vessel through the temple.' *Luke* (xix. 45–6) abbreviates and softens this statement. But in *John*, where, as we have said in § 157, the incident is placed a the beginning of the Lord's ministry (ii. 13–17), Jesus is stated

have made "a scourge of cords," probably, from the context,
drive out "the sheep and the oxen." There can have been no
se of physical force. Had Jesus and his followers made them-
elves by violence masters of any part of the temple area, they
ould have been immediately arrested, either by the temple
uard, or by the Roman garrison from the tower of Antonia
ear by. Even a symbolic use of force would have been quite
ut of keeping with the teaching of Jesus; but nothing is more
kely than that Jesus, outraged by the chicanery by which
ilgrims were fleeced in the sacred precincts, made a strong
nd, it may be, popular protest much resented by the temple
fficials.

A resolve to arrest and silence the troublesome prophet was
he natural outcome. The desire to avoid a disturbance in the
emple area led, according to the tradition, to the arrest of
esus in the garden of Gethsemane. The garden, as we have
aid, lay in the region of Bethany, the village where Jesus spent
ach night during his brief stay in Jerusalem. The arrest was
pparently made by a band of temple servants; and they were
uided by Judas Iscariot, the traitor among the twelve apostles.
There is said to have been a struggle in which one of the
ollowers of Jesus (*John* asserts that it was Simon Peter) drew a
word and struck off the ear of the servant of the high-priest.
Thereupon the followers of Jesus fled; and he himself was taken
n custody to the high-priest. *Mark* does not give the high-
riest's name: *John* says that Jesus was taken first to Annas and
hen to Caiaphas.

We have set out what seem to be the bare facts of the arrest.
But we must remember that all the stories of the Passion
robably assumed the forms which we know after being
epeatedly told at religious gatherings: they emerged from, and
vere largely intended for, liturgical use. They were welcomed
y people who wished to hear all that could be told of the death
f Jesus; and embellishments were the natural outcome of a
iety as simple as it was sincere.

Such an embellishment is certainly to be found in *Matthew's*
ccount (xxvii. 3–10) of the remorse and end of Judas Iscariot.
Mark (xiv. 10) says merely that Judas went to "the chief
riests, that he might deliver him unto them"; and they
romised to give him money. But *Matthew* (xxvi. 15) makes

cupidity the motive of the treachery; and tells us that Judas bargained for thirty pieces of silver. In his subsequent remorse the traitor threw the money into the sanctuary, went away and hanged himself. The priests thereupon used the silver to buy "the potter's field, to bury strangers in." "Wherefore that place was called, The field of blood, unto this day." The incident, like others in the gospel story, has been built upon an Old Testament text, deemed prophetic. But the collection of proof-texts which *Matthew* used has here played him false. His quotation was not, as he believed and asserted, from *Isaiah* but from *Zechariah* (xi. 13). The form which he gives diverges widely both from the Hebrew and from the Septuagint version. It should run, "So they weighed for my hire thirty pieces of silver. And the Lord said unto me, Cast it unto the potter, the goodly price that I was prized at of them. And I took the thirty pieces of silver, and cast them unto the potter, in the house of the Lord."

Such ornament of the story of the treachery of Judas is not to be condemned as the outcome of unrestrained fancy. It is based on what was regarded as a prophecy in the Jewish scriptures; its tone is sober: the moral lesson conveyed is admirable: there is none of the extravagance to be found in the apocryphal gospels. In fact, throughout the four gospels the Passion stories, even when we distrust their historicity, are manifestly the outcome of deep and reverent feeling, and of a desire to see the providence of God in the events which they narrate.

Certain analytical scholars tend to say that the whole incident of Judas Iscariot is an allegory introduced to give colour to a brief and bare story. Iscariot is normally assumed to mean "man of Kerioth"; but some modern philologists deny that such a derivation is possible. They contend that the name is more probably the corruption of an Aramaic word meaning "the betrayer." Judas Iscariot thus becomes "the traitor Jew" who falsely kisses Jesus; and the story is taken to be a reflection of hostility between Christians and Jews at the time when the gospels were written. In all probability such speculation should be dismissed as over-ingenious. In their stories of the Passion Christians were not afraid to admit, and even strongly to emphasize, failings of men who should have been loyal to Christ. Thus a traitor in the group of those nearest to

esus aided his arrest: at the time of that arrest all his other
ollowers showed themselves cowards and fled.

62. The Jewish trial of Jesus

As we analyse the records of the trial of Jesus which have
:ome down to us, we are led to think that an oft-told story
1as in the end become dramatized history. It may be that the
:arly followers of Christ knew practically nothing of his trial
ave that he was, after his arrest, summarily judged and con-
lemned. *Mark*, who is followed by *Matthew*, probably gives the
east doubtful account of what happened; but in it analytical
cholars can point to many reasons for uncertainty. According
o this account, Jesus was first brought before the high-priests,
who apparently summoned the sanhedrin to meet during the
very night of the passover! Even if we accept the date of the
ourth gospel, so that the sanhedrin was summoned during the
night before the passover, we are disturbed by the fact that a
nocturnal sitting for judicial purposes was contrary to Jewish
:ustom; and the practical difficulty of arranging at short
notice such a sitting must not be overlooked.

If the Marcan story of the examination before the sanhedrin
:an be trusted, Jesus was first accused of an intention to destroy
he temple, and made no reply to the charge. Then he was
asked by the high-priest whether he claimed to be "the Christ,
he Son of the Blessed." On his reply in the affirmative, the
igh-priest rent his clothes and declared that he had spoken
blasphemy. Then Jesus was condemned as worthy of death.

Luke modifies this record. According to him, the trial before
he sanhedrin did not take place until it was day. Jesus was
asked if he was the Christ, and replied with a somewhat
ndefinite avowal. His judges said that they had no further
need of witnesses: they rose up and brought him before
Pilate.

According to *John*, Jesus was brought first of all before
Annas (xviii. 13), "for he was father-in-law to Caiaphas, which
was high-priest that year." It seems that *John* thought that the
high-priesthood was an annual office. In point of fact, as we
have said in § 93, Annas was deposed in A.D. 15, having held
office for some nine years, while Caiaphas was probably high-

priest for the period A.D. 18–36. Annas is stated by *John* t
have asked Jesus as to his teaching, to receive the reply that h
had taught openly and that Annas should inquire of those wh
had heard him. An officer of the court then struck him, saying
"Answerest thou the high priest so?" After this incident n
condemnation is recorded. It is simply stated that Annas sen
Jesus bound to Caiaphas and that they led him from Caiapha
into the palace.

The discrepancies in the various stories are many, sufficien
to show the lack of detailed and accurate knowledge. But th
accounts are sober and not obviously fanciful. Behind then
probably lies a substantial basis of fact, which may have been
morning sitting of the sanhedrin at which it was resolved t
send Jesus for trial by Pilate.

163. The trial before Pilate

As regards the trial by Pilate all four evangelists differ
Such differences are to be expected. From the beginning th
trial will have been a subject of intense interest to all wh
belonged to, or joined, the Christian movement. The stor
will have been told a thousand times, with all the variation
that faulty memory and loving reverence brought to it.

Mark has the simplest record. Pilate asked Jesus whethe
he was the king of the Jews and received an affirmative reply
Then the chief priests accused him of many things; but Jesu
to Pilate's surprise, made no reply. Then, so we are told, Pilat
offered to release Jesus, inasmuch as there was a custom that a
the feast one prisoner should be released. But the peopl
clamoured for Barabbas. So Pilate, "wishing to content th
multitude," released Barabbas; "and delivered Jesus, when h
had scourged him, to be crucified."

Mark's record is the merest sketch of what may have hap
pened. There is in it no suggestion of legal formalities, no hir
of the need of an interpreter. And the story of Barabbas arouse
misgiving. For the alleged custom of release there is no evidenc
whatever outside the gospels. It suggests Eastern folk-lor
rather than Roman jurisprudence. Clemency could, of course
under Roman law, be exercised in favour of a prisoner; an
Pilate's right to exercise it in the case of Jesus would not be i
doubt. It seems as though the story grew up in an attempt t

ake from Pilate, as Roman procurator, any wish for the death of Jesus and to transfer his guilt to the Jews.

Similar stories with the same object appear in the records of he trial before Pilate as we have them in the other gospels. In *Matthew* we find, inserted into the narrative which he took rom *Mark*, the dream of Pilate's wife: "have thou nothing to do with that righteous man." This follows the statement taken rom *Mark* that Pilate knew that "for envy" the Jewish leaders had sent Jesus for trial. Finally, Pilate publicly washed his hands as a sign that he disclaimed a responsibility which the Jews accepted.

Luke alone records that Pilate sent Jesus to be examined by Herod Antipas, the tetrarch of Galilee, who was—or so it is asserted—in Jerusalem for the feast. Herod and his soldiers are said to have jeered at their prisoner and to have sent him back to Pilate, gorgeously attired. Pilate is made to say that neither he nor Herod find Jesus guilty of the charges brought against him. But he finally yields to the insistent demand for his crucifixion. The appearance of Jesus before both Herod and Pilate is mentioned in *Acts* (iv. 27) which, it will be remembered, is also by *Luke*. Many analytical scholars dismiss the story of the examination by Herod as fiction, intended to provide yet another assurance of the innocence of Jesus.

In the fourth gospel Pilate, in the first place, tells the Jews to take Jesus and judge him according to Jewish law. They reply that they cannot inflict the death penalty, a fact which some modern scholars dispute. Thereupon Pilate asks Jesus whether he is king of the Jews, and ultimately receives the reply, "My kingdom is not of this world." Pilate then goes out to the Jews, who would not enter his palace "that they might not be defiled but might eat the passover," and says that he finds no crime in Jesus. We ask whether a Roman governor, in formal session at a trial involving the death penalty, would so act. A series of visits to a clamorous mob in the courtyard of his palace was hardly dignified. However, according to *John*, Pilate makes two further attempts to release Jesus and only yields when he is threatened that release would imply that the procurator was not Caesar's friend. Even in the end he does not formally condemn Jesus, though he permits his crucifixion.

In such a confusion of varying statements as we find in the

four gospels exact truth evades us. Perhaps we may fairly conclude that a hasty trial before Pilate led him, somewhat reluctantly, to yield to Jewish pressure and to order the crucifixion of Jesus. On the other hand, Pilate may have been convinced that Jesus was a dangerous agitator, similar to others who appeared from time to time after the death of Herod the Great. The procurator probably had little sympathy with the people whom he ruled, and was quite prepared to execute an obscure religious teacher who seemed dangerous. That he was, as Christian tradition asserts, haunted later by remorse is unlikely: the incident will have rapidly passed from his mind. Roman rule in Palestine in the first century of our era needed, and used, rough methods.

164. The crucifixion of Jesus

Jesus was crucified. Tradition preserved the knowledge that he endured this terrible form of punishment at Golgotha, "the place of a skull," probably a rounded hill just outside the walls of Jerusalem; and that two thieves were crucified at the same time, one on each side of him. Such facts were readily ascertained and easily remembered. But it is doubtful how far a number of other circumstances of his death can with confidence be accepted as historical. Inevitably myths grew up around the death of the Saviour-Lord. Christians had to make the tragic and disgraceful end bearable to their feelings and acceptable to reason. They were sure that the Christ had died as he had lived, without bitterness or fear, kingly to the end. His death, moreover, must have been in accord with Messianic prophecy. It had surely been foreseen as part of the inscrutable providence of God. By searching the scriptures the relevant texts could be discovered.

There is thus good reason to think that some details, by which the fundamental facts were ultimately surrounded, were due to the industry and ingenuity of simple faith. The male followers of Jesus had fled, fearing to be implicated in his guilt and therefore condemned to a like punishment. *Mark*, however (xv. 40) followed by *Matthew* and *Luke*, states that "there were also women beholding from afar," and gives the names of a number of them. Some critics feel that this paragraph reads as though it were an afterthought, inserted when the desire for witnesses of the end had grown up; but surely the presence of the women at some distance from the cross was most natural.

There will have been near the cross a picket of soldiers, with an under-officer—a centurion is mentioned. They will have kept guard, bored during the heat of the day. Execution-duty will have been unpopular, though by a custom, which was formally recognized by the time of Hadrian (A.D. 117–38), the soldiers were entitled as a perquisite to the clothes of the condemned. *Mark* records (xv. 24), "And they crucify him, and part his garments among them, casting lots upon them, what each should take." On the other hand, it is just possible that the tradition derived this partition from a verse in a *Psalm* (xxii. 18) which has clearly influenced our records: this verse, "They part my garments among them, and upon my vesture do they cast lots," is actually quoted by *John* (xix. 24).

There is no doubt also that by a Roman custom a placard was put near or upon a condemned man, stating the nature of his crime. *Mark* (xv. 26) says of Jesus that "the superscription of his accusation" was "The King of the Jews." Each of the evangelists varies somewhat the form of words. Such variations suggest that the custom was actually observed in the case of Jesus, the exact form of words being modified by oral tradition.

Another incident which most probably is genuine history is the offering recorded by *Mark* (xv. 23), "And they offered him wine mingled with myrrh: but he received it not." There is a rabbinical tradition that Jewish ladies of high social rank, as a duty imposed by piety and pity, would prepare such a narcotic and personally hand it to condemned men about to be crucified. *Matthew* (xxvii. 34) writes of "wine mingled with gall," as though the drink was intended to be a bitter addition to the suffering of Jesus. The fact that he has misconceived the intention behind the offer renders it the more likely to have been made. He was probably influenced by a verse of a familiar *Psalm* (lxix. 21), "They gave me also gall for my meat; and in my thirst they gave me vinegar to drink." *Luke* was probably influenced by the second half of this verse when he says (xxiii. 36) that the soldiers mocked Jesus by offering him vinegar.

Scripture, deemed prophetic, and faith, rather than knowledge, seem to have determined some, at least, of the "words

M

from the cross." The influence of *Psalm* xxii, which, as we have said, can several times be traced in the record, is shown in the solitary utterance recorded by *Mark* (xv. 34) and *Matthew* (xxvii. 46), "My God, my God, why hast thou forsaken me?" *Luke* gives three sayings: we have (xxiii. 34), "Father, forgive them; for they know not what they do"; and also the concluding cry with a loud voice (xxiii. 46), "Father, into thy hands I commend my spirit." But, while both these sayings are completely in accord with the character of Jesus, we must allow it to be unlikely that, at the very end of such an agonizing and exhausting death as crucifixion, Jesus would have been able to cry loudly and articulately.

The third saying which *Luke* attributes to Jesus is his promise (xxiii. 43) to the penitent thief, "To-day shalt thou be with me in Paradise." The behaviour of the man to whom Jesus gives this promise is contradicted by the earlier narrative of *Mark* (xv. 32) which informs us that "they that were crucified with him reproached him." Analytical scholars conclude that the Lukan story of the two thieves is not to be regarded as historical.

Outside the sphere of history, equally, may be the sayings from the cross which *John* attributes to Jesus. We have already mentioned in § 135 that the fourth evangelist, against all probability, puts the mother of Jesus at the foot of the cross—had she been there, could the synoptists by any possibility have forgotten to record it?—and he entrusts her to the beloved disciple with the words (xix. 27), "Woman, behold thy son!" There follows a statement that Jesus, in order "that the scripture might be accomplished, saith, I thirst," whereupon they gave him vinegar upon hyssop. At the very end (xix. 30), just before death releases the sufferer, *John*, as against *Luke*, makes Jesus say, "It is finished." The critical objections just set out and the great divergence between the various gospel records force us to conclude that, as to the sayings from the cross attributed to Jesus, we can have little certainty. Preachers on Good Friday commonly assume that all are records of fact; and they gather them together by a process of accumulation which, though acceptable to simple religious feeling, cannot be accepted by critical scholarship.

It remains to be said that *John* alone records (xix. 34) that a soldier "with a spear pierced his side, and straightway there came out blood and water." In this supposed incident the symbolism of the fourth evangelist is especially noticeable: from the crucified Saviour come the water of baptism and the redeeming blood of the eucharist. A reference to the *First Epistle of John* makes clear that this symbolism is intended. We there read (v. 6), "This is he that came by water and blood, even Jesus Christ." Jesus, we read in the fourth gospel (xix. 30), "bowed his head, and gave up his spirit." In the epistle (v. 8) we read that, "there are three who bear witness, the Spirit, and the water, and the blood."

Natural additions to a grim story appear in *Mark* (xv. 33), who mentions that the veil of the temple was torn from top to bottom and says that there was darkness over the whole land from the sixth until the ninth hour. *Matthew* (xxvii. 51–3) recounts many marvels, including an earthquake, in which rocks were riven and tombs were opened, and the resurrection of "saints that had fallen asleep" who "entered into the holy city and appeared unto many." Myth and marvel become steadily more in evidence as our story moves to the burial and resurrection.

All visitors to Jerusalem will have seen the church of the Holy Sepulchre which covers Golgotha and the adjacent cave of the resurrection: many will have been surprised that the two holy places are only some thirty yards distant from one another. The authenticity of these sites has been much disputed and is difficult to defend. An account of their discovery—apparently in A.D. 326—was given by Eusebius in his *Life of Constantine* (iii. 25–6), probably written in A.D. 338. He tells us that Constantine built a house of prayer on the site of the resurrection; and that, in memory of his mother, he beautified the places connected with the Lord's birth and ascension where she had built churches. He does not tell us that Christian tradition guaranteed the identity of the sites: in fact, we are given to understand by later writers that the tomb of Jesus was rediscovered under the inspiration of the Saviour!

Jerome in a letter (lviii), probably written some twenty years after he had settled in Bethlehem in A.D. 386, states that, from the time of Hadrian until Constantine, there was an image of Jupiter on the site of the resurrection, and of

Venus on the site of the cross. It may well be that Hadrian, after the destruction of Jerusalem in A.D. 135, had erected such pagan shrines near a gate of the city: these cult sanctuaries would not have stood there before the Roman triumph of A.D. 70.

But we have to remember that Christians abandoned Jerusalem in A.D. 66, and that only a small community returned when the city was gradually rebuilt after Titus destroyed it. All memory of the actual sites would almost certainly have been lost during three centuries which embraced the double destruction of Jerusalem first by Titus and then by Hadrian; and only a general sense of the fitness of things will have led Constantine's officials to find the holy places of Christianity at shrines used for heathen worship. The birthplace of Jesus at Bethlehem was similarly discovered under a shrine of Adonis! One would like to believe that at any rate the site assigned to Golgotha is authentic; but no archaeological arguments in its favour carry conviction.

165. The essentials of the resurrection faith

The story of the resurrection is so intimately bound up with Christian feeling, and so strongly entrenched in Christian tradition, that the need to abandon belief in it as a physical fact causes much distress. Yet, as was made clear when miracles were discussed in chapter iv, we cannot, out of deference to religious sentiment, reject the principle of the uniformity of nature which is fundamental in the outlook created by modern science. The miraculous seemed a natural, even a necessary, concomitant of religious revelation when Christianity was born; but we know now that, in certain large-scale (finite as opposed to infinitesimal) domains of experience, the activity of God is in accordance with uniform laws which express the invariable character of His control of phenomena. We might possibly claim that the physical resurrection—the resuscitation of the dead body—of Jesus provided a single and momentous exception to the general law, if critical analysis of the New Testament records yielded overwhelming testimony in its favour. But the outcome of prolonged and many-sided inquiry is, as we shall see, to cast grave doubt on the story of the physical resurrection.

Before indicating the main outlines of such inquiry, we may rightly ask what was the origin of the resurrection story. The answer is undoubtedly to be found in the experience of the immediate followers of Jesus, and of those who came after them, that the Spirit of Christ was present with them. Jesus was, they were profoundly convinced, not a dead leader, but alive for evermore. Moreover, he was not living in some distant heavenly realm: he was active with and among his followers.

There is no little doubt as to whether the early Christians sharply distinguished between the Spirit of God, the Spirit of Jesus and the Comforter of the fourth gospel: and some Christian thinkers are of opinion that they were wise in avoiding distinctions in a realm where knowledge must be somewhat insecurely based on the collective experience of individuals. The writer of the fourth gospel had in mind the essentials of the resurrection faith when he said (xiv. 26), "the Comforter, even the Holy Spirit, whom the Father will send in my name, he shall teach you all things, and bring to your remembrance all that I said unto you." *Matthew* had, as we have seen, obvious limitations; but his work would not have been preferred by the church to the other gospels had he not had also exceptional spiritual insight. He, at the very end of his book, crystallized the resurrection faith of the Christian church in the words which he ascribes to the risen Jesus, "Lo, I am with you alway, even unto the end of the world."

Objection may be raised that the belief of early Christians that the Spirit of Jesus was present with them was mistaken: it can be maintained that they misunderstood the cause of their collective confidence and enthusiasm. In reply, we can point to the results of their belief. The early Christians, because of their belief, lived according to the teaching of Jesus. The discipline to which they subjected themselves was severe. Their faith led to a certainty which proved infectious: others imitated their conduct and equally felt the presence and power of the Spirit. The only test of a subjective certainty is its result in action. As Jesus said of false prophets, "By their fruits ye shall know them" (*Matthew* vii. 16). "A good tree cannot bring forth evil fruit, neither can a corrupt tree bring forth good fruit." The good fruit visible in the lives of Christians witnessed to the goodness and strength of the Power by which they were moved.

Throughout the Christian centuries belief in guidance given by God through the inward presence of the Spirit of Christ has never wholly disappeared: its strength has coincided with epochs of fine religious achievement. Great men, remarkable for their spiritual certainty, have had a profound conviction that they were guided by that Inner Light which is a witness to, no less than the result of, the activity of God as Jesus revealed Him. Their belief can no more be set aside than can the value of the influence of these men on human progress. Their Inner Light, surely, is none other than the Spirit of God flaming out in Jesus the Christ.

The resurrection is one of the great essential truths of Christianity. But it cannot be stated too often, or too emphatically, that this tenet of the Christian faith is quite independent of the question as to whether the body of Jesus was reanimated after his death. What matters is that Christians shall feel a spiritual power in their lives, which they can rightly interpret as that of the Spirit of Jesus revealing, as in his teaching in Galilee, the wisdom and righteousness of God. Those who do not accept the Christian faith will say that any feeling interpreted as such experience is mistakenly explained, just as those who do not accept theism say that we cannot reach God in prayer or meditation, or recognize His guidance in our lives. The crucial division between Christian and non-Christian lies in acceptance of the truth of such spiritual experience as was rationalized in the story of the disciples walking to Emmaus (*Luke* xxiv. 13–35): "Was not our heart burning within us, while he spake to us in the way, while he opened to us the scriptures?" The story ends, "He was known of them in the breaking of the bread." The teaching of Jesus and the familiar ritual are bonds uniting the Lord to his followers.

166. The burial of Jesus

All four gospels give an account of the burial of Jesus; but plainly in each case the Marcan record, or the source from which it came, has served as the basis. That record was intended to put beyond doubt the fact that the body of Jesus was not, like that of an ordinary criminal, flung into a common fosse, but was laid by itself with every care in a definite sepulchre. *Mark* says that the sepulchre was hewn out of a rock and that a stone was rolled against the door.

For the purpose of this interment the evangelist, or more probably the tradition which he follows, brings upon the scene Joseph of Arimathaea. The new-comer had to be of sufficient importance to have access to Pilate in order that he might obtain the body of Jesus; so the source used by *Mark* makes him "a councillor of honourable estate," presumably a member of the sanhedrin. Has *Mark* forgotten that he made the whole council deliver Jesus to Pilate? And when he tells, in connection with the burial, of the need of haste, because it was "the Preparation, that is, the day before the sabbath," has he forgotten that he was speaking of the day of the passover, which itself required a sabbath rest?

Mark further says of Joseph of Arimathaea that he "was looking for the kingdom of God." *Matthew* modifies the account and describes Joseph as a rich man "who also himself was Jesus' disciple." *Luke* corrects or amplifies *Mark*, and says that Joseph, though a councillor, was "a good man and a righteous (he had not consented to their counsel and deed)." *John* describes Joseph as "a disciple of Jesus, but secretly for fear of the Jews"; and with Joseph he associates Nicodemus, who never appears elsewhere than in the fourth gospel.

Of the sepulchre, *Matthew* says that it was Joseph's "own new tomb, which he had hewn out in the rock"; and he mentions a great stone rolled to the door of the tomb. *Luke* merely writes of "a tomb that was hewn in stone, where never man had yet lain." *John* writes that "in the place where he was crucified there was a garden; and in the garden a new tomb wherein was never man yet laid."

It is to be noticed that *Luke's* statement (xxiii. 53), following *Mark*, that the body of Jesus was taken down from the cross by Joseph does not agree with words in a speech attributed to Paul which we find in *Acts* (xiii. 29). In this second volume of *Luke's* work we read of dwellers in Jerusalem and their rulers, who asked of Pilate that Jesus should be slain; and we are told that "they took him down from the tree, and laid him in a tomb." In the resurrection tract of 1 *Corinthians* xv, we learn merely "that Christ died for our sins according to the scriptures; and that he was buried."

A survey of the different stories and of their variations makes clear that, as we have them in the gospels, they were told with the object of providing evidence that, if the sepulchre was found empty after thirty-six hours, Jesus must have arisen from the dead. *Matthew* (xxvii. 62–6) adds a story intended to provide additional evidence: he makes the chief priests and the pharisees ask Pilate to place a guard before the sepulchre. Such an addition, like others in *Matthew*, is typical of the mistaken and improbable emphasis which, usually in a more extravagant form, alienates us in the apocryphal gospels.

167. The Marcan story of the empty tomb

The first detailed account of the discovery of the empty tomb is given by *Mark* (xvi. 1–8). Three women, who are said to have been in the company of Jesus alike in Galilee and on the journey to Jerusalem, came to the tomb very early on the Sunday morning, when the sun was risen. To their surprise they found the great stone rolled back from the door of the tomb. Entering in they saw "a young man arrayed in a white robe," in other words, an angel, "sitting on the right side." He tells them not to be surprised, for "Jesus, the Nazarene, which hath been crucified: he is risen." He asked them to "tell his disciples and Peter, He goeth before you into Galilee: there shall ye see him, as he said unto you." With trembling and astonishment the women fled from the tomb and "said nothing to any one; for they were afraid."

Such is the end of *Mark's* story. An addition (xvi. 9–20) was subsequently composed: it is an obvious compilation, not to be found in some of our oldest manuscripts, though they are not earlier than the fourth century of our era.

Why does our earliest gospel end thus abruptly, with no mention of the actual resurrection or of any appearance of the risen Jesus? Some few writers, who assign an early date to the gospel, suggest that *Mark* had nothing more to add: details of the post-resurrection story were not known to him. The large majority of scholars contend that the narrative is plainly incomplete as it stands. It must have had an ending somewhat similar to that in each of the other gospels. That ending has been lost. Some attempt no explanation of the loss. Others say that the concluding paragraphs disappeared because the gospel, after its use by *Matthew* and *Luke*, was disregarded: at one time it "survived only in a single tattered copy."

A third explanation of the abrupt ending of the gospel has been put forward. In the passage from *Mark* which we have just quoted it is stated that the risen Jesus has gone into Galilee where he shall be seen. This is in agreement with an earlier statement in *Mark* (xiv. 28), a prophecy ascribed to Jesus, "After I am raised up, I will go before you into Galilee." These statements strongly suggest that the lost ending of *Mark* described one or more post-resurrection appearances in Galilee, whereas in *Luke* such appearances are placed in or near Jerusalem, while in *Matthew* the earliest appearance of Jesus is placed near the tomb. One modern scholar says, "The disappearance of the ending of Mark was at an extremely early time, so early that neither Matthew nor Luke shows any knowledge of it. . . . The real reason why the original ending of Mark did not survive was because the Church found it too difficult to maintain."

68. The resurrection according to *Matthew* and *Luke*

Even though the contradictions which may have been contained in the lost end of the second gospel are no longer an embarrassment, some confusion remains in our present sources. According to *Matthew* (xxviii. 1–10), two women came to see the sepulchre "as it began to dawn." There was a great earthquake; and an angel descended from heaven, rolled away the stone and sat upon it. The angel told the women to say to the disciples that they would see Jesus in Galilee. As they were departing, they met Jesus himself who confirmed the angel's words, "Go tell my brethren that they depart into Galilee, and there shall they see me." The first gospel ends (xxviii. 16–20) with the departure of the eleven disciples into Galilee "unto the mountain where Jesus had appointed them." There they saw him and he gave them his final message with its superb ending, "Lo, I am with you alway, even unto the end of the world."

The story in *Luke* (xxiv. 1–11) has certain significant differences. At early dawn on the first day of the week "the women,

which had come with him out of Galilee," came to the tomb:
they found the stone rolled away, and the sepulchre empty.
There is no mention of an earthquake, or of an angel rolling
away the stone. But two angels, described as men in dazzling
apparel, appeared to reassure them, saying, "He is not here,
but is risen: remember how he spake unto you when he was
yet in Galilee, saying that the Son of man must be delivered
up into the hands of sinful men, and be crucified, and the
third day rise again." The apostles—and the admission is
surprising in view of the prophecies said to have been made—
disbelieved the women: "these words appeared in their sight
as idle talk." It will be noticed that *Luke* says nothing as to
any resurrection appearances in Galilee: he is content to say
that Jesus, when he was in Galilee, prophesied his resurrection.
Luke, moreover, puts the appearances of the risen Christ in
or near Jerusalem, and his final ascension from "over against
Bethany."

From the summaries which we have given it is difficult
to avoid the conclusion that we are in the domain of religious
romance, not of religious history. The early Christians were
convinced that the Spirit of the Lord Jesus was with them. To
their great joy his peace rested upon them. His continual
guidance was their fundamental certainty. They received such
guidance when critical decisions had to be made. The Lord
himself was felt to be present at their gatherings, and particularly at "the breaking of bread." How came it that he was
thus present and active? He obviously must be alive. But, if
alive, he must have risen from the dead. The stories of the
empty tomb and of the resurrection appearances are attempts
to explain how he thus rose to eternal life, attempts to buttress
spiritual certainty by material fact. Religious conviction began
the story: the activity of faith with impressive seriousness added
details.

169. The resurrection according to the fourth gospel

We see such religious certainty at work in the record which
John gives. As has been stated (see also § 171), the last chapter
of the gospel as we now have it is a later addendum: the gospel,
when first completed, say in A.D. 110–20, ended with chapter xx.
The original ending was almost certainly based on a general

knowledge of the synoptic gospels, though differences in detail point to the existence of many variations in the fundamental story.

Among such differences we note that, not at sunrise, but while it is yet dark, one woman alone, Mary Magdalene, comes to the sepulchre and finds the stone taken away from the tomb. She hastens to Peter and to the beloved disciple; and the two men run to the sepulchre to discover in turn that only the grave-clothes remain. They go home; but Mary remains weeping. She looks again into the tomb, and sees two angels. Then she turns round; and Jesus reveals himself to her, saying, "Go unto my brethren, and say to them, I ascend unto my Father and your Father, and my God and your God." That same Sunday evening, "when the doors were shut where the disciples were, for fear of the Jews"—plainly the evangelist has in mind a eucharist—Jesus came and stood in the midst, saying, "Peace be unto you." Thomas was absent; and, subsequently, when told of the incident, doubted the appearance of Jesus. But at the eucharist a week later he is present, and is converted when the Lord appears again to show him his wounds. The lesson which *John* desires the story to convey is brought out by what he regards as the final and especially important words of Jesus, "Because thou hast seen me, thou hast believed: blessed are they that have not seen, and yet have believed."

70. The Emmaus story

Of all stories connected with the resurrection, the most moving is undoubtedly that of the walk to Emmaus. It is told (xxiv. 13–32) with *Luke's* consummate skill, so that, though we are left with the belief that it is not history, and that *Luke* himself did not give it as more than allegory, we feel that in it we are very near to the heart of Christianity. *Luke* has combined the necessity of the suffering Saviour-Lord, "Behoved it not the Christ to suffer these things, and to enter into his glory?" with the appeal, "Abide with us: for it is toward evening, and the day is now far spent"; and he follows up both the need and the entreaty by "the breaking of bread" where men's eyes are opened to know the risen Lord. Thus he emphasizes that in their common worship Christians find Christ.

171. The last chapter of the fourth gospel

Specific mention should perhaps be made of the last chapter (xxi) of the gospel according to *John*. It is a late addition, possibly of the middle of the second century of our era. Clumsily told, the story narrates the appearance of Jesus to some of his disciples, as they were fishing in the lake of Galilee. They had caught nothing during the night. At daybreak Jesus whom they did not recognize when he was standing on the shore, told them where to cast their net. There followed a miraculous draught of fishes: the disciples were not able to draw in the net for the multitude of the fishes. We have, in fact, a story which is told by *Luke* (v. 4–11) as an incident in the Galilean ministry. The beloved disciple said to Peter, "It is the Lord"; and Peter forthwith swam or waded to land. When the others arrived they found a "fire of coals there, and fish laid thereon, and bread." All knew that it was Jesus but dared not say so. "Jesus cometh, and taketh the bread and giveth them, and the fish likewise." There the first part of the story ends with the words, "This is now the third time that Jesus was manifested to the disciples, after that he was risen from the dead." This sentence is plain evidence that the author of the present last chapter of the fourth gospel had no knowledge of any post-resurrection appearances of Jesus to the disciples other than the two mentioned in the original last chapter of the gospel. He cannot have heard of the list in 1 *Corinthians* xv.

In the awkward narrative which we have just summarized, we obviously have another myth of the presence of the risen Jesus at a eucharistic feast, in which, however, fish replaced wine. It will be recalled that we have earlier pointed out in § 127 that the feeding of the five thousand on bread and fish is probably a eucharistic myth. The bread was a constant element in the common meal; but apparently in the beginning wine might be replaced by wine and water (see § 325), or by water (see § 189), or by fish.

172. The resurrection in the *First Epistle to the Corinthians*

We shall (§§ 224–226) subsequently consider the indications which lead to the view that the *First Epistle to the Corinthians* is composite; and, in particular, that the present chapter xv is a tract on the resurrection of Christ, and therefore of his followers.

he is "the firstfruits of them that are asleep." In this chapter, which neatly separates itself from those which precede and follow, Paul is made to say (xv. 3–8):

I delivered unto you first of all that which also I received, how that Christ died for our sins according to the scriptures; and that he was buried; and that he hath been raised on the third day according to the scriptures; and that he appeared to Cephas; then to the twelve; then he appeared to above five hundred brethren at once, of whom the greater part remain until now, but some are fallen asleep; then he appeared to James; then to all the apostles; and last of all, as unto one born out of due time, he appeared to me also.

If these verses are part of a genuine letter, as they purport to be, they must have been written about A.D. 54. They must, moreover, have constituted a most important and constantly repeated part of the teaching, not only of Paul and his companions, but also of all the early missionaries. The appearance to "above five hundred brethren at once" would have been of such overwhelming value as a piece of evidence for the resurrection that it would have been in the forefront of Christian apologetic. Yet we get no hint of it either in *Luke* or in the other two evangelists, *Matthew* and *John*, who wrote about, or somewhat later than, the end of the first century of our era. We are forced to the conclusion that it cannot be historical and that, as a story, it is much later than the time of Paul.

The appearance to James is not mentioned in any of our four gospels. It played, however, no little part in later Christian story. Jerome, writing towards the end of the fourth century, mentions a *Gospel according to the Hebrews*, now lost, in which the first resurrection appearance of the risen Christ was to James, who had taken an oath to fast until he had seen the Lord raised from the dead. When Jesus appeared, he "took the bread, blessed and brake it, and gave it to James," saying, "My brother, eat thy bread, for the Son of man is risen from the dead."

173. The survival of Christianity

We have now examined all the resurrection stories of the New Testament; and the question remains, What actually

happened immediately after the death of Jesus? Our quotations from *Mark* make it clear that the disciples fled to their
home country. The earliest tradition put the post-resurrection
appearances—"there shall ye see him"—in Galilee. We need
feel no surprise at the flight. The execution of Jesus showed
that Pilate was prepared brutally to crush the new movement.
The stay of Jesus in Jerusalem before his arrest had been so
short that he could have made few converts there: his followers
must have been almost entirely Galileans. They naturally
went home. With their return we should have expected the
movement to disappear. Memories and hopes, poignant and
precious, ought gradually to have faded.

Who was there to carry on the movement? Probably few
of the intimate followers of Jesus will have been able to write
with ease. They will normally have spoken Aramaic: their
knowledge of Greek will have been limited. They had, moreover, no social standing. After the crucifixion of Jesus they
were scattered fugitives, followers of a man who came to a
criminal's end, whose body quite possibly had been flung
ignominiously into a common malefactors' grave. By every
law of probability Christianity ought to have perished. That
it survived is—do we exaggerate?—the supreme miracle of
history.

How did it escape extinction? All will agree that we have no
adequate knowledge of what happened in the first year or two
after the death of Jesus. At the beginning of *Acts* we have the
sort of picture of events which *Luke* made some seventy years
later. But even that picture has been altered by the editorial
insertion (i. 3–11) which, as has been pointed out in § 130,
elaborates so extensively the story of the ascension as it is given
(xxiv. 50–53) in the third gospel. The process by which a
scattered group of frightened men became a resurgent community is hidden from us: the seed grew in secret.

But, as we have reiterated, the resurrection stories which
gradually arose express the conviction—the absolute certainty
—of the earliest members of the community that Jesus was
present with them. In the power given by his Spirit they
became missionaries: they grew increasingly confident that they
had a religious message of supreme importance. Probably
almost from the beginning, before the stories of the empty tomb

and of the post-resurrection appearances took shape as Christian beliefs, the earliest disciples of Jesus expressed their spiritual certainty by words such as "Christ is risen." *Luke* records (*Acts* iv. 2) that Peter and his associates in their early preaching "proclaimed in Jesus the resurrection from the dead." The followers of the Saviour-Lord thought of themselves as sharing his resurrection: they "were raised together with Christ" and therefore seeking "the things that are above, where Christ is, seated on the right hand of God" (*Colossians* iii. 1). Metaphor changes easily into myth, and myth into what is supposed to be history. When, at the beginning of *Acts*, an apostle had to be chosen in place of the traitor Judas, Peter is reported to have said (i. 21–22) that of the men who were constantly with Jesus, "of these must one become a witness with us of his resurrection." The implication is that the man chosen became a witness by sharing their experience of the risen Lord. To that experience there was soon joined a sense of God's presence such as was dramatized by *Luke* in the story of Pentecost (*Acts* ii. 1–42).

174. The ascension

Probably many years passed before the resurrection stories took the shapes in which we now find them in the gospels. The differences between these stories show myth-making in operation, not only until the time of *John*, chapter xx (say, A.D. 110–20), but until the final chapter of the fourth gospel was written, probably in the middle of the second century of our era. He who would understand this process should consider the part played by myth in Platonic teaching. Not until the accounts of the post-resurrection appearances were stabilized would the desire for a story of the ascension of Jesus emerge.

Whether *Mark* had any ascension story we do not know. *Matthew* plainly was satisfied by a formal farewell at the mountain in Galilee, "where Jesus had appointed them." The first gospel ends with what has well been called a magnificent theophany. On the other hand, *John* was satisfied to leave his risen Christ after Thomas had given him the supreme homage, "My Lord and my God."

Only in *Luke*, of all the four gospels, do we find an ascension story. The risen Christ, apparently on the Sunday of the resurrection, led them out until they were "over against

Bethany." Then he blessed them. "And it came to pass, while
he blessed them, he parted from them, and was carried up into
heaven. And they worshipped him, and returned to Jerusalem
with great joy: and were continually in the temple, blessing
God."

The story is naïvely pre-Copernican, its astronomy that of
the so-called Apostles' Creed. The risen Lord goes to heaven,
which is regarded as a place in the sky above the earth. We
cannot even guess at the date when the story took shape;
possibly, as *Matthew* and *John* make no mention of it, not
before the second decade of the second century of our era.

There seems to be no doubt, as we have said, that the earliest
ascension story put the event on the same day as the resurrection. Not only do we derive this impression from *Luke*, the only
gospel source of the story, but we also find it in the *Epistle of
Barnabas*. We shall discuss that work briefly in § 255. It suffices
now to say that it was probably written during the period
A.D.110–20; and that in it we find (chapter xv) the statement,
"we celebrate the eighth day with joyfulness, the day on which
Jesus rose also from the dead, and was made manifest, and
ascended into the heavens."

We must not omit to mention that, as we shall see in § 188,
the heretical *Gospel of Peter*, apparently written shortly before
A.D. 150, puts the ascension of Jesus at the moment of his
death.

A week is made to elapse in the fourth gospel between two
appearances of Jesus after his crucifixion. On the Sunday of
the resurrection he comes to the disciples in the absence of
Thomas; and a week later he reappears when Thomas is with
them. In *Acts*, *Luke* attributes to Peter a long speech before the
baptism of Cornelius, in the course of which he says of Jesus
(x. 40–1), "Him God raised up the third day, and gave him
to be made manifest, not to all the people, but unto witnesses
that were chosen before of God, even to us, who did eat and
drink with him [during several weeks] after he rose from the
dead." The words in brackets appear in a sixth-century manuscript known as the Codex Bezae, which contains a number of
interesting variants of the usual text. They show that some
scribe felt the need of harmonizing Peter's speech with the
story which now appears at the beginning of *Acts*.

That story, if the end of *Luke* is in its original form, must be, as we have briefly argued in § 130, a late insertion by some editor. In it we read (*Acts* i. 3) that Jesus "showed himself alive after his passion by many proofs, appearing unto them by the space of forty days, and speaking the things concerning the kingdom of God." We learn further that, "being assembled together with them, he charged them not to depart from Jerusalem," promising that they should "be baptized with the Holy Spirit not many days hence." Subsequently, "when they were come together," the time and place not being specified, Jesus made another short speech; "and when he had said these things, as they were looking, he was taken up; and a cloud received him out of their sight." Thereupon two angels, men in white apparel, appeared, and prophesied the Lord's return. The appearance of the angels is itself a warning that we are in the domain of religious romance.

To sum up, we may say that at first in Christian preaching the resurrection appearances were few and apparently all placed on the Sunday of the resurrection. Such probably was the state of the tradition, even half a century after the crucifixion, among those from whom *Matthew* derived his information. But almost simultaneously *Luke* accepted an ascension story which told of the return of the risen Christ to heaven after a quasi-material sojourn on earth: in *Luke* alone does the risen Jesus "eat before them." Probably a little later *John*, with a characteristic indifference to mere fact when symbolism was important, allowed a sojourn of a week that the risen Jesus might appear to "doubting Thomas." But the growth of belief in a terrestrial sojourn of many weeks was subsequent to the writing of the *Epistle of Barnabas* in, say, A.D. 110–20, and was, as will appear in § 327, probably unknown to Justin Martyr in A.D. 150. Its completed form, so far as it appears in the New Testament, is to be found in the editorial insertion in *Acts* (i. 3–11).

This insertion was to prove vastly convenient in later times. 'Forty,' as used in ancient Jewish writings, was a conventional number. It had no precise significance; and "forty days" meant merely a considerable, though undefined, period. But in due course ecclesiastics desired precision that they might have a settled church calendar; and a natural wish to make a

N

firm scheme brought into existence the sequence of Easter, Ascension Day and Whitsunday, as we now know them.

Far more important than a precise calendar was teaching apparently so authoritative that it could not be challenged. Even to-day any ecclesiastical dogma that seems in an especial degree to require the Lord's authority is, in certain Christian circles, attributed to the risen Christ, "appearing unto them by the space of forty days, and speaking the things concerning the kingdom of God."

CHAPTER X

PETER

175. Peter

AMONG the early followers of Jesus two men stand out pre-eminent: in fact, the book of *Acts* is mainly a record of their activities. The one is Simon, surnamed in Greek Peter, or in Aramaic Cephas, the rock. According to the Christian story he was with Jesus from the beginning of his ministry; and, though he deserted him at his trial and crucifixion, he was apparently for some time sole leader of the early Christian movement. At a later time, James, the brother of Jesus, became Peter's equal at Jerusalem; and, somewhat later, Paul became the chief leader of missionary movements outside Palestine. Unlike Peter, Paul had never seen Jesus; yet his influence on the development of Christianity has been greater than that of any other follower of his Lord.

Our knowledge of Peter rests in the main upon *Mark* and *Acts*. Fragments of additional information are to be found in *Matthew*, in the *First Epistle to the Corinthians* and in the *Epistle to the Galatians*.

According to *Mark* (i. 14–17), after John the Baptist had been thrown into prison, Jesus began his ministry in Galilee. Of this ministry the first recorded incident is that, as Jesus passed along the shore of the lake of Galilee, he saw Simon, and Andrew the brother of Simon; and he said to them, "Come ye after me, and I will make you to become fishers of men." Shortly afterwards, James and John, the sons of Zebedee, were "called." It would appear from the narrative that Zebedee was a man of some position, a fishing-smack owner, with "hired servants." Simon and Andrew were probably less well-to-do: we may think of them as working fishermen of independent status without capital. All fished at the northern end of the lake; and their trade seems to have been based on the large, and probably prosperous, village of Capernaum.

According to the gospel story, Peter was constantly with Jesus throughout his ministry. He, James and John are repre-

sented as Christ's closest followers. He was at the Last Supper
and also in the company of Jesus at his arrest. In fact, in the
fourth gospel we are told that it was Peter who, in a scuffle
drew a sword and cut off the ear of the high-priest's servant
The incident is narrated in all the synoptists; but Peter is no
mentioned by name save in *John*. While the trial of Jesus wa
taking place, Peter is said (*Mark* xiv. 66) to have been "beneath
in the court" and to have thrice denied that he was a followe
of "Jesus the Nazarene." The incident is told most graphically
Peter being recognized as a Galilean, probably, as *Matthev*
says, because of his accent. It is in such a story that w
seem to trace the existence in *Mark* of genuine reminiscence
of Peter.

176. Peter and the resurrection of Jesus

As we have seen in chapter ix, a very firm tradition connected
Peter with the first vision of Jesus after his burial. Our records
unfortunately, are allusive rather than descriptive. The gospe
according to *Mark* now ends, apart from the spurious addition
(xvi. 9–20), with the command of the angel at the tomb to the
three women who had brought spices, that they should go and
"tell his disciples and Peter, He goeth before you into Galilee
there shall ye see him, as he said unto you." In the account o
the post-resurrection appearances given in the *First Epistle to the
Corinthians*, we are told that (xv. 5) first of all "he appeared to
Cephas." This appearance is not described in any gospel
though in *Luke* (xxiv. 34) we are told how the Emmaus disciple
found the eleven gathered together, saying, "The Lord is risen
indeed, and hath appeared to Simon." In the editorial addition
which forms the present last chapter of the fourth gospel, Peter
plays the prominent part in a post-resurrection appearance
placed in Galilee; but, as we have said in § 171, the story has
every sign of being a late and fanciful development, better
worthy of a place in one of the apocryphal gospels than in the
New Testament.

177. Peter and the early church

The first dozen chapters of *Acts* contain all that we know of
the earliest development of the Christian movement, subsequent
to the resurrection of Jesus. They consist of history mixed with

improbable legends. In them Peter is the dominant figure. He
makes the speech which results in the election of an apostle in
succession to the traitor Judas. To him also is assigned a great
speech on the day of Pentecost, when the early disciples became
conscious of a new power in their midst. Subsequently, after a
miracle, he makes a speech in Solomon's porch of the temple.
These speeches, doubtless, are free compositions of *Luke*; but,
if only by reason of a quality which is shown in their primitive
theology, they are both well suited to their various occasions
and also probably embody early traditions. A little later
(*Acts* vi and vii) Stephen, as leader of the Greek-speaking
Christians at Jerusalem, appears to have succeeded Peter as
spokesman of the Christian community; and, when Stephen
was stoned, Paul, described as "a young man named Saul," is
mentioned for the first time.

There follow stories of the way in which Peter was led to
admit that "to the Gentiles also hath God granted repentance
unto life." These stories have to be read carefully in connection
with the sharp controversy of which Paul writes in his important, significant and early letter to the *Galatians*. Our authorities give us a confused, and possibly by *Luke* deliberately blurred,
account of the dispute. The admission of gentiles to the
Christian movement led finally to the breach with Judaism:
almost inevitably discussion as to the conditions of their
admission gave rise to grave differences within the Christian
community.

Subsequently, we are told (*Acts* xii. 1–19) of Peter's imprisonment by Herod (Agrippa I), who reigned from A.D. 41 to
A.D. 44: there follows the tale of Peter's miraculous escape.
The story ends, "And he said, Tell these things unto James, and
to the brethren. And he departed, and went to another place."
"As soon as it was day, there was no small stir among the
soldiers, what was become of Peter."

178. Peter's end

Where did Peter then go? What further part did he play
in the spread of Christianity? The only hint of an answer, if
it be allowed (see § 132) that the visits to Jerusalem recorded
in *Acts* xi and *Acts* xv are the same, is contained in Paul's
statement in *Galatians* (ii. 11), "When Cephas came to Antioch,

I resisted him to the face, because he stood condemned." Probably Peter, after thus visiting Antioch, never returned to Jerusalem. It may well be that his work was done. Our last glimpse of him is probably in the year A.D. 44; and, if he was an exact contemporary of Jesus, he would have been then some fifty years of age.

At the beginning of the *First Epistle to the Corinthians* (i. 12) there are references to divisions in the church of that large and vicious city, divisions associated with the names of Paul, Apollos and Cephas. Some scholars contend that the passage shows that Peter had been in person at Corinth; but surely such an inference is unwarranted. The name of Peter—the use of the Aramaic form Cephas is possibly significant—will have stood for the primitive Jerusalem tradition, the Judaic Christianity which doubtless had its followers at Corinth.

179. Peter a married man

Mark has an allusion to Peter that is copied by *Matthew* and *Luke*. We are told that (i. 29–31) Jesus healed Peter's wife's mother, who was "sick of a fever." The fact that Peter was married appears again in the *First Epistle to the Corinthians*, where (ix. 5) Paul inquires, "Have we no right to lead about a wife that is a believer, even as the rest of the apostles, and the brethren of the Lord, and Cephas?" We know singularly little of the domestic background of any of the chief men associated with the rise of Christianity. The passages just quoted establish conclusively that Peter was married.

180. Was Paul married?

The second of our two quotations seems to imply that Paul also was married; and this fact is asserted in what is called "the longer recension"—we shall discuss the variations in chapter xiv—of the letter of Ignatius to the *Philadelphians*. In that letter (iv) we read of "Peter, and Paul, and the rest of the apostles, that were married men." But it is highly doubtful whether the longer forms of any of the so-called letters of Ignatius are genuine: in fact, as we shall see later, the whole of the correspondence associated with the name of Ignatius, who is believed to have been martyred in the period A.D. 107–16, is suspect. Paul himself (1 *Corinthians* vii. 5–7) writes "by way of

permission, not of commandment" of the mutual obligations
of husband and wife; and continues, "Yet [or, for] I would
that all men were even as I myself." One reading seems to
imply that Paul was celibate, the other that his relations with
his wife were those which he commends. The former alternative would seem to emerge almost at once: "But I say to the
unmarried and to widows, It is good for them if they abide
even as I." But this verse leaves open the possibility that Paul
was a widower; and we have also to remember that much in the
first letter to the Corinthians may be by later writers.

Possibly the divergencies and ambiguities of our authorities
indicate that Paul had been married; but that, with the rise of
asceticism in the second century of our era, the fact was
suppressed. No certain conclusion can be reached: the discussion is complicated by considerations as to whether the *First
Epistle to the Corinthians* is, as it stands, a letter of Paul; or whether
it is not rather a short genuine letter into which a bundle of brief
early Christian documents has been thrust. Yet the belief that
Peter and Paul were both married was singularly persistent.
Eusebius, in his *Ecclesiastical History* (iii. 30), written at the
beginning of the fourth century of our era, quotes Clement of
Alexandria, who wrote towards the end of the second century,
as saying: "Peter and Philip were fathers of children, and Philip
even gave his daughters to husbands, while Paul himself does not
hesitate in one of his epistles to address his wife [*lit.* yokefellow]
whom, for the greater success of his mission, he did not take
with him." The reference is presumably to the *Epistle to the
Philippians* (iv. 3), "I beseech thee also, true yokefellow, help
these women, for they laboured with me in the gospel."

181. The so-called primacy of Peter

Another passage as to Peter, which occurs solely in *Matthew*, is
famous. It is recorded in different forms by the three synoptists
that Peter, in answer to a question from Jesus, said, "Thou
art the Christ, the Son of the living God." *Matthew* continues
(xvi. 17–18), "Jesus said unto him, Blessed art thou, Simon
Bar-Jonah: for flesh and blood hath not revealed it unto thee,
but my Father which is in heaven. And I also say unto thee
that thou art Peter, and upon this rock I will build my church;
and the gates of Hades shall not prevail against it. I will give

unto thee the keys of the kingdom of heaven: and whatsoever thou shalt bind on earth shall be bound in heaven: and whatsoever thou shalt loose on earth shall be loosed in heaven."

This saying, attributed to Jesus, is one of the passages in *Matthew* which come neither from *Mark* nor from Q. Like most of such passages, it is probably a late addition of no historical value. Jesus is represented as speaking of the church only here and in another passage of *Matthew* (xviii. 17); and immediately after the latter passage the same saying as to binding and loosing occurs again. The saying has an echo in the fourth gospel (xx. 23). It is out of harmony with those which come from Q; and, in type, it suggests a metaphor of some Jewish rabbi rather than the pure and undefiled religion of Jesus.

Moreover, it is a clumsy anticipation of later developments to make Jesus speak of "my church." The theme of his preaching was the kingdom of God. His mission, as he conceived it, was to call men to join this kingdom: he had not set out to found a church. As we have seen, he either expected that the kingdom would come with visible splendour in the near future, or else that its manifestation would be inward and spiritual. The early strata of the New Testament seem to show that the expectation of an earthly and visible kingdom was well-nigh universal during the first generation of Christians. Only as the hope died away were groups of expectant Christians gradually organized into what became branches of the church. At the beginning of the second century of our era, when *Matthew* was probably written, ecclesiasticism had begun: the alleged promise to Peter was to be one of its main buttresses.

The fame of Peter seems to have grown as the Christian movement expanded. He and Paul became in the Christian story the leading martyrs of the Church. Men wishing to commend their own expressions of the Christian faith wrote in Peter's name. We have in the New Testament the *First and Second Epistles of Peter*. Outside it, ranking among apocryphal books, we have a number of works including the *Gospel of Peter* and the *Apocalypse of Peter*. Such books, as we shall see, throw an interesting light on the rise of Christianity; but none of them can be ascribed to the apostle.

182. The death of Peter. Was he ever in Rome?

Where and when did Peter die? The traditional answer is that he died at Rome during the persecution of the Christians by Nero after the fire of Rome in A.D. 64. "He was bishop of Rome for twenty-five years, and was martyred in A.D. 67." So much emotion is bound up with this answer that to express doubt is to incur the risk of strong, if not angry, criticism. Yet such evidence as we have, if judicially considered, is adverse to the claim that Peter died in Rome. It is, in fact, most doubtful if he ever reached the city.

We have seen that, when we last hear of Peter in the New Testament, he is disputing with Paul at Antioch in about the year A.D. 44, after what is described as a miraculous escape from his imprisonment by Herod (Agrippa I). Now Paul wrote his epistle to the *Romans* in about the year A.D. 56. In the epistle there is no salutation to Peter, who is not even mentioned. The book of *Acts* finally brings Paul to Rome, probably during the period A.D. 60–2: once again Peter is not mentioned. In the epistles of the captivity (see § 238), written by Paul while a prisoner in Rome, there is silence as to Peter. If, at any of these times, Peter had been at Rome, as a leader of the church, it is incredible that the fact should have been ignored.

Against these perplexing silences we may recall that at the end of the *First Epistle of Peter* (v. 13) we read, "She that is in Babylon, elect together with you, saluteth you; and so doth Mark my son." In this passage, as in the *Apocalypse*, Babylon almost certainly stands for Rome: Mark's name is probably brought in because of the story of his association with Peter in the writing of the second gospel. But these facts merely emphasize that the *First Epistle of Peter* (see § 184) is a late anonymous work. A date such as A.D. 80 is commonly assigned to the booklet: it must, moreover, not be forgotten that the salutation which we have just quoted may even be a much later addition.

Outside the New Testament, we find among early Christian writers a passage which occurs in both recensions of the letter of Ignatius to the *Romans* in which the author says (iv), "I do not, as Peter and Paul, issue commandments unto you." But, even if this letter be a genuine composition of Ignatius, the statement merely proves that, at the beginning of the second century of our era, Peter and Paul jointly enjoyed the highest authority among Christ's followers. The letter, however, as will be argued in §§ 264–5, was probably not written before the middle of the second century.

The only fairly early witness to the belief that Peter and Paul were possibly martyred about the same time is contained in a work called the *First Epistle of Clement to the Corinthians*. There we read (v), after an enumeration of some, from Cain to David, who suffered through "envy" or "jealousy":

> But let us leave these examples of long ago and come to those who took up the struggle most recently. Let us take the noble examples of our own generation. By reason of jealousy and malice the greatest and most upright pillars were in their struggle pursued to the point of death. Let us set before our eyes the good apostles. Peter met with jealousy and injustice so that he suffered hardship not once, nor twice, but many times. So he bore witness as he went his way to his rightful place of honour.
>
> By facing jealousy and contention, Paul set up the prize of endurance for all to see; seven times in chains, forced into flight and stoned, he became a herald both in the East and in the West and so won noble renown for his faith. He taught righteousness to all the world and came to the furthest bounds of the West to bear his witness before its rulers. So he left the world and was carried up into the holy place, having become a very great pattern of endurance.

In this passage, which merits careful study in spite of its deplorable style, "our own generation" probably refers to those "born anew in Christ," and not to contemporaries of the writer.

We shall subsequently discuss Clement's letter in §§ 252–3. The letter in itself is anonymous but the writer must have been important at Rome; and his epistle was regarded in the early fifth century almost as holy scripture. It was at that time joined to the books of the New Testament in the Codex Alexandrinus, an early manuscript of the Bible in Greek, of great value and now in the British Museum. The writer is not called Clement save in the list of contents of the Codex; and he writes in the name of the church at Rome to the church at Corinth. In his epistle there is mention of an apparently recent persecution, which might be that supposed to have taken place in the year A.D. 95 under the emperor Domitian.

But the extract which we have given shows no personal knowedge of the end of either apostle. It is plainly based on vague tradition; and beneath its verbosity—the writer is making bricks without straw—there is no such clear recollection as would have survived if merely thirty years had passed since the martyrdoms: that the epistle was written as early as A.D. 96, a date often assigned to it, is most improbable. Possibly we should date the epistle about A.D. 125. Nothing is said, in the passage which we have quoted, as to Peter having ever been in Rome, or even of Paul having been executed there. At most we can infer that, when an otherwise unknown Clement wrote, the story of a practically simultaneous martyrdom of Peter and Paul in, or near, Rome was just beginning to be formed.

The development of this story took place during the middle and second half of the second century of our era. Eusebius, in his *Ecclesiastical History* (ii. 25), tells us that "a writer of the church named Caius," in a written discussion with a Montanist leader—the Montanist heresy was of the second half of the second century—stated, "I can show you the trophies of the apostles, for if you will go to the Vatican or to the Ostian way, you will find the trophies of the founders of this church."

In the next sentence of this same passage in Eusebius we are told that Dionysius, bishop of Corinth, in correspondence with the Romans, apparently of about the year A.D. 170, affirmed of Peter and Paul that "both of them in the same way came to our Corinth and started our growth and taught; and both in the same way came also to Italy to the same place and taught and bore their witness at the same time." So the legend grew, characteristically becoming more definite with the passage of time. In stories of the saints, truth is of little account as compared with edification. He who in hagiography expects to find nothing but historical fact will almost certainly be disappointed.

The appendix to the fourth gospel, which now appears as the last chapter of that work, was, as we said in § 171, possibly added towards the end of the first half of the second century of our era. In it (*John* xxi. 18–19) Jesus is made to prophesy in vague terms how Peter would die. If the appendix was written in Ephesus, it adds nothing to the probability of martyrdom in Rome.

As a result of this somewhat tedious examination of our authorities, we are left with the conviction that, though possibly

Peter was martyred, there is no adequate evidence that he was ever in Rome. He may well have died within twenty years of the crucifixion of Jesus and it is highly probable that, after leaving Palestine, he continued to live in Syria until his death.

CHAPTER XI

THE BOOKS ASCRIBED TO PETER

183. Authorship and ascription

AS is well known, it was, during the later pre-Christian
centuries, a common custom for Jewish authors to issue
their writings in the name of some person of distinction, who
possibly had died many centuries previously. Probably there
was little, if any, intention to deceive; though, let us say,
wisdom might seem the more certain if ascribed to Solomon.
The habit of thus ascribing the works of an unknown man to
some early leader or teacher persisted among Christians.
Copyright, before the discovery of printing, had no monetary
value; and many religious writers valued their message and its
success more than any *éclat* which it might bring to themselves.
Sometimes they wrote in the name of a great leader or renowned
teacher: sometimes, though more rarely, a book was issued
anonymously and the name of some revered man was attached
to it.

When Christian scholarship came into being towards the
end of the second century of our era, Christian scholars showed
surprisingly little critical sense. The ascription, for instance, of
such a book as the *Epistle of Barnabas* to Paul's fellow missionary,
the Levite Barnabas of Cyprus, was unanimous: yet no modern
scholar would allow such authorship. In view of these facts the
reader must not be surprised to learn that five more or less
important books were ascribed to Peter, that two of them are to
be found in the New Testament, and that not one of them is
genuine.

184. The *First Epistle of Peter*

There are, however, many scholars who would say that at
least the *First Epistle General of Peter* is from the apostle. This
work professes to have been written by Peter to Jewish Christians in Asia Minor. It gives, with dignity, sound advice: to
Christians as citizens—"fear God, honour the king": to those
who are household servants: to husbands: to wives. The

expectation of the second coming of Christ was still strong when the book was written. "The end of all things is at hand: be sober unto prayer." There are in the book several references to the sufferings of Christ, whose Father (i. 3) "begat us again unto a living hope by the resurrection of Jesus Christ from the dead." But there is singularly little in common between this work and *Mark* or the other evangelists.

There is, however, one curious, surprising and noteworthy development of the early Christian tradition: it is that Christ put to death in the flesh, was quickened in the spirit (iii. 19–20), "in which also he went and preached unto the spirits in prison, which aforetime were disobedient, when the longsuffering of God waited in the days of Noah." This theme of the descent into hell is adumbrated a second time in the epistle (iv. 6): at a later date it became firmly embedded in Christian belief.

For the rest, the writer expects, or observes (iv. 12), an outbreak of persecution: he urges that, if any man suffers as a Christian, he need not be ashamed: "let him glorify God in this name." On the whole it seems probable, from the character of this short work, that it was written about the year A.D. 80, or somewhat later, by an unknown Jewish Christian.

185. The *Second Epistle of Peter*

The *Second Epistle General of Peter* is a shorter work which no modern scholar whose scholarship was not fettered by ecclesiastical loyalties would attribute to Peter. None the less, the author describes himself as Simon Peter, a servant and apostle of Jesus Christ: he states (iii. 1) that his work is "the second epistle that I write unto you." The substance of this letter conveys a warning to Christians generally, to whom it is addressed, to avoid moral laxity, false teachers and destructive heresies: it thus covers much the same ground as the so-called *Epistle of Jude*.

Both works refer to Sodom and Gomorrah, and to Balaam. They seem to have been written to combat the extravagant theology and the sometimes deliberate immorality associated with the gnostic movement of the second century of our era. Internal evidence shows that the *Epistle of Jude* is the earlier of the two booklets: comparison with other writings suggests that the date of *Jude* is about A.D. 130.

It is of great interest that in the so-called second epistle of Peter our author buttresses his teaching by a reference to the epistles of Paul. The passage runs (iii. 15–16): "And account that the longsuffering of our Lord is salvation; even as our beloved brother Paul also, according to the wisdom given to him, wrote unto you; as also in all his epistles, speaking in them of these things; wherein are some things hard to be understood, which the ignorant and unstedfast wrest, as they do also the other scriptures, unto their own destruction."

We see from this quotation that, when our author wrote, Paul's epistles, or some of them, had been collected and ranked as scripture. When did this happen? In §§ 217–20 we shall indicate the probability that no collection of letters ascribed to Paul was known before A.D. 100; and that our first definite knowledge of any such collection is in connection with a violent controversy raised by a famous early heretic named Marcion. Such history as we have of movements within the Christian society in the first half of the second century is sadly inadequate; and, in particular, we have to learn of heretics from authors who wrote to combat their views. But it would appear that Marcion, who went to Rome from Sinope in the north of Asia Minor about A.D. 140, made a collection of ten epistles of Paul. We learn from Tertullian (c. A.D. 155–c. 230), who wrote against Marcion about A.D. 207 (see § 216), that Marcion's theology was strongly disliked by the party which, by triumphing, became orthodox. The *Second Epistle of Peter* apparently warns the orthodox against Marcion and his friends: the tract will thus have been written about A.D. 150.

186. The transfiguration of Jesus

In the so-called *Second Epistle of Peter* there is an interesting allusion to the perplexing story of the transfiguration of Jesus. It reads (i. 16–18), "We did not follow cunningly devised fables, when we made known unto you the power and coming of our Lord Jesus Christ, but we were eye-witnesses of his majesty. For he received from God the Father honour and glory, when there came such a voice to him from the excellent glory, This is my beloved son, in whom I am well pleased: and this voice we ourselves heard come out of heaven, when we were with him in the holy mount."

The story of the transfiguration is given in *Mark* (ix. 2–8), and from him was copied by *Matthew* (xvii. 1–8) and *Luke* (ix. 28–36). There has been much speculation as to its origin and significance. Some scholars have surmised that it was part of a series of myths connected with the ascension of Jesus; and this surmise has gained not a little support from the discovery, first published in the year A.D. 1910, of a further large fragment in Ethiopic of a work, highly influential during and after the second century of our era, known as the *Apocalypse of Peter.* There are distinct resemblances between the *Second Epistle of Peter* and the *Apocalypse of Peter.* The latter, for instance, accepts the stoic doctrine of the final destruction of the world by fire: the *Second Epistle of Peter*, alone among the books of the New Testament, states (iii. 7 and 10–12) that to perish in a general conflagration will be the fate of "the heavens that now are, and the earth."

187. The *Apocalypse of Peter*

The *Apocalypse of Peter* is probably a work of the first quarter of the second century of our era. It was thus written some thirty years before the *Second Epistle of Peter*; and careful examination leads to the conclusion that the reference in the latter to the transfiguration of Jesus is probably a reference to the story as narrated, not in the synoptic gospels, but in the *Apocalypse of Peter.*

What makes this *Apocalypse* of exceptional interest and importance is that it gathers together, and arranges quite differently, incidents, discourses and stories that are familiar in other settings in the New Testament gospels. It will be remembered that, according to Eusebius, Papias recorded—his words are given in § 124—that it was not in proper order that Mark, the interpreter of Peter, wrote down the sayings and doings of Christ.

The fragmentary condition of the available manuscripts of the *Apocalypse of Peter* leaves us in some doubt, but it seems that, in the original form of this work, the risen Christ, seated on the mount of Olives, is approached by his disciples, who inquire as to Christ's second coming and the end of the world. In the reply we have the parable of the barren fig-tree and its explanation. This is followed by a vivid account of the destruction by

re at the day of judgment "of those who have fallen away
om faith in God and have committed sin"; and by lurid
etails of the punishment of the wicked. Subsequently "my
,ord Jesus Christ our King" said, "Let us go unto the holy
iountain." Moses and Elias appear. Peter asks, Where are
ie patriarchs?; and Jesus shows him the fragrant garden where
iey live. Peter, as in the gospel account of the transfiguration,
roposes to make three tents; but he is sternly rebuked. Sud-
enly comes the voice from heaven: and then the heavens open
nd receive "our Lord and Moses and Elias." "Thereafter
ras the heaven shut, that had been open. And we prayed and
rent down from the mountain, glorifying God which hath
ritten the names of the righteous in heaven in the book of
fe."

Obviously, at a time when such a narrative could be written,
ie gospel story, as we now have it, was not regarded as
uthoritative and final. There was, instead of it, a floating
radition varying from place to place, genuine recollections of
Christ's teaching being mixed with fanciful developments. It
ras from a mass of such material that the author of the gospel
ccording to *Mark* shaped his story. That story became
uthoritative after it had been used, together with Q, by
Matthew and *Luke*. But probably it did not secure its unchal-
enged position before, let us say, A.D. 120, when the *Apocalypse
f Peter* will have already been written.

88. The *Gospel of Peter*

Only a fragment of the *Gospel of Peter* exists. It uses traditions
ontained in all our four gospels and is the first account of the
rucifixion and resurrection of Jesus, alternative to the accounts
i the New Testament, of which we have knowledge. It was
robably written shortly before A.D. 150. Of much interest is
ie statement that Jesus on the cross, just before he died, said,
My power, my power, thou hast forsaken me." Of even
reater interest is the statement, "And when he had so said, he
ras taken up." The ascension of Jesus thus occurs at the
ioment of his death. It may be added that the writer of the
ook is elsewhere tinged with the strange fancy, the docetic
eresy widely prevalent in the second century, that neither
he sufferings of Jesus, nor therefore his body, were real.

o

In the resurrection story of the *Gospel of Peter* two angels ente
the sepulchre and after an interval three men come out, "tw
of them upholding the other, and a cross following after them.
An inquiry was heard from heaven, "Hast thou preached t
them that sleep?" And an affirmative answer came from th
cross itself, which is thus made to witness to the descent of Jesu
into hell!

189. The *Acts of Peter*

The *Acts of Peter* is a lengthy religious romance, probabl
written towards the close of the second century of our er;
Such works seem to have had a great vogue among Christia
people and were probably regarded as edifying forms of fictioı
The book throws two clear side-lights on disputed facts. In oı
place we read that "they brought unto Paul bread and wate
for the sacrifice"; and the context makes it clear that, by th
sacrifice, the eucharist is meant. There exists other evidenc
though it is somewhat slight, that at times water was usec
instead of wine, in the Communion rite.

Again, we have a lengthy account of the crucifixion of Pete
head downwards, and of how a certain Marcellus took the bod
from the cross and cared for it. Peter afterwards appeared t
Marcellus, apparently in a dream. The story ends, "And Ma
cellus awoke and told the brethren of the appearing of Pete
and he was with them that had been established in the faith ı
Christ by Peter, himself also being stablished yet more unt
the coming of Paul unto Rome." Significantly the Latin text–
there are several versions extant of the martyrdom—omits th
last sentence which, if it were accepted, would be decisiv
against the tradition that Peter and Paul were well-nig
simultaneous martyrs in the persecution of Nero after th
burning of Rome in A.D. 64.

CHAPTER XII

PAUL

90. Paul and other pioneers

IT is sometimes said that, but for Paul, the Christian church would not exist, that he transformed into the Christian faith he devotion to Jesus and the regard for his teaching held by, t most, a few thousand men and women. Some go further and ontend that Paul, in the course of his missionary activity, nade extensive use of pagan religious ideas and of a degenerate udaism; and that, while developing, he twisted and coarsened he message and influence of Jesus. There is some truth, but nuch exaggeration, in these contentions.

Though Jesus did not found the church, yet many others esides Paul gave energy and enthusiasm to create it. Paul was .either the first, nor the only, great Christian missionary: by the hances of history he is the best known. Others first carried he gospel from Jews to gentiles: others were Christian pioneers n the great capitals of (Syrian) Antioch, Alexandria and Rome. 'aul was not even a Christian when Stephen, the leader of Greek-speaking Christians in Jerusalem, was stoned: a legend epresents him as having taken charge of the clothes of the xecutioners while they were busied with their horrible task.

Likewise, for many years after his conversion, Paul worked ither in obscurity or as assistant to the more attractive, if less ble and eloquent, Barnabas. Late in life his powers matured. s his natural force grew, his personality became impressive, nd perhaps oppressive. Disputes marked his career: his reaching, which never lacked decision and strength, seems to ave become more bravely outspoken. In the end a challenge the Roman authorities sent him as a prisoner to Rome; and, tradition can be trusted, to a trial before the emperor's ribunal ending in his death.

91. Evidences for Paul's career

He who would write a life of Paul finds himself sometimes affled by lack of information and, more often, perplexed by

the quality of that which he has. We have, it is true, no les
than thirteen letters attributed to Paul: some of them ar
virtually treatises or collections of tracts. From the letters w
get fragments of autobiography. The *Epistle to the Galatian*
is most important by reason of what Paul says of himself
elsewhere in the epistles we are sometimes at a loss to knov
whether Paul is writing or whether some later admirer is usin
his name.

The later and larger half of the *Acts of the Apostles* is th
story of Paul's missionary activity. Where it is based on
diary kept by a travelling companion of Paul it is undoubtedl
good history of its kind. But the book of *Acts*, as we hav
seen reason to believe, was written more than a generation afte
Paul's death, and more than sixty years after the crucifixio
of Jesus. Its early information as to Paul is not always easy t
reconcile with that given in *Galatians* and elsewhere; and in ou
own minds we must sharply distinguish such information fron
facts to be regarded as certain. This caution applies also to th
statements contained in the long speeches attributed to Paul i
the latter half of *Acts*. These are speeches composed by *Luk*
after the manner of ancient historians. They are not authenti
discourses of Paul preserved by a reporter present when the
are spoken: they represent beliefs held by the writer of *Act*
about the year A.D. 100.

192. Paul's origin and circumstances

Paul was in many ways a typical Jew. He was given th
name of Saul, as was natural inasmuch as he belonged to th
tribe of Benjamin. But in Greek *saulos* meant waddling: i
described the gait of the tortoise and had other considerabl
less creditable associations. So Paul changed his name—he wa
neither the first nor the last Jew so to act—for the more aristo
cratic Roman appellation of Paul: we may recall that Sergiu
Paulus held the high office of proconsul of Cyprus when Pau
was in the island (*Acts*. xiii. 7).

Paul seems to have been born of a prosperous Jewish famil
in Tarsus of Cilicia: though this information comes solely fron
Acts, it may be deemed trustworthy. The only hints we have o
his relatives are that he was born a Roman citizen (*Acts* xxii. 28)
which implies that his father had this status, and that he ha

a sister's son in Jerusalem (*Acts* xxiii. 16). The sister's son was able to tell him of a Jewish plot, and so probably was not a Christian: his use of the information which he had acquired shows typical Jewish clannishness. In the closing chapter of the *Epistle to the Romans* there are salutations to, or from, half a dozen people in Rome who are described as Paul's "kinsmen"; but the word probably should be translated "compatriots."

Paul learned the craft of a tent-maker: it was usual for students of Jewish Law to have a trade. He speaks of working with his own hands (1 *Corinthians* iv. 12), much as a well-to-do clergyman or professor might speak of working in his vegetable garden: he was emphatically not one who could be described as a manual worker. He was, too, a townsman, probably a well-to-do child of the ghetto: throughout his writings there is no feeling for nature, no understanding of the beauty of scenery, none of our modern delight in the austere dignity of the eternal hills. But he showed no little success in raising, among his converts in the Levant, the money which he took as a peace-offering to Jerusalem.

93. Tarsus

Tarsus was an ancient city, which had been a provincial capital well before the time of Alexander the Great, while the Persians still controlled Asia Minor. Throughout the centuries of Hellenistic domination it seems to have remained a centre of civilization. Its prosperity doubtless fluctuated: it was the capital of Cilicia, and Cilician piracy was troublesome in the Levant seas until it was put down by Pompey in 67 B.C. In Plutarch's *Lives* (*Pompey* xxiv) we learn that the Cilician pirates "made strange sacrificial offerings at Olympus [one of their strongholds in Cilicia] and there performed certain secret rites. Of these rites, those of Mithra which they instituted continue to the present time." Plutarch wrote about A.D. 100. He apparently had little knowledge of the worship of Mithra, the Persian god who, as we said in our account of the mystery-religions, was to prove so formidable a rival to Christ in the second and third centuries of our era.

Strabo, of whom we gave some account in § 93, wrote about the time of the birth of Jesus and seems to have desired to set

forth a knowledge of political and physical geography such a
would be useful to the Roman who might become a provincia
administrator. In his *Geography* (xiv. 5, 13) he emphasized tha
Tarsus was an important centre of learning, and especially o
philosophy. Those fond of learning in the city were all natives
yet even for them it was a university from which men passed to
study elsewhere.

Of Tarsus and its culture we have a less favourable picture
in the *Life of Apollonius of Tyana* (i. 7). This biography, it wil
be recalled from § 140, was written by Philostratus and published about A.D. 220. Apollonius, who brought Pythagorear
sympathies to the reform of paganism, was born about the same
time as Jesus. As a young man he went to study at Tarsus; and
he must have been a student there when Paul was emerging
from childhood. Apollonius is said to have found the atmosphere
of Tarsus little conducive to the philosophic life: the students
are described as luxurious and jesters: they paid more regard
to fine linen than the Athenians paid to wisdom. When
Philostratus wrote, some two centuries must have passed since
the student days of Apollonius; but the biography was based
on much earlier material.

194. Paul's education

In such an environment Paul passed his youth. He learned
Greek in a Jewish home; and he was probably as familiar with
the language as with his native Aramaic. But it appears from
his writings that his Greek reading was the Septuagint, the
Greek version of the Old Testament, rather than classical
Greek authors. He had not absorbed Greek culture as had his
elder contemporary Philo (c. 29 B.C.–c. A.D. 50) at Alexandria.
Paul's style and his mode of thought were Jewish rather than
Greek. We miss in Paul the high and sustained level of careful
argument which we find in the great Greek philosophers.

195. Paul's civic status

Paul's family, as we have said, was well-to-do, possibly
wealthy. What was its civic standing? According to *Acts*
(xxi. 39) he described himself as "a Jew, of Tarsus in Cilicia,
a citizen of no mean city." This is in agreement with the
conclusion, already drawn from *Acts* (xxii. 28), that his father

in Tarsus had the status of a Roman citizen, a standing inherited by Paul. The claim to such citizenship is, however, never made by Paul in his letters. He stresses rather his Jewish origin, as in the *Epistle to the Philippians*, one of his latest writings (iii. 5): "circumcised the eighth day, of the stock of Israel, of the tribe of Benjamin, a Hebrew of Hebrews; as touching the law, a Pharisee."

Here any suggestion of alien citizenship is, perhaps too emphatically, ignored. For neither Paul nor his father could have possessed full citizenship at Tarsus without worship of the city gods. At most they could have possessed potential citizenship: that is to say, they could have become citizens on demand if they had been willing to be apostates from Judaism. Some scholars are inclined to think that such was their status. But we have the awkward fact that at the end of his career Paul, because of his claim to Roman citizenship, appealed successfully to be tried before the emperor's tribunal at Rome; and there is no evidence that potential citizenship would have given him any such right.

We seem forced to conclude that the father, and in youth Paul himself, had apostatized, had given due homage to pagan gods, and to the *genius* of the emperor, in order to secure full civic status. Many a Jew, before and since, has acted similarly in a non-Jewish environment. But, if Paul had passed through this phase, his temperament would probably have brought him intimately into the atmosphere of the mystery-religions. In this connection we may usefully remember, as we have seen in § 193, that Mithraism was of fairly long standing in Cilicia— it reached the province at least a century before Christianity— and that the language of the mystery-faiths recurs frequently in Paul's letters.

196. Paul's religious changes

If any such conclusions are true—and it is difficult to avoid them—Paul must also have had early in life a violent revolt from paganism, a revolt which brought him to the most uncompromising form of orthodox Judaism: he became a pharisee. Such a revulsion of feeling is in line with the tendency of the Jew to pass to extremes. It will have been, moreover, the anticipation of another dramatic change of allegiance in Paul's life whereby the pharisee, who persecuted the church, became a Christian.

In *Acts* (xxii. 3) Paul is made to say that, though he was born in Tarsus of Cilicia, he was a Jew trained in Jerusalem at the feet of Gamaliel, who is known to have been a rabbi of eminence belonging to the liberal school of Hillel. But, as we have repeatedly said, the author of *Acts* had little accurate knowledge of the earliest phase of the Christian movement. He makes the young Saul take an indirect part in the stoning of Stephen at Jerusalem; and goes on to say (ix. 2) that the young man obtained from the high-priest letters to the synagogues in Damascus authorizing him to bring, bound to Jerusalem, "any that were of the Way."

Such powers of action in a foreign city were in themselves most unlikely; that they should have been given to a quite young man is incredible. Moreover, though Paul several times says that he persecuted the church before his conversion, he also writes, in the autobiographical passage in *Galatians* (i. 17), that after his conversion near Damascus he did not "go up" (we should have expected "return") to Jerusalem and that (i. 22) some years later he "was still unknown by face unto the churches of Judaea which were in Christ." Obscurity hangs somewhat thickly over the youth and early manhood of Paul.

197. Paul's physical characteristics

What was Paul's personal appearance? The book called the *Second Epistle to the Corinthians* is (see § 222) an amalgam of at least two letters to which some extraneous matter has probably been added. It is highly probable, however, that Paul himself writes (x. 10) that "his letters, they say, are weighty and strong; but his bodily presence is weak, and his speech of no account." As against this low estimate of his oratory we read in *Acts* that, when Paul and Barnabas were at Lystra in Asia Minor, the natives (xiv. 12) "called Barnabas, Zeus; and Paul, Hermes, because he was the chief speaker." The fact that Paul normally employed an amanuensis and that, when he wrote in his own hand, he made "large letters" (*Galatians* vi. 11), suggests weak eyesight. The picture we construct from meagre information is that of a Jew from the Levant, ungainly, blear-eyed, quick of speech, with uncommon force of character, shrewd, able and ready for any emergency, with great powers of endurance.

198. The chronology of Paul's early life

When was Paul born? We cannot make even a guess which does not arouse misgiving. It is sometimes assumed that Paul was an almost exact contemporary of Jesus; but, as we shall see, it is more likely that he was as much as ten years younger. The chronology of his life, moreover, is perplexing.

After his conversion, as we learn from *Galatians* (i. 17), Paul spent some time in Arabia. "Then after three years" he went up to Jerusalem. "Then after the space of fourteen years" he went again to Jerusalem. Subsequently Cephas came to Antioch (ii. 11) where Paul "resisted him to the face." This none too amicable meeting must have taken place, as we have said, about the year A.D. 44: it can hardly have been later if we are to have enough time for all Paul's subsequent activities before he went to Corinth when Gallio was proconsul in A.D. 51–2. Yet, if we assume that the meeting with Peter at Antioch took place in A.D. 44, we must also assume that the fourteen years just quoted included the previous three years which we have mentioned. Even in that case we have to place Paul's conversion about the year A.D. 30, the martyrdom of Stephen in A.D. 28–9, and the crucifixion of Jesus in A.D. 26–7. The data of *Luke* lead many scholars to put the crucifixion in A.D. 29–30: a recent careful examination by an expert in ancient chronology leads to A.D. 33. Obviously no certainty can be reached: some of our data must be erroneous.

199. The conversion of Paul

It need hardly be said that, for the future of the Christian church, Paul's conversion was of immense importance. Seldom has the violently rapid psychological change which we term conversion had such far-reaching results. *Acts* gives three accounts of this spiritual crisis. The two later of these occur (xxii. 6–16 and xxvi. 12–18) in speeches attributed to Paul: the earlier objective account (ix. 3–9) tells in essentials the same story, which is familiar to every instructed Christian child. Paul is approaching Damascus when light shines round him:

he falls to the ground and hears a voice saying, "Saul, Saul, why persecutest thou me?" He replies, "Who art thou, Lord?" The answer comes, "I am Jesus whom thou persecutest." When he opened his eyes, he could not see for three days until a certain Ananias, a disciple at Damascus, laid his hands upon him. To the great crisis of his spiritual life Paul himself refers in *Galatians* (i. 15): he describes it as an occasion "when it was the good pleasure of God, who separated me, even from my mother's womb, and called me through his grace, to reveal his Son in me, that I might preach him among the Gentiles."

There is probably a reference to Paul's conversion in the *Second Epistle to the Corinthians* (xii. 2–4), "I know a man in Christ, fourteen years ago (whether in the body, I know not; or whether out of the body, I know not; God knoweth), such a one caught up even to the third heaven. And I know such a man (whether in the body, or apart from the body, I know not; God knoweth), how that he was caught up into Paradise, and heard unspeakable words, which it is not lawful for a man to utter."

There is no doubt that this passage was written by Paul —its style is typical—and that Paul is writing of his own experience. He uses the third person to give emphasis, just as Jesus used the term "the Son of man" of himself. Paul is, moreover, writing of his greatest spiritual experience, the experience which, as he believed, gave him both courage to triumph over persecution and weakness, and authority against those who challenged his teaching. A serious difficulty arises as to "fourteen years." The *Second Epistle to the Corinthians* is probably a collection of two or three documents, all written during the years A.D. 52–55. Paul thus seems to assign his conversion to about the year A.D. 40, at least six years later than the probable date. No plausible explanation of the discrepancy can be put forward.

Practically all text-books on religious psychology discuss Paul's conversion. It differed from normal conversion in that it does not seem to have arisen as the climax of a reaction against a life deemed sinful. It was rather the discovery that, in persecuting those who were "of the Way," Paul had made a profound mistake. With this discovery there went what he believed to be a vision of the risen Jesus, who was in future years to dominate his life: "I live, yet no longer I, but Christ liveth in me," as he writes in the letter to the *Galatians* (ii. 20).

There is no need to associate Paul's great experience with an epileptic attack: many of the quasi-medical discussions of what happened are more fanciful than wise. Paul's own language corresponded to the strangely confused background of his upbringing. In his letters he frequently makes perplexing statements; in fact, it is hardly an exaggeration to say that the more closely experts study his writings, the more difficult of interpretation do they find them.

We can, in connection with his conversion, with advantage emphasize that Paul gained, and knew that he could gain, nothing on earth by his acceptance of Jesus as the Christ, the Messiah. His whole life-history goes to show that he was honest in joining the ranks of those whom he had persecuted. There are probably legendary elements in the Lukan story, thrice told in *Acts*. But we have every reason to think that Paul in his letters described his great experience as truthfully as was possible to him. We need to remember that spiritual happenings must be expressed in words primarily devised to describe material change.

200. The first Christian years

According to the *Epistle to the Galatians* (i. 17), Paul, after his conversion, left Damascus for Arabia, probably for a period of quiet. He then returned for a three years' stay in Damascus. At the end of this period he went to Jerusalem and, of all the apostles, saw only Cephas (that is, Peter) and James, "the Lord's brother." Subsequently, according to his own story in *Galatians*, he went to Syria and Cilicia, where apparently he worked in obscurity for fourteen—the wording makes it possible that it was, in our counting, for thirteen—years. Then, with Barnabas and Titus, he went again to Jerusalem and (*Galatians* ii. 9) received "the right hand of fellowship"—the phrase suggests a form of reconciliation—from "James and Cephas and John."

Soon after "when Cephas came to Antioch" controversy between him and Paul broke out anew. Of this controversy and of the visits to Jerusalem and of Paul's earlier activity in

Damascus our authorities, as we have reiterated, give confused records. The story of the end of the stay at Damascus, as given in the second letter to the *Corinthians* (xi. 32–33), is not easily harmonized with that which we find in *Acts* (ix. 23–25). The visits to Jerusalem recorded in *Acts* xi and in *Acts* xv are, as we have pointed out in § 132, probably different versions of the same mission—which Paul himself describes in *Galatians* (ii. 1–10). What seems clear is that ultimately, after formulae of compromise between the Jewish and gentile sections of the growing Christian body had been accepted as satisfactory, further disputes arose. Between Paul and Peter, and apparently also somewhat later between Paul and Barnabas after the "sharp contention" described in *Acts* (xv. 39), there was no reconciliation. Neither Jerusalem nor Antioch could under such conditions be Paul's headquarters. He left Antioch for Asia Minor and Greece, working henceforth with subordinates and returning only once more to the Syrian capital.

201. Paul in Asia Minor

Asia Minor proved to be a region where missionary work flourished. In Paul's time, and somewhat later, it was at the height of its prosperity. The cities mentioned in the *Apocalypse* were, as archaeological researches show, wealthy and beautiful. Their flourishing commerce had attracted a large Jewish population, somewhat lax in its religious duties. Paul had previously (*Acts* xiii and xiv) journeyed with Barnabas through Phrygia and South Galatia: after their separation he returned to the same region. Working at first through the synagogues, and thus reaching proselytes in addition to Jews, he and his companions spread anew the Christian message and made further converts.

The writer of *Acts* records how, from time to time, the missionaries felt themselves moved by the Spirit: the sense of direct divine guidance, explain it how you will, was strong. Sometimes by deliberate planning, sometimes under a sense of pressure by a compelling spiritual Power, Paul and those with him travelled through Asia Minor, preaching the new faith with varying success. Finally, when they had reached the seacoast in the historic region of Troy, a vision appeared to Paul in the night (*Acts* xvi. 9), a man of Macedonia, standing and saying, "Come over into Macedonia, and help us." So Paul came to Europe.

202. Paul in Europe

We have already pointed out in § 132 that, with the determination to cross the sea to Macedonia, the famous "we-passages" of *Acts* begin. Henceforth the author of *Acts* had for his guidance a travel-diary kept by a travelling-companion of Paul, who was without doubt his physician Luke, a younger man of pagan origin. The diarist gives a vivid picture of the rebuffs and hardships endured by the missionaries: their pertinacity never failed, though their resources must often have been meagre. They constantly felt the pressure of Jewish dislike. They were frowned on, and at times ill-treated, by the Roman authorities. But, thrust out of one city, they carried their tactics and their message to another: their persistence was proof of moral, no less than of physical, courage. Paul had not the attractive grandeur, the compelling simplicity, of his Master; but no fair man, after reading what would seem to be genuine in the epistles ascribed to him and also the extracts from the diary which are enshrined in *Acts*, can deny that he was a constructive religious leader of outstanding eminence.

The experience of Paul and his companions (*Acts* xvi. 12–40) at Philippi, a Roman colony and the first important city at which they stayed in Macedonia, was in many ways typical. They preached at a place outside the gate by the river-side where women congregated—it may be that clothes were washed there; and they made a convert of a woman named Lydia, who probably had a prosperous, if small, business in dyes and cosmetics. With her they stayed—her house must have seemed a haven of rest—until the time came when Paul cured an hysterical or half-mad girl whose wild utterances were a source of profit to those who kept her. Then the profiteering protectors of the girl felt aggrieved. They brought the missionaries before the civic magistrates, who had them beaten with rods and put in prison. According to the story, the behaviour of Paul and Silas during an earthquake shock procured their release. The magistrates, moreover, were perturbed when they learned that the prisoners, whom they had publicly beaten, claimed to be Roman citizens. They told them to leave the city; and doubtless were much relieved when such disturbers of the peace set out for Salonica.

At Salonica, the mission appears to have had no little success with many devout Greeks and not a few important women. But the Jews of the city instigated a riot, and again Paul and those with him were brought before the "rulers of the city." They again, naturally, wished to be rid of such troublesome visitors; "and the brethren immediately sent away Paul and Silas by night unto Berœa."

203. The travelling missionary

Probably the missionaries passed into Europe in about the years A.D. 47–48. If Paul was an exact contemporary of Jesus he must then have been some fifty-four years old. It is hardly credible that a man well past middle life could have endured without a breakdown in health the sort of existence of which we have given a brief sample. We shall therefore be wise to assume that Paul was at least some ten years the junior of Jesus. Even so, he was about forty-three years of age when he passed to Europe. His powers of endurance must have been exceptional, or he would have collapsed under so wearing a life.

The details of Paul's journeys are only of interest as showing how the new faith was spreading a quarter of a century after the crucifixion of Jesus. The wandering philosopher, his teaching primarily ethical, was a familiar figure of the age: with his short cloak and his independent speech he was recognized as a citizen of the world, spreading culture and new ideas. Paul, to the casual passer-by, must have approximated to this type, as doubtless did Barnabas, Apollos and many another early Christian leader. A century later Justin Martyr, of whom we shall write in §§ 319–328, similarly travelled and taught, arguing not unskilfully, as we learn from his writings, in defence of Christianity.

204. Paul at Athens

After Paul and his friends had spent some time at Berœa, Jews from Salonica stirred up trouble and a hurried departure became necessary. The missionaries moved to Athens which even then, though Greece was woefully depopulated and poverty-stricken, was a university city of outstanding eminence.

We cannot honestly say that, in the time of Paul, Athens possessed philosophers worthy of lasting fame; but she was the city where Socrates, Plato and Aristotle had taught; and her reputation as a centre of speculative thought remained so long as regard for learning persisted in the Graeco-Roman world.

The account of Paul's visit to Athens is doubly interesting. On the one hand, the author of *Acts* makes it clear that the missionaries met with practically no success: the intellectuals of the age were scornful. On the other hand, we are given the sort of speech which *Luke*, writing about A.D. 100—it may even have been somewhat later—thought that Paul would have made. It is a speech midway between the primitive appeal of the Galilean missionaries in Jerusalem and the fully developed apologetic of writers like Aristides (see § 318) and Justin Martyr in the middle of the second century of our era.

Scholars point out that it is highly unlikely that Paul would, in fact, have seen an inscription (*Acts* xvii. 23) "to an unknown god." He might have seen an altar with no inscription, or he might have seen one inscribed "to unknown gods," set up by some person who wished to propitiate the divinities of a spot felt to be sacred. To pass, as Paul is made to pass, from popular deities to a vague theism was, however, common among educated people in the age of the Antonines (*c.* A.D. 120–180).

Luke, moreover, shows the growing interest in classical culture of the Christian society by making Paul quote "certain even of your own poets." The verse "in him we live and move and have our being" seems to be taken from a poem by Epimenides, entitled *Minos*. Epimenides, "one of themselves," is also the author of the disparaging remark about the Cretans, "always liars, evil beasts, idle gluttons," which is quoted in the *Epistle to Titus* (i. 12). Modern scholars, as we shall see in § 216, are generally agreed that this epistle "to Titus" is a writing of the middle of the second century of our era.

The words "for we also are his offspring" are to be found in a poem of Aratus of Soli in Cilicia—would not Paul naturally quote a fellow-provincial? Aratus, who lived somewhat earlier than 250 B.C., left two poems, one of none-too-good astronomy, and the other dealing with the somewhat unpromising subject of the weather. The poems had a wide and long-lasting influence: one was translated into Latin by Cicero. From Aratus, Virgil seems to have derived not a few of his stoic conceptions.

205. Corinth and Gallio

As Athens obviously offered no scope to Paul and his companions, they left it for the great seaport of Corinth, famous for its wealth and luxury, notorious for its vice. At this stage of their activity we get for the first time information which enables us to assign a definite date to particular events. We are told (*Acts* xviii. 2) that they found in Corinth a Jew of Pontus named Aquila, with his wife Priscilla, and that the pair had lately come from Italy because the emperor Claudius had banished all Jews from Rome. As we shall describe later in § 311, the historian Suetonius narrates that Claudius banished the Jews who "at the instigation of Chrestus continually raised tumults": the date normally assigned to his edict is A.D. 49. Further, we learn that Paul taught "the word of God" at Corinth for eighteen months; and that then, when Gallio was proconsul of Achaia, the Jews brought him before the judgment seat. Now there is an inscription at Delphi which goes to show that Gallio's term of office covered the second half of A.D. 51 and the first half of A.D. 52. Our dates thus seem to agree satisfactorily.

Gallio belonged to a family of Romanized Spaniards. He was a brother of Seneca (*c.* 4 B.C.–A.D. 65), the well-known stoic philosopher—perhaps we should say essayist and preacher—who was, by a strange chance, a tutor and afterwards the victim of the emperor Nero. Nero, dying before the age of thirty-one, left behind a record of infamy seldom, if ever, surpassed. Gallio was also an uncle of Lucan, the Latin stoic poet. The whole family fell under Nero's displeasure; and Gallio in A.D. 66 had to commit suicide because suspected by the emperor of conspiracy against him.

When Paul was accused before the proconsul, Gallio dismissed the charge in a short speech of barely veiled contempt; and *Luke*, commenting, gives us the oft-quoted saying, "And Gallio cared for none of these things." It is generally held that from Corinth, in about A.D. 51, Paul wrote whatever came from his pen in the two epistles to the *Thessalonians*.

206. Ephesus and Apollos

After his successful mission at Corinth, with its varied commerce and its cosmopolitan population, Paul crossed the Aegean to the great city of Ephesus. We are told very shortly (*Acts* xviii. 20–23) that from Ephesus after a brief stay he returned to Syria, and that after spending some time in Syrian Antioch, following possibly upon a visit to Jerusalem, he went anew to Galatia and thence to Ephesus once more. Such travelling, with the means of transport available to Paul, must have been protracted and exhausting. If we may judge by the fact that it is described by *Luke* in three fairly short sentences, the diarist was probably not in Paul's company when the long journey was undertaken. Some scholars think that *Luke's* sources were in confusion and doubt whether this particular tour was ever made.

What interests us especially, in connection with Paul's absence from Ephesus, is the brief reference to Apollos. Apollos, we are told, was a Jew of Alexandria, a learned man, "mighty in the scriptures." He had been instructed in the way of the Lord: "he spake and taught carefully the things concerning Jesus, knowing only the baptism of John." It would thus appear that in Alexandria a form of Christianity had sprung up differing as regards the sacrament of baptism from that of Paul. The latter, on his return, seems to have baptized, in the name of the Lord Jesus, some of the converts made by Apollos: he laid his hands upon them, and "the Holy Ghost came on them."

Obviously, behind these simple statements there lies the possibility of violent controversy and fierce rivalry: "I am of Paul: and I of Apollos." During the period of Paul's revised teaching and amplified sacramental practice, Apollos was absent from Ephesus, having gone to Greece. The impression left by the story, as narrated in *Acts*, is that the writer felt it necessary to indicate that, as between Apollos from Alexandria and Paul from Antioch, there were noteworthy differences; but that he wished, so far as possible, to say little of the inevitable friction to which they led.

207. The years at Ephesus

After Paul's return to Ephesus there followed a vigorous and successful missionary campaign, in the city and district, of some

P

three years' duration. Ephesus became a centre from which
converts began to carry their new faith to adjacent cities. While
at Ephesus at this time, possibly in the years A.D. 52–55, Paul
was distressed by controversies and moral disorders among his
Corinthian converts. Portions of several letters written by him
during his stay at Ephesus, together in all probability with later
material, comprise the two *Epistles to the Corinthians* which we
shall analyse later.

Paul's missionary activity in Ephesus was brought to an end
by a riot in the theatre, instigated by craftsmen who made
silver shrines of Artemis. Artemis—called Diana in the English
version of *Acts*—was a primitive goddess at Ephesus, who had
received a Greek name: her most sacred idol—should we say
dwelling-place?—was a meteorite "which fell down from
heaven." The fame of this deity was widespread; and the
commercial ramifications of her worship were extensive.
Christian converts were, of course, contemptuous of her silver
shrines; and from what we know of the later development of
Christianity we can be sure that, where possible, they avoided
food which had been offered to her or to any other pagan
deities. Some sixty years later, probably in A.D. 112, Pliny, as
imperial legate in the north of Asia Minor, had to deal with the
problem of the Christians. He makes it clear, as will be seen
in § 307, that at that time they had abandoned the temples and
took no part in pagan festivals, while the flesh of animals killed
sacrificially found among them no buyers. We can well
understand that religious fanatics, with the cry, "great is
Diana of the Ephesians," ultimately aroused in Ephesus such
hostility towards Paul that he dared not continue within its
walls. In peril of his life, he left the scene of his most successful
activity.

208. From Asia Minor to Jerusalem

There followed a visit to Macedonia and Greece. It would
appear that, while in Greece, Paul visited Corinth for the last
time. This visit can be inferred from the *Second Epistle to the
Corinthians* (xiii. 1). It will have taken place in A.D. 55–56; and,
during his stay, Paul will have written such parts of the *Epistle
to the Romans* as are genuinely his. A return to Macedonia was
followed by a sea-crossing to Troas. Then a voyage to some of

he islands of the Aegean finally brought Paul and his com-
anions to Miletus.

Ephesus, some fifty miles away from Miletus as the crow
lies, was too dangerous for Paul to venture into it. But he
ent for the leading men of the church at Ephesus to see him at
Miletus: and, if in *Acts* (xx. 18–35) we have Paul's own words,
he made to them a singularly moving speech: "And they all
wept sore, and fell on Paul's neck, and kissed him, sorrowing
most of all for the word which he had spoken, that they should
behold his face no more." It was the end of an epoch in Paul's
life: he never again saw the scenes of the missionary work of so
many years.

From Miletus Paul continued on his journey, travelling by
ea to Caesarea in Palestine and finally reaching Jerusalem for
his last visit. In Jerusalem he "went in with us unto James;
and all the elders were present." He gave a detailed account
of the success of his ministry; and, in reply, was told of the
thousands of Jewish converts recruited in Jerusalem, "all
zealous for the law." He was, moreover, asked, as being himself
a Jew, formally to associate himself with a vow (apparently
a Jewish purification rite) taken by four Jewish Christians and
to pay their incidental expenses.

There was evidently much anxiety as to whether Paul in the
mission field had completely abandoned Jewish customs. He
clearly was eager to emphasize his own loyalty to the Law;
and, "all things to all men," agreed to the suggestion made, and
"the next day purifying himself with them went into the
temple." When the seven days of the vow were almost completed, he was seen in the temple and accused of bringing Greeks
into the holy place. Jewish fanaticism in the first century of our
era was easily aroused, especially by an act which seemed to
profane the temple. Paul would undoubtedly have been
murdered had he not been rescued by the military tribune of
the cohort of soldiers which kept order in Jerusalem.

According to the story in *Acts*, Paul, as he was being brought
into the fortress—the tower of Antonia—where the Roman
garrison was kept, obtained permission to speak to the crowd;
and his speech is reported at considerable length. The incident
is almost certainly fictitious. To have allowed an address to an
infuriated Jewish mob by a prisoner, rescued from their clutches

by the hated Roman authorities, would have been to throw o[i]
on fierce flames.

209. Paul in custody

The story continues that the tribune, when Paul was i[n]
custody, ordered him to be examined by scourging; and tha[t]
then Paul claimed to be a Roman citizen by birth, and s[o]
exempt from the cruelties by which the Romans obtaine[d]
evidence from those who were not citizens. The claim wa[s]
allowed; and, in order to discover the cause of the tumult, th[e]
tribune called what was apparently a meeting of the sanhedrin[n].
It was disorderly: between Paul and the high-priest Anania[s]
there was recrimination; and in the end Paul stirred u[p]
dissension between sadducees and pharisees. He was remove[d]
lest he should be torn in pieces; and then, learning of a plot t[o]
assassinate him, the tribune sent him under a strong guard t[o]
Felix, the procurator of Judaea, at Caesarea.

As we read of the arrest of Paul, and of the subsequen[t]
proceedings in Judaea before he was committed for trial a[t]
Rome, we have to remember that, especially after the death o[f]
Herod the Great, Palestine was a distracted country. Judae[a]
from A.D. 6 was governed directly by the Roman procurator[.]
Other areas of Palestine under client-kings were indirectl[y]
subject to the authority of Rome. Everywhere, until thei[r]
ruthless overthrow by Hadrian in about A.D. 134, the Jews—
and they seem to have numbered about five millions—wer[e]
probably the most troublesome element within the Roma[n]
empire.

In Palestine their hatred for the conqueror was made wors[e]
because of social bitterness. The Romans favoured the uppe[r]
classes, predominantly sadducees: they who were thus favoure[d]
were the great landowners and from them the high-priest[s]
were chosen. The mass of the people sympathized with th[e]
pharisees, and wished a re-division of the land in accordanc[e]
with Mosaic Law. Quarrels were furious: a Jewish tendency t[o]
extremes constantly showed itself. Moreover, between th[e]
Romans and the Jewish populace there was no understanding[.]
The Roman procurators were continually exasperated; an[d]
consequently failed to show that administrative wisdom whic[h]
generally characterized Roman government.

The Christian movement during the first century of its exist-
nce must have appeared to the Roman authorities generally as
half-mad religious growth within a pestilentially troublesome
eople whose religion was an aggressive nuisance. All other
orms of faith within the empire co-existed in friendly rivalry.
he Christians, like the Jews, were uncompromising in their
epudiation of paganism as being false and idolatrous. But,
efore its destruction in A.D. 70, the Jewish authorities went so
ar as to offer sacrifices for the emperor in the temple at
erusalem: no equivalent sign of religious respect was forth-
oming from the Christians. Judaism was, and remained, even
uring the savage conflicts with Vespasian and Hadrian, a
olerated religion: Christianity seems never to have gained
uch a status until towards the end of the third century of our
ra.

10. Paul before Felix and Festus

Paul seems to have been the first man to bring the legal
osition of Christianity formally before the Roman judicial
uthorities. The scales were weighted against him from the out-
et. He was a Jew, claiming to be a Roman citizen; and at the
ame time he was the apparent cause of yet another of the never-
nding series of *fracas* and riots in Jerusalem and elsewhere, by
vhich the Roman procurators, legates and proconsuls were
estered.

The high-priest Ananias with a professional advocate went
o Caesarea to impeach Paul before Felix. We are given what
uke represents as the advocate's speech, together with Paul's
eply. Felix is somewhat surprisingly described as "having
nore exact knowledge concerning the Way": though he post-
oned his verdict he ordered that Paul should be treated
eniently. Subsequently, in company with his wife, Drusilla,
aughter of (Herod) Agrippa I, he sent again for Paul; but
gain remanded him, hoping now for a bribe. After two years,
aul being still in prison, Felix was succeeded by Porcius
estus.

From non-Christian authors we know not a little of Felix; and
vhat we know is unfavourable to his memory. He was a
rother of the freedman Pallas, who was financial secretary to
he emperor Claudius. The freedmen by whom Claudius

surrounded himself were clever and unscrupulous: by th
Roman nobility they were hated for their arrogance an
rapacity. Felix undoubtedly owed his appointment, in A.D. 52
as procurator of Judaea, to the influence of Pallas. In thi
position he not only, as *Luke* states, took bribes but, accordin
to Josephus, he was secretly in league with the assassins wh
killed the high-priest Jonathan. Even though his conduct wa
thus an affront to decent government, he retained his positio
because Pallas could shield him. But Claudius died in A.D. 54
poisoned by Nero's mother; and Nero removed Pallas early i
A.D. 55. We do not know when Felix had to give place t
Festus; but it is hardly likely that he lasted longer than, at th
most, three years after the protection of Pallas was withdrawn

At the beginning of the term of office of Festus, Paul wa
brought before him. Rather than be tried at Jerusalem, th
prisoner uttered the famous words, "I appeal unto Caesar."
Then followed, according to *Acts*, an examination of the case b
(Herod) Agrippa II, who was Drusilla's brother; and, onc
again, an impressive speech was made by Paul. The protracte
series of inquiries is said to have ended with Agrippa's verdic
(xxvi. 32), "This man might have been set at liberty, if he ha
not appealed unto Caesar."

211. The journey to Rome

In charge of a centurion, Paul and certain other prisoner
set sail for Italy, probably in, or shortly before, A.D. 58. Th
journey was unfortunate. The ship reached Crete; but, becaus
the harbour there "was not commodious to winter in," they se
sail again, ran into a gale in the south of the Adriatic and wer
finally wrecked on Malta. After a stay of three months in th
island, they made for Rome, *via* Syracuse and Puteoli. Pau
probably reached the capital not later than the spring o
A.D. 60. In Rome he "was suffered to abide by himself wit
the soldier that guarded him."

212. Paul in Rome

Within three days of his arrival in Rome, Paul is said to hav
called together "those that were the chief of the Jews." Th
story is most perplexing because, after a short address by Paul
the Jews said, "We neither received letters from Judaea con-

erning thee, nor did any of the brethren come hither and report
r speak any harm of thee." As we reflect upon this surprising
tatement, we remember that four or five years previously Paul
ad written his *Epistle to the Romans*, a letter of which the last
hapter is full of personal salutations. We remember, further
§ 205), that by A.D. 49 Christianity had made such progress in
Rome that the Jews were expelled by the emperor Claudius
because of the riotous disputes which arose. Doubtless they
eturned quickly enough, but so doubtless did the Christians
among them. Leading Jews in Rome must have heard of Paul
as a dangerous teacher with little regard for the Law. We are
herefore forced to conclude that the author of *Acts* had a quite
mistaken impression of the situation at Rome in about A.D. 60
—we must not forget that he wrote some forty years later—and
he cannot have known of the *Epistle to the Romans*. But, in fact,
he cannot have known of any of Paul's epistles. Had he had
uch knowledge, their composition, and the controversies and
anxieties which went with it, must have found a place in his
tory of Paul's life.

13. Paul's end

Acts ends with the words, "He abode two whole years in his
own hired dwelling, and received all that went in unto him,
preaching the kingdom of God, and teaching the things concerning the Lord Jesus Christ with all boldness, none forbidding
him." Of Paul's trial, of his fate, not a word!

Throughout the centuries Christians have found the abrupt
silence provocative. It was quite early assumed that at the end
of the two years he was acquitted. Remembering his expressed
intention in the *Epistle to the Romans* (xv. 28), "I will go on by
you unto Spain," those who assumed his acquittal believed that
he then travelled as a missionary to the western Mediterranean.
They further assumed that he subsequently returned to Rome, to
be engulfed in the persecution of the Christians by Nero which
followed the great fire of Rome in A.D. 64.

We have already quoted in § 182 the passage from the *First
Epistle of Clement* in which such highly speculative conclusions
are beginning to find a place. They are also hinted at in the
Second Epistle to Timothy (iv. 16) where Paul is made to say, "At
my first defence no one took my part, but all forsook me: may

it not be laid to their account." He adds—thereby emphasizin,
that a first defence led to a first acquittal—that the Lord stoo
by him, and he was delivered out of the mouth of the lion. Bu
neither of these two documents can be much, if at all, earlie
than A.D. 125: the *Second Epistle to Timothy* (see § 216) i
probably at least twenty years later.

There is little doubt that the author of *Acts* was aware that
when after "two whole years" Paul was brought to tria
probably in A.D. 62, he was condemned and executed. But, a
was said in § 131, our author had ended his first volume with th
crucifixion of Jesus by order of a Roman procurator: he did no
wish to end his second volume with the death of Paul, con
demned by the emperor's tribunal. His two volumes wer
designed to commend Christianity to the Roman authorities
There were certain awkward facts which he could not ignore
but, whenever possible, he laid stress on the friendly interes
or leniency of Roman officials. So at the end he leaves Pau
in honourable captivity, preaching the kingdom of God, non
forbidding him.

CHAPTER XIII

THE BOOKS ASCRIBED TO PAUL

214. The *Epistle to the Hebrews*

IN the New Testament there are fourteen books ascribed to Paul. Of these the *Epistle to the Hebrews* is certainly not his work. Different views as to its authorship existed in the early church; and in the end it was only ascribed to Paul because Jerome and Augustine, at the close of the fourth century of our era, were won over to the view that Paul wrote it. We have previously indicated its quality in §§ 109, 110.

215. The pastoral epistles

Three other epistles, two to *Timothy* and one to *Titus*, are commonly called the pastoral epistles. Many scholars, even to-day, claim either that they are genuine letters of Paul or that they incorporate genuine fragments of his correspondence. But in style and vocabulary they differ markedly from the main body of writings ascribed to Paul. If we turn over the pages of a dictionary of New Testament Greek, words occurring only in the pastoral epistles at once attract attention. Moreover, the subject-matter of these short works brings before us an organized church with a well-established discipline. The eager enthusiasm of earlier days has vanished. Faith is now acceptance of a tradition, to be firmly held against those who would change the bases of Christian teaching. "Sound doctrine" must be preserved against "itching ears." Foolish and ignorant questionings must be refused: from disputes of words come "envy, strife, railings, evil surmisings, wranglings of men corrupted in mind and bereft of the truth, supposing that godliness is a way of gain" (1 *Timothy* vi. 4–5).

Evidently the anonymous author who so wrote was waging war against the speculative and dangerously attractive theology of the second century known as gnosticism. But he was also afraid of more sober teachers whose influence he regarded as disruptive; and there appear to have been a number of preachers with whom financial gain was the main motive of their activity. Are such men ever absent from an organized church? The warnings and denunciations of the pastoral epistles are expressed in strong terms; but it is not fanciful to say that they lack the pungency of Paul's rebukes.

216. Their date

By reason of the fortunate wording of a charge, professedly addressed to Timothy, we can fairly accurately date the pastoral epistles—all three obviously come from the same source. There are, at the end of the *First Epistle to Timothy* (vi. 20–21), a couple of verses often quoted by amateur theologians, clerical and lay, who dislike such conclusions of science as contradict traditional beliefs. "O Timothy, keep that which is committed to thy trust, avoiding profane and vain babblings, and oppositions of science falsely so called: which some professing have erred concerning the faith." All translation involves interpretation; and the translation of the Authorized Version of the Bible just given leads to misunderstanding. The first verse may be rendered, "O Timothy, guard the deposit, avoiding impious verbiage and the *Antitheses* of *gnosis* [theological knowledge] falsely so called."

Now the most important, and possibly the most violent, of the controversies of the first half of the second century of our era centred round Marcion. Of this remarkable man we know not a little—and the worst—through his denunciation, in or after A.D. 207, by Tertullian in a book bearing the title, *Against Marcion*. Marcion, of whom we have written in § 185, was born in the north-east of Asia Minor, where his father was a Christian bishop. The chronology of his life is most obscure; but apparently he went to Rome about the year A.D. 140. The New Testament was not then in existence, though a number of its books were being accepted as authoritative.

Marcion set forth as Christian scripture a modified version of the *Gospel according to Luke* and a collection of ten epistles attributed to Paul. They were the epistles now generally received, which we shall shortly consider, save that the *Epistle to the Ephesians* was apparently termed the *Epistle to the Laodiceans*. Marcion justified his selection of scripture, and the theology which he based upon it, in a work termed *Antitheses*; and it is this work which "Timothy" is explicitly told to avoid. If we knew that an unknown Christian writer of the nineteenth century had warned his fellow Christians against dangerous speculations as to the origin of species, we could feel sure that his warning was later than A.D. 1859, when Darwin's book was published. Marcion's fate was that of other pioneers; and he was expelled from the church at Rome about A.D. 144. Evidently the so-called *First Epistle to Timothy* was written shortly after this date; and the other two pastoral epistles will have been written about the same time.

217. The *Epistle to the Ephesians*

If we reject as non-Pauline the *Epistle to the Hebrews* and the pastoral epistles, we are left with ten books of the New Testament which have been, until recently, commonly attributed to Paul. Of late years there has been increasing suspicion as to the *Epistle to the Ephesians*. As has been said, it does not appear under that title in the list of epistles attributed to Paul by Marcion. Study of it reveals that the writer elaborates the "high" doctrine of Christ developed in the *Epistle to the Colossians*. Neither its vocabulary nor its style are characteristic of Paul's writings, though there is not only a similarity of thought but also an occasional identity of language between *Ephesians* and *Colossians*.

We may go so far as to say that in places *Ephesians* is a mosaic of fragments of Paul. But its style lacks Paul's rugged force: some describe it as bad. Its laborious smoothness is to some extent concealed by translation; but long and involved sentences are retained. The writer makes Paul talk (iii. 4–5) of "my understanding in the mystery of Christ; which in other generations was not made known unto the sons of men, as it hath now been revealed unto his holy apostles and prophets in the Spirit." Such a sentence, or part of a characteristically clumsy sentence, is in itself, according to many scholars, enough to show that *Ephesians* belongs to a generation later than Paul.

We are then left with nine epistles, ascribed to Paul, which call for examination. At the beginning we must repeat what was said in § 132, that the author of *Acts*, writing about the year A.D. 100, or even a little later, shows no knowledge of any of these writings. Yet, as he tells us at the beginning of the gospel according to *Luke* (i. 3), he took pains to trace "the course of all things accurately from the first." We must, therefore, conclude that the nine epistles, so far as any of them were published, had no wide circulation. On the other hand, these epistles, plus the *Epistle to the Laodiceans* (*Ephesians*), were set forth for reading in church by Marcion about A.D. 140. We are thus forced to conclude that, in the first forty years of the second century, letters which Paul had written, possibly more than half a century earlier, were gathered together, and, having probably been joined to other material, were edited and widely published by some Christian enthusiast. Before the end of the second century they were generally accepted as inspired scripture.

218. The witness of the Apostolic Fathers

Outside the New Testament there are four early Christian authors, commonly called the Apostolic Fathers, who seem to have written before, or not long after, the middle of the second century. They are Clement, from whose *First Epistle* we have already (§ 182) quoted a much-used, though singularly vague, account of the labours and sufferings of Peter and Paul; Ignatius, to whom is ascribed a somewhat bulky series of letters, of which the texts differ remarkably; Polycarp; and a pseudo-Barnabas. There are also in the same period a work of fiction called the *Shepherd of Hermas*; fragmentary remains of Papias from which we have previously quoted; and, more important and probably earlier than any other of these writings, a Christian hand-book called the *Didache*. These works we describe more fully in chapter xiv. They have naturally been searched with the greatest care to see how far they quote from, and thus show a knowledge of, the epistles of Paul.

As will appear when the *Ignatian Letters* are discussed in §§ 260–264, their date and origin are so doubtful as to make them valueless as witnesses to the use before A.D. 150 of the epistles ascribed to Paul.

In the *First Epistle of Clement to the Corinthians* we read (xlvii), "Take up the epistle of the blessed apostle Paul. What did he write to you when he began to spread the gospel? With true spiritual insight he gave you his bidding about himself, and Cephas, and Apollos, because you had even then formed partisan groups." Here there is a definite allusion to Paul's *First Epistle to the Corinthians* (i. 12). We have, however, in § 182 seen fit to date the letter of Clement about A.D. 125; and, in the very chapter from which we have just quoted, Clement speaks of the "ancient church of the Corinthians."

In Clement's epistle there is another possible quotation, also from Paul's *First Epistle to the Corinthians*. We have (xxxiv), "For *the scripture* saith, Eye hath not seen, nor ear heard, neither have entered into the heart of man, the things which he hath prepared for them that wait for him." The writer may be referring to 1 *Corinthians* ii. 9, though equally he may have before him the source of a verse which is itself of the nature of a quotation.

In the *Letter of Polycarp to the Philippians* (iii) we read, "For neither I, nor any other such one, can come up to the wisdom of the blessed and glorious Paul. He, when among you, accurately and stedfastly taught the word of truth in the presence of those who were then alive; and also, when absent from you, wrote letters by studying which you can establish yourselves in the faith given you." Most scholars, however (see § 265), date Polycarp's letter a little later than A.D. 150.

In the work called the *Epistle of Barnabas*, probably written about A.D. 110–120, there occurs what seems to be the first quotation from a New Testament book with the authoritative formula, "it is written." The passage runs (iv), "Let us beware lest we be found *cast out*, as it is written, 'many are called, but few are chosen.'" It is to be observed, however, that the quotation comes, not from an epistle of Paul, but from the *Gospel according to Matthew* (xxii. 14).

Beyond the statements just made, it may be said that verbal resemblances between books of the New Testament and passages in the Apostolic Fathers are numerous. Such vague resemblances, unfortunately, are of little aid to critical scholarship.

A new era in Christian literature began with the rise of the cultured defenders of Christianity in the middle of the second century. When Justin Martyr (*c.* A.D. 105–165) wrote his *First Apology*, addressed to the emperor Antoninus Pius about A.D. 152, he cited the gospels with a frequency without earlier parallel. But he never mentions Paul; and (see § 319), though he says that the prophets and gospels ("memoirs of the apostles") were read at Sunday worship, there is no suggestion that the Pauline epistles were so used.

219. The nine " genuine " epistles

From the evidence thus before us, it appears that nine epistles of Paul, which Marcion seems to have given in the order, *Galatians*, 1 and 2 *Corinthians*, *Romans*, 1 and 2 *Thessalonians*, *Colossians*, *Philemon*, *Philippians*, were, together with *Laodiceans*, generally known and accepted by A.D. 140. All were practically unknown forty years earlier. They were probably collected and published about the end of the first quarter of the second century. This meagre knowledge—or surmise—makes us ask a whole series of questions to which no answers can be given.

Who gathered together these letters of Paul? Where had they been in the meantime? In what condition were they when they were prepared for publication? Were they tattered manuscripts? Were they in rolls or, as is more probable, in book form? Had scattered pages been tied up with other early Christian tracts, sermon-notes, or fly-sheets? How did the man, or men, who published the material determine what in it was actually from Paul: almost certainly there was nothing in his handwriting—he will only have autographed the concluding sentences in the earliest original of any letter.

Although none of these questions can be answered, it is well that they should be asked because too often it is assumed that an epistle, as we have it, must be entirely from Paul or entirely from some other source. We have, however, in fact no right to assume, save as the result of a careful examination of internal evidence, that even the best-attested epistle is, in its entirety, Paul's work.

220. Tests of authorship

Resemblance of style and language, it should be observed, is by no means decisive. Alien matter in Paul's epistles will have been written by men who, within half a century of Paul's death, were familiar with the religious thought and worship to which he had notably contributed. Paul wrote the popular Greek of his time, modified by the language of the Septuagint. The influence of the Septuagint remained with the early church: the form of popular Greek changed but slowly. Ideas,

in short, are a surer criterion of date than language. Ideas
reflect the influence of the changing social order. A church,
growing rapidly in a hostile environment, will change quickly
from within as it reacts to pressure from without: both its
organization and its thought tend to develop rapidly under
such circumstances.

All that is genuine in Paul's letters was written between, at
earliest, A.D. 48 and, at latest, A.D. 64: more probably such
material must be placed in the period A.D. 51–62. Now in their
English dress the letters show a deceptive uniformity of
language—in the Greek this uniformity is by no means
invariably present—and their range of ideas, which are sometimes so unintelligible as to seem irrational, is great. Is this
range not at times greater than we should expect from an
elderly man in the last dozen years of his life?

The upshot of our argument is that, while we can be certain
that the nine "genuine" epistles of Paul faithfully reflect the
changing thought of fairly representative Christians during the
last half of the first century of our era, we cannot with equal
certainty attribute to Paul all the teaching and advice which
they contain.

221. The two *Epistles to the Thessalonians*

We have seen that Paul must have arrived at Salonica about
the year A.D. 48–49. He probably reached Corinth about A.D. 50,
and left for Ephesus towards the end of A.D. 52. As we have
previously stated in § 205, it is thought that he wrote his first
letter to the *Thessalonians* when he was in Corinth about
A.D. 51. This letter is believed to be the earliest Christian
document, known to us, to which we can assign an approximate date. The letter, apart from a possible insertion which we
shall mention shortly, bears every mark of genuineness. It
opens with a salutation from Paul and his two fellow-mission-
aries, Silvanus and Timothy. At the very beginning (i. 3)
there is a reference to "your work of faith and labour of love
and patience of hope in our Lord Jesus Christ, before our God
and Father." In this passage we have the triad of Christian
virtues, faith, hope and love, which recurs in one of the most
famous passages in the New Testament (1 *Corinthians* xiii).
Paul then praises his Thessalonian converts because, notwith-

standing their "affliction," the ostracism and worse of Chris
tians in a pagan community, they were an example to othe
converts in Macedonia and Greece. He had wished to visi
them from Athens, but was compelled to send Timothy with a
message of comfort.

Then follows a strong blunt warning against sexual laxity
Such warnings against the low standards of social behaviour o
the pagan world recur throughout early Christian literature
They serve to emphasize, what we too easily forget, tha
Christianity was primarily a Way of life. Its strength lay in the
manner in which belief in God, and in Jesus as His Christ, wa
combined with an inspiration to clean and kindly living.

As we read Paul's epistles, we are too apt to concentrate
attention on theological teaching which may border on the
absurd; and on religious expectations which proved false. Such
teaching and such expectations existed; but the essence of the
gospel was something quite different. It was the belief ir
God which Jesus had taught. This belief was combined
with reverence for Jesus, who had sealed his own faith
by his death and whose Spirit was with his followers. Belie
and reverence were expressed in high standards of persona
conduct.

Paul, in this his first known letter, unless indeed (iv. 15–v. 4)
is an intrusion by a later writer, wrote at no little length as to
the second coming of Christ, which he expected almos
immediately. "The dead in Christ shall rise first: then we tha
are alive, that are left, shall together with them be caught up
in the clouds" (iv. 16–17). "The day of the Lord so cometh as
a thief in the night." In spite of this mistaken expectation, the
letter shows Paul as a wise, kindly leader, with a warm persona
regard for the little congregation which he has gathered
together, "working night and day that we might not burder
any."

The *Second Epistle to the Thessalonians* opens with practically
the same salutation as the first letter. But it lacks the persona
warmth of the first epistle and might have been written by one
who had studied that letter. Whoever was its author, he
wished to emphasize some aspects of the earlier advice and
teaching and, in particular, to give fuller instruction as to the
second coming of Christ. The belief that the Lord Jesus would

oon come again was widespread in the early church; and there
an be little doubt that it was frequently the subject of preach-
ng and of short tracts or fly-sheets. One such was probably the
pasis of what is called "the little apocalypse" (*Mark* xiii).
Possibly another was used in chapter ii of our second letter to the
Thessalonians. The day of the Lord will, we are told, not be,
"except the falling away come first, and the man of sin be
evealed." Many smile at these fantastic expectations. But
hey tend to revive in Christendom in every period of great
listress. Is such revival not to be expected? All Christians
pray daily for the coming of the kingdom of God on earth.
When its coming seems hopeless, there arises an eager desire,
a confident expectation, that God will exert His power and the
Lord descend from heaven.

22. The two *Epistles to the Corinthians*

So far as can be estimated, Paul was at Ephesus, the scene
of his most successful missionary work, during the years
A.D. 52–55. During these years a crisis in the Corinthian church
arose and Paul wrote several letters to the Corinthians. In
connection with the crisis, we must admit that the sequence of
events, and the number and nature of the letters written, leave
room for argument and doubt. It would seem clear, however,
hat there was a "previous epistle," now wholly lost, to which
reference is made in 1 *Corinthians* (v. 9–11). "I wrote unto you
in my epistle to have no company with fornicators . . . but now
write unto you . . ." At a later time, in some anxiety as to
he position at Corinth, he wrote what is genuine of our *First
Epistle to the Corinthians*.

Then it would appear from 2 *Corinthians* (ii. 1–11) that Paul
paid a second visit to Corinth, unrecorded in *Acts*, which ended
most unpleasantly. On returning from this visit he wrote a
"severe" letter, of which the latter part only is to be found in
chapters x–xiii of the *Second Epistle to the Corinthians*. In the
chapters which seem to belong to this "severe" letter he says
twice over, (xii. 14) and (xiii. 1), "This is the third time I am
ready to come (I am coming) to you." The "severe" letter was
carried by Titus: the messenger was able to bring back better
ews; and in profound thankfulness Paul sent a letter of
econciliation which is now to be found in 2 *Corinthians* (i–ix).

Q

This last letter seems to have been written after he had left Ephesus.

We infer these facts chiefly from two passages in the letter. In the first place we read (2 *Corinthians* ii. 12–13), "When came to Troas for the gospel of Christ, and when a door was opened unto me in the Lord, I had no relief for my spirit, because I found not Titus my brother: but taking my leave of them, I went forth into Macedonia." In the second place we read in 2 *Corinthians* (vii. 13), "We have been comforted: and in our comfort we joyed the more exceedingly for the joy of Titus, because his spirit hath been refreshed by you all." The sense of happy relief in 2 *Corinthians* (i–ix) is in strong contrast to the anxiety and self-assertive despondency of the second part of the same epistle; and the only way of explaining the contrast seems to be to assume that two letters (or parts of letters) have been joined together in the wrong order. This assumption is now fairly generally accepted.

In itself, perhaps, the number of the letters to the Corinthians is not an important matter. But it is highly significant that many of our best scholars agree that in the *Second Epistle to the Corinthians* there has been a serious dislocation of manuscripts. If in this second epistle two letters, one of them mutilated, could have been joined together in an order opposite to that in which they were written, stray documents might equally well have been thrust into another letter of Paul, to make the long and very varied document which we call the *First Epistle to the Corinthians*.

223. The *First Epistle to the Corinthians*

This work is one of the most important documents of the New Testament. If it only contained the great Praise of Love (chapter xiii), it would be noteworthy. But it gives important teaching (chapter vii) with regard to sex, marriage and divorce. We find advice (chapter viii) as to the eating of things sacrificed to idols. There is a highly significant parallel (chapter x) between the bread and wine of the eucharist and "the things which the Gentiles sacrifice." In chapter xi there are somewhat surprising arguments with regard to men and women at worship. The same chapter, moreover, contains what is often asserted to be the earliest record of the Last

Supper: the record contains an account of the words attributed to Jesus which includes the command, "This do in remembrance of me." Then we have in chapter xii a varied list of spiritual gifts and in chapter xv what we can best describe as a short tract on the resurrection of Christ and his followers. Finally, in the last chapter we have personal touches: a collection for poor Christians, Paul's plans, a friendly reference to Apollos, and a final "salutation of me Paul with my own hand."

224. Is the *First Epistle to the Corinthians* composite?

The question as to whether all the varied teaching just mentioned comes from Paul is highly controversial. The controversy is sharpened by the fact that, as regards the Last Supper, the evidence of the manuscripts makes it clear (see § 288) that the original text of *Luke* has been expanded by use of the passage in 1 *Corinthians* xi: thus not one of the gospels originally stated that Jesus said, "This do in remembrance of me." If the account of 1 *Corinthians* xi was actually written by Paul about the year A.D. 54, such a vital omission in all three synoptic gospels is extremely hard to understand. Further, the total omission of any record of the Last Supper, in such a book as the fourth gospel with its emphatic sacramental teaching, is inexplicable; and, moreover, the form of prayer at the eucharist given in our earliest Christian service book, the *Didache* (see §§ 244–251), which apparently dates from the end of the first century, is completely bewildering.

We shall later in chapter xvi discuss teaching ascribed to Paul in connection with the origin and nature of the eucharist; but plainly we should be less perplexed could we assume that in the first place developments of worship, associated with the "breaking of bread," led to the story given in *Mark*. We can imagine that this story was subsequently accepted with variants by *Matthew* and *Luke*, editorial additions of the second century being in all cases possible. Some Christian late in the first century may have given his development of the same story in a tract ascribed to Paul. This tract with alterations must ultimately have been joined to the Corinthian letters and will have become the central portion (verses 17–34) of 1 *Corinthians* xi.

225. A tract on the resurrection?

There are other signs that early tracts or fly-sheets, written one or two generations after Paul but ascribed to him, have gone to make up some of the very varied chapters of the *First Epistle to the Corinthians*. Take, for instance, the teaching as to the resurrection which finds a place in chapter xv of the epistle. Incidentally we read, "If after the manner of men I fought with beasts at Ephesus, what doth it profit me?" (1 *Corinthians* xv. 32). Paul, writing from Ephesus, would never thus have spoken of an experience there. Moreover, as a Roman citizen, he would not have been condemned to face wild beasts in the arena. It may be argued that Paul used a surprisingly violent metaphor, and that he wrote from some country place outside Ephesus. But, much more probably, the verse is due to some follower who, many years after Paul's death, exaggerated his perils and forgot that the *First Epistle to the Corinthians* was written from Ephesus.

Furthermore, the account of the post-resurrection appearances of the risen Christ includes an appearance to "above five hundred brethren at once, of whom the greater part remain until now, but some are fallen asleep" (xv. 6). Here is evidence for the fact of the resurrection which, by reason of the number of witnesses, is far more conclusive than we get elsewhere. Had such an account been authoritative in Paul's teaching in A.D. 54, the gospel records, as we have argued in § 172, would not have been as meagre as they are.

As a third argument we may recall that it is most unusual for Paul to show any sign of classical Greek culture: few scholars believe his speech at Athens to be genuine. But, in the chapter which we are now considering, the verse (xv. 33), "Evil company doth corrupt good manners," is thought to be quoted, as we have said in § 41, from the poet Menander (*c.* 320 B.C.).

As a fourth consideration we may mention the appearance of the risen Jesus to "the twelve": the writer has forgotten the treachery of Judas Iscariot.

We are thus tempted to attribute our resurrection tract to some early second-century Christian apologist.

226. Other documents included in the epistle

In the varied teaching with regard to matters connected with sex that we find in chapter vii, there is much to suggest that we have rules and advice which are not the answer to problems raised by a group of newly made converts, but directions needed by a church established for some considerable time. There is, in particular, a passage of great difficulty in I *Corinthians* (vii. 36–8), relating to "virgins." It runs:

> But if any man thinketh that he behaveth himself unseemly toward his virgin *daughter*, if she be past the flower of her age, and if need so requireth, let him do what he will; he sinneth not; let them marry. But he that standeth stedfast in his heart, having no necessity, but hath power as touching his own will, and hath determined this in his own heart, to keep his own virgin *daughter*, shall do well. So then both he that giveth his own virgin *daughter* in marriage doeth well; and he that giveth her not in marriage shall do better.

Here the revisers in their translation have wrongly inserted the word "daughter." Almost certainly the writer of the passage is alluding to a queer practice of "spiritual marriage," in which a man and woman lived together as celibates. This custom existed in the Christianity of the second and third centuries; but it was an ascetic growth which could hardly have arisen at the very beginning of the spread of the Christian faith.

In chapter x we have a tract on food sacrificed to "demons," in other words, to the gods of paganism. The tract begins with strange and most fanciful Judaic parallels to baptism and the eucharist—there are a few verses which one critic unkindly terms "sacramental babbling"—and it ends with an assertion of Paul's virtuous conduct, "Be ye imitators of me, even as I also am of Christ," which tends the more to cast doubt on its authenticity. An elaborate parallel between food offered to idols and that of the table of the Lord, between the cup of the Lord and the cup of devils, suggests a somewhat prolonged influence of pagan cults on Christian worship.

The fact that the so-called *First Epistle to the Corinthians* is composite is perhaps most clearly brought out by the advice given as to women and preaching. In I *Corinthians* (xi. 5) we are told that, "every woman praying or prophesying with her head unveiled dishonoureth her head : for it is one and the same thing as if she were shaven." In 1 *Corinthians* (xiv. 34) we read, "Let the women keep silence in the churches : for it is not permitted unto them to speak." The two passages are irreconcilable ; and the efforts of commentators to reconcile them are more ingenious than convincing.

Finally, it is worth while to draw attention to the famous "Praise of Love" (chapter xiii). Nothing could be less like Paul's tumultuous flow of words than this carefully written prose-poem. Quite possibly it was inspired by Paul's salutation in his first letter to the Thessalonians (i. 3), "your work of faith and labour of love and patience of hope." But much skill and care went to its writing : it shows a literary excellence which is not found in any other passage attributed to Paul. Moreover, the phrase (xiii. 2), "though I understand all mysteries and all *gnosis*," suggests, not Paul's early preaching of Christianity, but repudiation of claims of leaders of the gnostic movement of the early part of the second century of our era.

What, further, are we to make of the words, "if I give my body to be burned"? Burning was not a Roman punishment for those who refused to worship the State gods, and Paul was in no danger of such a fate. To some scholars the phrase recalls a story, *The Passing of Peregrinus*, told by the satirist and public lecturer, Lucian of Samosata. Peregrinus seems to have been a religious adventurer who ended his career by burning himself alive about A.D. 165, shortly before Lucian wrote. It may be recalled that Lucian tells us that Peregrinus for a time belonged to the Christians : they repudiated him after he had been seen to eat what were probably pagan sacrificial meats.

We may well doubt Paul's authorship of the "Praise of Love." But, whoever was its author and whenever it was written, it must speedily have become a favourite passage for reading in churches ; and its inclusion in a composite group of writings ascribed to Paul was natural.

227. The *Second Epistle to the Corinthians*

Possibly the *Second Epistle to the Corinthians* is not, to anything like the same extent as the first letter, an amalgam of writings by persons other than Paul. Much in it seems to have the true ring of Paul's voice.

In chapters x–xiii, which were, as has been suggested, originally part of the "severe" letter, Paul vigorously defends himself against critics who sought to minimize the importance of his work and his status in the Christian movement. "I reckon," he says (xi. 5), "that I am not a whit behind the very chiefest apostles." He enumerates the perils and suffering that had been associated with his ministry. There is a reference (xi. 32–33) to an escape through a window in the city wall of Damascus which (see § 200) in detail differs from the story in *Acts* (ix. 23–25). The mention of Damascus leads Paul naturally to a recollection of that revelation of the Lord which, as he asserts, had been granted to him fourteen years before he wrote. To this perplexing dating we have already referred in § 199.

As has been already stated, the first nine chapters of the Second Epistle form the substance of Paul's final letter to the Corinthians. They belong to a letter of reconciliation, probably written from Macedonia about the year A.D. 55, after Paul had left Ephesus. This letter is especially remarkable for the Christ-mysticism which occurs in the latter part of chapter v (14–19). It is barely intelligible, yet contains sentences which will probably endure as long as Christianity. "We henceforth know no man after the flesh: even though we have known Christ after the flesh, yet now we know him so no more. Wherefore if any man is in Christ, he is a new creature: the old things are passed away; behold, they are become new. . . . God was in Christ reconciling the world unto himself."

228. The *Epistle to the Galatians*

The Galatians were descendants of Celtic invaders who thrust themselves into western parts of Asia Minor about 275 B.C. But the Roman province of Galatia included not only these Celts in its northern half, but also an older Phrygian-Lycaonian population in its southern half, where were such towns as Lystra and Derbe. There is much dispute as to where the converts lived to whom Paul wrote. Before his letter was sent, he *seems* (iv. 13)—the evidence is not conclusive for "the first time" may more accurately be "originally"—to have made at least two journeys to these converts. If they lived in northern Galatia, this fact would apparently imply that his visits were those mentioned in *Acts* (xvi. 6) and *Acts* (xviii. 23). The

Epistle to the Galatians may then have been written about the year A.D. 55, shortly before the final letter to the *Corinthians*. The similarity between *Galatians* and the *Epistle to the Romans* makes many scholars ready to accept this date.

It should, however, be said that a reference in the letter (ii. 13) to Barnabas, as though he were personally known to those to whom the letter was addressed, suggests that it was written to southern Galatians, who were visited twice (*Acts* xiv) while Paul and Barnabas were still working together: it may, then, date from within the period A.D. 48–52, and so is possibly the earliest writing of Paul that has survived. In any event it is the most personal of all the letters ascribed to Paul. Its language is strong and direct: one passage (*Galatians* v. 12) in a controversy as to the necessity of circumcision, shows an anger that does not escape coarseness, "I wish that those who are unsettling you would proceed from circumcision to self-mutilation."

Paul is primarily concerned to defend his own authority. He is, he says at the outset, an apostle, not from men neither through a man, but through God and Christ, Christ who gave himself for our sins to take us out of this present evil world, and whom God raised from the dead. In a sentence we are thus given the man and his message. Paul proceeds to claim that the gospel which he preached was not received from man, but came to him directly by revelation of Jesus Christ. He then writes of his conversion and of the years which followed, during which "the gospel of the uncircumcision" (ii. 7) was committed to him. This leads naturally to an account of the disputes with Peter at Antioch; but the blaming of Peter loses itself in a statement that men are "justified," not by "works of the law" (ii. 16), but by faith in Christ.

229. Paul and Judaism

The dispute as to whether Christian converts need be circumcised died a natural death as Christianity separated itself from Judaism; but it evidently and inevitably led to no little tension while it lasted. It was associated with the larger issue as to whether Christians were subject to the Law of Moses, which was alike the binding force of Judaism and the essence of the teaching of the rabbis. In *Galatians*, and more elaborately in *Romans*, Paul argues against the Law: he is vehement, sometimes unfair and, it must be added, sometimes unintelligible. The essence of his argument is that Abraham, four hundred and thirty years before the Law came into existence, was justified by faith: he believed God and it was counted to him for righteousness. The blessing of Abraham can, therefore, come upon gentiles through faith in Jesus Christ. "If ye are Christ's, then are ye Abraham's seed, heirs according to promise" (iii. 29).

In chapter iii of *Galatians*, Paul thus sets faith in Jesus Christ in opposition to the Law: in chapter vii of the *Epistle to the Romans*, he considers the connection between sin and the Law. There are probably no passages in all the writings ascribed to Paul from which the Christian humanist of the modern world finds himself so alienated. To the humanist the opposition between faith and law, of which so much is made in *Galatians*, is largely unreal. There were in the Mosaic Law a number of food regulations and ritual observances that might well, together with the rite of circumcision, have been set aside by Paul's converts as troublesome or trivial, and unnecessary. But, to the Jew, his Law was a scheme for wholesome and happy living. He could say truly that he took delight in the commandments of the Law. At its base was a fine monotheism. It embraced a strict and lofty moral code. Jesus had said of the Law that he came not to destroy but to fulfil; and his attitude might well have been an example to Paul. To every student of early Christianity Paul is a perplexing figure; and one of the most perplexing aspects of his personality is that he, who claimed that he had been a strict pharisee, should have become so hostile to the religion of his people that he could write of being "redeemed from the curse of the law" (*Galatians* iii. 13). The pious rabbi or strict pharisee was not a man who, naturally and almost of necessity, combined hypocrisy and arrogant fanaticism with ritual trivialities: he was, because of the Law, clean-living and honourable, kindly and charitable. The Law taught him to be a lover of things pure and true and beautiful: he could smell the rose and thank God for its fragrance. Paul in his polemic seems to have forgotten such fundamental facts.

230. The invective against the Law

The situation is worse in the *Epistle to the Romans*. There Paul actually brings himself to say that the Law leads to sin. "I

had not known sin, except through the law: for I had not
known lust, except the law had said, Thou shalt not lust"
(*Romans* vii. 7). He had previously written (v. 13), "Until the
law sin was in the world: but sin is not imputed when there is
no law." And he had added (v. 20), "The law came in beside,
that the trespass might abound; but where sin abounded, grace
did abound more exceedingly." Some scholars have surmised
that such teaching, which must needs largely apply not only
to the Mosaic Law but to all law, cannot have come from a
Jew carefully brought up in the traditions of his people. It
must be due, they think, to some man of a primitive mentality,
whose speculations with regard to social conduct were as
confused as those of an untaught adolescent grappling with a
fundamental philosophical problem.

We have, of course, to remember that Paul found himself,
as he thought, in a difficult position. To the Jew a crucified
Christ was a stumbling-block. Paul had to justify the death of
his Lord. If he allowed that righteousness came through the
Law, "then Christ died for nought" (*Galatians* ii. 21). The
notion that innocent suffering in itself had a redemptive power
seems never to have lodged in his mind. So he denied the value
of the Law; and he pressed home his denial by asking his
Galatian converts whether they "received the Spirit by the
works of the law, or by the hearing of faith" (iii. 2).

This strange teaching seems to assert that a good life does
not lead to possession of the Christ-Spirit. Men are, on the
contrary, said to be "justified" by faith. They are (*Galatians*
iii. 26) "sons of God, through faith, in Christ Jesus."

Paul states (ii. 20) that he lives in faith, "the faith which is
in the Son of God, who loved me, and gave himself up for me."
To the Galatians he describes the certainty that was his, and
the experience that had led to it, in the words, "I have been
crucified with Christ; yet I live; and yet no longer I, but
Christ liveth in me" (ii. 20). Apparently various metaphors,
"to be in Christ," "to put on Christ," "to feel Christ dwelling
in one," mean the same certainty that a profound spiritual
change has taken place. Paul asserts *tout court* that it results
from baptism, to which he attaches a mechanical and magical
efficiency: "As many of you as were baptized into Christ did
put on Christ" (iii. 27).

31. Paul and humanism

All such teaching as we get in *Galatians*, and it is even more highly developed in the *Epistle to the Romans*, is, of course, repellent to the modern Christian humanist who views the world as it is described by men of science. Such a man sees the majestic sweep of evolution slowly leading to higher types of life, as God reveals Himself in creation. The varied splendour and beauty of nature, to which man himself belongs, witness to the greatness of the indwelling Spirit, alike immanent and transcendent. With such a vision a man can rise above his failures; and, as he fixes his gaze on the triumphs of an illimitable future, is drawn to God Whose law controls the universe. So a divinely based optimism expresses his reaction to the world to which he belongs. The man gives of his best that he may work with and for his Creator. In his life good works are good service. He accepts law as the obligation to right conduct. Is such an one more remote from Jesus, the Christ, than the writer of *Galatians*?

In the teaching ascribed to Paul profound pessimism is coupled with strange arguments and irrational beliefs. Yet, curiously, it has left an indelible mark on Christian theology; and it tends to revive in periods of exhaustion and despair. Apparently, in its repudiation of the necessity of good works, it corresponds to some deep-seated religious craving in man. Paul, or whoever wrote in his name, knew the nature of the satisfaction reached in a common type of conversion. The spiritually anxious sinner suddenly finds his soul flooded by light and happiness: the indwelling Christ has come. He has been saved, not by works, but by faith. The gift is so great that his former struggles and strivings for a higher life are forgotten: he almost exults in the desperate wickedness of his unregenerate days. He cannot explain what has happened and delights in the thought that his whole experience is irrational. He proclaims that God is beyond reason.

Yet in the end contact must be established between such ecstasy and ordered religious life: explanation or dogma must link the convert to his church or group. The moral dangers of such an experience and of the dogma which may be associated with it are obvious. Paul and his associates were well aware of them; and they were never weary of warning their converts

against evil living, and of inculcating what we now call th
Christian virtues. The *Epistle to the Galatians* virtually ends with
a detailed warning against the works of the flesh (v. 16–24
followed by wise and kindly exhortations to well-doing (v. 25-
vi. 10).

232. The *Epistle to the Romans*

As we have said in § 208, Paul probably wrote the *Epistle t
the Romans*, or such part of it as came from his pen, from
Corinth in A.D. 55–6. Some scholars would put the date two
years later. Paul had never visited Rome; and we know
nothing of those who first carried Christianity to the capital
of the empire. But, beyond a doubt, Christianity spread like a
contagion among the disinherited, the unhappy proletariat, o
the ancient world. "The kingdom of God is coming. Change
your hopes and your way of life. Believe the good news"—
such appear to have been watchwords to which oppressed and
anxious people, whose lives were drab and uncertain, eagerly
turned. God's anointed had appeared in Judaea. Though
he—the Christ—had been crucified for saying that he was king
of the new kingdom, he was still alive: his Spirit was active
among his followers. Soon he would come again with power
and great glory.

The message spread by its own momentum; and, wherever it
went, men and women began to prepare themselves for the new
order. For many decades the expectation of the immediate
return of Christ was strong. Even when it began to fade away
a resolve to create the new kingdom remained vigorous: those
among whom it was shared naturally formed groups whose
manner of life was a common bond. Whether they had for the
most part any theology, such as the letters ascribed to Paul set
forth, is most doubtful. They had inherited Jewish monotheism
as expressed in the Septuagint, the Greek translation of the Old
Testament. But a manuscript copy of this work, if in small
volumes, must have been a bulky series of books; and few will
have possessed it. Apart from a theological background thus
inherited, early Christians will all have believed in the presence
and power of the Spirit of Jesus the Christ. They knew that God
had raised Jesus from the dead, because they felt him to be
with them at their gatherings and in their lives. Thus there

came first the hope of the new kingdom: then came the certainty of the presence of the Spirit of Christ: only at a later stage was a specifically Christian theology formulated.

33. Christian morality

Far more important than a common theology was a common way of life. We tend to take for granted, and to pass over as uninteresting, the moral exhortations which recur with such frequency and force in the New Testament. But the new standards of life quietly became the distinctive marks of the Christian. To other citizens his absurd beliefs, as they regarded them, may well have seemed negligible. Yet he showed himself different from those among whom he lived by shunning foul talk, by avoiding the opportunities for sexual licence which were all too common, and by his honesty in business. He was peculiar in that he would not buy or eat meat that had come from the pagan sacrifices. His refusal to join in the ceremonial expression of patriotism must have been a source of deep-seated anger, though in the absence of conscription his pacifism was not practically troublesome.

34. Christians and their reputation

Yet a Christian was one who, though not a Jew, refused the formal incense-worship of the emperor and the State. *Ipso facto* he was a bad citizen. He had a way of life different from his pagan neighbours. They assumed, and quickly believed, that outward professions of honesty and piety concealed the gravest and foulest sins. It therefore became all the more important that, in every way possible, the behaviour of the Christian should be above reproach: sins which in the community at large were so common as not to call for comment, were in the Christian plain proof of gross hypocrisy. Equally it was imperative that the Christian should be law-abiding, ready to pay taxes and customs-dues, showing proper respect to State and civic authorities.

One would have thought that a historian of first-rate quality such as Tacitus, writing about the year A.D. 115, would have realized that Christians were good citizens and that the horrible and disgraceful charges brought against them were sheer calumny. Yet, when he writes of the burning of Rome in

A.D. 64, Christians are, as we shall see in § 306, a class of men "hated for their abominations": their creed is a "pernicious superstition" which had broken out in Rome, "where everything foul and shameful from any source collects and finds a following." Groundless accusations brought against an unpopular religious sect can be amazingly persistent!

What has just been written will perhaps give a background for Paul's letter to the Romans. It may explain why, in writing to a large group, or to several groups, of converts whom he had never seen, he gives such stern and elaborate moral teaching as is to be found in the last part of chapter i of his epistle. Some scholars say that such teaching must have come from a tract which was, at a later date, thrust into Paul's letter: and, indeed, it would be, to say the least, tactless—we might describe it as an exhibition of deplorably bad manners—to warn, at the opening of a presumably friendly letter, unknown fellow-believers against misconduct including filthy vices. The unpopularity of the Christian movement will, in any case, have been a reason for the firm advice as to the duties of citizenship given in chapter xii (1–7). To this advice we shall recur in § 303.

235. Baptism into the death of Christ

We have already, in describing the *Epistle to the Galatians* written of Paul's surprising theories of the Mosaic Law and sin as developed in his letter to the *Romans*. This latter epistle connects his theory of sin and grace with baptism. In chapter v (1–14) he affirms that baptism into Christ Jesus is baptism into his death. Hence, just as Christ was raised from the dead, so the baptized shall walk in newness of life: having died with Christ, they shall live with him: being made free from sin, they shall have in the end eternal life (vi. 22). This theory with singular exactness equates Christ to the Saviour-god of a mystery-religion: the worshipper symbolically dies with his Lord to gain, through that Lord's redemptive activity, eternal life. No man could have evolved such a theory of baptism unless—we may refer to what was written in § 66—he had been profoundly influenced by some oriental mystery-faith. To such a theory it is a long journey from the ministry in Galilee and from the early preaching of Peter, James and Stephen in Jerusalem: that Paul himself travelled so far in less than thirty years may perhaps be doubted. Yet it must be observed that precisely the same teaching recurs in the *Epistle to the Colossians* (ii. 12).

236. The two Adams

Another theological development in *Romans* (v. 12–21) is the doctrine of the two Adams: it also appears in that chapter (xv. 21–23 and 45–50) of the *First Epistle to the Corinthians* which, as we have seen reason to think, was originally a separate tract on the resurrection. This curious and fantastic fragment of theological speculation uses the old myth of *Genesis* (ii. 7–iii. 19), familiar to every child who has had a Bible training.

The story goes that God created a first man, Adam—the writer never dreamt of the evolution of man from the higher apes—and placed him in the garden of Eden. There, tempted to disobedience, he ate of the fruit of the tree of knowledge of good and evil. Lest he should go further and eat of the fruit of the tree of life and thereby become immortal, he was expelled from the garden and condemned to that life of toil which is the common lot of humanity. This story, misunderstood or wrested from its true meaning, is taken by Paul, or by someone writing in his name, to teach that, through the sin of the first man Adam, death came. By an assertion of the inheritance of acquired characters, which to-day would hardly win acceptance from the most thorough-going Lamarckian, it is assumed that, because of the first Adam's disobedience, condemnation came to all men; the many were made sinners. But, the writer continues, there is a second Adam, a life-giving Spirit, Jesus Christ. Through his obedience shall the many be made righteous. "As in Adam all die, so also in Christ shall all be made alive" (1 *Corinthians* xv. 22). Much of the theology associated with the gnostic movement of the early second century of our era surprises us by its mixture of ingenuity and naïveté : the doctrine of the two Adams has these characteristics so definitely that one is tempted to assign it to a period some forty or fifty years after Paul's death.

The author of the doctrine deserves credit for trying to explain a serious difficulty. If God be good and the world his creation, how can there be evil in it? The question is for us, with our limited knowledge and understanding, ultimately unanswerable. But the story of the first Adam seemed, to the writer or writers whom we have been considering, to explain the origin of human sin; and on it was built a doctrine of 'original sin' which, with various modifications, has had a profound influence on Christian theology.

Those whose outlook has been transformed by the conclusions of modern biologists see, in selfishness and lust, by-products of instincts implanted to secure the continuance of the individual and the race. Man with his ethical conscience has moved far from the animals whence he has sprung. Thus there has arisen a tension between moral duty and inherited instinct. When conduct falls below the level demanded by conscience, sin results: a man is then disloyal to the Christ-spirit seeking fulfilment in himself. We may go so far with Paul as to assert that all Christians agree that man conquers his weakness by the grace which comes from the indwelling Spirit of Christ.

237. Personal information as to Paul in *Romans*

While, as we have seen, grave doubts assail the critical reader who begins with the belief that the whole of *Romans* is due to Paul, it remains to be said that towards its close it undoubtedly contains precious personal information as to the great apostle. We learn (xv. 19) that his missionary activity had extended from Jerusalem "even unto Illyricum," apparently the hinterland of what we now call the Dalmatian coast. He also says that he was planning to go to Spain, and that on his way he hoped to visit Rome (xv. 24). At the time of his letter he was intending to visit Jerusalem with money which had been raised in Macedonia and Greece to help the poverty-stricken converts at Jerusalem. Plainly he was somewhat apprehensive (xv. 31) as to the reception that he might receive in Judaea: he prays that he "may be delivered from them that are disobedient" there, and trusts that the money which he has collected "may be acceptable to the saints" in Jerusalem. The story in *Acts* (xxi. 20–26) shows that his fear of a somewhat suspicious reception in Jerusalem was well-founded.

The last chapter of the epistle consists almost entirely of personal salutations, so surprisingly numerous in view of the fact that Paul had never been to Rome, that it has been surmised that they were originally attached to some other letter, now lost. For this surmise there is some early manuscript evidence, recently discovered in Egypt: a papyrus of about the year A.D. 200 puts the doxology at the end of chapter xv instead of at the end of chapter xvi.

238. The epistles of the captivity

The epistles to the *Colossians*, the *Philippians* and *Philemon* are sometimes called the epistles of the captivity, as they are thought to have been all written by Paul when he was a prisoner in Rome, approximately during the years A.D. 60–62. They would thus be the latest genuine, or partially genuine, letters of Paul which have come down to us. We have no clear indication of the order in which the letters were written.

239. The *Epistle to the Colossians*

Colossae was a town in Asia Minor, not far from Laodicea and roughly one hundred and thirty miles due east of Ephesus: in the time of Paul, it seems to have shared in the general prosperity of Asia Minor. Paul had apparently (ii. 1) never been to either Colossae or Laodicea; but in Rome he was visited by a Christian teacher named Epaphras (i. 7), who had been a missionary in the region of these cities. From Epaphras he seems to have heard of certain teaching which, so far as we can learn from Paul's condemnation of it, was due to the infiltration of a sort of orientalized Judaism. The teaching stressed the observance of certain days and included regulations with regard to meat and drink. It seems also to have contained a type of pseudo-philosophy which involved the worship of angels.

240. Bondage to " elementals "

This degenerate religion certainly attached importance to, and probably sought to propitiate, "rudiments" or "elementals" (ii. 8 and 20). These entities appear to have been thought of alike as the four elements (earth, water, air, fire) of ancient physics, as astral spirits, as angelic powers, and as spiritual beings associated with phenomena and places. In ancient speculation, especially as shaped by stoic monists, they were not only the four simple substances which by their opposition and blending gave rise to all phenomena of the visible world; but they were also spiritual elements, regarded as quasi-material

R

(see § 42), which animated earthly and celestial bodies. As such they were objects of pagan worship. We may, perhaps, best think of these gods, or "godlings" as cosmic energies: such a concept could actually be made to harmonize happily with the modern view that matter is a form of energy, provided it were coupled with the baseless though plausible assumption that, as energy is fundamental in all known activity, it is not only the field of operation, but also a manifestation, of the divine. A warning against "bondage" to these elementals had previously been given to the *Galatians* (iv. 3 and 9). The ancient world had a profound belief in omnipresent spiritual powers: it was "plagued—and sometimes blessed—by demons of its own imagining." Such crudities of popular and of pseudo-intellectual religion, naturally enough, entered into the outlook of Christian converts: they were an important feature of second-century gnosticism.

241. The "pleroma" in Christ

Paul, as against these degenerate developments, sets out a doctrine of God and Christ which, to some scholars, seems permeated by the same atmosphere. The whole "pleroma," that is to say, the fullness of God's being, the aggregate of Divine attributes, virtues and energies, dwells in Christ, according to *Colossians* (i. 15–20 and ii. 9–10). Christ is the image of God the unseen: he is the first-born of all creation. For in him all things, seen and unseen, angelic powers of every degree, were created. He is also the head of the church, the beginning, the first-born from the dead. Such words give form to what we may fairly term a blaze of enthusiastic praise. But beneath the well-nigh unbounded veneration of the writer for "the Son of God's love" there is restraint in the rhapsody. Jesus, as the Christ, is never termed God.

In the *Epistle to the Colossians*, as so often in the epistles ascribed to Paul, there is a direct and stern warning against the sins and failings which in ancient paganism were even more common than in our own civilization. The new and higher morality of the Christian Way was evidently regarded as of fundamental importance for converts at Colossae as elsewhere: doctrinal controversies could not obscure the need for clean, wholesome and honourable living. The epistle also contains kindly advice

to family life, the mutual obligations of husband, wife,
ildren and servants.

In the salutations with which the letter ends we learn that
Mark, the cousin of Barnabas" is with Paul, and that there
as some intention of his visiting Colossae. Luke, the beloved
aysician, was also in Rome. There is no mention of Peter
ther here or in any other letter of the captivity. The letter
ids "Remember my bonds. Grace be with you."

2. The *Epistle to the Philippians*

This epistle must have been written about the same time as
ae letter to Colossae. But Paul is now writing to a church
hich he had himself founded, to converts who had generously
elped him (iv. 15–16) when he was in need at Salonica. There
·e, in consequence, a number of intimate personal touches in
ae letter. In its present form it seems to be composite. Near
ae very end (iv. 18), Paul speaks of "having received from
paphroditus the things that came from you." But earlier
i. 25) he states that he "counted it necessary to send to you
paphroditus . . . since he longed after you . . . he was sick
igh unto death. . . . I have sent him therefore." Fragments
f two letters thus seem to have been joined together in reverse
rder.

The most noteworthy feature of the letter is teaching with
·gard to Christ (ii. 6–7), "who, being in the form of God,
ounted it not good fortune to be on an equality with God, but
mptied himself, taking the form of a servant, being made in the
keness of men." There follows an enthusiastic outburst
cclaiming Jesus as Lord, "God highly exalted him, and gave
nto him the name which is above every name; that in the
ame of Jesus every knee should bow, of things in heaven and
iings on earth and things under the earth, and that every
ongue should confess that Jesus Christ is Lord, to the glory of
rod the Father."

The earlier part, especially, of this praise of the exalted
esus likens him, as Lord, to the Saviour-gods of the mystery-
aiths. Though not God, he was on an equality with Him
·efore he came to earth to endure the humiliation of the cross.
Ie is thus thought of as having been both pre-existent and
ivine. Paul does not use the term *Logos*; but his teaching

244 THE RISE OF CHRISTIANITY

here is almost identical with that of the prologue to the fourt
gospel. The passage from which we have just quoted ha
naturally had immense influence in the development of th
doctrine of the person of Christ: stress upon it has caused th
human Jesus of Nazareth to be virtually lost in the divine pre
existent Lord, who emptied himself to become man. Wheth
this teaching, together with the corresponding teaching :
Colossians, actually came from Paul is perhaps open to som
doubt: it might be a development at the end of the first centu
of our era.

In the letter to the *Philippians* there is an undercurrent
apprehension and weariness. Paul complains that there a
those around him who "raise up affliction for me in my bonds
(i. 17). To his bonds he refers more than once: there is also a
allusion to "the defence and confirmation of the gospel" (i. 7
as though his trial had taken place and he was awaitir
judgment. He has a "desire to depart and be with Chris
for it is very far better" (i. 23). The clouds were gatherir
thickly, the end drawing nigh.

Yet there is, midway through the letter (iii. 4–11), an ou
burst characteristic of Paul, emphasis on his Jewish origin an
youthful orthodoxy as a pharisee, followed by a statement of h
willingness to suffer all things that he might "gain Christ.
There is no warning against specific sins; but in its place th
moving exhortation (iv. 8), "Whatsoever things are true, wha
soever things are honourable, whatsoever things are just, wha
sover things are pure, whatsoever things are lovely, whatsoeve
things are of good report; if there be any virtue, and if the
be any praise, think on these things." This appeal is, of cours
one of the most famous passages in religious literature.

At the end of the epistle we have a salutation from "th
saints," "especially they that are of Caesar's household." Th
gospel had thus apparently made its way up into the ranks-
possibly the lower ranks—of the civil service of the empire
in the emperor Domitian's time (*c.* A.D. 95) it was to reac
close relatives of Caesar himself.

243. The *Epistle to Philemon*

This document is the shortest "book" in the New Testamen
and is also the only private letter of Paul that has survived. I

nds with saluations from Epaphras, Mark, Aristarchus, Demas
nd Luke, who also send salutations towards the close of the
pistle to the Colossians: it was therefore probably written about
ne same time as the latter document, and may indeed have
een sent with it. The letter was written to Philemon, who was
pparently a well-to-do Christian convert known to Paul. It
as been conjectured that he lived at Colossae though, as Paul
ad never visited this city, he may have lived in some neigh-
ouring city of Asia Minor where Paul had ministered.

Paul wrote on behalf of a slave named Onesimus, who had
un away from his master, Philemon, possibly with some of the
atter's possessions. The letter is somewhat elaborately tactful,
riendly in its approach, but delicate almost to humility in its
equest that Onesimus shall be received back without punish-
nent. The relation of master to slave, when both were
Christians, was, at first, no doubt, a problem of no little
lifficulty. Paul had written, actually in his letter to the
Colossians (iii. 11), that in Christ "there cannot be Greek and
ew . . . bondman, freeman: but Christ is all, and in all." Of
ecessity Christianity brought a new relationship between
naster and slave: the master had to be more humane, the slave
elt the freedom born of religious equality. Under Christianity,
lavery lasted long, because the Christianity was superficial
ather than real. But, wherever Christianity has been deeply
nfluential, slavery has been felt to be a denial of the fact that
ll men are equal in Christ Jesus. Ultimately, as a result, it has
een brought to an end. Doubtless the letter to Philemon was
ften quoted for guidance in Christian communities: probably
or that reason it survived.

CHAPTER XIV

EARLY CHRISTIAN WRITINGS OUTSIDE THE NEW TESTAMENT

OUTSIDE the New Testament there are, as we said in § 218, a few books which throw light on the early growth of Christianity. They give us some slight insight into conditions in Christian communities at, or fairly soon after, the beginning of the second century of our era; and to some extent they show what were the sympathies and tastes of the members of these groups. These writings, however, are few in number, of doubtful dates, and not very illuminating. We learn from them practically nothing of the political situation in which Christians found themselves. As to the social difficulties of Christians in a pagan society there is a virtual silence. During the first century after the death of Jesus, Christians were, for the most part, humble folk, strongly puritan in their way of life, kind and helpful to one another, unworldly, without political enthusiasms or social ambitions, interested in their worship and in stories and traditions connected with their faith: they were probably only too content that the politico-social organization of the Roman empire should leave them forgotten or, at least, unmolested.

244. The *Didache*

Of paramount importance among early Christian writings not admitted to the New Testament is the *Didache* or *Teaching of the Twelve Apostles*. The *Didache* is an ancient church hand book, written in Greek, which for long was lost, though its existence had been surmised, while its contents were to a considerable extent known to scholars.

It was discovered in a small, thick, manuscript volume containing seven separate works bound together, one of which was the *First Epistle of Clement*, which we shall discuss shortly. This volume was found in a monastery at Constantinople in A.D. 1873. The actual writing of the volume was completed by "Leo, notary and sinner," in A.D. 1056. The *Didache* was first printed in A.D. 1883. Since its publication, the importance of its evidence as to the development of early Christianity has been increasingly recognized. That evidence is in some ways so disturbing to traditional beliefs, especially as to the origin of the eucharist, that repeated attempts have been made to discredit its reliability and to disparage its witness. Yet all must be adjudged to have failed. It is now known that later works were based on the *Didache*, that translations from it into Latin, Syriac and Ethiopic were made. It probably passed through several editions, differing in detail though not in general plan.

The *Didache* is short: the original manuscript, whose discovery we have described, was contained on ten pages of leaves. It is a brief hand-book, instructing the Christian primarily as to the moral law and as to church worship. It gives what may be called a picture of normal church life some sixty or seventy years after the crucifixion of Jesus. Its background is Jewish, not gentile. We have already realized that pagan and Hellenic influences are many and strong in books of the New Testament: in these books we see Christianity as it grew and changed outside Palestine. In the *Didache* the growing Christian church has retained much of the atmosphere, sober thought combined with prayer, fasting and righteousness, of its earliest period in Jerusalem.

245. The discarding of the *Didache*

Why, it may be asked, was the *Didache* ignored and ultimately forgotten, if it is thus valuable? The answer is, though some scholars demur, that the church found that the account of the Last Supper, common to the *First Epistle to the Corinthians* and the synoptic gospels, could not be maintained if the form of the eucharist in the *Didache* were admitted to be primitive. The form which survived was highly congenial to converts from paganism: it gave a Christian setting to old practices and beliefs. The closest parallels could be drawn, as indeed they are drawn in the *First Epistle to the Corinthians* (x. 14–22), between, on the one hand, bread and wine, asserted to be a communion of the body and blood of Christ, and, on the other hand, heathen sacrifices: converts had left the table of devils to partake of the table of the Lord. Outside the New Testament and the *Didache*, the Christian eucharist is first described by

Justin Martyr, as will appear subsequently in §§ 284 and 325,
He gives (*First Apology*, 66), with some variations, the New
Testament account of the Last Supper, and adds, "this th
wicked demons have imitated in the mysteries of Mithra
ordering it to be done." These words probably date from the
year A.D. 152: we could ask for no clearer evidence as to
the close affinity between the Mithraic communion and the
form of Christian eucharist which ousted the primitive communion of the *Didache*.

The *Didache* is possibly quoted in the *Epistle to Titus* (i. 9,
which, as in § 216 we have seen reason to think, belongs to a
period shortly before the middle of the second century of our
era. A bishop, we read in this letter, must hold "to the faithful
word which is according to the *Didache*." In the so-called
Epistle of Barnabas, which we shall discuss in § 255, there is an
exposition of "the Two Ways," very like that which we find at
the beginning of the *Didache*. It is introduced (chapter xviii) by
the words, "Let us pass on to yet another knowledge and
Didache." One can argue that *Didache*, or Teaching, is such a
common word that in each of these places there is no intention
to refer to the book before us: but some scholars incline to the
opinion that such a reference is intended, at any rate in the
Epistle of Barnabas.

246. The character of the *Didache*

The *Didache* is a presentation of Christianity which appeals
especially to the modern Christian humanist. It does not contain any of the miraculous stories which, to one who accepts the
finite-scale uniformity of nature, impair the actuality of the
gospels. The tendency to theological extravagance, which we
find at times in the epistles attributed to Paul, is equally
absent. Yet the book is completely Christian, firmly based on
belief in God as taught by the great Hebrew prophets and by
Jesus.

It can be divided into three unequal parts. The first and
largest part sets forth some principles of Christian morality.
Then follows a section dealing with Christian worship and
church organization. The book ends with only a few sentences
as to "the last days" when, after persecution and trial, the
Christian hope will be realized: it affirms that then there will be

a resurrection of the righteous dead and "the world shall see the Lord coming upon the clouds of heaven."

This conclusion of the book is brief—perhaps surprisingly brief. Clearly the visible return of Christ in glory, after a period of grave moral disorder and "fiery trial," was expected when it was written. Between such expectations and those which find a place in the synoptic gospels there is the closest likeness. It has been suggested that all the writers, alike of the synoptic gospels and of the *Didache*, who looked for the spectacular coming of Christ in clouds of glory, were influenced by Jewish tracts. Such tracts, prophesying the end of the then world-order, may have been published in the period of emotional stress of A.D. 70, when Titus besieged and took Jerusalem. Acceptance of these tracts may have led to novel expectations, which were intruded into the *First Epistle to the Thessalonians* and which the *Didache* mentioned but briefly. Possibly, when Christianity was originally proclaimed, its message with regard to the future was simply the speedy coming of the kingdom of God, as the social expression of new moral standards. But, as we have previously said in chapter viii, there is no clear evidence as to what Jesus himself expected.

247. The *Didache* and the synoptic gospels

Teaching as to "the last days" is not the only bond of likeness between the *Didache* and the synoptic gospels. The *Didache* (viii) gives the Lord's prayer substantially as we have it in *Matthew*. Now the prayer, notwithstanding its supreme place in Christian thought and worship, occurs in the New Testament solely in *Matthew* and *Luke*. There are enough similarities in its wording to show that these two evangelists drew upon a common Greek source, presumably Q. But it is a surprising fact that there is no reference to the prayer elsewhere in the New Testament. Outside the first and third gospels, the *Didache* is the earliest witness to its existence.

The *Didache* also (vii) orders baptism "into the name of the Father, and of the Son, and of the Holy Spirit." It thus prescribes the formula which occurs at the end of *Matthew* (xxviii. 19). The primitive formula was of baptism "in the name of Jesus Christ," as in *Acts* (ii. 38). This formula had not apparently gone out of use when the *Didache* was written, for

we are told (ix) that none may be admitted to the eucharist
save "such as have been baptized into the name of the Lord."
There is thus reason to think that the *Didache* and the first
gospel may be of about the same date; and it is quite possible
that the *Didache* was the earlier of the two.

The book does not profess to be a history of Jesus or com-
pendium of Christian theology. It was plainly intended to
help the average Christian of the end of the first century to live
the Christian life. The crucifixion of Jesus is not explicitly
mentioned; but (xvi) the coming of Christ will be heralded by
a sign, which is plainly the sign of the cross, in the sky; and,
moreover (viii), fasting was to be "on the fourth day (Wednes-
day) and the preparation (Friday)": obviously the Friday fast
was in memory of the crucifixion. To the writer Jesus was the
child, the servant or son, of God, who had made known life
and knowledge and faith and immortality, and was to come
again. Maran atha, the Lord cometh, was still the watchword.

248. " The Two Ways "

The *Didache* begins, "There are two ways, one of life and one
of death." The first four chapters of the book expound in
detail the way of life: the fifth chapter describes the way of
death. There is clear evidence that these chapters come from
a tract, probably Jewish and possibly pre-Christian, which had
deservedly a considerable vogue. Detailed use was made of this
tract by the writer of the *Epistle of Barnabas* (chapters xviii–xx),
a work of no great value which we describe subsequently in
§ 255. But, in the *Didache*, the beginning of the tract has been
filled out by passages from the Sermon on the Mount, that is to
say, from Q. The conclusion of the moral teaching of the two
ways is (vi), "Take heed lest any make thee to err from this
way of teaching, seeing he teacheth thee not according to God.
For if indeed thou art able to bear the whole yoke of the Lord,
thou shalt be perfect. But, if thou art not able, do what thou
canst." The advice is typical of the sober good sense of the
whole work.

249. The eucharist in the *Didache*

As has been previously stated, the instructions with regard
to the eucharist give to the *Didache* its outstanding importance.

Until the discovery of the book it was generally assumed that the eucharist was the continuation of a mode of sacramental worship enjoined by Jesus at the Last Supper, the evening meal before his arrest, trial and crucifixion. It was thus "ordained by Christ himself." This mode of worship was thought to be the practice referred to at the beginning of *Acts* as "the breaking of bread." In the earliest Christian period the eucharist, whatever its origin or initial form, was associated with a complete meal, as we realize from the *First Epistle to the Corinthians* (xi. 20–22). But the fact that, alike in this epistle and in all three synoptic gospels, substantially the same story of its origin was told, was deemed proof positive that it was based upon the action and command of Jesus. This belief, as we shall see in chapter xvi, can no longer be easily held.

In the *Didache*, baptism and the eucharist are set forth as the two main rites of the church. Baptism is regarded as such a grave step that not only he who is baptized, but also he who performs the rite, "and such others as are able," are to fast.

250. The chief eucharistic prayers of the *Didache*

The term "eucharist" properly means thanksgiving and blessing: it rapidly came to denote the feast of thanksgiving, or Holy Communion, which conveyed God's blessing to those who took part in it. In the *Didache* no one is to come to the eucharist who has not been baptized. The feast was evidently regarded as the central bond of worship of the Christian community. Members of the church joined together to share a common meal of food deemed "holy." The words of the primary prayer, corresponding to the later prayer of consecration in the eucharist, are set out as follows (ix):

In the service of thanksgiving, called the eucharist, give thanks thus. First, for the cup: "We thank thee, our Father, for the holy vine of David thy child, which thou hast revealed to us through Jesus thy child. Thine is the glory for ever." Then, for the broken bread: "We thank thee, our Father, for the life and knowledge which thou hast revealed to us through Jesus thy child. Thine is the glory for ever. Even as this broken bread was scattered over the mountains and was brought together and made one, so may thy church be brought together from the ends of the earth into thy kingdom. For thine is the glory and the power through Jesus

Christ for ever." But let no one eat or drink of your eucharist save those who are baptized into the name of the Lord. For the Lord spoke, in fact, of this food, saying, "Give not what is holy to the dogs."

It will be noticed that here we have, as one of the material elements, the bread that has persisted through all transformations from the earliest "breaking of bread" to "the Mass." The cup—and this is undoubtedly primitive—is mentioned before the bread. The "holy vine of David" is plainly the Messiah or, in Greek, the Christ. The wine is thus symbolical of him. The broken bread is similarly symbolical of the life and knowledge which Jesus brought to men: with the bread goes the prayer that, as it was made from scattered grains of wheat or other corn, so may the church, built up of scattered units, be gathered from the ends of the earth into the kingdom of God. Thus the bread and wine are already truly sacramental, outward and visible forms of inward and spiritual grace. But there is no hint that bread and wine were, or ever had been when the *Didache* was written, associated with the body and blood of Christ. There is no suggestion that the eucharist arose by command of Jesus, or that it was associated with words and actions of his at the Last Supper. It was a natural growth: gradually the common meal of Christian believers was taking a spiritual significance.

These facts are emphasized by the words of the "post-consecration" prayer (x):

After eating your fill, thus give thanks: "We thank thee, holy Father, for thy holy name which thou hast sheltered in our hearts as in a tent; we thank thee for the knowledge, for the faith and for the immortality which thou hast revealed to us through Jesus thy child. Thine is the glory for ever. Thou, Lord and ruler of all, hast created all things for thy name's sake, and hast given food and drink to men for their enjoyment, that they might thank thee. To us thou hast vouchsafed spiritual food and drink and everlasting life through thy child. Above all things we thank thee that thou art mighty. Thine is the glory for ever. Remember, Lord, thy church, to ward off from it all evil and to make it perfect in thy love; bring it together from the four winds, made ready in holiness, into thy kingdom which thou hast prepared for it; for thine is the power and the glory for ever. Let grace come and let this world pass away. Hosanna to the God of David. Whoever is holy, let him come: whoever is not, let him repent. Maran atha, Amen."

251. Primitive church order

This prayer is followed by the instruction, "But suffer ye the prophets to give thanks [*or*, to celebrate the eucharist] as pleaseth them." When the *Didache* was written, the eucharist was gradually taking a set form; but it was not felt wrong for "a prophet," some born religious leader, to shape the prayers as he was moved by the Spirit of God. "Apostles and prophets," wandering ministers and evangelists, were clearly at the time prominent in the church's life. Regulations are given with reference to their reception and behaviour; and it was plainly necessary to distinguish between true and false prophets. In the advice there is a happy combination of worldly wisdom and religious earnestness.

Already Sunday worship was the rule, as is evident from the injunction (xiv), "And on each Lord's day of the Lord gather together, break bread and give thanks, after confessing your transgressions, that your sacrifice may be pure." But there is no evidence that Christians met for worship before dawn; though, as we know from a letter of Pliny to Trajan of about A.D. 112, which will be set out and discussed in §§ 307–309, this custom had at that time arisen in the north of Asia Minor. Finally, we may observe that, though the *Didache* enjoins "fasting baptism," it knows nothing of "fasting communion." We have said that the *Didache* probably passed through several editions. The earliest draft cannot well have been later than A.D. 95.

252. The *First Epistle of Clement* to the Corinthians

Some light is thrown upon the development of thought and feeling among Christians, probably somewhat less than a century after the crucifixion of Jesus, by the work called the *First Epistle of Clement*. This work, as we have written in § 182, was highly esteemed, inasmuch as, together with a *Second Epistle*, it is appended to the books of the New Testament in the fifth-century manuscript known as the Codex Alexandrinus. Reference to it is frequently made by ancient Christian writers.

In itself it is anonymous, being written by "the church of God which sojourneth at Rome to the church of God which sojourneth at Corinth."

The writer begins by referring to "the sudden and repeated calamities and reverses which are befalling us." Apparently there had been some outbreak of persecution in Rome which had caused the reply to inquiries from Corinth to be delayed. In Corinth itself a violent dispute seems to have arisen through the action of "a few rash and self-confident persons." The church at - Corinth, says the writer, had been sincere and uncorrupted, honourable and happy. But (iii) "the worthless rose up against the honoured, those of no reputation against such as were renowned, the foolish against the wise, the young against the elders." And the cause of it all was an unrighteous and ungodly jealousy. Against "jealousy" and its consequences the Corinthians are warned by examples taken from the Old Testament; and by a reminder of the labours and end of Peter and of Paul, which we have already quoted in § 182.

There follows an exhortation to repentance based upon the Old Testament. Then (xiii) comes an exhortation to humility in which the gospel source Q is loosely quoted: we are bidden to "remember the words of the Lord Jesus which he spake." The words are an echo of *Matthew* (vi. 12–15; vii. 2) and *Luke* (vi. 31 and 36–38): "Be merciful that ye may obtain mercy; forgive that ye may be forgiven; as ye do, so shall it be done unto you; as ye judge, so shall ye be judged; as ye are kind, so shall kindness be shown to you; with what measure ye mete, it shall be measured to you." In a subsequent chapter (xvi) Christ is praised as an example of humility; but the writer does not refer to any particular event in the gospel story.

Throughout his lengthy and painstaking moral teaching *Clement* gives no hint of the actual social or political circumstances, either of himself or of those whom he addresses. He does not seem concerned with problems of poverty and wealth, of political freedom or social justice. He writes of the peace and order of the universe with a sort of superficial complacency. It is a relief when we pass from the laborious quoting of texts and stories, mainly from the Old Testament, to such an approach to actuality as the advice (xxi), "Let us fear the Lord Jesus Christ, whose blood was given for us. Let us reverence our rulers. Let us honour the aged among us. Let us train up the young men in the fear of God. Let us guide our women to that which is good."

Clement, whoever he may have been—possibly the son of a Jewish freedman of the Flavians, the imperial house at Rome which ended with Domitian—is plainly familiar with the *Epistle to the Hebrews*, which he quotes several times. He also refers (xlvii) explicitly, as we have already said in § 218, to Paul as the author of a quotation which comes from the *First Epistle to the Corinthians*, "whose was a stedfast and ancient church." He is familiar (xlix) with the hymn in Praise of Love (1 *Corinthians* xiii). He wrote (xxiii) at a time when the expectation still continued that Christ would speedily come again. Of a future resurrection he says (xxiv) that "God has rendered the Lord Jesus Christ the first-fruits by raising him from the dead."

253. The mental background of Clement

The difference between the mental background of the early Christians and our own must have been enormous. It is well brought out by what *Clement* deems to be a proof of the power of God to raise from the dead those who have piously served him, which he (xxv) derives from the fable of the phoenix. We give it at length:

Let us look at this strange portent which occurs in Eastern lands, actually in the regions round Arabia. For there is a bird known by the name of the Phoenix, which is a unique creature and lives for five hundred years. When it has come to the time of its dissolution in death, it builds itself a coffin of frankincense and myrrh and other sweet-smelling things; and when its time is completed, it enters this coffin and dies. But as its flesh rots a kind of worm is born, which feeds on the juices of the dead creature and so grows wings. Then it comes to its full strength and takes up the coffin which contains the bones of the earlier creature. Carrying these it travels from the land of Arabia to the city in Egypt known as Heliopolis; and there by daylight, in full view of everyone, it swoops down on to the altar of the sun, sets down its load and so begins its homeward journey. The priests then inspect the records of times and discover that it has come on the completion of the five hundredth year. Are we then to consider it so great a miracle if the Creator of the universe is intending to bring about the resurrection of those who have laboured righteously for him, in the assurance of a good faith, when even through a bird he shows us how mighty is his promise?

This fantastic story reveals how uncritical could be a good man who apparently held an important place in the church at Rome. We have no means of satisfactorily ascertaining who he was or when he wrote. A hint of his date is given by the fact that in his time the orders of the ministry consisted of bishops and deacons: the separation of bishops and priests had not apparently taken place. Probably, as we have said in § 182, the book was written about A.D. 125.

254. The *Second Epistle of Clement*

The so-called *Second Epistle of Clement* is shown by its style to be by a different writer: it was almost certainly written at a later time. It is a moral exhortation, largely built up on Old and New Testament texts; and from it, unfortunately, we can infer nothing as to the then interaction of Christians and the world around them. There is in it, however, an interesting quotation, said by a later writer to come from the *Gospel according to the Egyptians*. Jesus, asked when his kingdom would come, replied, "When the two shall be one, and that which is without as that which is within, and the male with the female, neither male nor female." Have we here a genuine recollection of some characteristic warning of Jesus that the coming of the kingdom of God on earth would be delayed far longer than his enthusiastic followers, misled by their hopes, believed? The saying is tantamount to a statement that the kingdom, in the form expected by his hearers, would not come until the world as they knew it had disappeared.

255. The *Epistle of Barnabas*

At one time the work called the *Epistle of Barnabas* must have had a considerable vogue. In the early and highly important biblical manuscript known as the Codex Sinaiticus, bought from the Soviet government in A.D. 1933 and now in the British Museum, the epistle finds a place at the end of the New Testament, with much of a symbolical story known as the *Shepherd of*

Hermas. The epistle seems to have been written (xvi) after the destruction of the temple by Titus in A.D. 70 and before its renewed and final overthrow by the emperor Hadrian in A.D. 135. We do not know who its author was. Ancient opinion, from the end of the second century of our era onwards, was unanimous that it was written by Barnabas, whom we know to have been the companion of Paul in his early missionary work. No modern scholar would endorse this belief: it is but another instance of the absence of critical insight in the collapsing Graeco-Roman civilization.

The work is valueless, save as showing the mentality of its author and of those who esteemed what he wrote. It exists, as it were, in the void, an attempt by a fanciful interpretation of Old Testament passages to show that Christians, and not Jews, were the true Israel, heirs of the ancient promises. The writer prides himself on his *gnosis*, secret knowledge of things divine. For instance (ix), he makes his own deduction from two passages in the book of *Genesis*, and states that "Abraham circumcised ten, and eight, and three hundred men of his household." He goes on to say that ten is denoted by I and eight by H: these two letters signify Jesus. He adds that the number three hundred anticipates T, the sign of the cross. Puerilities of this kind, in which the writer takes great pride, surprise us by the low level of intelligence that they reveal. But *Barnabas* goes to even lower depths: his attempt to give spiritual significance to Mosaic food laws (x) is a mixture of nastiness and foolishness.

Our author has clearly a strong controversial hostility to the Jews: and he couples it with a determination to use every possible argument, good or bad, as he inquires (xiii) "whether the covenant is for us or for them." He is widely read in the Old Testament and had possibly belonged to some heretical Jewish group before being converted to Christianity: his story of the goat sent away into the wilderness (vii) is not from orthodox Judaism.

From internal evidence we infer that, when *Barnabas* wrote, the gospel story was not widely known, although, as we have said in § 218, he quotes (iv) the saying, "Many are called, but few are chosen," with the formula "as it is written." If we assign his work to about the years A.D. 110–120, we shall probably not be far wrong. It was pointed out in § 174 that *Barnabas*, like

S

Luke, seems to have believed that the resurrection and ascension of Jesus took place on the same day; for he writes (xv), "W celebrate the eighth day with joyfulness, the day on which Jesus rose also from the dead, and was made manifest, and ascended into the heavens." As we have previously said in discussing the *Didache*, the epistle ends by incorporating practically th whole of the Jewish tract on *The Two Ways* which the author of the *Didache* also used.

256. The *Shepherd of Hermas*

The Codex Sinaiticus is probably, after the Codex Vaticanus the earliest manuscript of the whole New Testament which exists: it also contains much of the Septuagint. In it, as a sor of appendix, the *Shepherd of Hermas* (in a now mutilated form appears, as we have said in § 255, together with the *Epistle of Barnabas*. The fact proves that these two works hovered on th edge of the New Testament, before being in the end excluded from it. Neither work really deserved inclusion. The *Epistle of Barnabas*, as we have seen, is of no great merit. On the othe hand, the *Shepherd of Hermas*, though verbose and prolix, ha distinct merits as an allegory. It seems to have enjoyed among early Christians as much popularity as Bunyan's *Pilgrim's Progress* in the English-speaking world of the last three cen turies. It is not great as a work of art: it lacks the force and imaginative power of Bunyan's masterpiece. But Hermas ca invent scenes with skill; and, though his book is far too long, i is not intolerably dull.

His theme is the building of the church. It gives him th opportunity of describing the virtues of those who are fit fo membership and of warning his readers against those sins whic true Christians should avoid. *Hermas* is familiar (command ment iv. 1) with the teaching of Jesus with regard to divorce, a we have it in *Matthew* and *Luke*; but he tacitly sets aside th Roman possibility of a wife divorcing her husband which, as w have seen in § 128, finds a place in *Mark* (x. 12). We mus confess, however, that he comparatively seldom uses languag that suggests a knowledge either of the Jewish or of the Christia scriptures. Yet he writes continually of God and "the Lord" and references to the Holy Spirit and to the Son occur no infrequently.

257. The social position of Christians when Hermas wrote

The *Shepherd* gives us little information as to conditions, either within the church or in the world outside, at the time when it was written. We infer, however, that the expectation of the second coming of Christ was fading away. Christians, in the locality known to *Hermas*, were to some extent ceasing to be objects of general ill-will: their virtues were giving them recognition and even wealth. *Hermas* writes sadly (commandment x. 1) of those who, having never searched for the truth, but having simply believed, "become mixed up with business, and wealth, and heathen friendships, and many other occupations of this world": "their minds are thus darkened, they are corrupted, and become sterile." Warnings against luxury, useless dainties and drinks, are necessary.

Hermas, on occasion, can even go so far as to view with favour dispossessing the rich of their wealth (vision iii. 6). "When they shall be deprived of their wealth which leads their souls astray, they will be useful to God." "When you were rich, you were useless." The rich, however, are regarded with more favour than by Jesus in the gospels. There is no command, such as we find in *Mark* (x. 21), "Sell whatsoever thou hast, and give to the poor." On the contrary (similitude ii), "Poor men, pleading with the Lord on behalf of the rich, add to their riches; and the rich again, aiding the poor in their needs, add to their prayers. Both, therefore, are partners in the righteous work."

258. Hermas on sin after baptism

In the sphere of doctrine *Hermas*, of course, regards baptism as the great rite of the Christian life. The righteous dead need the preaching of the gospel and also baptism that they may be saved (similitude ix. 16). Though *Hermas* thus associates preaching with baptism, it seems not unfair to say that he attaches to the rite a magical significance. Those who are baptized "descend into the water dead, and they arise alive." His tower, which is the church, is built upon the waters, "because your life has been, and will be, saved through water." With such a view of the rite, the question of sin after baptism became acute. *Hermas* is led to say (commandment iv. 3), "If any one is tempted by the devil, and sins after that great and

holy calling, he has one opportunity to repent." Plainly the
barriers of primitive rigour are breaking down. If one sin be
no final impediment to eternal life, why not two? The way i
opening to the system of confession, repentance and absolution
of later ages.

It is noteworthy, however, that fasting is commended
(similitude v. 3), not as an ecclesiastical habit, but as an aid to
practical charity. "On the day on which you fast you will taste
nothing but bread and water; and having reckoned up the
price of the dishes of that day which you would have eaten, you
will give it to a widow or orphan or to some person in want."
The same advice, as we shall see in § 318, occurs in the *Apolog*
of Aristides.

259. The date of the *Shepherd of Hermas*

A fragmentary document known as the Muratorian Canon
probably of the later part of the second century of our era
tells us that "the *Shepherd* was written recently, in our own time
at Rome by Hermas, while bishop Pius, his brother, wa
occupying the chair of the Roman church." Because its origin
was thus known, men were clear that it was not written by an
apostle, or under apostolic authority; and it was therefore
adjudged unsuited to a place among the authoritative books of
the New Testament. It was probably written at varying dates
during the period A.D. 130–50. Though it seems to have come
from Italy, the language originally employed was Greek
Perhaps for this reason it was more popular in the eastern
churches than in those of the west.

260. The letters attributed to Ignatius

Until quite modern times there was a convention that the
writings of the New Testament were to be b e taken at their face
value: critical inquiries into date and authorship were tacitly
deemed unbecoming unless, indeed, they led up to and confirmed traditional opinions. But no such convention protected
other Christian writings. In consequence the letters attributed
to Ignatius have for three centuries been a battleground of
scholars.

261. The martyrdom of Ignatius

Of Ignatius himself little is known. He is said to have been a bishop of (Syrian) Antioch and to have been martyred in Rome under Trajan a few years before or after A.D. 110. But the account of his martyrdom, which professes to have come from those who went with him on his final journey to Rome, is probably of a later date. It refers to Trajan in a manner which, to say the least, would have been highly injudicious while that emperor was alive. It represents the emperor as having condemned Ignatius at Antioch and as having ordered him to be sent to Rome, to be exposed there to wild beasts in the arena for the gratification of the people. Such a sentence from an emperor who, about the same time, advised Pliny with kindly good sense as to his treatment of the Christians, is highly unlikely. It sounds like the invention of a hagiographer, indifferent to truth as he sought to edify credulous readers long years after the events which he describes.

This same writer makes Ignatius on his voyage stop at Smyrna and there greet its bishop, Polycarp. The church there seems, with other churches of Asia, to have been untouched by the persecution of Trajan. We are further told—the statement is most improbable—that both Ignatius and Polycarp had been disciples of John the Apostle. Finally, after Ignatius had been devoured by the wild beasts at Rome, "only the harder portions of his holy remains were left"; and they were conveyed to Antioch, "an inestimable treasure" for the church there. We may well doubt whether the cult of relics of the saints had begun within a century of the crucifixion of Jesus. In brief, the story of the martyrdom of Ignatius is edifying legend, not contemporary history.

262. The different versions of the Ignatian letters

What of the so-called Ignatian letters? There are, in all, fifteen such epistles. Eight are, by general consent, spurious. Of the remaining seven, we possess two Greek editions, a longer and a shorter, differing at times somewhat markedly. Controversy with regard to these writings has burst out vigorously from time to time since the middle of the seventeenth century. Many scholars of eminence in western Europe have asserted that none of these writings is genuine; but perhaps the dominant opinion has been in favour of the genuineness of the shorter Greek version. In the middle of the nineteenth century a still shorter Syriac version of three letters, those to the *Ephesians*, the *Romans* and *Polycarp*, was found. The discoverer asserted that there had thus been brought to light the only true and genuine letters of Ignatius.

Why, it may be asked, should such prolonged controversy have been deemed worth while? The answer is that loose quotations from, and references to, gospels and various epistles of the New Testament are fairly numerous, in particular in the so-called letter of Ignatius to the *Ephesians*; and if even the shorter Greek versions of this and other letters are genuine writings of a man who died not later than A.D. 117, the gospels of *Matthew*, and probably *John*, together with several epistles of the New Testament, must have been documents which, by the beginning of the second century of our era, were already regarded as authoritative.

Opinion, however, during the present century has hardened against the belief that the Ignatian correspondence is genuine. Internal evidence is conclusive against such an early date for the letters as would make them valuable witnesses, at the beginning of the second century, to the use of the gospels and Pauline epistles as authoritative documents.

263. The shorter version of the Greek letters is the original

We can, first of all, dismiss the contention that the Syriac version of the so-called Ignatian letters is the original. It is, on the contrary, a bald and unsatisfactory *précis* of three of the Greek letters.

In the second place, even a cursory examination makes clear that the longer Greek version of the letters has been filled out from the shorter by the use of New Testament texts.

Take, for example, the form of the teaching in the letter to the *Smyrnaeans* (iii) that Christ after his resurrection was possessed of a body. In the shorter version we have: "He said to them, Lay hold, handle me and see that I am not an incorporeal spirit. And immediately they touched him and believed, being convinced both by his flesh and spirit. For this cause also they despised death. . . ." But in the longer version we have, after the words "incorporeal spirit": "For a spirit hath

ιοt flesh and bones as ye see me have. And he says to Thomas,
Reach hither thy finger into the print of the nails, and reach
ιither thy hand, and thrust it into my side; and immediately
they believed that he was the Christ. Wherefore Thomas also
says to him, My Lord and my God. And on this account also
did they despise death. . . ." The longer version has quite
obviously been filled out by the use of *Luke* (xxiv. 39) and *John*
(xx. 27–8).

264. Arguments in favour of a late date for the Ignatian letters

It remains then to inquire whether the shorter version of the
seven Greek letters ascribed to Ignatius can possibly date from
about A.D. 110. We are forced to reply that they represent a
later development of Christian belief and speculation. We find,
for instance, an early creed in *Smyrnaeans* (i) which in the longer
version is still further expanded.

The threefold ordering of bishops, priests and deacons has
taken place, though no man is to do anything connected
with the church without the bishop. Without the bishop it is not
lawful to baptize or to celebrate the eucharist. There is also,
even in the shorter version of the letters, an emphasis on the
authority of the bishop which points to the need of strong
government to combat speculative heresy. For instance, in
Smyrnaeans (ix) we get, "It is well to reverence both God and
the bishop. He who honours the bishop has been honoured by
God: he who does anything without the knowledge of the
bishop, serves the devil." Or again, in the letter to *Polycarp*
(vi), "Give heed to the bishop, that God also may give heed
to you."

The reiterated emphasis on the authority of the bishop is so
extravagant as at times to cause a smile. Even a young bishop
must not be treated familiarly: he must receive all reverence.
The need for the exercise of a firm authority in Christian
churches was plainly great.

Again, "the gospel" has become a body of teaching which
can be set against the Jewish scriptures. In *Philadelphians* (viii)
the writer controverts the opinion, "If I do not find the gospel
in the ancient writings, I will not believe it." He goes on to say
(ix), again in the shorter version, "The beloved prophets had a

message pointing to Christ, but the gospel is the perfection c
immortality."

Warnings against heresy are many. Especially strong i
teaching directed against what is known as "the doceti
heresy," the strange belief that Jesus only seemed to suffer
Such teaching is several times repeated. In *Trallians* (ix) it i
said that Jesus Christ was truly born and did eat and drink
was truly persecuted, was truly crucified, was truly raised from
the dead, the writer seeking by repetition to set reality agains
appearance.

From the considerations just brought forward we may
conclude, briefly, that the letters reflect, not the time, say
A.D. 110, when *Luke* and *Acts* had been recently written,
but an emphasis on belief and discipline necessary thirty
or forty years later when the gnostic movement was in ful
spate.

The most famous passage in the so-called Ignatian letters
comes from the letter to the *Romans* (iv). There Ignatius is
made to say, "I am the wheat of God, and I am to be ground
by the teeth of wild beasts, that I may be found the pure bread
of Christ. I would have you entice the wild beasts that they
may become my tomb, and may leave nothing of my body, that
when I sleep in death I may be no burden to anyone." In a
genuine letter this would be an improbable passage unless it
were an hysterical outburst; but we can well imagine it being
written by some later enthusiastic admirer of Ignatius. Significantly, the passage is not quoted until Irenaeus, who will have
written probably some time after A.D. 170; and he does not
name its author.

265. Writings relating to Polycarp

Closely associated with the so-called letters of Ignatius are a
Letter of Polycarp to the Philippians and an account of Polycarp's
martyrdom. Polycarp is said to have lived to the age of eighty-
six; and Irenaeus, whose chief work was published about
A.D. 185, was his disciple. Polycarp's letter appears to be
genuine and shows a knowledge of most books of the New
Testament. Many scholars think that there has been in its
chapter xiii an interpolation to recommend the letters of
Ignatius. It was probably written shortly after the middle of

the second century of our era, and the Ignatian letters may themselves be of that date.

The account of the *Martyrdom of Polycarp* may be based on a contemporary record of, say, A.D. 155–165; but the miraculous stories in it show the labour of a later editor. The attempts to persuade Polycarp to abandon his faith, which occur in the story of the martyrdom, almost certainly reflect faithfully the attitude of government officials in the middle of the second century of our era. For instance, we read (viii), "They endeavoured to persuade him, saying, What harm is there in admitting that Caesar is Lord, and in sacrificing, with the other formalities observed on such occasions, and so making sure of safety?" A little later, we learn that the proconsul sought to persuade Polycarp to deny Christ saying, "Swear by the fortune of Caesar: repent and say, Away with the atheists." In reading such a passage we have to remember that the common accusation against the Christians was that they were "atheists," because they denied the existence of the pagan gods. The "fortune" of Caesar appears as the Greek equivalent of the Latin "*genius*" of Caesar; but it may be usefully recalled that when, in March, A.D. 161, the emperor Antoninus Pius was dying, he commended Marcus Aurelius as his successor and caused the gold statue of fortune which he worshipped to be transferred to Marcus's room.

The account of Polycarp's end is one of the earliest stories of the death of a Christian martyr. In its chapters xv and xvi we learn, among other marvels, that when the flesh of the martyr was burning there was a fragrant smell as of incense and that when the saint was stabbed a dove came forth. This disregard of truth is characteristic of similar records which were subsequently produced in large numbers. We must remember that their primary object was edification. Hagiography, the praise of good men who have died for their faith, can seldom be regarded as history: it is usually fiction masquerading as history in the service of piety. On a meagre basis of fact a vast edifice of fiction was not infrequently raised: hence the lives of the saints abound in fantastically improbable statements and their writers show childish credulity. Probably neither they nor their readers accepted seriously all that they wrote. Works of fiction are in modern times secular; but a liking for fiction was strong when men deemed it their duty to produce only works commending their faith.

266. Conclusion

We have now given a brief review of the more important books in the early Christian literature which lies outside the New Testament. The result is to show that we have no certain witness to the epistles of Paul earlier than Marcion, say in A.D. 140. About the same time the gospels became authoritative. The New Testament, as we have it, indicates the limits to speculative Christian theology which were maintained by the church's leaders towards the middle of the second century.

So far as we can reconstruct the historical situation, it would appear that, by about A.D. 125, there were arising within the church wild theories that would only too probably have led to its disintegration. There followed a struggle against extravagant types of theology—gnostic heresies, as they are sometimes called—which went on for more than half a century. In the end these extravagances were conquered by limiting inspired authority to a collection of books which was practically the New Testament as we now have it. "Heresy" was not then finally overcome; but the framework of Christian theology had henceforth to be found in the authoritative scriptures. The historian can now see that some of the claims made for such scriptures were not justified. Their authors had no personal knowledge of the beginnings of the Christian movement; and the writings betray the presence of religious ideas other than those of Jesus. The struggle against "gnosticism" was long and severe; but in the end the church preserved, not only Christ's teaching as to God and as to man's duty and destiny, but also, with comparatively little contamination, the essentials of the message of the Christian missionaries of the first century.

CHAPTER XV

BAPTISM

A T the outset of any discussion of the two so-called "Dominical sacraments of the Christian church," we must emphasize that, in the opinion of the large majority of independent scholars, Jesus neither instituted sacraments nor founded a church. An independent scholar we define as one who does not feel bound to reach conclusions prescribed by the Christian communion to which he belongs.

267. John the Baptist in the synoptic gospels

According to the gospel story Jesus, before he began his ministry, went to John the Baptist and was baptized by him. All the synoptic gospels give an account of this baptism, and echoes of it occur in the *Gospel according to John*.

Anyone who has heard of gospel criticism and who wishes to investigate for himself the connection between the gospels may well begin by carefully comparing the accounts of John the Baptist and his baptism of Jesus which are to be found in *Mark* (i. 1–11), *Matthew* (iii. 1–17) and *Luke* (iii. 3–22). He who makes this comparison will see at once that the material, which *Matthew* and *Luke* have in common with *Mark*, has come from a single document. The sequence of sentences and the turns of phrase are such as would have been impossible if different spoken traditions had been written down by the different evangelists. The document which is the common basis has been used freely, so that the copying has not been exact. But the three synoptists, so far as this common material is concerned, depend upon a single literary source. This source we know to be *Mark*: the arguments by which this conclusion was reached have already been set out in §§ 115–19 in connection with the general investigation of the gospel sources; and the same conclusion will be justified by the inquiry to which we now proceed.

268. The synoptic record of the Baptist's preaching

In the story of John the Baptist, it was *Mark* who first quoted the words of the prophet *Isaiah* (xl. 3), "The voice of one crying in the wilderness, Make ye ready the way of the Lord, Make his paths straight": the other two synoptic evangelists followed his example. It is *Mark*, moreover, who says that John preached "the baptism of repentance unto remission of sins." *Luke* copied this phrase exactly: *Matthew* merely quotes from *Mark* that the people were "baptized of him in the river Jordan, confessing their sins." Similarly *Mark* (i. 7) records that John the Baptist said, "There cometh after me he that is mightier than I, the latchet of whose shoes I am not worthy to stoop down and unloose. I baptized you with water; but he shall baptize you with the Holy Spirit." *Luke* (iii. 16) and *Matthew* (iii. 11) (with a minor variation) repeat these words. But *Matthew* and *Luke* both add, after "Holy Spirit," the words "and with fire": in this addition they are following a different authority. They go on to say, in almost identical words, "whose fan is in his hand, throughly to cleanse his threshing-floor, and to gather the wheat into his garner; but the chaff he will burn up with unquenchable fire." In these words, which are also absent from *Mark*, they are using one and the same document, their other authority which we know to be Q. This document also contained the Baptist's teaching, which we get repeated almost exactly in *Matthew* (iii. 7–10) and in *Luke* (iii. 7–9).

Thus when the story of John the Baptist and his baptism of Jesus is closely examined, the result is to show conclusively that *Matthew* and *Luke* were working with the same two documents: one of these was *Mark* and the other we have called Q.

There are also, in addition, a few statements peculiar to either the first or the third of the evangelists: they seem to have come from neither *Mark* nor Q. *Matthew* alone says (iii. 2) that the Baptist's message was, "Repent ye; for the kingdom of heaven is at hand": he thus attributes to him the substance of the message of Jesus as we have it in *Mark* (i. 15), "The time is fulfilled, and the kingdom of God is at hand: repent ye, and believe in the good news." *Luke* alone (iii. 10–14) records the advice which the Baptist gave to the well-to-do, to tax-gatherers and to soldiers. It is characteristic of *Luke* that he should thus emphasize the social aspects of John's teaching. More significantly *Matthew* alone (iii. 14–15) records that John protested that he should rather have been baptized by Jesus, and received the reply, "Suffer it now: for thus it becometh us to fulfil all righteousness." The vagueness of this reply, which few scholars would deem historical, shows a certain bewilderment on the part of the writer. Jesus, according to this writer's belief—it will be remembered that he was writing at the close of the first century—needed no change of heart or baptism of repentance unto remission of sins.

We notice further that *Luke* alone (iii. 1–2) tries to give the historical background of the Baptist's mission, and that he alone tells us at this stage (iii. 19–20) of the Baptist's imprisonment by "Herod the tetrarch" (Herod Antipas). In fact, he tries to be a good historian.

269. The baptism of Jesus in the fourth gospel

After having thus examined the story of the baptism as we find it in the first three gospels, it is enlightening to read what is recorded in the fourth gospel. There we see at once that *John* is not copying either Mark or Q. But he has read the synoptic story as it occurs in *Mark*. He repeats the prophecy from *Isaiah*. He knows (i. 27) John the Baptist's saying that he was not worthy to untie the shoelaces of Jesus (*Matthew* had written "carry his shoes"). He implies, but does not explicitly state, that Jesus was baptized; and he does *not* record that a voice came from heaven, saying, "Thou art my beloved Son; in thee I am well pleased." He also knows the story told by all the earlier evangelists that, when Jesus was baptized, the Holy Spirit descended upon him as a dove out of heaven. But, instead of endorsing this story, he says that the Baptist was told that "Upon whomsoever thou shalt see the Spirit descending, and abiding upon him, the same is he that baptizeth with the Holy Spirit."

270. The implications of John's baptism

We come now to the crux of all the narratives. What is the implication of John the Baptist's baptism? Is it likely, or even possible, that he used the language attributed to him? We are told (*Mark* i. 4) that he "preached the baptism of repentance

unto remission of sins." The phrase is not particularly intelligible: perhaps we may translate, "baptism, conditional
on repentance, to obtain forgiveness of sins." But again
we ask, what meaning lies behind these words? Was
acceptance of baptism merely the sign of that change of
heart which ensured Divine forgiveness: or was the baptism
itself supposed to have some such effect as washing away the
stain of sin?

Such questions lead up to others, much more puzzling and
theologically important. What is the meaning of the statement,
attributed to the Baptist, that Jesus shall "baptize you with the
Holy Spirit"? All the gospel writers evidently attach great
significance to baptism with the Spirit. The Q document
seems to have known the phrase and to have added to it, so
that we get the prophecy that Jesus "shall baptize you with the
Holy Spirit and with fire." Coupled with this addition, however, is a reminder that, after threshing, wheat is stored but the
chaff is burned with fire. We are thus led to inquire as to the
significance of this spiritual baptism, linked to the burning up
of that which is worthless. How comes the term so naturally to
the lips of a Jewish preacher of righteousness? John was a desert
ascetic, a Jewish prophet. His background was the religious
tradition of his race: we must seek it in the Old Testament and
in later pre-Christian Judaism.

Now there seems to be some evidence that, when a man
became a Jewish proselyte, he was baptized by immersion to
get rid of ritual impurity: his life as a gentile had been cere-
monially unclean. But, according to the gospel story, John's
baptism was a cleansing from moral impurity; while at the
same time he himself said that Jesus, coming after him and
mightier than he, would "baptize with the Holy Spirit," thus
using a theological phrase that, so far as we know, is strange to
earlier Judaism. In the Septuagint translation of the Old
Testament the term "Holy Spirit" occurs only in a *Psalm*
(li. 11) and in a late chapter of the book of *Isaiah* (lxiii. 10 and
11): in the *Apocrypha* it is to be found—we have given a quotation in § 39—in the contemporary *Wisdom of Solomon* (ix. 17).
The use of the term corresponds to a strengthening under
Hellenic influences of the idea of divine immanence.

271. Josephus and John the Baptist

We can perhaps throw some light on our inquiry by recalling that Josephus, in his *Jewish Antiquities* (XVIII, v. 2), makes mention of John the Baptist. There is no reason to doubt the authenticity of the passage which, in a free translation, runs:

> Some of the Jews thought that the destruction of Herod's army came from God as a just punishment of his action against John who was called the Baptist. For Herod slew him: he was a good man and told the Jews who were training themselves in virtue, to show righteousness towards one another and piety towards God, and to receive baptism. For he said that baptism would be acceptable to him only in those who used it, not to escape from sins, but for purification of the body, if the soul also had previously been thoroughly cleansed by righteousness. Now when many crowded to him, much moved by hearing his words, Herod feared that his great influence would lead to some rebellion, for they seemed ready to do anything that he should advise. Herod therefore thought it best, by putting John to death, to anticipate any mischief he might cause, rather than find himself in difficulties through a revolution and then regret it. Accordingly, through Herod's suspicion John was sent a prisoner to Machaerus and was there put to death.

Josephus almost goes out of his way to insist that John's baptism was not a baptism unto remission of sins. It was for the purification of the body, if the soul had been previously cleansed by righteousness. Thus, according to Josephus, it was not, in any way, sacramental. In the gospels, on the other hand, John's baptism appears to have had a mildly sacramental character; but a mightier sacramental quality, involving the presence and direct action of the Holy Spirit of God, was to attach to the baptism of Jesus.

272. Jesus and baptism

Yet, as we read the synoptic gospels, we find no mention of any baptism by Jesus. He is made to commend the rite in *Mark* (xvi. 16); but this passage occurs in the late addendum to the gospel which replaced the original ending now lost: this addendum, which we mentioned in § 167, is probably a compilation of the second century of our era. Also, at the end of *Matthew* (xxviii. 19) there is the very famous passage, "Go ye therefore, and make disciples of all the nations, baptizing them into the name of the Father and of the Son and of the Holy Spirit." But the use of this formula of baptism in the name of the Trinity, instead of the earlier formula of baptism "in the name of the Lord Jesus," shows that this passage represents, not an early tradition, but late Christian opinion as to what the risen Christ should have said. It must have been formulated many years after the crucifixion of Jesus. Clearly the early tradition preserved no record either that Jesus himself baptized or that he instructed his disciples so to act.

The fourth gospel, as we know, gives us theology under the guise of history. When John the evangelist wrote, baptism was a recognized and fundamental rite, as we see from the passage (*John* iii. 5), "Except a man be born of water and the Spirit, he cannot enter into the kingdom of God." It is, consequently, not surprising that in the fourth gospel there are three explicit statements (iii. 22, iii. 26, and iv. 1) that Jesus himself baptized: what is surprising is that they are followed by a parenthesis (iv. 2), "although Jesus himself baptized not, but his disciples," which looks like an editorial correction.

As a result of this detailed examination, we reach the conclusion that Jesus, before his Galilean ministry, associated himself for a time with a Jewish puritan movement, led by John the Baptist. In this movement baptism by total immersion was a symbol of the change of heart demanded by John. Jesus left the movement, though possibly the complete severance only came after John's death; but it continued for a number of years in a more or less friendly rivalry with the Christian movement. By the time the fourth gospel was written, say A.D. 110–20, the relative success of the two movements was clear, for the Baptist is made to say (iii. 30), "He must increase, but I must decrease."

273. The growth of the practice of baptism

At an earlier stage, say in A.D. 54, we catch a significant side-light on the interaction of the two movements: it is the story of Paul and Apollos at Ephesus, which we have mentioned in chapter xii. We recall that Apollos was a successful Christian missionary, "a learned man," "mighty in the scriptures," who had been "instructed in the way of the Lord." He taught carefully the things concerning Jesus, but knew only the baptism of John (*Acts* xviii. 24–25). When Paul asked the Ephesian converts of Apollos, "Did ye receive the Holy Spirit when ye believed?" they seemed ignorant of the very existence of the Holy Spirit; and so had to be more adequately baptized "into the name of the Lord Jesus" (*Acts* xix. 1–7). Thus, some quarter of a century after the crucifixion of Jesus, new developments in the theology of baptism were taking place: the baptism of John, which had been taken over by the earlier Christian missionaries, was falling into disrepute; and Paul was teaching that Christian baptism had an especial character, derived from its association with the Holy Spirit of God.

Notwithstanding these developments, it is practically certain that, when Jesus began his own ministry, he abandoned the rite of baptism just as he abandoned the Baptist's asceticism. It was not from John that Jesus derived his knowledge of God and message for men. In his teaching and mode of life he drew upon his own religious experience, showing independent understanding and strength: to these qualities *Mark*, and more especially Q, bear clear witness.

Even if Jesus had commanded his followers to baptize, it is unlikely that he would have spoken of "baptism with the Holy Spirit." It is, in fact, doubtful if he ever used the term "Holy Spirit." The famous sentence (*Luke* xi. 13), "your heavenly Father shall give the Holy Spirit to them that ask him," is from Q. But in the corresponding passage in *Matthew* (vii. 11), "your Father which is in heaven" is mentioned, but not the Holy Spirit. *Luke*, in fact, refashioned his excerpt from Q; and used language natural to the time when he wrote his gospel. We noticed a similar change of language when, in § 120, we discussed the problem of doublets. We saw then that, when *Luke* gives "Holy Spirit," *Matthew* gives "Spirit of your Father"; but in one of the Lukan doublets, Jesus is represented as using the first person singular instead of either expression. We conclude that the idea of "baptism with the Holy Spirit" was foreign to the thought, and absent from the teaching, of Jesus.

274. Baptism with the Holy Spirit

How then did the idea arise? Plainly, when the Christian movement began to gain strength, there was need of some rite

T

of admission to the society of believers. Remembering the association of Jesus with the Baptist's movement, and their Master's own baptism, the early missionaries, with the Galilean apostles as their nucleus, began to baptize their converts. The picture of the early progress of Christianity, as we have it at the beginning of *Acts*, is idealized history; it was written up from tradition, possibly with the aid of a few meagre documents, some sixty or seventy years later than the events which it records. But there is clear evidence that, as the new faith was preached, whether at Jerusalem or in gentile cities, its success was often accompanied by contagious religious enthusiasm. A transformed record of such religious excitement, with its incoherent cries and ecstatic certainty, appears in the account of the happenings of the day of Pentecost (*Acts* ii), when Jews from divers countries caught the fervour of the early disciples. Such spiritual exaltation was naturally attributed to the influence of the Holy Spirit of God; or, for the distinction, if in the beginning it existed at all, was very fine, to the influence of the Spirit of Christ.

A new and significant stage in the spread of Christianity was reached, according to *Luke*, when, as a result of Peter's preaching, the gift of the Holy Spirit was poured out on the gentiles: "They heard them speak with tongues and magnify God." This presence of the Spirit was regarded by Peter as a sufficient reason why gentiles should be baptized (*Acts* x. 44–xi. 18). In this instance, there was first the gift of the Spirit and then baptism. Sometimes the sequence was inverted. Thus we read in *Acts* (viii. 12–17) that, though men and women were baptized in the name of the Lord Jesus, the gift of the Holy Spirit was only observed subsequently when leaders of the movement came, as it were, to set the embers aflame.

275. The growth of the theology of baptism

But gradually practice and expectation became stereotyped. There arose the belief that baptism by John was relatively feeble. Christian baptism, on the contrary, was regarded as baptism with the Holy Spirit. In it there was believed to be the direct influence of God, the infusion of His Spirit: it gave the recipient a new birth: he was born again, regenerated. Sometimes such baptism enabled, or was thought to enable, the convert to speak in divers languages; he could prophesy and even—so it was believed—work miracles: the gifts of the Spirit are set out in a well-known passage in the *First Epistle to the Corinthians* (xii. 1–11).

As we have thus traced the development of Christian baptism, and of the spiritual powers supposed to be given by the rite, we have realized that, though the story of the baptism of Jesus is historical, such terms as "baptism of repentance unto remission of sins" and, still more, "baptism with the holy Spirit" cannot have been in use before Jesus began his ministry. They belong to the later period, at which *Mark* and Q wrote, when a completely sacramental view of the rite had developed. By that time baptism had become the outward and visible sign of an inward and spiritual grace which was thought to be conveyed by the rite. In so far as the rite followed conversion, it was not magical; but magic lay just round the corner. Needless to add, all magical and semi-magical ideas are importations into Christianity. There is no sign of them in the teaching of Jesus, or in that of the great Hebrew prophets of whom he was the greatest successor. They flourished, however, in the atmosphere of the pagan mystery-religions.

276. Baptism, ancient and modern

It needs no little imaginative understanding for a modern Christian to realize why baptism was regarded as of such profound importance in the first century of Christianity. He knows that it is now customary for an infant, soon after birth, to be baptized: it is thus formally admitted to the church, of which its membership in later years is only too likely to be more nominal than real. If an interested onlooker makes inquiry of the minister as to the meaning of the "regeneration" supposed to be effected by the rite, he will almost certainly learn that an inheritance of "original sin" has been removed. He will probably be further told that "original sin" is inherited from a first man Adam, who ate forbidden fruit. As the inquirer regards Adam and the talking serpent as equally legendary, he will receive the explanation with bland incredulity. Privately he will wonder whether the minister has ever heard of the science of experimental psychology; and whether an inquiry by that science would show a higher standard of conduct on the part of those "regenerated from original sin" than appears in others who have been subjected to no such rite.

Contrast such "christening" with baptism in the early church. Then a convert took a step of vital significance. He gave up the easy laxity of life and speech common to pagan friends and neighbours. He joined a body of men and women who were hated and derided by the populace, and who lived under the menacing frown of the imperial government. At any moment persecution might break out; and the step which he had taken would expose him to vindictive rancour. He would, however, know that many who had been baptized had, in or after the ceremony, felt the Christ-spirit taking possession of them. The Spirit of Christ was the divine power moving among Christians. They were waiting for Christ to come to create a new order, visible in all its moral beauty and religious splendour: meanwhile, they were preparing themselves and their little world to be ready for Christ's kingdom. The convert would know, further, that not a few who had taken the decisive step of joining the church, with all the danger which it entailed, had felt a vast elation. Before taking the step they had been "sore let and hindered," dogged by memories of evil habits and practices. But the sense of sin had suddenly gone. The Christ had come.

It was true that such spiritual freedom and joy were not universal. But by general consent they were to be expected. The convert was prepared for them by prayer and fasting. He, a few friends, and the man who was to baptize him, all fasted, as we learn alike in the *Didache* (vii) and from Justin's *First Apology* (61). The preparation was solemn and doubtless, like the rite, secret. The convert was treading a most dangerous path, renouncing the possibility of civic honours, losing social safety and esteem. Would the spiritual splendour that others had known and that he hoped for—"illumination" and baptism were often used as equivalent words—be worth his renunciation of so many worldly hopes and ambitions? The decisive day came. A new member was added to the church. What was his religious experience? For an answer we grope amid obscurity. Few can describe inward spiritual move-ments and certainties. Yet, after baptism, many a Christian convert must have been greatly satisfied, or he would have speedily left the dangerous society which he had imprudently joined.

It is only as we realize how profound was the social and civic importance of baptism, and how joyful the spiritual ecstasy that it must often have brought, that we can examine, with the reverence they deserve to receive, the various theories of baptism that were put forward. Coldly considered, a theory may seem quite unworthy of patient consideration until one remembers that it is an attempt to explain a supreme emotional experience.

277. Infant baptism

In view of what has just been written, it is hardly necessary to say that there is no evidence for infant baptism in the early church. It is sometimes argued that infant baptism is implied in the statement (*Acts* xvi. 15) that Lydia "was baptized, and her household." The argument will only carry conviction to those who wish to be convinced. As against any such practice the rules as to fasting before baptism are decisive. One may doubt if any mother would let her infant fast "one or two days before": a fast of even a few hours would be impracticable.

278. Baptism in "living" water

Originally, as we learn from the *Didache* (vii), baptism by total immersion in "living water," that is to say, in a running stream, seems to have been regarded as the ideal. However, if running water was impossible, still water would suffice; and, if there were no cold water available, warm could be used. In default of total immersion, water might be thrice poured on the head. Probably "living" water was used, in part, because Jesus was baptized in the flowing Jordan; and, in part, to emphasize the connection of baptism with the new birth in Christ, regeneration by the Holy Spirit. The convert, according to the theory set out in the fourth gospel (iii. 3–8), was "born of water and the Spirit" that he might enter the kingdom of God. *John*, in his usual elusive way, does not commit himself to the view that baptism ensures the gift of the Spirit. But the living water is more than a means of purification: it is a symbol of the life eternal which comes from Christ.

279. Pauline or pseudo-Pauline theories

An entirely different theory of baptism is to be found, as we have seen in § 235, in the *Epistle to the Romans* (vi. 3–11). There baptism is associated, not with life, but with death. "All we who were baptized into Christ Jesus were baptized into his death. We were buried therefore with him through baptism into death: that like as Christ was raised from the dead through the glory of the Father, so we also might walk in newness of life." In such a passage the influence of the pagan mystery-religions is dominant. As we stated in chapter iii, the man who was initiated into such a religion symbolically suffered the painful experience of the Lord of his faith, and thereby shared his triumph. A mysterious kinship had been established between the Saviour-Lord and the man who sought salvation by his aid. The victory of the Saviour-Lord, after suffering and death, was by a sort of sympathetic magic communicated to whosoever was rightly initiated.

Paul, or whoever wrote in his name, thinks of baptism as an initiation whereby the convert symbolically dies and is buried with Christ. "We were buried therefore with him through baptism into death." But just as Christ was gloriously raised from the dead to life eternal, so the Christian rises after baptism to a new life. We recall the fact, to which we have already drawn attention in § 258, that at a later time the *Shepherd of Hermas* says of the baptized that they "descend into the water dead, and they arise alive." Of Christ, Paul says (*Romans* vi. 10–11), "In that he died, he died unto sin once; but the life that he liveth, he liveth unto God. Even so reckon ye also yourselves to be dead unto sin, but alive unto God in Christ Jesus."

There is a close association between sin and death in Pauline teaching. In the passage just cited, Paul seems to say that the victor over death is also the victor over sin. The Christian convert can similarly die unto sin and live unto God, if in baptism he shares the death of Christ. Baptism is thus not the efficacious symbol of redemption but, it would seem, the sacramental condition.

But we must, in the region of the mystery-faiths, be always on our guard against a desire for logical precision. It has been well remarked, in connection with the infiltration of oriental beliefs into Roman paganism, that the West eschewed absolute affirmations: it was content with metaphors and preferred to use obscure expressions which admitted of differing interpretations. Studied ambiguity has its uses elsewhere than in diplomacy.

280. Baptism for the dead

A most curious development in the early church appears to have been the baptism of the dead by proxy. We find mention of it in the tract on the resurrection, which now forms chapter xv of the *First Epistle to the Corinthians*. There we read (xv. 29–30), "Else what shall they do which are baptized for the dead? If the dead are not raised at all, why then are they baptized for them?" Unsuccessful attempts have been made to show that the translation conveys a wrong meaning. But evidently it was felt unfair that those who had died before having had the knowledge that they could obtain redemption to eternal life by baptism, should be excluded from regeneration. They were therefore baptized by proxy. The practice naturally died out when Christianity ceased either to be a new movement or to be spreading into new regions.

281. Sin after baptism

As we have tried to make clear, baptism in the early church was the believer's transcendent experience. It was the new birth in which the stain of old sins was removed. The baptized convert was "in Christ." There seems reason to believe that in some of the mystery-religions the rite of initiation could be repeated: most certainly a man could have himself initiated into different faiths. Christianity, however, would not come to terms with any rival religion; and, by a sound psychological judgment, never permitted repetition of a baptism that was not deemed defective.

With such practice and with the beliefs which we have set forth the problem of sin after baptism gradually became acute. As we read the Pauline letters and the *Epistle to the Hebrews*, we are left with the impression that the writers believed that he who was in Christ could not fall into sin. The same teaching appears in the *First Epistle of John* (iv. 15), "Whosoever shall confess that Jesus is the Son of God, God abideth in him, and he in God."

As the church established itself, while the expectation of the immediate return of Christ died away, sin among baptized Christians became all too obvious. What was to be done? We have seen in § 258 that in the *Shepherd of Hermas*, probably written in the period A.D. 130–50, the possibility of a single repentance for sin after baptism is held out. Gradually more opportunities had to be allowed: in the end the ecclesiastical discipline of confession and absolution became standardized. None the less, for centuries the danger of sin after baptism was deemed so great that many Christians postponed baptism until they were at the point of death. Such postponement was reasonable, if not edifying. Granted that baptism annulled all past sins, a death-bed baptism made a man safe in the world to come. Strange that men did not perceive that an assumption which logically led to such a conclusion must be false!

CHAPTER XVI

THE EUCHARIST

282. Modern conclusions as to the eucharist

IF not from the beginning, at any rate from shortly after the death of Jesus, entrance to the Christian community was, as it were, ratified by baptism. Baptized members of the community, also from very early days, joined in a common religious rite, originally described as "the breaking of bread." This rite, apparently at first an introduction to an actual meal though afterwards the food was symbolic, became the principal rite of the organized community. Various terms have been used to describe it, among the more common being the Lord's Supper, the Holy Communion, the Mass. We shall, as heretofore, use an early Greek term, from a word which, as we have said in § 250, means both a thanksgiving and a blessing, and call it the eucharist. Though we may describe the eucharist as the principal rite of the early Christians, we must not be thought to ignore the fact that they had other regular meetings for worship in which hymns, prayers and the reading of sacred or edifying books seem to have been conjoined.

At the beginning of a discussion of the eucharist, it is well to state two facts to which reference has already been made. In the first place, a majority of independent scholars are of opinion that at the Last Supper Jesus did not say, "Do this in remembrance of me." Secondly, a minority of such scholars, which seems to be steadily growing, would add that the sentences, "This is my body," "This is my blood," are equally unhistorical. Scholars in this minority contend that the story, as we have it in slightly different forms in the *First Epistle to the Corinthians*, in the synoptic gospels, and in the *First Apology* of Justin Martyr, grew up as an attempt to give Christ's authority to the existing cult-practice of the common meal. When a religion has a rite in general use, it must have an explanation of, or authority for, that rite. The story of the Last Supper commended and explained the "breaking of bread."

283. The " breaking of bread "

There is no reason to doubt that, during the Galilean
ministry, when Jesus and his followers shared their simple
meal, it was his custom, after a short prayer of thanksgiving,
to break and distribute the bread. He thus assumed the position
of host when they ate together. In memory of him, his apostles,
after his death, solemnly broke bread when they, and their
converts, made the common meal a part of their primitive ritual.
Such formal meals, as we have seen, had parallels in the feasts
of the pagan mystery-faiths. Perhaps in consequence, the risen
Christ was gradually thought to be present as host when the
bread was broken. The stories of his post-resurrection appearances, as we have them in *Luke* and *John*, must have been
written long after the crucifixion of Jesus. But, as we pointed out
in §§ 169–171, confidence in the presence at the eucharist of the
risen Christ has been preserved. We recall that in *John*
(xxi. 13), "Jesus cometh and taketh the bread, and giveth
them." In *Luke* (xxiv. 35), the disciples of the walk to Emmaus
"rehearsed the things that happened in the way, and how he
was known of them in the breaking of bread."

At the beginning of *Acts*, *Luke* seems to have preserved a
faithful recollection of early days when he says that, after the
notable outburst of spiritual enthusiasm on the day of Pentecost
(ii. 42), "they continued stedfastly in the apostles' teaching and
fellowship, in the breaking of bread and the prayers."

The association of prayers with the breaking of bread will
have been primitive. There is every reason to think that Jesus
was brought up in, and was loyal to, the customs of strict
Jewish piety. At the beginning of a meal in which he acted as
host, he will have spoken a prayer of thanksgiving. Another
prayer will have ended the meal. We thus have "the breaking
of bread and the prayers" by which the new converts showed
their fellowship with the apostles whose teaching they accepted.

Even a hundred and twenty years later, as we shall see
(§ 325) in Justin Martyr's account of the eucharist, one of the
assembled brethren, acting as president, gave thanks "at
considerable length" over bread and a cup of wine mixed
with water, which had been brought and placed before him.
The only set words of his prayer seem to have been comprised
in the statement that he "gives praise and glory to the Father

of the universe, through the name of the Son and of the Holy
Spirit." In Justin's time "the water mixed with wine" has
come to occupy a place as important as that of the bread; but
here are indications, as we have seen for example in § 189,
that the wine might at times be replaced by water: wine was an
accessory of, and not a fundamental element in, the eucharistic
rite.

184. The institution of the eucharist

At first sight, the evidence for the institution of the eucharist
by Jesus on the night of his betrayal seems exceptionally satisfactory. We have, in the first place, the brief but definite statement in the *First Epistle to the Corinthians* (xi. 23–26), an epistle
which, in so far as it is genuine, must have been written in, say,
A.D. 54, only about a quarter of a century after the crucifixion
of Jesus. Then we have the account in the gospel according to
Mark (xiv. 22–25). As we have seen, it is impossible to assign a
definite date to this gospel, but perhaps A.D. 75 is not far wrong.
The account in the gospel according to *Matthew* (xxvi, 26–29) is
obviously based on that in *Mark*; but *Luke* (xxii. 15–21), writing
about the end of the first century of our era, preserves an
independent tradition which seems to contain all that is
essential in the other records. It is true that in the gospel
according to *John* there is no account of the Last Supper; but
there is explicit eucharistic teaching which seems to assume a
knowledge of the synoptic story: there is, for instance, the
teaching (vi. 53–54), "Except ye eat the flesh of the Son of man
and drink his blood, ye have not life in yourselves. He that
eateth my flesh and drinketh my blood hath eternal life; and I
will raise him up at the last day." Finally, in the *First Apology* of
Justin Martyr (chapter 66), which was written about A.D. 150,
we have in substance the usual story: it is stated to come from
"the apostles, in the memoirs which have been handed down
from them, which are called gospels." Witnesses thus seem to
come forward with undeviating testimony. In fact, evidence
appears to be piled upon evidence—until we begin a careful
sifting of our authorities. Then, as we proceed to show, the
story disappears into a haze of doubt.

At the outset we may set aside the account of the Last Supper
in Justin Martyr, which will be given in full in § 325: it is almost

certainly an imperfectly remembered blend with the synoptic
records of the narrative in the *First Epistle to the Corinthians*. By
the time of Justin the gospels and, very probably, the more
important epistles attributed to Paul were deemed authoritative
and existed in substantially the forms in which we know them.

285. The Last Supper according to the *First Epistle to the Corinthians*

As we proceed to investigate our other authorities we will
put out, in the first place, the story given in the *First Epistle to
the Corinthians* (xi. 23–26). It runs:

> For I received of the Lord that which also I delivered unto you,
> how that the Lord Jesus in the night in which he was betrayed
> took bread; and when he had given thanks, he brake it, and said,
> This is my body, which is for you: this do in remembrance of
> me. In like manner also the cup, after supper, saying, This cup
> is the new covenant in my blood: this do, as oft as ye drink it,
> in remembrance of me. For as often as ye eat this bread, and
> drink the cup, ye proclaim the Lord's death till he come.

We have previously in §§ 224–226 set out reasons for the belief
that the *First Epistle to the Corinthians* consists of a short genuine
letter into which a bundle of notes, fly-sheets and memoranda
has been inserted. Such material may well have been accumu-
lated during the last half of the first century of our era; and the
final insertion may have been made at any date before the
appearance of the Pauline epistles in connection with the
controversy raised by Marcion at Rome about A.D. 140. We
have, further, to bear in mind the common practice of ancient
Jewish authors, who believed themselves to be giving the views
of some important person, to write in his name. A modern
teacher would say, "There is good reason to believe that Paul
received directly from his Lord, in such a vision as that on the
way to Damascus, the following account of what took place at
the Last Supper." Among the Jews an ancient teacher, accepting a long-established convention, would say, "I, Paul,
received of the Lord this revelation." In accordance with such
custom, the teaching of *John* the evangelist is in the fourth
gospel ascribed to Jesus: *John's* beliefs are set out in what purport
to be the very words of his Lord. Such action conformed to com-

non practice and therefore would probably not be misunderstood. We may doubt whether anyone, for instance, imagined that the *Wisdom of Solomon*, probably composed when Jesus was a child, was written by the renowned Hebrew monarch a thousand years earlier.

If we assert that Paul did actually in A.D. 54 write the passage just quoted, we must confess ourselves bewildered as to his meaning. He could only have received information from his Lord in a vision; and a vision conveying such detailed information as he gives is incredible. We cannot accept the plea that the words attributed to Paul merely imply that he had received his account of the Last Supper from disciples who were present. In *Galatians* (i. 11–12) he firmly asserts that the gospel preached by him was "not after man." "For neither did I receive it from man, nor was I taught it, but it came to me through revelation of Jesus Christ." We are forced back on the belief that we have the words of a follower of Paul, writing, maybe, half a century after his death, who knew of doubts as to the Marcan story of the origin of the eucharist, and wished to dispel them.

86. The Last Supper according to *Mark*

If the pseudo-Pauline account be thus set aside, our earliest record of the Last Supper is that in the gospel according to *Mark* (xiv. 22–25). It is convenient to give the passage in full:

> And as they were eating, he took bread, and when he had blessed, he brake it, and gave to them, and said, Take ye: this is my body. And he took a cup, and when he had given thanks, he gave to them: and they all drank of it. And he said unto them, This is my blood of the covenant, which is shed for many. Verily I say unto you, I will no more drink of the fruit of the vine, until that day when I drink it new in the kingdom of God.

As we compare this account with the pseudo-Pauline story, we notice at once that the command to repeat the rite is missing. The words, "This do in remembrance of me," which are twice repeated in the record attributed to Paul, are simply not there. Secondly, "the new covenant in my blood" has now become "my blood of the covenant, which is shed for many." Finally, we recall that the pseudo-Pauline account ends with the words, "as often as ye eat this bread, and drink the cup, ye proclaim the Lord's death till he come"; but, in *Mark*, Jesus says, "I will no more drink of the fruit of the vine, until that day when I drink it new in the kingdom of God." The first account gives what purports to be Paul's understanding of the significance of the rite: the second has been thought by some scholars to show that the record of the institution of the eucharist has been inserted into what had been the story of a meal anticipating the feast of the redeemed in the kingdom of God.

Endless controversy has taken place as to the meaning of the verb in the sentence, "this is my body." Jesus must have spoken Aramaic, in which language the word "is" would not occur; but to take literally the statement—assuming that he made it—that the bread which he was breaking was actually his body, is plainly impossible.

In connection with the phrase, "the blood of the covenant," we may quote the book of *Exodus* (xxiv. 8), where "Moses took the blood, and sprinkled it on the people, and said, Behold the blood of the covenant, which the Lord hath made with you . . ."

287. The Last Supper according to *Matthew*

If the reader will consult any arrangement of the gospels in which parallel passages are set out side by side, he will see that *Matthew* practically repeats *Mark*. The one change of importance is that the blood of the covenant is now said to be shed for many "for the remission of sins." This addition is obviously intended to leave no doubt as to the meaning of *Mark's* phrase. Thus the blood of Jesus, now about to be shed, is alike in *Mark* and *Matthew* the blood of an atoning sacrifice.

288. The Last Supper according to *Luke*

In spite of repetition, it is necessary to give in full the story as told by *Luke* (xxii. 15–21), in order to make clear that we have in his gospel a different tradition. For some reason, either because his copy of *Mark* was imperfect, or because he thought that he possessed better information than was contained in the Marcan story, he did not use that story. *Luke's* variant runs:

> With desire I have desired to eat this passover with you before I suffer: for I say unto you, I will not eat it, until it be fulfilled in the kingdom of God. And he received a cup, and when he had

given thanks, he said, Take this, and divide it among yourselves: for I say unto you, I will not drink from henceforth of the fruit of the vine, until the kingdom of God shall come. And he took bread, and when he had given thanks, he brake it, and gave to them, saying, This is my body [which is given for you: this do in remembrance of me. And the cup in like manner after supper, saying, This cup is the new covenant in my blood, even that which is poured out for you]. But behold, the hand of him that betrayeth me is with me on the table.

In this account we notice, first of all, that near the middle of t there is that suggestion of an anticipation of the feast of the redeemed which comes at the end of the Marcan story. In the second place, we notice that the cup is mentioned twice, once before and once after the bread. We should be sorely puzzled by this duplication were it not that a series of manuscripts, embodying what is called the Western Text, omit the words which we have put in brackets. This omission undoubtedly takes us back to *Luke's* original text: it leaves us with one cup (which comes before the bread), and it omits the words, "this do in remembrance of me." What happened is clear. Some scribe, dismayed by the difference between *Luke's* story and that attributed to Paul, filled out the one by the other. None of our complete manuscripts is older than the fourth century of our era; but, of course, all have been copied from older manuscripts. Plainly, after *Luke's* gospel had become authoritative, his account of the Last Supper was felt to be so inadequate that it was altered.

Henceforth we will deal with the original Lukan story, omitting the bracketed verses. We notice that, on the assumption that this text gives a true account of the words of Jesus, the command, "This do in remembrance of me" has vanished from all the gospels. Jesus did *not* "in his holy Gospel command us to continue, a perpetual memory of that his precious death," as the words run in the consecration prayer of the English Prayer Book. The only narrative, according to which Jesus commands the repetition of the rite, is the pseudo-Pauline story which, as we have seen reason to think, is a late insertion into the *First Epistle to the Corinthians*.

We notice next that *Luke* puts the cup before the bread. He is thus in accord with an early tradition which finds a place in a further fragment of eucharistic teaching inserted in the *Firs[t] Epistle to the Corinthians* (x. 16), "The cup of blessing which w[e] bless, is it not a communion of the blood of Christ? The brea[d] which we break, is it not a communion of the body of Christ?' The same order is retained in the *Didache* (ix), as we hav[e] already seen in § 250.

We notice, further, that, according to *Luke*, Judas partici- pated in the Last Supper. The record of his presence un- doubtedly belongs to an early tradition, for it has shocke[d] ecclesiastics through the centuries. If Judas was admitted t[o] communion by Jesus, who in the world can be excommuni- cated? The answer, assuming that the story of the Last Suppe[r] is a record of fact, would appear to be that the eucharist shoul[d] be used to help towards a "godly righteous and sober life," an[d] not, by its deprivation, as a mode of punishment.

Still further, from the story in *Luke* we are given to under- stand, even more clearly than in the other two synoptic gospels, that the Last Supper was actually the passover meal and tha[t] after it Jesus expected to "suffer," in other words, that he had at the meal a foreknowledge of his crucifixion. Most scholars, as we have seen in § 160, hold that the Last Supper could not possibly have been the passover meal.

289. The last Supper and a new covenant

The important question now arises as to whether we ca[n] accept either the Marcan story, or the shortened form of the story in *Luke*, as a record of fact. The story in *Mark* arouses grave misgivings because Jesus is made to say that his blood would establish a new covenant. But his actual teaching i[n] Galilee had called men to enter the kingdom of God. He thought of himself, not as destroying, but as more truly ful- filling the old Law. A new covenant is foreign to his whole outlook as we find it in the synoptic gospels: it belongs to the ideas of Paul, or of a pseudo-Paul, to whom Jesus was the second Adam. In short, behind the Marcan story lies the redemption theology attributed to Paul.

We are then left with the shortened form of the Lukan story. Can we accept it as a record of fact? The answer is almost certainly in the negative.

In the first place, even from *Luke's* story the idea that the

leath of Jesus is an atoning sacrifice is not altogether absent.
The broken bread is "my body." Though the words "which is
given for you" be omitted, we have a suggestion of redemption.
The language and the thought are not such as belong to the
eaching of Jesus and of his early Jewish followers. Yet we must
not expect to find decisive evidence in the books of the New
Testament for a conclusion adverse to the Lukan story. From
hese books all sharp contradictions, if they existed, have been
emoved. The books were, for the most part, made authorita-
ive in the second century of our era; and we must assume that
hey were then edited so as to remove harsh discrepancies. If
a book could not be so edited it was discarded. For this reason
he *Didache* was set aside. As we saw, its account of the eucharist
shows a development of the early "breaking of bread," which
accorded naturally with Jewish piety. In it the eucharist is
epresented as the principal rite of the church; and yet there is
no hint of a knowledge of the Lukan story. The latter, in fact,
belongs to the type of Christianity which grew up when the
gospel was preached to gentiles, a type of which Paul is the
best-known exponent. It owes its form to the influence of the
mystery-faiths, in which, as we have seen in chapter iii, mystical
participation in the death of the Saviour-God leads to a share
n his immortality.

90. The Last Supper and the fourth gospel

Among the authoritative books of the New Testament is the
fourth gospel. In it there is a silent challenge to the Lukan
story of the Last Supper. As we have more than once pointed
out, *John* never formally corrects the other evangelists: he
ndicates his dissent obliquely. Thus he ignores nearly all that
other evangelists say of the last meal and places his eucharistic
eaching (vi. 22–65) after the miracle of the feeding of the five
housand (vi. 4–13). This miracle, which cannot be a statement
of fact, is plainly a eucharistic myth. It has been contended that
John gave no account of the institution of the eucharist because
each of the other evangelists recorded it. This argument will
not hold good, because each of the other evangelists gives an
account of the feeding of the five thousand—to say nothing
of the fact that its duplicate, the feeding of the four thousand,
also appears in *Matthew* and *Mark*. We are forced to the con-

U

clusion that, though *John* accepted the full sacramental significance of the eucharist, he did not believe that the synoptic story of the Last Supper was good history.

291. The general conclusion

To sum up, we gather from our inquiry that Jesus did not say at the Supper, "This do in remembrance of me"; and it is highly improbable that he spoke the sentences, "This is my body," "This is my blood." Those sentences, and the story in which they are embedded, grew up in a gentile environment, probably in the latter half of the first century of our era. The story will have rapidly won acceptance because it enhanced the significance of the common meal which, after baptism, was to Christians their formal bond of union. The pagans in their mystery-religions had similar common meals: in particular, as we learn from Justin Martyr (see § 325), the form of the eucharist was very like that of the communion of the followers of Mithra, the Persian god of the unconquerable sun. When in chapter iii we described the mystery-religions which intruded themselves into Roman paganism, in and shortly before the first centuries of the empire, we pointed out that Mithraism was centuries older than Christianity; and, though Christianity seems to have progressed with at least equal rapidity in the period A.D. 50–150, the two faiths were in acute rivalry until the end of the third century of our era. If any rival faith had for its communion a myth which emphasized the high sacramental significance of the rite, it was natural that a similar myth should make its appearance within Christianity.

What can we save of the story of the Last Supper? Such a question cannot be answered with any confidence; but it may well be that the cult-story was inserted in the record of an early tradition, in which Jesus replaced the feast of preparation for the passover by a meal foreshadowing the unity of his followers in the kingdom of God. "With desire I have desired to eat this passover with you before I suffer: for I say unto you, I will not not eat it, until it be fulfilled in the kingdom of God." "I will no more drink of the fruit of the vine, until that day when I drink it new in the kingdom of God."

292. The relative importance of baptism and the eucharist in the early church

After having thus dealt with the historical basis of the eucharist, we have now briefly to examine the significance attached to the rite in the New Testament, and particularly in the writings attributed to Paul and in the fourth gospel.

In the epistles of Paul, speaking generally, much more significance is attached to baptism than to the eucharist. Naturally so, for, as we have emphasized in chapter xv, it was for the early Christian by far the more important rite. He who was baptized took a step which severed him from his fellow-citizens. He cut himself off from the usual expression of loyalty to the emperor. He avoided all civic ceremonies in the local temples. In a social environment where "the priest was the butcher, and the butcher the priest," he would not purchase meat which came from animals slaughtered in the sacrifices. He attached himself to a "poisonous superstition," of which horrible stories were told. The eucharist was, *per contra*, merely the cult meal of those who had been baptized. It only became of primary importance when all the world was nominally Christian; and, with its growing importance, its theology became, as some would say, more adequate; as others would say, more extravagant. Later developments, however, do not here concern us: they belong, not to the rise, but to the later growth of Christianity.

293. Eucharistic theology in the fourth gospel

The passage in the fourth gospel which contains the evangelist's eucharistic teaching is too long to quote in full. In form, it is teaching which Jesus himself gives: in fact, *John* ascribes to Jesus his own doctrine. Without misrepresenting this teaching, we may quote:

> Verily, verily, I say unto you, It was not Moses that gave you the bread out of heaven; but my Father giveth you the true bread out of heaven. For the bread of God is that which cometh down out of heaven, and giveth life unto the world. . . . I am the bread of life: he that cometh to me shall not hunger, and he that believeth on me shall never thirst. . . . I am the living bread which came down out of heaven: if any man eat of this bread, he shall live for ever.

In the above passage we have extracted a number of sentences from the earlier part of the Johannine eucharistic teaching (vi. 32–51). In them, plainly, the bread is the symbol of the spiritual salvation to eternal life which Jesus brings to men. But subsequently we have further teaching, which at first sight seems to be as crude in its magical realism as that which, as we shall see in § 326, was given a generation later by Justin Martyr. We may quote the sentences (vi. 53–6):

> Except ye eat the flesh of the Son of man and drink his blood, ye have not life in yourselves. He that eateth my flesh and drinketh my blood hath eternal life; and I will raise him up at the last day. For my flesh is meat indeed, and my blood is drink indeed. He that eateth my flesh and drinketh my blood abideth in me, and I in him.

There are hidden depths in the fourth evangelist: he likes to give with one hand and to take away with the other. The sentences just quoted have a crudity which should suffice the most thoroughgoing believer in the existence of a spiritual presence in the consecrated elements. *John* himself suggests that the disciples felt the teaching to be "hard"; and then in a single sentence he rejects all its magical implications. "It is the spirit that quickeneth; the flesh profiteth nothing: the words that I have spoken unto you are spirit, and are life" (vi. 63). The dexterity of this *volte-face* is not realized at a hasty reading; but it is characteristic of the man who supremely among New Testament writers combined the truest mysticism with rugged common sense. According to *John*, the bread and wine of the eucharist are indeed the flesh and blood of Jesus, but they are so mystically. In themselves they are the flesh "which profiteth nothing." It is the spirit of God that quickens men: Christ's teaching brings that spirit and gives life.

294. Eucharistic teaching in the eleventh chapter of the *First Epistle to the Corinthians*

The eucharistic teaching of Paul, or more probably of a follower writing in his name, is to be found in the *First Epistle to the Corinthians*. We have already in § 285 quoted the pseudo-Pauline account (xi. 23–6) of the institution of the rite by the Lord Jesus. This account is followed by teaching embodying

beliefs so primitive that there is much difficulty in assuming
them to have come from an educated Jew. We quote
(xi. 27–31):

> Wherefore whosoever shall eat the bread or drink the cup of
> the Lord unworthily, shall be guilty of the body and the blood of
> the Lord. But let a man prove himself, and so let him eat of the
> bread, and drink of the cup. For he that eateth and drinketh,
> eateth and drinketh judgement unto himself, if he discern not the
> body. For this cause many among you are weak and sickly, and
> not a few sleep. But if we discerned ourselves, we should not be
> judged.

This passage is none too easy to understand, as we do not
know the precise significance of the words translated, "discern
not the body." But plainly the rite is not thought of as a pure
sacrament, whereby a moral and spiritual link is formed between
the worshipper and his Lord. The bread and wine used in it are
thought to acquire physical properties. If they are wrongly
taken, they are a poison, making men weak and sickly, and
even causing death. The consecrated elements, in fact, are a
test of worth: if you are good, they will do you good; but if
you are bad, they may kill you. We move in the region of ideas
from which comes the practice of throwing a suspected witch
into water.

The teaching cannot be taken seriously. Nor, surely, can it
be ascribed to Paul: it is well below the level of his spiritual
understanding. The passage, in fact, might have been ignored
did it not follow immediately as a comment upon the account
of the institution of the eucharist which, as we have argued, is
equally not by Paul.

295. Eucharistic teaching in the tenth chapter of the *First Epistle to the Corinthians*

Other eucharistic teaching in the *First Epistle to the Corinthians*
appears in the tenth chapter which, in all probability, was
originally a separate fly-sheet, or the substance of an address,
by some Christian living in a gentile environment a generation
or more after Paul's death. It was plainly not written by the
author of the eleventh chapter, for the latter in his account of
the Last Supper puts the bread before the cup, whereas the

order is reversed in the chapter now under consideration: the two writers had inherited different traditions. The present tradition, which is that of the uninterpolated Lukan story and of the *Didache*, is almost certainly the earlier.

We have already in § 226 made reference to this chapter with its strange opening, comprising references to ancient Hebrew legends and far-fetched analogies. But it is the later specifically doctrinal passage (x. 16–21) which now calls for quotation:

> The cup of blessing which we bless, is it not a communion of the blood of Christ? The bread which we break, is it not a communion of the body of Christ? seeing that we, who are many, are one bread, one body: for we all partake of the one bread. Behold Israel after the flesh: have not they which eat the sacrifices communion with the altar? What say I then? that a thing sacrificed to idols is anything, or that an idol is anything? But I say, that the things which the Gentiles sacrifice, they sacrifice to devils, and not to God: and I would not that ye should have communion with devils. Ye cannot drink the cup of the Lord, and the cup of devils: ye cannot partake of the table of the Lord, and of the table of devils.

The sentences in this passage seem roughly thrown together, and suggest notes for an address rather than a finished statement. We notice, first of all, that the author at the beginning does not say explicitly that the bread of the eucharist is the body of Christ: he is content to say that the common cup gives communion in Christ's blood: the loaf which is broken gives communion in his body. The rite is thus truly sacramental, for by it the many worshippers become one body. But our author, after an allusion to "Israel after the flesh," proceeds to establish the closest possible analogy between the Lord's Supper and a pagan sacrificial meal. The pagan gods are asserted to be demons or devils—as is usual with second-century Christian apologists. Christ is contrasted with these demons; but the bread and wine of the eucharist are regarded as strictly parallel to the oblations on pagan altars.

296. Christianity and pagan sacrifices

At a pagan feast, when the flesh of a sacrificial animal was eaten, the worshipper did not think that he was eating the god; but, by means of the meal, he was establishing a mystical union between himself and the god. This union was other than a simple influence emanating from the god: it was to be likened to possession of the worshipper by the god. So too, it would seem, by analogy, in the eucharist the worshipper did not with the bread eat the flesh of Christ, neither did he in drinking the wine drink Christ's blood; but, by means of the meal, he established a mystical union between himself and his Saviour: he became possessed, as Paul had felt himself possessed, by the Christ-Spirit. "I live, and yet no longer I, but Christ liveth in me" (*Galatians* ii. 20).

Now we are so accustomed to these ideas that they seem to many Christians to belong to Christ's teaching. It comes as a shock to them to learn that at bottom such ideas are pagan, not Jewish. The Jewish sacrifices were offerings by which the favour of God was sought: they were the expression of reverence and faithfulness. Our author is, it would seem, not satisfied by such a conception. He will have it that the Jewish sacrifices establish what he terms "communion with the altar": he hesitates to say "communion with the God of Israel," for such language would mean too violent a breach with the traditional language of Judaism. As he sees the situation, there is between his Lord and pagan gods the strongest opposition, but also a sinister similarity. These gods are evil rival devils. Though idols are nothing and though things sacrificed to idols are nothing, yet by pagan sacrifices it is possible to make communion with devils. Such sacrifices are, in fact, real with the horrible reality of a Black Mass: they are an intolerable affront to Christ. For a member of a Christian community to go to a pagan sacrificial meal is "to provoke the Lord to jealousy." And our author asks grimly (x. 22), "Are we stronger than he?"

297. The Christian refusal of compromise

This teaching is plainly directed against a tendency to abandon the firmly exclusive policy of the early Christians, a policy which was alike the foundation of the strength of the Christian movement and a main cause of its unpopularity. When our author wrote, the various mystery-religions of the Graeco-Roman world were, as we have seen, not mutually exclusive rivals of one another. A man might be initiated into several of these cults. There must have been a period when the

Christian religion, with its Saviour-God, and its eucharist like
to a pagan sacrifice, seemed but another mystery-faith. Whoever wrote the passage we have been considering saw the
danger of any process of accommodation. So he emphatically
asserted that whoever came to the table of the Lord must
fiercely shun "the table of devils."

The temptation to form tacit alliances with other religious
movements, in some ways remarkably similar, must have been
strong. Such an alliance would, however, have meant the
ultimate repudiation of all that was most characteristic in the
teaching of Jesus. Because Christianity refused compromise
with other faiths, it survived to become, until practically our
own time, the nominal, and not wholly ineffective, religion of
Europe. Whether, by reaffirming the teaching of Jesus in its
undeviating severity, Christianity can resume its hold on the
hearts and minds of men, is a question of great importance as
regards the ultimate fate of European civilization.

CHAPTER XVII

THE CHRISTIAN MOVEMENT AND THE ROMAN EMPIRE

298. Christianity, socialist, pacifist, internationalist

IN its early authoritative documents the Christian movement is represented as essentially moral and law-abiding. Its members desired to be good citizens and loyal subjects. They shunned the failings and vices of paganism. In private life they sought to be peaceful neighbours and trustworthy friends. They were taught to be sober, industrious and clean-living. Amid prevailing corruption and licentiousness they were, if loyal to their principles, honest and truthful. Their sexual standards were high: the marriage tie was respected and family life was pure. With such virtues they could not, one would have thought, have been troublesome citizens. Yet they were for long despised, maligned and hated.

As we seek to understand the reason for the unpopularity of the Christian movement, we observe that it had within itself a strong vein of socialism. It had had an epoch of communism; and, in its official teaching, the dangers of wealth, and of the misuse of wealth, were almost fanatically exposed and denounced. Moreover, the movement was anti-nationalist. At the beginning it had held aloof from Jewish nationalism; and, as it developed within the Roman empire, it claimed to regard with equal favour free citizens and slaves, Jews, cultured Greeks and barbarous Scythians from the Russian steppes. The Roman authorities naturally regarded it as unpatriotic, and were confirmed in this opinion by its pacifism. Its founder was reported to have said at the crisis of his life that he could receive, if he so wished, more than twelve legions of angels for his protection (*Matthew* xxvi. 53); and he had refused to summon such aid. His followers, who preserved this story, naturally held aloof from military service.

We thus have a notable paradox. A movement which encouraged its members to be the salt of the earth, which created such puritans as are the strength of a nation, was

regarded by the authorities with profound aversion. For three
centuries a succession of emperors sought at intervals to suppress
it. Its leaders, from its founder onward, were from time to time
executed. Again and again there were outbreaks of persecution,
sometimes quite horrible in their nature. There was, in fact,
between the imperial government and a religious sect which
abjured the use of force a struggle that lasted for three hundred
years. In the end the sect, socialist, pacifist, anti-nationalist,
won. The modern world may well consider whether the same
sect, if it returns anew to its old ideals, will not have a similar
triumph on an even larger scale.

299. Christians and taxation

The gospels give us the teaching of Jesus, as it was preserved
and, it may be, modified by his followers. We can seldom be
sure that we have his actual words; but there is such coherence
in the teaching attributed to him that it can rarely misrepresent
his attitude to life.

All three synoptists give the story of the tribute to Caesar,
which must have been copied by *Matthew* and *Luke* from *Mark*
(xii. 13–17). It will be a true incident in the ministry of Jesus:
the dexterity of his reply is characteristic in its simple, though
quick, shrewdness. The pharisees and Herodians, religious
leaders and supporters of the dynasty, tried to catch him in his
talk. Is tribute to Caesar, of whom Herod was but a client,
lawful? The patriotic Jew had no affection for the Roman
emperor under whose shadow he lived; and a negative answer,
however dangerous to him who gave it, would have been
welcome. "Show me a coin," said Jesus. "Whose head is on
it?" They said unto him, Caesar's. Quickly comes the
answer: "Render unto Caesar the things that are Caesar's, and
unto God the things that are God's."

Whenever, for centuries to come, a Christian was in doubt as
to his duty towards the State, he turned to Christ's authoritative
teaching. He would pay taxes: the dues levied might be heavy
—they became intolerable before the collapse of the Western
Empire—but the Christian would endure them. He would
likewise accept all other State obligations, provided he was not
called upon to render unto Caesar the things that belonged to
God. In that proviso lay the seeds of unending strife.

300. Christian pacifism

Of all Roman virtues, probably the patriotism, which was ready, if need be, to meet death in war, was the most highly esteemed. By the bravery of her citizens and their readiness to die in her service, Rome had conquered the civilized world, as it was then known. The disciplined courage of her troops protected the frontiers. A refusal to fight was treachery to the beloved and eternal City. Unfortunately for their happiness, such refusal was part of the creed which Christians held and taught.

The passage in *Matthew*, in which Jesus said that he could summon legions of angels, amplifies the corresponding story in *Mark* (xiv. 47–50). There can be little doubt that it was intended to emphasize the pacifism inherent in the teaching of Christ, a pacifism which the gospels derive from Q. Obviously, a sect which took seriously such texts as, "Blessed are the peace-makers" (*Matthew* v. 9), "Resist not him that is evil" (*Matthew* v. 39), "Love your enemies, and pray for them that persecute you" (*Matthew* v. 44), could not countenance the doing of evil that good might come, which is the essence of war. The Christian attitude to war is crystallized by *Matthew* (xxvi. 52) in the sentence, "Put up again thy sword into its place: for all they that take the sword shall perish with the sword." Somewhat surprisingly, it recurs in the *Apocalypse* (xiii. 10), "If any man shall kill with the sword, with the sword must he be killed. Here is the patience and the faith of the saints."

Although the pacifism of the Christians was regarded with angry contempt, it was probably not the main cause of the detestation in which they were held. The Roman government does not seem to have needed, during the period covered by the first two centuries of the Christian movement, to have recourse to conscription in order to maintain at full strength the armies on the frontiers. The population of the empire at the end of the first century of our era is estimated to have numbered seventy millions: the strength of the army varied, but may have averaged six hundred thousand, less than one per cent of the population. The civil wars at the end of the Roman republic had largely eliminated the good fighting material of Italy; and increasingly troops were recruited on the frontiers. The urban proletariat, among which Christianity most effectively made headway, was not promising military material.

But though Christian pacifism was in all probability not a source of serious trouble to the army authorities, the Christian attitude towards enemies who were always threatening the frontiers must have been deemed both absurd and mischievous. The barbarians beyond the frontiers were regarded as being little better than savages, whose existence was a perpetual menace. But the Christian affirmed that to them also the gospel should be preached: they also were children of God the Father. In Christ, as we read in *Colossians* (iii. 11), there could not be "Greek and Jew, circumcision and uncircumcision, barbarian, Scythian, bondman, freeman: but Christ is all, and in all."

301. Christians and the *genius* of the emperor

Because Christianity thus declined to recognize national boundaries, because it was not nationalist but internationalist, it was regarded as unpatriotic. This estimate of its nature was confirmed by the unfortunate fact that Christians, by reason of the stern monotheism which is central in the teaching of Jesus, felt bound to refuse to offer incense on pagan altars. The normal expression of loyalty, alike to the emperor and to the imperial City, was to burn incense to his *genius* and to the *genius* of Rome. The Christian held that such action was to offer worship to gods or divinities that he did not recognize. He was thus not only unpatriotic, rebellious in spirit, but he was also an "atheist." His offence was both political and religious. It was as though to-day in England a man should refuse to stand up for the national anthem, because he did not acknowledge God.

The Christian believed that he had his Lord's example to confirm him in his obstinacy. The developed form of the story of the temptation of Jesus, which is given in *Matthew* (iv. 1–11) and *Luke* (iv. 1–13), almost certainly comes from Q. In it Jesus is said to have been told by the devil that he might have all the kingdoms of the world and the glory of them, if he would give to the devil worship; and the answer had been, "Thou shalt worship the Lord thy God, and him only shalt thou serve." Rome and the emperor were accordingly flouted by religious enthusiasts who acknowledged themselves to be pacifists, internationalists and, in the current acceptance of the term, atheists.

302. Christianity and the rich

Even such a catalogue of political and religious heresies as we have just made is incomplete. The Christian was also dangerous because of his condemnation of the rich. The teaching which he venerated would, taken literally, have made him a communist; and there can be no doubt that such teaching fully implied that equality of material well-being which is the aim of modern socialism. Under the early Roman empire, during the rise of Christianity, as was said in § 78, great landowners and large trading corporations flourished. The need of limiting the oppressive power of wealth was shown by imperial legislation. To give "the small man" a chance, Hadrian, who reigned from A.D. 117 to A.D. 138, sought to help smallholders in agriculture and petty contractors in the mines: he tried in business to eliminate the middleman. But the methods of capitalism none the less easily maintained their supremacy. The shipping magnates, in particular, and the companies which they controlled, were immensely powerful.

The abuses of the power of wealth, when Christianity was spreading, were probably even greater than within our modern Western civilization. The rich were closely allied with the government and used the alliance, especially when the taxes were farmed, to exploit the common people. Under the early emperors, contractors and contracting companies collected the indirect taxes. Then, to prevent abuses, imperial controllers were appointed to watch the levying of State duties and taxes. Finally, the emperors' own officials took over the collection. It would appear that simultaneously the distinction between the enormous private wealth of the head of the State and that of the State itself began to disappear. But, though a vast system of State-socialism thus developed, the existence of slavery, and the denial of any right of combination on the part of the workers, allowed the exploiting of the poor. It has been well said that, during the second century of our era, the empire was governed by the upper-middle classes for the upper-middle classes.

One need not read the first three gospels with any great care to realize how harsh the pressure of wealth was felt to be. Jesus had said—the teaching comes from Q—that men could not "serve God and mammon," mammon being the personification of unrighteous riches. And *Luke* (xvi. 19–31), shortly after this teaching, gives point to it by one of his most famous parables, that of the Rich Man and Lazarus. Read that parable carefully; and it will appear that the Rich Man went to hell, simply because he was rich and—as it is implied though not stated—unmoved by the misery of Lazarus. In all literature it would be difficult to find a more unsparing denunciation of the moral insensitiveness that wealth can create than we find in stories in the synoptic gospels.

303. Official Christian teaching as to citizenship

Perhaps enough has now been said to explain why the Christian was loathed by the Roman government: he was pacifist, socialist, internationalist, atheist, in spirit a rebel. All the more necessary was it that he should proclaim himself a good and loyal citizen, so far as was possible to him. Such necessity, doubtless, lay behind the teaching as to obedience to the State given in the *Epistle to the Romans* (xiii. 1–7). It runs:

> Let every soul be in subjection to the higher powers: for there is no power but of God; and the powers that be are ordained of God. Therefore he that resisteth the power, withstandeth the ordinance of God: and they that withstand shall receive to themselves judgement. For rulers are not a terror to the good work, but to the evil. And wouldest thou have no fear of the power? do that which is good, and thou shalt have praise from the same: for he is a minister of God to thee for good. But if thou do that which is evil, be afraid; for he beareth not the sword in vain: for he is a minister of God, an avenger for wrath to him that doeth evil. Wherefore ye must needs be in subjection, not only because of the wrath, but also for conscience sake. For for this cause ye pay tribute also; for they are ministers of God's service, attending continually upon this very thing. Render to all their dues: tribute to whom tribute is due; custom to whom custom; fear to whom fear; honour to whom honour.

As we have already said in §§ 208 and 232, the epistle in which this clumsily worded advice occurs was probably written about the year A.D. 56. Possibly in the use of the term "tribute" there is a recollection of gospel teaching, for *Luke* (xx. 22), in recounting the inquiry of Jesus as to tribute to Caesar, uses the same Greek word as Paul, though it does not occur in *Mark* or

Matthew. The advice given to the Roman converts is unexceptionable in its content. Christians were urged to go so far as they possibly could to render all due honour to "the powers that be": these powers, they are reminded, are ordained of God.

Similar imperative advice is given in the *First Epistle General of Peter* (ii. 13–17), a work which, as we have in § 184 seen reason to believe, was probably written by an unknown Jewish Christian about the year A.D. 80. We read:

> Be subject to every ordinance of man for the Lord's sake: whether it be to the king, as supreme; or unto governors, as sent by him for vengeance on evil-doers and for praise to them that do well. For so is the will of God, that by well-doing ye should put to silence the ignorance of foolish men: as free, and not using your freedom for a cloke of wickedness, but as bondservants of God. Honour all men. Love the brotherhood. Fear God. Honour the king."

The king to whom honour is to be given is, of course, the emperor. At first sight the advice of the *Epistle to the Romans* is almost exactly repeated. But, in the *First Epistle of Peter* just quoted, the emperor is explicitly mentioned: moreover, it is stated that he is to have, not worship, but honour. We notice, further, that all men are to be honoured. There is thus a definite implication that the emperor is as other men: tacitly, but very delicately, the worship of his *genius* is repudiated. But Christians are told to obey the laws and regulations, alike of the emperor and of his legates and other officials. By well-doing they are to silence the ignorant clamour rising against them. The advice was good: there was evidently, among Christians in the second half of the first century of our era, a sincere and honest attempt to secure favourable notice as good citizens. It failed. After the *Epistle to the Romans* was written came the persecution that followed the fire of Rome in A.D. 64. After the *First Epistle of Peter* came the persecution of about A.D. 95 under the emperor Domitian. The latter persecution led to the half-mad resentment which we find in the *Revelation of St. John the Divine*. Typical of the writer's fury in this apocalypse is a passage in which, as he dare not name Rome, he denounces "Babylon the great, the mother of the harlots and of the abominations of the earth. And I saw the woman drunken with the blood of the saints, and with the blood of the martyrs of Jesus" (xvii. 5–6).

304. Early Christianity in non-Christian writers

Christians tried to conciliate the authorities without yielding as to their principles. We should much like to have first-hand contemporary records of the reaction of the imperial government to these efforts. None such are to be found. There is no definite non-Christian evidence of the mere existence of Christianity that can be dated earlier than A.D. 110. The absence of any mention, friendly or hostile, of Christianity in pagan writers during the first century of our era is surprising. Probably, to a considerable extent there was a deliberate silence as to the movement: it was felt to be, not only discreditable, but also dangerous. The silence cannot be due to the fact that Christianity was not spreading. There were, according to Tacitus, as we shall shortly see, "vast numbers" of Christians in Rome at the time of the fire in A.D. 64. In Bithynia, according to Pliny, some fifty years later, the "infectious superstition" involved large numbers, not only in the cities but in the villages and rural districts. A widespread movement of such magnitude would, one might think, have compelled notice from, say, a stoic moralist like Seneca, who died in A.D. 65. We find in his pages no mention of it.

305. The witness of Josephus

The first dubious mention of Christianity in a non-Christian writer occurs in the *Jewish Antiquities* (xviii, 3, 3) of Flavius Josephus, whose books we described in § 92. The paragraph in which this mention occurs arouses immediate suspicion because it breaks the sequence of the narrative. It begins: "About that time lived Jesus, a wise man, if man he may be called, for he did wonderful works—a teacher of those who joyfully received the truth. He won to himself many Jews and many Greeks. He was the Messiah (the Christus). . . ."

We need not complete the paragraph. Though its style resembles that of Josephus, the passage is surely not genuine. It is not to be imagined that a Jew, living in court circles in Rome in the last decade of the first century of our era, would call Jesus the Messiah, or express doubt as to whether he could rightly be called a man. The reference to Christ has been for centuries a subject of contention. It was known to, and accepted by, Eusebius, who quoted it (*c.* A.D. 320) in his *Ecclesiastical History* (i. 11). But we need have no hesitation in terming it a forgery.

There is, however, an approach to the mention of Christianity in Josephus which was possibly in the original text of the Jewish historian. We read in the *Jewish Antiquities* (xx, 9, 1) of an illegal action by the high-priest Ananus, probably in A.D. 62. It occurred in Judaea after the death of the procurator Festus, and during the interregnum before his successor arrived. Ananus summoned the sanhedrin; and brought before it "the brother of Jesus, who was called Christ, whose name was James, and some others": these he accused of breaking the law and he ordered them to be stoned. Even assuming, however, that this brief reference is genuine, it gives no hint that Christianity was a religious movement of widespread activity.

306. Tacitus

The first two pagan references to Christians which are undoubtedly genuine, and, we may add, highly important, must have been published within a few years of one another. They come respectively from Tacitus and from the younger Pliny.

We take first the account given by the great historian Tacitus (*c.* A.D. 55–*c.* A.D. 120). Tacitus was born in the reign of Nero and must have been a boy, some six years old, when Paul reached Rome. He had a distinguished official career, during which he was consul in A.D. 97, and proconsul of Asia about the year A.D. 112. He married the daughter of Agricola, who during the years A.D. 77–84 completed the conquest of Britain, and built a line of forts between the Clyde and the Forth.

Tacitus, by his career, was well fitted to write the history of the first century of our era: it is a sad loss that so much of his work has not survived. Though he has been variously judged, it is probably true that "he never forgoes the first duty of a historian, laborious and critical investigation of evidence in order to reach a true and impartial account." In view of this

X

verdict, his account of the Christians is the more surprising. It occurs in his *Annals* (xv. 44), a work of his maturity, probably published after A.D. 115, and written shortly before that date. Tacitus, describing the fire of Rome in A.D. 64, states:

> But no human resource, no imperial munificence, no propitiation of the gods, banished the slanderous belief that the fire had happened by order. To crush the rumour therefore Nero provided as culprits, and punished with every form of severity, persons who were hated for their abominations and generally known as Christians. This name had originated with one Christus, who had been put to death by the procurator Pontius Pilate in the reign of Tiberius. The pernicious superstition had been suppressed for a time; but was breaking out again, not only in Judaea, where the trouble had started, but even in the City, where everything foul and shameful from any source collects and finds a following. Self-confessed Christians were arrested first; then on their evidence vast numbers were convicted, not on charges arising from the fire, but for hatred of mankind. As they died they also provided sport, by being wrapped in the skins of wild animals and torn to death by dogs, or by being fastened to crosses so that, when daylight was past, their burning gave light by night. Nero had offered his own garden for this show; and provided a performance at the circus, either mixing with the crowd himself, dressed as a driver, or standing in his own chariot. As a result these men, though their wickedness deserved exemplary punishment, aroused sympathy since their death was occasioned, not by needs of state, but to satisfy the savagery of a single individual.

The loathing and fierce contempt for the Christians, shown by Tacitus in this passage, are the more noteworthy as he makes clear that, though "vast numbers" were convicted, their crime was not arson, but "hatred of mankind." One would have thought it singularly difficult to initiate criminal proceedings on such a charge! We find no evidence, in spite of a paragraph in Suetonius which we shall mention in due course (§ 311), that any special laws against the Christians were, either then or subsequently, enacted. Proceedings after the fire of Rome seem to have served as a precedent for a legal maxim that it was unlawful to be a Christian, and that the punishment for the offence was death. So at least we must infer from the correspondence between Pliny and Trajan which we shall shortly give.

As Tacitus was a child at the time of the fire of Rome, he must have relied for his information on some earlier writer, whose dislike of the Christians will have been strong. But we would emphasize that he himself, writing about A.D. 110 in the middle of the reign of Trajan, was a man well over fifty years of age, who had occupied from time to time great administrative offices in the empire: none the less, he uses towards the Christians the language of studied vituperation.

307. Pliny

The younger Pliny (*c.* A.D. 61–*c.* A.D. 114) is so called because he was the nephew of an elder Pliny, whose *Natural History* is famous and who perished, a victim of scientific curiosity, in the eruption of Vesuvius which overwhelmed Pompeii in A.D. 79. The younger man had a distinguished official career, during which he was consul in A.D. 100. A panegyric of his, delivered in the same year, shows that he found life well-nigh intolerable in the later years of Domitian; but he was happy in his relations with the emperor Trajan. This emperor sent him in A.D. 111 as governor, or special commissioner, to Bithynia, in the north of Asia Minor. Many of Pliny's *Letters* have survived; and of particular importance for the early history of Christianity is that (x. 96) which he wrote to Trajan:

> One of my principles, Sir, is to refer to you anything which raises doubts in my mind, for no one is better equipped to guide me in uncertainty or to enlighten me in ignorance. I have never been present at any enquiries involving Christians and so know neither what to do nor how far to go in punishment or enquiry. I am also very uncertain whether to discriminate on account of age; or if no difference is to be made between the young and their elders; whether repentance should earn a pardon, or if, when a man has once been a Christian, he gains nothing by leaving the sect; whether nominal Christianity without crime deserves punishment or only when crime is coupled with it.
>
> In the meantime this is the procedure I have adopted when any so-called Christians have been brought before me. I asked them if they were Christians. If they admitted it, I asked them a second and again a third time, adding threats of death. If they still claimed to be Christians, I gave orders for their execution. For I had no doubt that, whatever the nature of the guilt which they admitted, their stubbornness and rigid obstinacy should

at all events be punished. There were others equally infatuated but, as they were Roman citizens, I remitted them to the capital.

Soon in the usual way the investigation itself led to further accusations, covering several types of charge. An anonymous accusation appeared, containing many names. Some of those named denied that they were Christians or ever had been. As they joined with me in invocations to the gods and offered supplications with incense and wine to your Majesty's ikon, which I had had brought in with the divine images for this purpose, and finally cursed Christ, I thought they could be discharged, as it is said that genuine Christians cannot be forced into these acts. Others whose names were quoted by the informer said they were Christians but soon withdrew the plea; to be sure, they had once been Christians but they had ceased, some three years before, some for a longer time and a few even for twenty-five years. All these worshipped your Majesty's ikon and the images of the gods; and cursed Christ.

But they claimed that the extent of their crime or wrong-doing had been merely that they used to meet on a fixed day before dawn to sing in alternate verses a hymn to Christ, as to a god, and to bind themselves by oath, not for any criminal purpose, but that they would not commit theft, robbery or adultery, or break their word, or fail to return a deposit on request. After this, they said, they usually went away and then met again for food—but for normal and innocent food. They claimed, however, to have given up even this practice after my decree, in which I had forbidden secret societies by your Majesty's command. I was therefore all the more anxious to discover the truth, even by torture, from two slave girls who were said to be "ministers." But I found nothing, save a crazy and unrestrained superstition.

I have therefore adjourned the enquiry and hasten to seek your advice. For the case seemed to justify asking advice, particularly in view of the number of persons in jeopardy. For many people of every age, of every class and of both sexes are being, and will be, brought into danger. This infectious superstition has spread not only to the cities but even to the villages and countryside; but it can apparently be checked and cured. One thing is certain: temples which were almost deserted are now beginning to be crowded; and sacred festivals, long since abandoned, are being revived. There is also a good market for sacrificial animals, which previously hardly ever found a buyer. From this it can be clearly seen how many could be brought to mend their ways if they were given a chance of repentance.

Trajan's reply, short, kindly and statesmanlike, shows the emperor in a most favourable light:

> My dear Pliny, you have adopted the right method in examining the cases of the Christians who were brought before you. For there can be no general rule which could establish a fixed procedure. There should be no search made for Christians; though, if they are summoned and convicted, they must be punished. But the method should be that anyone who denies that he is a Christian and proves it by his actions, namely by worshipping our gods, whatever suspicion he may previously have incurred, should earn pardon by repentance. Public accusations by anonymous persons should have no place in criminal practice. Such a procedure would be thoroughly bad and out of keeping with the spirit of our age.

308. Imperial methods of repression of the Christians

The letter of Pliny just quoted was probably written from Bithynia in A.D. 112. It enlists our sympathy, for it shows him to have been careful and conscientious. He was plainly the best kind of Roman governor, resolute to maintain order, but honest and impartial, reluctant to punish unless compelled by his duty. For these reasons certain sentences in his letter are the more noteworthy. When the accused are brought before him, he inquires if they are Christians. If he receives an affirmative reply, he puts the question again, adding the threat of capital punishment. On a third affirmative he orders execution. There is but one case of exception: Roman citizens are sent for trial to Rome. Pliny must throughout have acted in accordance with recognized practice; but we are shocked by the cold determination and harsh inflexibility of the whole process.

It should also be noticed that, when Pliny sought to obtain evidence from the two female "ministers"—they were plainly deaconesses—they were, as a matter of course, tortured. We understand from this sentence in his report why it was that, as the Christian movement spread, its members not only refused service in the army, but also declined to act as magistrates. They would not kill, neither would they connive at torture.

The tests applied to those who denied that they were Christians are significant. In the first place, they had to show that they were not "atheists": they repeated after Pliny an invocation to the gods. In the second place, they had to demonstrate their patriotism by the customary offerings of wine and incense on an altar before a statue, a bust, or a picture of the emperor. Finally, they were told to curse Christ. The existence of such a scheme of tests is clear proof of earlier systematic attempts—apparently quite unsuccessful—to prevent Christianity from spreading.

309. The Christian movement as Pliny saw it

We notice further that those who confessed themselves Christians described, as the whole of their guilt, simple worship combined with a solemn pledge to be loyal to a high standard of conduct. Evening worship—the Lord's Supper—had been abandoned. Like the followers of Mithra, the Christians of Bithynia met before the dawn on a certain "fixed day," doubtless on Sunday, the day of Christ, but also the day of Mithra, the god of the Sun. There is no mention of any "breaking of bread": a hymn to Christ, as to a god, sung in alternate verses, is the description which Pliny gives of their liturgy.

But we must not omit to notice that Pliny speaks of their separating and then reassembling to partake of food, but "normal and innocent food." Plainly there is an allusion here to the common belief that Christians partook of cannibal feasts, a misunderstanding easily derived from such words as eating and drinking the body and blood of Christ. Probably the common meal for which they reassembled was a eucharist at which the worshippers were "filled." Such a meal is described in the *First Epistle to the Corinthians* (xi. 20-2) and in the *Didache* (x).

The moral teaching repeated so often in the New Testament epistles had evidently become effective. The Christians at their worship bound themselves by a solemn oath to avoid dishonesty, theft, adultery and falsehood. They prided themselves on faithfully restoring on demand goods entrusted to them, an important fact when our modern banking facilities and safe-deposits did not exist.

Finally, we notice that, according to Pliny, Christianity had spread through all ranks and ages. Men and women were equally involved—had he in mind that Mithra had no women in his congregations? And Christianity was no longer confined to the cities: it had spread to villages and rural districts.

310. Pagan and Christian writings contrasted

The extracts from Tacitus and Pliny which we have given are brief; but they differ markedly from the secondary Christian writings of the same period. Even in a translation we can recognize that they come from educated men accustomed to express their thoughts with precision and to convey essential information with orderly brevity. For the most part, early Christian writings are full of catchwords, *clichés*, quotations. They are verbose, disfigured by repetitions, and they convey singularly little information. The gospels and some parts of some epistles do not deserve such condemnation. *Luke*, for instance, was a practised writer; and whenever we get what appear to be genuine sayings or parables of Jesus, his brilliancy of speech shows the impress of his fine mind, a quality of greatness difficult to assess.

But, speaking generally, as compared with Tacitus and Pliny, contemporary Christians had the faults of relatively uneducated persons. They had not learned the art of concise and clear statement. They were muddled in thought and clumsy in expression. As a result they seem at times indifferent to truth. The success of the movement and their willingness to face persecution prove, however, their fundamental honesty, though not their accuracy. One who in war-time has seen the chairman of a conscientious objectors' tribunal questioning simple Christian pacifists can appreciate the intellectual gulf between Pliny and the majority of the Christians of his province.

311. Suetonius

Suetonius (*c.* A.D. 75–*c.* A.D. 150) was a voluminous Latin writer, most of whose work has perished. He was befriended by the younger Pliny, entered the imperial service, and became private secretary to the emperor Hadrian. From this post he was dismissed for lack of respect to the empress. His *Lives of the Caesars*, already mentioned in § 104, ends with Domitian, who died in A.D. 96. It was published in the period A.D. 119–21.

In this work of Suetonius (*Claudius*, 25) we have mention of what is apparently a phase of the Christian movement earlier than can be found in any other pagan author writing before the second-century Christian apologists arose; for Suetonius writes, as we have already stated in § 205, that Claudius, it would seem in A.D. 49, banished from Rome the Jews who "at the instigation of Chrestus continually raised tumults." The sentence recording this expulsion stands by itself between a notice of an exemption from tribute of the people of Ilium and permission for the envoys of the Germans to sit in the orchestra seats, presumably at the circus. It is a characteristic fragment of gossip. We may conjecture that the early preaching of Christianity in Rome created a turmoil in the Jewish community; and that, mistakenly reading some contemporary authority, Suetonius imagined that a certain Chrestus had come to Rome and had made trouble.

Suetonius (*Nero*, 16) also, after a paragraph relating to the sale of food in taverns, and before another as to the diversions of the chariot drivers, writes: "Punishment was inflicted on the Christians, a class of men given to a new and mischievous superstition." Thus we learn that penal measures were taken against Christians in the time of Nero. Suetonius may be referring to the persecution described by Tacitus in the passage which we have quoted; but some scholars think that permanent regulations were then made which guided future administrative action.

312. The dearth of second-century historians

After the death of Vespasian in A.D. 79, there is for a whole century a deplorable lack of contemporary writers on Roman history. What has survived of the *Histories* of Tacitus does not go beyond A.D. 70. Suetonius, writing about A.D. 120, gives, as we have seen, not ordered history but interesting gossip for the period which begins with Julius Caesar (100–44 B.C.) and ends in A.D. 96 with the death of Domitian. Subsequently, as regards historians, we have a blank of a century. The silence ends with the one historian of importance from whom we get a connected narrative for the period which followed the Flavians, that is to say, for what is loosely called the age of the Antonines, ending with the death of Commodus in A.D. 192. This writer is Cassius Dio or, as he is sometimes called, Dion Cassius. He wrote in Greek with a background of administrative experience, for he had held important posts in the empire. In particular, he was twice consul, the second time with the then emperor in A.D. 229. But Dio could have had no contemporary knowledge of events before the death of Marcus Aurelius in A.D. 180.

Unfortunately, even of Dio's history we have only, for the period from A.D. 54 to A.D. 222, an epitome by an eleventh-century Byzantine scholar. The result is that our sources for Roman history during the reigns of Trajan (A.D. 98–117), Hadrian (A.D. 117–138), Antoninus Pius (A.D. 138–161) and Marcus Aurelius (A.D. 161–180) are lamentably meagre. Of the Christian movement, as it appeared to contemporary Roman officials, during this long and highly important time of its development, we know practically nothing. There must have been, one would think, non-Christian writers of ability describing events during an era which, externally at least, was a brilliant epoch during the decline of Graeco-Roman civilization. If such writers existed, what they wrote has perished.

313. A possible cause

It may be, however, that beneath the material splendour of the time of Hadrian and the tranquil glory of Antoninus, there was, as we suggested in § 80, rapid intellectual decay, although civic generosity and social sympathy, if we may judge by inscriptions, increased. It may be, also, that as the Christian movement later became more powerful, pagan writers were deliberately neglected. Our speculations are necessarily inconclusive.

In favour of the opinion that an epoch of literary sterility began under Hadrian about A.D. 120, a number of facts may be adduced. Subsequent to that date we can discover no new developments in architecture or sculpture. No improvements were made in the art of war or in agriculture: there is, in fact, reason to believe that agriculture became less efficient. Even in the great university of Alexandria, mathematics and astronomy ceased to progress. Medicine began to deteriorate: there is one great name, that of Galen who was physician to Marcus Aurelius: but, though he was a voluminous writer, he breaks no new ground.

Men's thoughts seem, after the beginning of Hadrian's reign, to have turned away from the external order of things. They lost desire to enrich the civilization of which they were the heirs. The aloofness from, and, at times, even the repudiation of, the glories of humanism—and there is little appreciation of such glories in the New Testament—must have infected the whole Graeco-Roman world. Men do not eagerly write a history of their own times when pessimism is widespread and when the thoughts of such as value religion are set on schemes of redemption which by Christ, Isis, Mithra, or some rival cult, shall lead to eternal life beyond the grave.

So we have to reconstruct the history of the rise of Christianity during the second century, not from classical historians, but from incidental statements in Christian writings: they can at best give but a partial picture.

314. The *Meditations* of Marcus Aurelius

An interesting side-light on the disappearance of ancient writings is given by the book commonly described as the *Meditations* of Marcus Aurelius. The private thoughts of the stoic emperor, who has been called the saint of paganism, receive no mention for nine centuries after they were written down. It was, moreover, not until A.D. 1558 that they became generally known, through their publication from the single manuscript which preserved them and is now lost. Their combination of moral elevation and pessimism, the brooding sense of futility dominating noble aspirations, seldom fails to win from their reader sympathy and pity.

Marcus has but a single reference to the Christians. He writes (book xi): "The soul should be ready, when the hour of release from the body comes, to be extinguished or to be scattered or to survive. But such readiness should proceed from inward conviction, and not come of mere perversity, as with the Christians: it should result from a temper rational and grave, and—if it is to convince others—it should be unostentatious."

315. Marcus Aurelius and the Christians

To Marcus the Christians were merely perverse: he implies that in their beliefs they were irrational and ostentatious. One would have expected a fundamental sympathy between the Christians, waiting in righteousness for the coming of the kingdom of God, and the great stoic to whom life was "more like wrestling than dancing." Marcus Aurelius was a Romanized Spaniard, akin by temperament and, it may be, by race to a number of persons of Spanish origin who have been venerated as Christian saints. Yet, possibly because of his upbringing, there was between him and the Christians no instinctive regard.

If our authorities are trustworthy, Marcus allowed the execution about the year A.D. 165 of the brave and honest Christian apologist Justin Martyr. Moreover, there seems unfortunately to be no doubt that, about the year A.D. 177, towards the close of his reign, there was a deplorable outburst of persecution at Lyons in France: of it detailed and obviously authentic particulars have been preserved in the *Ecclesiastical History* (v. 1) of the Christian historian Eusebius. It has been said that, if Marcus permitted the Lyons atrocities, he was merely following administrative practice as it had been laid down by Trajan. More probably he was so harassed by wars on the northern frontiers and by a succession of crises, caused by pestilence, poverty and rebellion, that he failed to exercise due personal supervision of provincial administration. In our ignorance we must suspend judgment.

It should, however, be emphasized that, at the time of the Lyons persecution, the true nature of Christianity ought to have been known to every educated official, the emperor included. Popular charges such as "Thyestean banquets, Oedipodean incests" (see § 329), ought for officials to have passed into the limbo of baseless calumnies. The State had everything to lose by public punishments which, as at Lyons, showed the steadfastness of old men and the bravery of young girls. When everyone knew that the officials had no religious convictions, the Christians showed that they themselves were sure and certain in their trust in God and in their loyalty to Christ. While the State was harsh in repression, the Christians won converts by simple kindness. They, and not the stoic emperor, were destined to emerge as victors in the conflict, because they offered to mankind the more valuable gifts.

CHAPTER XVIII

THE EARLY APOLOGISTS

WE have said, towards the close of chapter xvii, that, for nearly a century after the death of the emperor Domitian in A.D. 96, there are practically no contemporary writers to tell us of the history of the Roman empire. Something can be learned from inscriptions and coins which have survived. But an eleventh-century epitome of a history by Cassius Dio, itself written probably later than A.D. 220, is almost our sole non-Christian authority for the first three-quarters of the second century of our era. In chapter xiv we have already discussed some of the earlier Christian writings which have survived: for the most part, they deserve praise neither for their thought nor for their style. It now remains to describe a group of works of about the middle of the second century, in which men of some education sought to defend the Christian faith. These men are known as the early apologists; but it must be understood that, in the description, the word "apology" is used for a reasoned defence, and without any suggestion of excuse for a misguided or wrongful action, such as we usually attach to it.

316. The general outlook of the second-century apologists

It would appear that, following the advice of the emperor Trajan in his letter to Pliny, his immediate successors, Hadrian and Antoninus Pius, showed moderation, and even possibly an aloof toleration, in their dealings with Christians. In consequence, several Christian men of letters sought to present to the emperors the Christian case. Their reasoned arguments, so far as they have survived, are set out carefully and, for the most part, with an evident desire to avoid giving offence. They write, not for their fellow-Christians, but for the world outside the church. They seek to win the good-will of the pagans, not to influence the converted. Naturally, they have a general likeness one to another. In certain ways they use developments of the ideas put by *Luke* into the mouth of Paul at Athens (*Acts* xvii. 22–31).

Current developments of Platonism were almost everywhere leading intellectuals from Greek and Roman mythology to a sort of monotheism. Without giving great offence it was possible to attack the outmoded polytheism of the time. Quasi-philosophic theories as to the *Logos* established a sort of bridge between current paganism and Christian doctrine, though it is difficult to say how far such speculations conveyed a clear meaning to either side.

All the apologists accept and defend the story of the virgin birth of Jesus. All insist on his physical resurrection. But all find their soundest arguments in the good lives of Christians. That Christians abstained from the vices and treacheries of the paganism by which they were surrounded was urged—and surely not unfairly—as proof that the God whom they worshipped was the source of goodness and truth. They could rightly claim that their founder was the Christ of God when his teaching and example so transformed their lives.

317. Quadratus

Of the man who seems to have been the earliest apologist of the second century of our era, nothing survives. We read of him in the pages of the ecclesiastical historian Eusebius (iv. 3), whose information is usually trustworthy. He was a certain Quadratus; and he addressed his *Apology* to the emperor Hadrian. According to Eusebius, who possessed a copy of the apology, Quadratus mentioned persons whom Jesus raised from the dead, and asserted that some were still alive when he wrote. Of persons thus recalled to life, so few are mentioned in the gospels that we must conjecture that Quadratus accepted a different tradition from that preserved in the New Testament.

318. Aristides

Eusebius (iv. 3) also mentioned an *Apology of Aristides*, whom he described as "a man of faith devoted to our religion." He said that it likewise was addressed to Hadrian. Of this apology nothing certain was known until a manuscript Syriac translation was discovered in A.D. 1889: it was first published two years later. Discovery of the text showed that Eusebius was mistaken; and we must admit that he does not say that he possessed a copy of the work. The *Apology* was addressed, not to Hadrian, but to his successor, Antoninus Pius, after his adoption by Hadrian. Such a mistake, as the result of a hasty reading, was natural, inasmuch as Antoninus received most of Hadrian's names on his adoption. We might smile at the way in which distinguished Romans changed their names, did not some of our own citizens, in passing from the chrysalis commoner to the peerage butterfly, take pleasure in even more fantastic changes. Internal evidence goes to show that the *Apology of Aristides* was probably written fairly early in the second century: we are therefore tempted to assign to it the date A.D. 140, soon after the accession of Antoninus.

It has been happily said that Aristides is well-trained in creed and well-practised in ethics: he is not so much a philosopher as a simple enthusiast. The natural dignity of his subject gains by the simplicity of his treatment; and his work is worthy of a place by the side of the best Christian writing of his time.

He opens with a defence of the Christian doctrine of God; and, in particular, affirms that God made all things for man. This belief was subsequently the object of an especial attack by Celsus, the pagan controversialist who wrote about A.D. 178. Of the work of Celsus we have extensive knowledge, by reason of an elaborate reply to it which Origen wrote towards the middle of the third century. Celsus had almost certainly read Aristides.

Aristides himself had read the moral handbook known as *The Two Ways* which, as we have seen, was used alike in the *Didache* and in the *Shepherd of Hermas*. It is, however, doubtful if he had actually read either of these works; probably he went to an earlier fountain-head.

He has an easy task in discrediting the deities of Olympus, by reason of the immoralities attributed to them in generally received legends. He shows (xii) no little knowledge of Egyptian religion, as it was exported in the early centuries of our era. But, speaking generally, he avoids the mystery-religions of his age, although among rival expressions of spiritual enthusiasm they were, in fact, after Christianity the most successful. Possibly they were too like certain aspects of his own faith to be easily challenged by him.

One sign of the probably early date of his book is its friendly tone towards the Jews. Its ethical atmosphere is that of Jewish piety. Aristides consciously accepts their monotheism, though he remarks (xiv) that "in the methods of their actions their service is to angels and not to God." But there is no such hostility to the Jews as we find in, for instance, *The Martyrdom of Polycarp*. We notice, also, as a sign of the early date of Aristides, that fasting is not yet a mere ecclesiastical discipline. As in the *Shepherd of Hermas* (see § 258), so Christians, according to the *Apology of Aristides* (xv), "fast two or three days that they may supply the needy with their necessary food."

When Aristides writes alike of the virgin birth of Jesus and of his resurrection, he replaces a definite statement by a cautious "*on dit*." Thus (ii) we read, "It is said that God came down from heaven and from a Hebrew virgin took and clad himself with flesh and in a daughter of man there dwelt the son of God." So also, "They say that after three days he rose and ascended into heaven." Of Jesus, Aristides tells us that "he was pierced by the Jews" and that "he is about to come as judge."

Dominant throughout the whole *Apology* is insistence on the fact that Christians accept and loyally observe a lofty moral code. We can be sure that the calumnies commonly at the time alleged against Christians were constantly in the writer's thoughts. But his praise of Christian morality is not merely defensive: he is proud that Christians shun the vices and untrustworthiness all too common among pagans.

319. Justin Martyr

The most important defence of Christianity written during the second century of our era consists of several works having for their author Justin, commonly from the manner of his death called Justin Martyr. Justin, as he himself tells us, was born at Flavia Neapolis, the modern Nablous, in Palestine. He was thus by birth a Samaritan; and we may conjecture that, though his father and grandfather had respectively Roman and Greek names, he was of Semitic origin. He was possibly born somewhat earlier than the year A.D. 110; and he was probably martyred towards A.D. 165, when Marcus Aurelius was emperor.

The genuine writings of Justin that have survived are known as the *First Apology*, the *Second Apology*, and the *Dialogue with*

Trypho the Jew. A brief *Martyrdom* of Justin and others exists and is probably based on a contemporary record. There are a number of other works, or fragments of works, written in defence of the Christian position or of some of its cardinal doctrines, which are also ascribed to Justin. They probably are of the later part of the second or of the third century of our era; and they indicate that, when Christianity was struggling not without success against persecution, those who wrote in its support were fairly numerous.

For the facts of Justin's life we have to search his writings. It seems that in youth he was a wandering scholar who studied in various centres of learning; and, though he had no particular philosophic grasp, he acquired a knowledge of Platonism as it was then taught. His travels naturally brought him into contact with Christians. He was impressed by their endurance under persecution. He writes (*Second Apology*, 12):

> For I myself, while I was rejoicing in the teaching of Plato, heard the Christians abused. But I saw that they were afraid neither of death, nor of anything usually thought fearful, and I considered it was impossible that they were living in wickedness and promiscuity.

About the year A.D. 133, when he was still a young man, he himself became a Christian. Thenceforth he was a wandering religious teacher, of a type common in that era; but his message was the Christian faith and not some variant of the ethical philosophy of the time.

It is likely that he was converted at Ephesus, then, as earlier, a strong Christian centre. At Ephesus, about the year A.D. 135, he had a prolonged series of arguments with a learned Jew named Trypho. The disputation was afterwards written up and published by Justin under the title, the *Dialogue with Trypho the Jew*. The date of the publication can only be surmised: perhaps the year A.D. 155 is not far wrong. The *Dialogue* is portentously long, so elaborate that most modern readers turn over its pages with impatience. But in the most careful way Justin quotes the Old Testament to show that Jesus is rightly to be regarded as the Messiah, the Christ. His is the first systematic attempt thus to challenge Jewish incredulity.

The *First Apology* of Justin is his most valuable work. It was addressed to the emperor Antoninus Pius and was probably written about the year A.D. 152. The *Second Apology* is a much slighter work in which, by an appeal, nominally to the Roman Senate but really to public opinion, Justin first protests against the condemnation by the then prefect of Rome of three unfortunate Christians whose story he tells: he subsequently offers a defence of Christians generally. In this short work he allows that he expects martyrdom, and even mentions in connection with his foreboding an enemy named Crescens, "that lover of bravado and boasting."

Justin, as might have been expected, had a wide knowledge of the Old Testament. The books which he most frequently quotes are, in order, the *Book of Isaiah*, the *Psalms* and the *Book of Genesis*. But already the gospels, to which he refers as "memoirs of the (*or*, his) apostles" (*Dialogue*, chapters 101, 103), are authoritative. Direct references to *Mark*, alike in the *Dialogue* and in the *First Apology*, are probably few: we cannot form a definite opinion as to their number because *Mark* is, as we know, the ultimate authority for practically all the material common to the three synoptic gospels. Quotations from *Matthew*, however, are numerous; and those from *Luke*, though possibly not so abundant, range from the birth story to the last words from the cross.

There is, however, in Justin's writings no passage which conclusively shows that he was acquainted with any of the epistles of Paul. He must have heard of these works in connection with the violent storm aroused during the years A.D. 140–4 by the teaching of Marcion; and one would have thought that he would have found certain arguments in the epistles most useful in his controversy with Trypho. Justin's silence suggests that, when he wrote, the so-called Pauline literature was, if not suspect, at any rate little known. In support of this surmise, we may recall that Justin states (*First Apology*, 67) that at the Sunday worship of Christians, "the memoirs of the apostles or the writings of the prophets are read, as long as time permits." Apparently, though we cannot be completely certain, the epistles of Paul were not read.

In the *Dialogue* there is (chapter 81) a reference to the thousand years' reign of the saints in Jerusalem, prophesied by

Y

"John" in a "revelation": evidently the *Apocalypse* was known to Justin: its author he deems an apostle. There is also in the *First Apology* (61) a definite reference to the fourth gospel (iii. 5). Justin is, so far as our knowledge extends, the first writer to assign to the gospels an authority equal to that of favourite books of the Old Testament.

320. Justin and Christian history

Justin twice refers to Marcion (*First Apology*, 26, 58). On the second occasion he writes: "The demons put forward Marcion of Pontus, who is even now teaching men to deny that God is the maker of all things in heaven and on earth, and that the Christ predicted by the prophets is His Son: he preaches another god besides the Creator of all things, and likewise another son." There is thus every reason to think that Marcion, who came to Rome about A.D. 140, and was expelled from the Christian church there a few years later, was still teaching as a notorious heretic when Justin wrote his *First Apology*.

But, though Justin seems to be reliable as regards his own time, his history is sometimes at fault. He makes Quirinius (see § 92) the first procurator of Judaea (*First Apology*, 34). He supposes (35) that in his own day "Acts" of Pontius Pilate existed in Rome containing a detailed account of the crucifixion of Jesus: he even suggests (48) that readers might go to these "Acts" for confirmation of Christ's miracles of healing.

He is especially interested in Simon Magus (*Acts* viii. 9–24), probably because he too was a Samaritan; and he asserts (26) that, because of Simon's skill in magic in the reign of Claudius, a statue was erected on the Tiber with the inscription, "Simoni Deo Sancto." Actually in A.D. 1574 there was found, on an island of the Tiber, the base of a statue with the inscription "Semoni Sanco Deo Fidio Sacrum," the dedication being to the old Sabine deity Semo Sancus. We get the impression that Justin was an honest man, but not always accurate, and not at home in the official Roman world.

321. Justin and other faiths

Justin, as a wandering philosopher-preacher, naturally knew of the mystery-religions of the empire. We have already said that, after his brief account of the eucharist (*First Apology*, 66), he states that "the wicked demons have imitated it in the mysteries of Mithra." But there is another interesting reference to Mithraic worship (*Dialogue*, 70), which runs:

> And when those who record the mysteries of Mithra say that he was begotten of a rock, and call the place where those who believe in him are initiated a cave, do I not perceive here that the words of Daniel, that a stone was cut out of a great mountain without hands, have been imitated by them?

Justin is plainly at pains to show that the rival faith, successfully thrusting itself forward, is a base imitation.

We can, I think, agree that no little ingenuity was needed thus to extract a phase of the Mithra story from the book of *Daniel* (ii. 45). But, in the *First Apology* (54), Justin even derives, from a famous passage in the book of *Genesis* (xlix. 10–12), the origin of Bacchic worship. The passage is certainly obscure:

> The sceptre shall not depart from Judah,
> Nor the ruler's staff from between his feet,
> Until Shiloh come;
> And unto him shall the obedience of the peoples be.
> Binding his foal unto the vine,
> And his ass's colt unto the choice vine;
> He hath washed his garments in wine,
> And his vesture in the blood of grapes:
> His eyes shall be red with wine,
> And his teeth white with milk.

But Justin derives from this fragment of ancient poetry the conclusion that the demons, having heard these prophetic words, said that Dionysus was the discoverer of the vine. "They reckon wine among his mysteries"; and "taught that, having been torn in pieces, he ascended into heaven." Plainly Justin had the interest of an inquisitive theologian in the mystery-faiths of his time: the cult of Dionysus-Zagreus (see § 67) was not unknown to him. Plainly, also, he found connections between different faiths where, in fact, none existed. He is, in short, fantastically ingenious; and, by our standards, he is without the restraint needed for rational inquiry.

322. Justin and Christian morality

These limitations show themselves throughout the *First Apology*. None the less, the work deserves very high praise by reason of the earnestness, the sincerity and the complete honesty of the writer. At times his subject gives him a moving eloquence, as in a deservedly famous passage in chapter 14:

> We who formerly delighted in promiscuity now embrace chastity alone. We who formerly used magic, dedicate ourselves to the good and unbegotten God. We who above all valued the acquiring of wealth and goods, now bring what we have into a common stock and give to everyone in need. We who hated and destroyed one another, and would not share hearth or fire with foreigners, now that Christ has come, live intimately with them and pray for our enemies; and try to persuade those who wrongly hate us to live as Christ taught, that we all may share the joyful hope of God's reward.

Such a passage shows that what we have called the socialist, pacifist ideals of early Christianity were still strong in Justin's time, and that he regarded loyalty to these ideals as a reason why Christians should receive toleration from the imperial authorities.

He boasts proudly (*First Apology*, 39): "We who formerly used to murder one another do not only now refrain from making war upon our enemies, but also, that we may not lie nor deceive those who examine us, willingly die confessing Christ." Justin can also express fierce indignation, as when he writes (27) of the exposure of children, and of the way in which those exposed were brought up to be instruments of vice. The passage is bluntly outspoken: evidence from other sources goes to show that Justin did not unfairly describe the moral pollution of decadent paganism.

323. Justin's method of argument

We feel at one with Justin in his moral earnestness and in his hatred of harsh cruelty and foul iniquity. But, in the arguments which at times he uses and in the beliefs which he tolerates, we realize that he belongs to a pre-scientific age in which credulity had apparently no bounds. Take, for instance, such an argument as the following in defence of the virgin birth and healing miracles of Jesus (22): "And if we even affirm that he was born of a virgin, accept this in common with what you accept of Perseus. And in that we say that he made whole the lame, the paralytic, and those born blind, we assert what is very similar to the cures said to have been wrought by Aesculapius."

Again, when seeking to defend belief in the resurrection of Jesus, he writes (*First Apology*, 21): "For what shall I say of Ariadne, and of those who, like her, have been declared to be set among the stars? And what of the emperors who die among you, whom you deem worthy of deification, and on whose behalf you produce some one who swears he has seen the burning Caesar rise to heaven from the funeral pyre?" Such arguments either imply extraordinarily muddled thinking on the part of our author, or point to his acceptance of beliefs now long outgrown. They suggest that the dogmas of the virgin birth and physical resurrection are, as it were, fossil forms of religious truths that would have received different expression had Christianity arisen in the modern world.

Justin, of course, insists that Christians are neither rebels nor bad citizens who try to escape taxation. In the *First Apology* (11) he says: "When you hear that we look for a kingdom, you suppose, without making any inquiry, that we speak of a human kingdom; whereas we speak of that which is with God." And further, in chapter 17, he protests that "everywhere we, more readily than all men, endeavour to pay to those appointed by you the taxes, both ordinary and extraordinary." He naturally goes on to repeat the teaching of Jesus, when inquiry as to tribute to Caesar was made of him (*Mark* xii. 13–17).

324. Early Christian worship as described by Justin

In the *Didache* we have a description of Christian worship at a time some sixty years after the crucifixion of Jesus. In Justin's *First Apology* (chapters 61–67), we have a description of such worship which must be dated another sixty years later. The changes and developments which have taken place in the interval are, of course, of great interest.

Baptism, the eucharist and Sunday worship continue, with some significant differences. In Justin's time we read, in connection with baptism, that those "who are persuaded and believe that what we teach and say is true, and undertake to live accordingly, are instructed to pray and to entreat God with fasting, for the remission of their past sins, we praying and fasting with them." So far, the parallel with the *Didache* is almost exact. But, whereas in the *Didache* no quasi-magical effect was attached to the rite of baptism, in Justin (*First Apology*, 61) the name of God is pronounced over him who chooses to be born again, in order that "he may obtain in the water the remission of sins formerly committed." Baptism is thus not merely symbolic, a sign of repentance; but it effects that change in God's attitude to the individual which is termed remission of sins. As there is no rational connection between the rite and the result which is supposed to be produced, the whole conception must be adjudged magical.

After his baptism, the convert was brought to a meeting of the brethren. We learn (65) that prayers were offered, including a petition that all might "be found good citizens and keepers of the commandments." The prayers ended, "we salute one another with a kiss." Thereupon the eucharist follows. As in the *Didache*, only those who have been baptized are admitted to communion: in addition one thus admitted must be "so living as Christ has enjoined."

325. Justin and the eucharist

In the eucharist, as it is described by Justin (*First Apology*, 65), "bread and a cup of water mixed with wine" are brought either "to the president of the brethren," or possibly "to that one of the brethren who is presiding." He takes them, "gives praise and glory to the Father of the universe, through the name of the Son and of the Holy Spirit, and offers thanks at considerable length that we are counted worthy to receive these things at his hands." Thereupon all the people say, Amen. Then "those who are called by us deacons give to each of those present to partake of the bread and of the wine mixed with water over which the thanksgiving was spoken, and to those who are absent they carry away a portion."

From the account which Justin gives there appears to have been no set form of consecration prayer. The president acts as the prophets (see § 251) in the *Didache* could act: he gives thanks as it pleases him. But, if the primitive practice still remained, its interpretation was changing under the influence of the story of the Last Supper. Justin goes on to say (66):

> For not as common bread and common drink do we receive these gifts; but just as Jesus Christ our Saviour, having been made flesh by the *Logos* (Word) of God, had both flesh and blood for our salvation, so likewise have we been taught that the food which is blessed by the prayer of the *Logos* (Word) which comes from him, and from which our blood and flesh in some process of metabolism are nourished, is the flesh and blood of that Jesus who was made flesh. For the apostles, in the memoirs written by them which are called gospels, have thus handed down to us what was told them: that Jesus took bread and when he had given thanks, said, "This do ye in remembrance of me, this is my body"; and that, in the same way, having taken the cup and given thanks, he said, "This is my blood"; and gave it to them alone. This the wicked demons have imitated in the mysteries of Mithra, ordering it to be done. For that bread and a cup of water are placed with certain invocations in the mystic rites of initiation, you either know or can learn.

326. Justin's eucharistic theology

The passage, of course, is highly significant. The story of the Last Supper has in Justin's time (*c.* A.D. 150) not yet made such headway that it is incorporated into the so-called consecration prayer. One of the brethren still acts as president and prays as he will. But, by virtue of the words of Jesus in the story of the Last Supper, it is now held that, as the president prays, a magical change takes place in the bread and wine: they become the flesh and blood of Jesus. The president's words are likened to invocations or incantations in the mystic rites of Mithra. He need but pray to God in the name of the Son and of the Holy Spirit, and the change results. Thus mystically, spiritually, really—for spiritual reality transcends physical fact—the bread and wine become the body and blood of Christ. By eating the bread and drinking the wine, it is possible to partake of Christ. Will "specious foolishness" be your comment on such teaching? Say, rather, that Christianity, in an era of intellectual deterioration, is taking a step which shall more closely assimilate it to the mystery-religions. We have travelled far from the spiritual wisdom of the Master in Galilee.

In later ages, the essence of the consecration effecting the magical change was held to reside in the sentences, "This is my body," "This is my blood," said over the bread and wine. In Justin's time no such formulae were supposed to be necessary. Bread together with wine mixed with water, prayer coupled with thanksgiving to God in (*or,* through) the name of the Son and of the Holy Spirit—these sufficed.

In the ancient world, as we said in describing Egyptian religion in § 10, belief in the power of words was widespread. Especially strong was belief in the might of a revered name to effect great changes. Given the right formula of incantation, even the dead might be raised. To us, "open sesame" belongs to the realm of make-believe, appropriate to children's stories: we cannot take it seriously. But in the second and subsequent centuries of our era, when human civilization was decaying and human scepticism was losing its cleansing strength, the wildest beliefs were increasingly accepted with simple and unquestioning credulity.

327. Sunday worship

In the *Didache*, we learned that "on each Lord's day of the Lord" Christians gathered together to break bread and to give thanks. In Justin's *First Apology* (67), "on the day which is called the day of the Sun" Christians assemble for weekly worship. "All who live in the cities or in the country" gather together: the gospels or the prophets are read "as long as time permits." Then follows an address by the president. Next all stand for prayer; and then comes the eucharist. In describing the weekly worship, Justin twice over emphasizes the practice of charity. "The rich among us help the needy, and we always keep together." "They who are well-to-do, and are willing, give what each thinks fit; and what is collected is placed with the president, who helps the orphans and widows, the sick and needy, prisoners and indigent visitors." Such is a brief summary of Justin's words.

Justin explains that Christians met on Sunday because it is the day on which Jesus Christ rose from the dead: "on the day after that of Saturn, which is the day of the Sun, having appeared to his apostles and disciples, he taught them these things which we have submitted to you for your consideration."

This passage is like several others in suggesting that the day of the resurrection of Jesus was also the day of his ascension.

328. Justin and the empire: his end

Justin began his *First Apology* by saying to the emperor that he was writing on "behalf of men of all races who are unjustly hated and wronged, being myself one of them." Throughout he has in mind the harsh repression to which his fellow-Christians were exposed. At the end (68), he begs the emperor "not to decree death against those who have done no wrong, as you would against enemies." He adds sternly: "We forewarn you, that you shall not escape the coming judgment of God, if you continue in your injustice."

Justin, however, ultimately went to a martyr's death. We could hardly have expected any other end to a man who, in defending Christian morality, dared to write (29) of Hadrian's scandalous favourite Antinous to Hadrian's adopted son. A narrative of the end of Justin and others, itself a work of unknown date and authorship, has for its title *The Martyrdom of the Holy Martyrs*. It tells in some detail of Justin's examination by a certain Rusticus, prefect of Rome; and bears internal evidence of being well-informed. We learn from it, for example, where Justin was lodging (above a certain Martinus at the Timiotinian bath), and that he was then living in Rome for the second time. With four equally resolute Christians he was sentenced by the prefect to be scourged and beheaded. So a brave man died; and Christianity continued to spread.

Attached to the *First Apology* is a letter of the emperor Hadrian to a certain Minucius Fundanus, which seems to be genuine. In it the emperor allows accusations against Christians to be brought in a court of law, but proof must be furnished that the accused committed offences that are contrary to the laws. Mere calumny will bring punishment upon the accusers.

There exists also what professes to be a letter of the emperor Marcus Aurelius to the Senate, in which he describes how Christians were the cause of a notable victory near Carnuntum. It is obvious forgery by a Christian of a somewhat later age. But it is of interest because the emperor is made to say that when, after praying in vain to his gods, he made inquiry for Christians, he found a vast number of them. "They began the battle, not by preparing weapons, nor arms, nor bugles, for such preparation is hateful to them, on account of the God whom they bear in their consciences." But "they prayed not only for me, but also for the whole army as it stood." Their prayers were answered; and the emperor directs that henceforth Christians shall not be punished merely for their faith. The interest of this naïve invention lies, of course, in the writer's apologetic pacifism. The great stoic emperor is made to witness that the Christian wins his victories, not by force of arms, but by prayer. Yet, though the Christians are represented as unwilling so bear arms, they are ready to pray for victory. The original Christian attitude is changing: war is no longer condemned as wrong.

329. Athenagoras

Among a number of works written in defence of Christianity in the second half of the second century of our era, the *Plea* (or *Embassy*) *of Athenagoras* deserves mention. The writer is described as an Athenian, a philosopher and a Christian. He dedicates his book to the emperors Marcus Aurelius and his son Commodus: we may probably date it about A.D. 177. Athenagoras is well-read. He writes elegantly: I fear that we must add that, like most philosophers of his time, he is somewhat sterile.

He urges that Christians suffer unjustly, contrary to law and reason. They ought not to be hated and punished merely because they are Christians, but tried on definite charges. He emphasizes (i) the pacifism of Christians and their refusal to go to law: "We have learned not only not to return blow for blow, nor to go to law with those who plunder and rob us, but to those who smite us on one side of the face to offer the other also, and to those who take away our coat to give likewise our cloak."

Three things, he says (iii), are alleged against them: atheism, Thyestean feasts, Oedipodean intercourse. It will be remembered that, in Greek mythology, Thyestes was said to have unwittingly eaten his own children, and Oedipus to have married his mother. As regards the charge of atheism, Athenagoras sets out the Christian doctrine of God. As against the charge of eating human flesh, he reminds his readers (xxxv) that Christians refuse to go to gladiatorial shows, that they condemn abortion as murder, that they will not expose children: how then can they be accused of murder or cannibalism? We notice, however, that he is silent as to the eucharist with its suggestion of eating the flesh and drinking the blood of the Lord. As regards stories of forbidden intercourse between the sexes, which arose from the practice of greeting one another "with a holy kiss," he quotes (xxxii) the teaching of Jesus (*Matthew* v. 28) as to looking on a woman to lust after her; and he states that Christians are most careful that their bodies should remain undefiled and uncorrupted. "The kiss should be given with the greatest care, since if it be mixed with the least defilement of thought, it excludes us from eternal life."

For the rest, Athenagoras writes at length of the gods of Olympus, freely quoting Homer and Herodotus among other classical writers. He shows (xxii) a fairly intimate knowledge of Egyptian mysteries. And, like Justin, he delights (as in chapters x and xxiv) in developing theories concerning the connection between God, the *Logos* who is the Son of God, and the Holy Spirit. To us, who have learned to build on the understanding of the universe given by science, backed by personal religious experience and historical inquiry, such theorizing seems in large part fanciful and useless.

330. Celsus

Probably at the very time when Athenagoras was writing to defend Christianity, a well-read pagan named Celsus wrote a reasoned attack on the rising faith. We should be quite ignorant of the *True Discourse* of Celsus were it not for the long and detailed reply to it made by Origen (*c.* A.D. 185–254) about the year A.D. 246. Origen himself seems to have come upon Celsus's book by a lucky chance and obviously knew nothing of its author. From internal evidence it has been conjectured that the book was written towards the end of the reign of Marcus Aurelius, say in A.D. 178.

It must be allowed that Celsus, whom we only see through the eyes of an opponent, impresses us favourably. There is in his writing no clumsy denunciation or violent invective. He has acquired some knowledge of the gospels; in fact, they were probably the main source of his knowledge of the origin of

Christianity. He has had personal acquaintance with Christians: he recognizes the existence within the movement of different sects: he appreciates the moral elevation of the teaching and conduct which the gospels set forth and enjoin: he does not believe that Christians indulge in the licentious orgies of popular calumny. But, to him, Christianity is a foolish superstition, unworthy of acceptance by reasonable men. He desires to convert Christians to a more rational faith, in which a doctrine of the *Logos* might find its place. But, in so far as they are good citizens, he does not desire their extermination. Let them, rather, abandon alike their pacifism and their refusal to act as imperial or civic officials. Christianity then might well take its place as one of the religions of the empire, living in friendly rivalry with other faiths.

Plainly there is a new note in the *True Discourse* of Celsus. The writer was prepared to refute in detail the beliefs which lay at the basis of Christianity; but he realized that it had become too strong to be destroyed by force. A situation had arisen in which the new religion must be tolerated and, perhaps, killed by kindness.

The State, towards the end of the reign of Marcus Aurelius when Celsus wrote, was in none too happy a condition. We are ill-informed as to the history of the latter part of the reign of Marcus. But we know that barbarian pressure on the northern frontiers was continuous. There was added to this ever-present menace a financial crisis which came to a head about the year A.D. 170. About the same time there was a most serious outbreak of pestilence. With a knowledge of these calamities we learn without surprise that the provincials were sorely impoverished by heavy taxation: to avoid increasing their burdens, Marcus even sold the treasures of his palaces. Against a violent epidemic the medicine of the time would be powerless: pestilence raging in the camps must have profoundly weakened the armies. Possibly it was the general discontent which in A.D. 175 allowed an able legate, Avidius Cassius, a Syrian by origin, to threaten by revolt the stability of the empire.

Under such circumstances, an intransigent minority, steadily growing stronger, was a grave danger. Celsus, if from the pages of Origen's refutation we can form a just estimate, saw the need of a new policy.

331. Christians and military service

A careful review of all the information available goes to show that, until the time of Marcus Aurelius, no Christian became a soldier; and no soldier, after becoming a Christian, remained in military service. Against this conclusion it can be argued that, according to *Acts* (x. 1-48), Cornelius, a centurion of the Italian band, was baptized, together with others, after he had received Peter in consequence of the direction of "a man in bright apparel"—the usual description of an angel—who appeared before him; that, according to *Acts* (xiii. 12), Sergius Paulus, the proconsul of Cyprus, "believed," after Paul had blinded Elymas the sorcerer; and, finally, that the jailer at Philippi (*Acts* xvi. 23-34) was baptized after a miraculous earthquake in which "every one's bands were loosed." Stories in which such miraculous embellishments appear cannot be regarded as sober history: we have, in fact, seen reason to hold that, in the first part of *Acts*, fact and fancy are blended so as to make a record which is sometimes allegory and sometimes literal truth.

What can be fairly deduced from these stories is that early Christians recognized that some officials and some soldiers could be good men, worthy of a place within the Christian movement. *Luke* would be concerned to emphasize this opinion as he earnestly desired, by his writings, to commend Christianity to the imperial government. But, apart from *Luke's* stories, there is no trace of the existence of Christians who were either officials or soldiers before the year A.D. 170. In the writings of Tertullian, which can be dated A.D. 200-210, we have the earliest record that we possess that some Christians actually accepted military service; but we also learn from him that in his day many soldiers left the army when they were converted to Christianity.

332. Origen's reply to Celsus

An appeal of Celsus, which Origen records and to which he replies, makes clear that in A.D. 178, when the *True Discourse* was written, Christians with practical unanimity refused aike magisterial office and military service. In his reply, Origen shows that in the middle of the third century of our era Christians still, for the most part, persisted in such refusal. Origen

writes cogently and at length. We give, without abbreviation
a passage (*Against Celsus* viii. 73) which unambiguously sets out
his position:

> In the next place, Celsus urges us "to help the emperor with
> all our strength, to work with him in maintaining justice, to fight
> for him and, if he requires it, to serve under him, and to share
> military command with him." To this our answer is that we do,
> when occasion requires, help the emperor, with a help which is,
> so to say, divine, "putting on the whole armour of God." And
> this we do in obedience to the command of the apostle, "I exhort
> therefore, first of all, that supplications, prayers, intercessions,
> thanksgivings, be made for all men; for emperors and all that are
> in high place"; and the more a man excels in piety, the more
> effective help does he give to the emperors, even more than is
> given by soldiers who go forth in battle order and kill as many of
> the enemy as they can. And to those strangers to our faith who
> ask us to bear arms for the commonwealth and to kill men we
> would reply: Among you, priests at certain shrines, and temple
> wardens of your so-called gods, keep their hands unstained by
> blood that they may offer the appointed sacrifices to your gods
> with hands unstained and free from blood; and whenever war
> comes, you do not conscript priests. If then it is reasonable so to
> act, how much more so, that while others are serving in the army,
> Christians also should do their service as ministers and priests of
> God, keeping their hands pure, and striving by prayers to God on
> behalf of those who are fighting in a righteous cause and also for
> him who reigns righteously, that all things opposed and hostile
> to those who act righteously may be overthrown? And, as we by
> our prayers vanquish all demons who stir up the passions of war
> and encourage the violation of oaths, and disturb the peace, so
> we give more help to the emperor than those who fight on the
> field of battle. We do take our part in public affairs, when we
> pray with righteousness, in exercises and meditations which
> teach us to despise pleasures and not to be led away by them.
> And none fight better for the emperor. We do not serve as soldiers
> with him, even though he require it: but we fight on his behalf,
> forming a special army—an army of piety—by making our
> prayers to God."

333. Christianity after Origen

Origen died in A.D. 254 and most scholars would endorse the
opinion that his moral qualities were as remarkable as his

intellectual gifts. In the passage which we have just quoted he was defending a losing cause. Yet only gradually did Christians tolerate military service. Only gradually did the earlier rigorism of the church disappear. The growth of moral laxity, of which we have spoken in § 257 in connection with the *Shepherd of Hermas*, continued at an increased rate during the third century, a period of military disaster and social disorder when the empire almost foundered. It seems to be generally agreed that, after the reign of the emperor Gallienus (A.D. 260–8), the number of Christian officers and soldiers in the army gradually increased; and the military authorities began to connive at Christian absence from the official pagan sacrifices. Concurrently Christians became magistrates. None the less, bloodshed on the battlefield, capital punishment, the torture of witnesses—all continued to arouse profound misgiving among Christians even during the fourth century of our era.

With Constantine, early in the fourth century, the Christian church gained in some measure control of the Roman state: thenceforth it was to be expected that Christian morality should gradually come to terms with paganism. Before the fifth century had well begun, such leaders of orthodoxy as Athanasius and Augustine had written approving of wars in a righteous cause—was there ever a war which, for those taking part in it, did not come within that description?

With their rise to power Christians ceased to be pacifist, socialist, internationalist. No longer persecuted as "atheists," their triumphant orthodoxy, as time passed, could use the resources of the State to persecute pagans and heretics. The unfortunate Mithraists felt their heavy vengeance after the emperor Julian, "the apostate," fell in battle in A.D. 363. During a slow process of extermination, mithraea were destroyed, or profaned by the corpses of refractory Mithraic priests: archaeologists from time to time still find pathetic witness to the barbarity of decadent Christians. "Heresy" was similarly suppressed with partisan anger.

During the third century Christian missionaries had carried the gospel across the frontiers of the Roman empire. But the view of the nature of the person of Christ, which to them was conservative orthodoxy, became Arian heresy in the fourth century of our era, and so added to the bitterness of military warfare and civil strife. As classical civilization collapsed, Christianity ceased to be the noble faith of Jesus the Christ: it became a religion useful as the social cement of a world in dissolution. As such it assisted at the rebirth of western European civilization after the Dark Ages. It has endured to be the nominal creed of clever and restless peoples who are ceasing to give even lip-service to its ideals. As to its future, who can prophesy?

334. The strange story and the final questions

In the preceding pages we have carried the story of Christianity from its obscure beginning to its worldly triumph. It is a most strange tale, which would be incredible were it not true. In the background of the story we have a succession of men, prophets who during several centuries arose within two obscure, and none too highly civilized, groups of Semitic tribes. These men fashioned ethical monotheism, the conviction that humanity is the creation of a God who is good and who demands the service of goodness.

Then there emerged in Galilee a peasant artisan, profoundly convinced of the truth of the prophets' message, who felt that he knew God and was called to serve Him. This man for a brief year or so taught in a remote district, speaking of God with an intimate and beautiful certainty. Finally, because of teaching which expressed his loyalty to God, he was executed as a common criminal.

All memory of him ought rapidly to have vanished. But it would seem that his personality was so strong, his religious sureness so great, his moral and spiritual influence so powerful that his followers could not forget him. As they repeated his teaching they gained an unshakable certainty of his continuing presence. So a new religion grew up, ethical monotheism centred on Jesus the Christ.

The new faith, like its founder, taught its adherents to lead clean, honourable and kindly lives. It led them to ignore many of the motives of worldly prudence by which men are normally guided. Christians believed that the Spirit of Christ bade them distrust the use of armed force, renounce the power of wealth and even forgo the appeal to established law. They lived in the conviction that, apart from such help, goodness and good-will shown in speech and deed would in the end prevail. After being persecuted for well-nigh three centuries by the authorities of an empire to whom its tenets were an affront, the Christian faith triumphed—and forthwith its adherents began to forsake their distinctive outlook on life. The salt lost its savour. An opportunist monotheism, at its best stoic rather than Christian, remained. Expediency—the higher expediency which God may be thought to approve—became the all too common guide of the Christian in the perplexities and dangers of his earthly life.

Yet there remained—and remains—the memory of him whom men still call God's anointed, the Christ. The Spirit of Christ perturbs even the churches which have largely forsaken his teaching. Beyond the churches his influence persists. Amid unpromising surroundings it repeatedly emerges with renewed strength in a way that confounds critics and joyfully surprises anxious followers of Jesus. Men captured by the thought and personality of the Christ never apologize for their faith, though they may often be ashamed of the weakness of their loyalty. Some exalt the importance of religious forms and ceremonies and thus instinctively seek to excuse to themselves their failings. Uneasiness is seldom, if ever, thus overcome. But after failure the search for religious reality begins anew. Out of apparently dead formulae and empty ritual the Spirit of Christ emerges as buds in springtime appear on what seemed lifeless twigs. Intellectual groups, perplexed by a struggle to understand a Universe obviously too vast for man's apprehension, joining heart to mind, give homage to Christ. So his followers are led to claim for Jesus the Christ a supremacy that time cannot end. Because his Spirit does not die they worship him as Son of God.

What was the quality of that Sonship? Had it a perfection given to none other? Is the faith centred on the Christ the supreme expression of religious truth? These questions each man must answer for himself, using the understanding which comes from suffering, joy and peace. As he gropes for truth so he will shape his life.

z

BOOKS WHICH MAY BE CONSULTED

AS has been said in the Foreword, the number of books relating to various aspects of the rise of Christianity is enormous. The following list is limited to comparatively recent works in the English language.

Of the Bible the revised version has been used: the authorized version should be at hand for comparison.

As regards the text of the New Testament, reference should be made to:

> F. G. Kenyon: *The Text of the Greek Bible.* 1937. *Our Bible and the Ancient Manuscripts.* 1939.

When it is desired to compare the different gospel records, the reader may employ:

> J. M. Thompson: *The Synoptic Gospels arranged in parallel columns.* 1910.

It has been seen that the books of the New Testament should at times be compared with other early Christian writings, ultimately rejected by the church. Translations of the more important of these writings are to be found in:

> M. R. James: *The Apocryphal New Testament.* 1924.

Among general works of reference:

> *The Cambridge Ancient History*: Vols. I–XII. 1923–39,

is especially important: it contains elaborate bibliographies.

A short but brilliant history is:

> M. Rostovtzeff: *A History of the Ancient World.* 2 vols. 1930–3.

Reference may also be made to the early chapters of a work by one who was distinguished alike as scholar and man of affairs:

> H. A. L. Fisher: *A History of Europe.* 1936.

A book well documented and singularly attractive in style is

> S. Dill: *Roman Society from Nero to Marcus Aurelius.* 1920.

English Biblical scholarship of the beginning of the twentieth century is represented by the conservative

> *Dictionary of the Bible*: ed. J. Hastings. Vols. I–V. 1900–4,

and by the radical, though occasionally fanciful

> *Encyclopaedia Biblica*: ed. T. K. Cheyne and J. S. Black. 1899–1903.

A Dictionary of Christian Biography. 4 vols. 1877–87, contains a mass of well-arranged material.

A convenient summary of the classical culture of Greece and Rome is to be found in two books:

A Companion to Greek Studies: ed. L. Whibley. 1916.
A Companion to Latin Studies: ed. J. E. Sandys. 1910.

English translations of many works of Greek and Latin authors to which reference has been made are to be found in the admirable

Loeb Classical Library,

where text and translation are simultaneously before the reader as he refers to any particular passage.

For the geographical background of the rise of Christianity the reader may usefully consult

George Adam Smith: *The Historical Geography of the Holy Land*. 1894 and often later.

The same author's

Atlas of the Historical Geography of the Holy Land, 1915, has a wider range than its title suggests.

A short list of books is appended which may be consulted in connection with various chapters of the present work. When a book has once been named no further mention of it is made, even though it may serve as a useful commentary upon statements in later chapters. Mention of a book must not be taken to imply agreement with the conclusions of its author.

CHAPTER I
Marcellin Boule: *Fossil Men*. 1923.
R. Broom: *The Coming of Man*. 1933.
J. L. Myres: *Who were the Greeks?* 1930.
V. G. Childe: *The Dawn of European Civilization*. 1939.
H. R. Hall: *The Ancient History of the Near East*. 1920.
J. H. Breasted: *History of Egypt*. 1909.
J. Wellhausen: *Prolegomena to the History of Israel*. 1885.
W. Robertson Smith: *The Religion of the Semites*. 1889.
W. F. Albright: *From the Stone Age to Christianity*. 1940.

CHAPTER II
G. Glotz: *The Aegean Civilization*. 1925.
J. B. Bury: *History of Greece*. 1922.
z*

G. Murray: *Five Stages of Greek Religion.* 1925.
W. W. Tarn: *Hellenistic Civilization.* 1930.
E. Bevan: *The House of Seleucus.* 1902.
W. E. Heitland: *Short History of the Roman Republic.* 1909.
H. Stuart Jones: *The Roman Empire.* 1908.
E. V. Arnold: *Roman Stoicism.* 1911.

CHAPTER III

F. Cumont: *The Mysteries of Mithra.* 1910.
F. Cumont: *The Oriental Religions in Roman Paganism.* 1911.
S. Angus: *The Mystery-Religions and Christianity.* 1925.
A. D. Nock: *Conversion.* 1933.

CHAPTER IV

F. J. A. Hort: *The Way, the Truth, the Life.* 1897.
A. C. Headlam: *The Miracles of the New Testament.* 1914.
C. J. Wright: *Miracle in History and in Modern Thought.* 1930.
M. Planck: *Where is Science going?* 1933.
A. S. Eddington: *New Pathways in Science.* 1935.
J. H. Jeans: *Physics and Philosophy.* 1942.

CHAPTERS V AND VI

Ch. Guignebert: *Jesus.* 1935. With an extensive bibliography.
B. W. Bacon: *The Story of Jesus.* 1927. *Jesus the Son of God.* 1930.
F. C. Burkitt: *The Gospel History and its Transmission.* 1906.
W. Whiston: *The Works of Flavius Josephus in English.* 1737, and often reprinted.
C. Gore: *Belief in God.* 1921. *Belief in Christ.* 1922. *The Holy Spirit and the Church.* 1924.
J. F. Bethune-Baker: *Early Traditions about Jesus.* 1929.

CHAPTERS VII, VIII AND IX

B. H. Streeter: *The Four Gospels.* 1926.
W. Sanday (ed.): *Studies in the Synoptic Problem.* 1911.
G. W. Wade: *The Documents of the New Testament.* 1934.
F. J. Foakes Jackson and Kirsopp Lake: *The Beginnings of Christianity.* 5 vols. 1920–32.

E. F. Scott: *The Fourth Gospel, its Purpose and Theology.* 1908.

W. F. Howard: *The Fourth Gospel in recent Criticism and Interpretation.* 1931. With a good bibliography.

C. H. Roberts: *An unpublished Fragment of the Fourth Gospel.* 1935.

T. R. Glover: *The Jesus of History.* 1917.

Chapters X–XIII

A. Jülicher: *Introduction to the New Testament.* 1904.

K. Lake: *The Earlier Epistles of St. Paul.* 1911.

A. Schweitzer: *Paul and his Interpreters.* 1912.

A. D. Nock: *St. Paul.* 1938.

C. G. Montefiore: *Judaism and St. Paul.* 1914.

Chapters XIV–XVIII

J. B. Lightfoot: *Apostolic Fathers.* 3 vols. 1889.

C. Taylor: *The Teaching of the Twelve Apostles.* 1886.

H. M. Gwatkin: *Early Church History to A.D. 313.* 2 vols. 1909.

W. M. Ramsay: *The Church in the Roman Empire before A.D. 170.* 1895.

T. R. Glover: *The Conflict of Religions in the Early Roman Empire.* 1912.

C. J. Cadoux: *The Early Christian Attitude to War.* 1940.

G. H. Rendall: *Marcus Aurelius Antoninus to Himself.* 1898.

J. R. Harris and J. A. Robinson: *The Apology of Aristides.* 1893.

INDEX

The numbers refer to the pages.

Abilene (Abila), 76, 77, 112
"Abomination of desolation," 27
Abortion, Christians and, 331
Abraham, 20, 233, 257
Accountancy, Egyptian, 57
Achaia, 208
Acquired characters, inheritance of, 239
Acts of the Apostles, 110 *et seq.*, 179, 196,
    231, 249, 273, 274, 282, 322, 333
  authorship of, 113 *et seq.*
  chapters xi and xv describe the
    same mission, 115, 204
  legendary history in, 115
  miracles in, 64
  Paul's life as told in, 196 *et seq.*, 204
    et seq.
  Peter and the early church in, 180,
    181
  the ascension in, 177
  travel-diary in, 113 *et seq.*, 196
Adam, 239, 275
Adam, the second, 288
Adams, the two, doctrine of, 239, 240
Adonis, 164
Adornment of man, early, 2
Aesculapius, cures of, 325
Africans, 26
Africanus, Julius, 72
Against Celsus, see Origen
Against Marcion, see Tertullian
Agricola, Roman general, 305
Agriculture, beginning of, 3
Agrippa (Herod) I, 107, 124, 181, 185,
    213
Agrippa (Herod) II, 77, 112, 214
Ahaz, king of Judah, 70
Ahriman, spirit of falsehood, 19
Ahura-Mazda, the Wise Lord, 19, 58, 59
Akhenaten (Ikhnaton), 9, 18, 20
Akhetaten, now Tell el-Amarna, 9
Alalia, battle of, 40
Alexander the Great, 15, 16, 23, 25, 88,
    197
Alexander, Tiberius, procurator, 113
Alexandria, 25, 34, 110, 195, 209
  a university centre, 26, 64, 313
  serapeum in, 57
Alexandrinus, Codex, 186, 253
Alphabet, invention of, 22
Alphaeus, 118
Altamira cave, in Spain, 2
Amarna letters, 9

Amenhotep IV (Akhenaten), 9
Ammon, 10
Ammonite, 26
Amon-Ra, 9
Amos, Hebrew prophet, 16
Ananias, disciple, 202
Ananias, high-priest, 212, 213
Ananus, high-priest, 305
Andrew, apostle, 179
Anemones in Palestine, 129
Angels, 27, 65, 71, 89, 168, 169, 170,
    171, 177, 194
  worship of, 241, 319
Annas, or Ananus, high-priest, 76, 77,
    155, 157, 158
Anshan, 13
Antinous, 329
Antioch (Syrian), 38, 115, 181, 182,
    185, 195, 201, 203, 204, 209, 232,
    261
Antiochus Epiphanes, 27, 36, 37, 79
Antiochus the Great, 27
Antipas, Herod, 81, 112, 146, 147, 159,
    269, 271
Antipater, 28
Anti-Semitism, 38, 42
Antitheses of Marcion, 218
Antonia, tower of, 155, 211
Antonines, age of the, 207, 312
Antoninus Pius, emperor, 221, 265, 313,
    316, 318, 321
Antony, Mark, 28, 45
Apes, origin of man in the, 1, 239
Apocalypse, the, or *Revelation of St. John
    the Divine*, 79, 92, 93, 94, 116, 118,
    204, 303
  and pacifism, 299
  known to Justin, 322
Apocalypse of Peter, 143
Apocrypha, the, 26, 30, 35, 270
Apollo, 87
Apollonius of Tyana, at Tarsus, 198
  Life of, 126, 198
Apollos, early missionary, 84, 182, 206,
    209, 220, 227, 272, 273
Apologists of second century, 23, 32,
    chap. xviii
Apology, First, of Justin Martyr, 221,
    276, 281, 283
Apology of Aristides, see Aristides
Apology of Quadratus, 317
Apostasy, Paul's presumed, 199

"Apostles' Creed," 64, 139, 176
Aquila, 208
Arabia, 201, 203, 255
Arabian desert, 5
Aramaeans, 12
Aramaic, 12, 30, 31, 82, 83, 109, 133, 156, 174, 179, 286
Aramaic papyri, 29
Aratus, poet, 115, 207, 208
Archelaus, son of Herod, 74, 75, 81
Ariadne, 325
Arian heresy, 335
Arimathaea, Joseph of, 167
Aristarchus, astronomer, 23
Aristarchus, Paul's companion, 245
Aristides, Apology of, 260, 317, 318, 319
Aristides, second-century apologist, 207, 318
Aristion, 105, 106
Aristotle, 23, 207
Army, strength of Roman, 299
Artemis (Diana), 210
Aryan invaders of Italy, 47
the Peloponnese, 21
Aryan races and Semitic faith, 18
religion and Mithra, 58
Aryans, Kassites, 6
Medes, 14
nature gods of, 19
Zoroaster, 19
Ascension, on the day of the resurrection, 111, 176, 258, 328, 329
Day, 178
of Jesus, 111, 175, 176, 177, 178, 192, 258
Asia Minor, 9, 10, 25, 116, 119, 189, 190, 200, 204, 218, 245, 252
western, prosperity of, 92, 204, 241
Asiatic churches and the close of the pascal fast, 151, 152
Assize, the Great, 141
Assyria and Assyrians, 12, 13, 14, 53, 70
Astronomy, Babylonian, 9
Greek, 22, 23
Athanasius, 335
"Atheism" of Christians, 121
Atheists, term applied to Christians, 265, 300, 309, 330
Athenagoras, apologist, 330, 331
Athenagoras, Embassy (or *Plea*) *of*, 330
Athenian, Athenagoras an, 330
Athenians, 198
Athens, 23, 25, 30, 51, 54, 224
a university centre, 94, 206, 207
Paul's speech at, 32, 115, 206, 207, 228, 316
Attis, saviour-lord, husband of Cybele, 55, 56, 57
Augustan peace, the, 46
Augustine, 43, 217, 335

Augustus (Octavian), emperor, 28, 45, 74, 75, 76, 87, 88, 121
and the Julio-Claudians, 46
divus, 48
Aurelius, Marcus, emperor, *see* Marcus Aurelius
Avidius Cassius, Syrian, 332

Baal, Syrian god, 42
worship of, 17
Babel, tower of, 5
Babylon, 13
synonym for Rome, 92, 185
Babylonia, 9
clergy in, 24
epics of, 41
Babylonian empire, 6
archives of, 11
end of, 14
Bacchic orgies, 51
worship, 323
Balaam, prophecy of, 91
reference to, 190
Balkan emperors, 43
Baptism, chapter xv
ancient and modern, 276
and "original sin," 275
formula of, 249, 250, 272
in the name of the Trinity, 272
infant, 277
into death of Christ, 238, 278
magical, with Hermas, 259
Justin, 326
Paul, 234, 278
of Jesus, by John, 142, 267 *et seq.*
of the dead by proxy, 279
sin after, 259, 260, 279, 280
with the Holy Spirit, 209, 269, 270, 271, 272, 273, 274
Baptisms, rival, of Paul and Apollos, 209, 272, 273
Barabbas, 158
Barnabas, 98, 99, 115, 189, 195, 200, 203, 204, 206, 220, 232, 257
Barnabas, and heretical Jewish group, 257
Barnabas, Epistle of, 176, 177, 189, 221, 248, 250, 256 *et seq.*
Barren fig-tree, parable of, 192
Bartimaeus, blind, 149
Batanaea, 77
Bedouin, 82
Beelzebub, the prince of the devils, 37, 137
Beloved disciple, the, 122
"Benefactors," 133
Benjamin, tribe of, 196, 199
Berbers, 40
Beroea, 206
Bethany, 111, 149 *et seq.*, 155, 170

Bethlehem, 69 *et seq.*, 163, 164
Bethsaida, 146
Bezae, Codex, 176
Birth of Jesus, day of, 79
    year of, 46, 74 *et seq.*
    stories of gospels, agreements in, 69, 70
    date of, 69
    divergence between, 71
Bishop, need for authority of, in Ignatian letters, 263
Bishops and priests, separation of, 256, 263
Bithynia, 304, 307, 309, 310
Black Mass, 295
Black Sea, 24
Blind man, cure of, 120
Boeotia, 24
Boghaz Keui, site of Hittite capital, 10
Bondage to "elementals," 241, 242
"Breaking of bread," 37, 170, 171, 172, 173, 227, 251, 282
Britain, conquest of, 305
British Museum, 186
Bronze age, the, 3, 22
Bunyan, John, 119, 258
Burial of Jesus, 166 *et seq.*
Burials, early Egyptian, 4
Butcher, the, as priest, 291
Byzantine epitomist, 313

Cadiz, 38
Caesar, 244, 265, 298, 302, 325
    appeal to, 214
    Augustus, 46, 74; *see* Augustus (Octavian)
    Julius, *see* Julius Caesar
    tribute to, 298, 302, 325
Caesar's household, 62, 244
Caesarea, 105, 211, 212
Caesarea Philippi, 145
Caiaphas, high-priest, 76, 77, 151, 155, 157, 158
Caius, ecclesiastical writer, 187
Caligula, Gaius, emperor, 47
Camel, the, in Palestine, 131
Cana of Galilee, miracle at, 96, 121
Cannibal feasts, alleged against Christians, 310, 315, 330, 331
Canon, Muratorian, 260
Capernaum, 179
Cappadocia, 126
Captivity, epistles of Paul's, 241
Caria, in Asia Minor, 10
Carnuntum, 329
Carpenter's son, the, 86
Carthage, culture of, 41
    destruction of, 41, 44
    government of, 40
    human sacrifice in, 18, 42
    "new town," 40

religion of, 42
    struggle with Rome, 41
Carthaginians, 55
Cassius Dio, or Dion Cassius, historian, 121, 312, 313, 316
Celibacy of Jesus, 128
Celsus, 318, 331 *et seq.*
Celsus, True Discourse of, 331, 332, 333
Celts, 231
Census of Quirinius, 69, 71, 74 *et seq.*, 113
Centurion, 85
Cephas, Aramaic name of Peter, 173, 180, 181, 182, 203, 220
Chemosh, god of Moab, 17
Children, ancient exposure of, 324
Chrestus, 208, 312
Christ, *see* Jesus
    argumentative, of fourth gospel, 118
    God's anointed, 68
Christ-mysticism, 231
Christian era, beginning of, 78
    gospels, Persian dualism in, 19
    help to the poor in Justin's time, 328
    humanist, outlook of, 235
    message, the early, 236
    morality and the apologists, 317, 319, 320, 324, 330, 331
    worship, early, 247 *et seq.*, 310, 324 *et seq.*
Christianity, a movement among the proletariat, 71
    a Way of life, 224
    central fact of, 125
    early, in non-Christian writings, 304 *et seq.*
    legal status of, 213
    reaches Rome, 56
Christians and citizenship, 302, 303
    estimate of, by Marcus Aurelius, 314
    loyalty, 291, 300
    pacifism, *see* Pacifism, Christian
    slavery, 245
    taxation, 298, 302, 325
    wealth, 301
Christmas Day, 79
Church, the, in *Matthew*, 183, 184
Cicero, 43, 94, 208
Cilicia, 115, 196, 199, 203, 207
    pirates of, 197
Circumcision, Paul and, 232
City, the, meaning Rome, 85, 300
Claudius, emperor, 47, 48, 56, 115, 124, 208, 213, 214, 215, 302
Claudius, Life by Suetonius, 311
Cleansing of the temple, 146, 154, 155
Clement of Rome, 187, 255
Clement, First Epistle of, to the Corinthians, 116, 186, 215, 220, 221, 246, 253 *et seq.*
    probable date of, 187

Clement, Second Epistle of, 253, 256
Clement's story of the phoenix, 255
Clyde, the river, 305
Cnossos, capital of Crete, 21
Codex Alexandrinus, 186, 253
  Bezae, 176
  Sinaiticus, 256, 258
  Vaticanus, 258
Colossae, 241, 242, 243, 245
Colossians, Epistle of Paul to the, 219, 241, 242
Comforter, the, 165
Commodus, emperor, 312, 330
Communion rite, 194; *see* Eucharist
  Mithraic, 290
Constantine, emperor, 43, 163, 335
Constantinople, 246
Contradictions, removal of, in New Testament books, 72
Conversion of Paul, 201, 202, 203
Copernicus, 23, 176
Copper, discovery of, 3
Copyright in antiquity, 189
Corinth, 62, 114, 201, 208, 223
Corinthians, Epistles to the, 210, 225, 226
  First Epistle to the, 116, 179, 221, 226 *et seq.,* 255, 281, 283, 284, 287, 288
  Second Epistle to the, 202, 230, 231
  the "severe" letter, 225, 231
1 *Corinthians* xv, a tract on the resurrection, 172, 173, 228
Cornelius, centurion, 176, 333
Cos, Ionian island, 23
Creative activity of God, 66
Credulity in ancient world, 65
Creed, an early, in *Smyrnaeans,* 263
  so-called Apostles', 64, 139, 176
Crescens, enemy of Justin, 321
Cretans, libel on, 32, 207
Crete, 21, 53, 214
  neolithic civilization in, 3
  Philistines and, 10
Cross, last words from the, 161, 162, 193
  Mary at the, 119, 162
Crucifixion of Jesus, 31, 113, 160 *et seq.*
  date of, 201
Crucifixion, origin of practice, 43
Cuneiform inscriptions, 7
Cup and bread, order of, in eucharist, 252, 293, 294
Cybele, the Great Mother of Ida, 55, 56, 57
Cybele-Attis rites in Rome, 56
Cyprus, 94, 189, 196, 333
Cyrenaica, 24
Cyrus, Persian king, 13, 14

Daibon (Dibhon), 17
Dalmatian coast, 240

Damascus, 12, 38, 142, 200, 201, 202, 203, 204, 231, 284
Daniel, book of, 16, 20, 27, 36, 66, 79, 323
Darius, Persian king, 14, 19
Dark Ages, 336
Darwin, 219
David, king, 12, 20, 27, 41, 69, 71, 72, 73, 75, 78
  descent of Jesus from, 73
  holy vine of, 252
  rise of, 12
  romantic stories of, 16
Deaconesses, slave girls in Bithynia, 308, 309
Dead Sea, 12
Decapolis, 82, 83, 145
Dedication of the House, festival of, 80
Deification of the emperors, 48, 88, 325
Delos, Aegean island, 25
Delphi, 25, 208
Demas, companion of Paul, 245
Demons and disease, 23, 128
Demons or devils, the gods of paganism, 65, 229, 294, 295, 296, 322, 323, 327
Derbe, in southern Galatia, 231
Descent into hell, the, 190
Destruction of the world by fire, 192
Deuteronomy, 80
Dialogue with Trypho the Jew, Justin, 319, 320, 321, 323
Diana (Artemis), 210
Didache, the, 220, 227, 246 *et seq.,* 276, 277, 288, 289, 294, 310, 318, 325, 326
  discarding of, 247, 289
Dion Cassius, historian, *see* Cassius Dio
Diogenes Laertius, 87
Dionysiac ritual, 96
Dionysius, bishop of Corinth, 187
Dionysus, Thracian god, 52 *et seq.,* 323
  rites of, 24, 31, 121
Dionysus-Zagreus, 53, 323
Diplomacy, Aramaic the language of, in western Asia, 12
Disciple, the beloved, 122
Divorce in 1 *Corinthians,* 226
  in Hermas, 258
  in *Mark* and the other synoptists, 110
divus, by decree of the senate, 48, 88, 121
Docetic heresy, 193, 264
"Dominical sacraments," 267
Dominus et Deus, Lord and God, 121
Domitian, emperor, 121, 244, 255, 303, 307, 312, 316
Doublets in the gospels, 102, 103, 109, 273
Dove, the, at baptism of Jesus, 142, 269
  at martyrdom of Polycarp, 265

Drusilla, wife of Felix, 213, 214
Dualism, Persian, 19

Earth, the, a sphere, 23
  radius of, 23
  rotation round the sun, suggested by
    Aristarchus, 23
Easter, 151, 154, 178
Ecclesiastes, 16, 29
Ecclesiastical History of Eusebius, *see*
  Eusebius, *Ecclesiastical History*
Ecclesiasticus, 16, 30, 36, 98
Eclipses, cycle for, 9
Economics, teaching of Jesus as to, 131
Eden, garden of, 5, 239
Edom, Hebrew tribe, 10
Edomites (Idumaeans), 28
Education in Palestine, 63
  level of, among early Christians, 64
Egypt, Hebrews in, 6
  neolithic civilization in, 3, 4
  papyrus fragments from, 122, 138
  pyramids of, 5
  ten plagues of, 11
  twelfth dynasty in, 6
Egyptian civilization and the Romans,
  57
  religion, 7, 20, 24, 328, 331
Egyptians, Gospel according to the, 256
"Elementals," or godlings, 241, 242
Elephantiné, 29
Eleusinian mysteries, 54, 57
Eleusis, 24, 31, 51
Elias, 193
Elijah, 16
Elijah-Elisha cycle of stories, 66
Elisabeth, mother of John the Baptist,
  71, 73, 74
Elisha, 16
Elymas, sorcerer, 333
Embassy (or *Plea*) *of Athenagoras*, 330
Emigration, early Greek, 24
Emmaus, 166, 171, 180
Emperor, in Greek, king, 189, 303
  sacrifices for the, 213, 237
English Prayer Book, consecration
  prayer in, 287
entos, meaning of, 138
Entrails, inspection of the, 9, 39
Epaphras, 241
Epaphroditus, in attendance on Paul,
  243
Ephesians, Epistle to the, or *to the Laodi-
  ceans*, 218, 219, 220, 222
Ephesians, letter of Ignatius to the, 262
Ephesus, 23, 32, 62, 94, 96, 105, 107,
  119, 122, 123, 209, 210, 223, 228,
  231, 241, 272, 320
Epimenides, poet, 32, 115, 207
Epiphanius, ecclesiastic, 107

*Epistle of Barnabas, see Barnabas, Epist
  of*
Epistles of Paul, ignored by *Luke*, 115
  so-called "genuine," 222
  pastoral, 217
Esdraelon, plain of, 12
Essenes, Jewish sect, 37
Ethical monotheism of Hebrew pro
  phets, 16, 18, 336
Ethiopic, *Apocalypse of Peter* in, 192
  Didache, translated into, 247
Etruria, 38, 39
Etruscans, 9, 38
  artistic ability of, 39, 44
  legacy of Rome, 39
  vices of, 39
Eucharist, 171, 172, chap. xvi
  alternatives to wine in, 172, 194, 289
    326
  in Justin Martyr, 326, 327
  in the *Didache*, 251, 252, 253
  meaning of term, 251
euergetes, benefactor, royal title, 133
Euphrates, the, river, 1, 4, 5
Europe, Paul in, 205
Eusebius, 106, 192
  Ecclesiastical History, 72, 105, 123, 15
    183, 187, 305, 315, 317
  Life of Constantine, 163
Excommunication, 288
Exile of the Jews, 13
Exodus from Egypt, 6
Exodus, book of, 11, 151, 153, 286
*Exposition of the Oracles of the Lord
  Papias*, 107
Ezekiel, book of, 16
Ezra, book of, 15

Faith, the resurrection, essentials of, 16
  et seq.
Famine "in the days of Claudius," 11
"Fasting baptism," 253, 276
"Fasting communion," 253
Fasting in *Hermas* and *Aristides*, 260, 31
Feeding of the five thousand, 108, 109
  146, 172, 289
  four thousand, 108, 109, 289
Felix, procurator, 212, 213, 214
Fertility, Greek, exhaustion of, 24
Festus, Porcius, procurator, 213, 214
  305
Finite-scale uniformity of nature, 66
Fire, destruction of heaven and eart
  by, 192
Fire of Rome under Nero, *see* Rome
  fire of
First-born, sacrifice of, 42
"Five hundred brethren," resurrectio
  appearance to, 173, 228
Flavia Neapolis, now Nablous, 319

Flavians, dynasty of the, 75, 255, 312
Flavius Josephus, see Josephus, Flavius
Forth, Firth of, 305
"Fortune" of Caesar, equivalent to genius of, 265
"Forty days," 177, 178
Forum, the, at Rome, 55
Fourth Gospel, see John, Gospel according to
Friday, day of the preparation, 250

Gabriel, the angel, 71, 88
Gadara, intellectual centre in Decapolis, 64, 82
Gaius (Caligula), emperor, 47
Galatia, 209, 231
south, 204
Galatians, 231, 232
Galatians, Epistle of Paul to the, 115, 179, 181, 196, 201, 203, 204, 231 et seq., 242, 285
Galen, physician, 64, 313
Galilean accent of Peter, see Peter
missionaries, 207
Galileans, 149, 174
Galilee, 31, 73, 74, 75, 76, 80, 81, 82, 83
lake of, 81, 127, 145, 146, 172, 179
"Galilee of the Gentiles," 83
Galilee, resurrection appearances in, 168, 169, 170, 174, 175
Gallic invasions of Italy, 39
Gallienus, emperor, 335
Gallio, proconsul of Achaia, 114, 201, 208
Gamaliel, rabbi, 112, 113, 200
Gathas, ancient Persian hymns, 19
Gauls, the, 26, 39, 45
Genealogies of Jesus, 72
Genes in the living cell, 66
Genesis, book of, 5, 11, 16, 78, 91, 239, 257, 321, 323
genius, 48, 88, 265
of the City (Rome), 48, 85, 300
of the emperor, worship of, 48, 85, 265, 300
Geography of Strabo, 77, 198
Germans at the circus, Suetonius, 312
Gethsemane, garden of, 150, 155
Gladiatorial shows, 39, 331
gnosis, theological knowledge, 218, 230, 257
Gnosticism, 107, 217, 266
Gnostic movement, 190, 230, 239, 264
God and Jesus, 129, 142 et seq.
"Goddess of a thousand names," Isis, 57
Golgotha, 160, 163, 164
Gomorrah, city of, 190
Good Friday, preachers on, 162
Good Samaritan, parable of, 104

Gospel according to the Egyptians, 256
according to the Hebrews, 173
of Peter, 176
Gospels, the, chap. vii
"memoirs of the apostles," 321
miracles in the, 64 et seq.
Graeco-Roman civilization, 26
decay of, 64, 257, 313, 314
"Great Assize," the, 141
Great Mother of Ida, Cybele, 55, 56, 57
Greece and Persia, war between, 15
depopulated, 206
Greek art, 22, 31
epigrams, Meleager, 82
fertility, 39
influence on Christianity, 31, 32
knowledge of, by Jesus, 83, 133
of Luke, Semitic influences in, 110
politics, 25
religion and morality, 25
Semitic, of Apocalypse, 118
of Septuagint, 30
words in Christianity, 31
Greeks, the, 22 et seq.
qualities of, 15, 22

Hades, 93, 141, 183
Hadrian, emperor, 15, 34, 163, 164, 212, 213, 257, 301, 311, 313, 329
Hagiography, nature of, 261, 265
Hammurabi, 6
Hannibal, 41, 55
and John, virtually the same name, 41, 42
Hasmonaean family, 27, 79
princes, dispute between, 28
opposition of pharisees to, 36
princess, wife of Herod the Great, 124
Hebrew patriarchs, era of, 6
prophecy, 20
prophets, 16, 17, 18
Hebrews, 6
Hebrews, Epistle to the, 90, 91, 92, 96, 217, 219, 255, 279
Gospel according to the, 173
Heliodorus, Seleucid treasurer, 26
Heliopolis, 255
Hellenes, the, 22
Hellenistic civilization, nature of, 25, 26
Heracleitus, 32, 33, 94
Heresy, 190, 191, 263, 264, 266, 335
Heretical Jewish group, Barnabas and, 257
Hermas and divorce, 258
and moral laxity, 259, 335
and the rich, 259
and the second coming of Christ, 259
on sin after baptism, 259, 260, 279, 280

Hermas, Shepherd of, 220, 258 *et seq.,* 278, 280, 318, 319
  date of, 260
  origin of, 260
Hermes, 200
Herod Agrippa I, 107, 124, 181, 185, 213
Herod Agrippa II, 77, 112, 214
Herod Antipas, tetrarch, 81, 112, 146, 147, 159, 269, 271
  leaven of, 147
Herod the Great, 15, 28, 69, 70, 71, 74, 124, 160, 298
  death of, 29
Herodians, 298
Herodotus, 331
Hierapolis, 105
Hieroglyphics, Egyptian, 7
Hillel, Jewish rabbi, 35, 200
Hippocrates of Cos, physician, 23
Hippocratic tradition, disappearance of, 64, 313
Hittites, 10, 11
Holy Communion, 194, 281; *see* Eucharist
  Spirit, use of the term, 270 *et seq.*
"Holy vine of David," 251, 252
Homer, 331
Hosea, 16, 17, 70
Human sacrifice among Semites, 17, 18, 42
Humanism, possibility of a, both scientific and Christian, 34
Humanist, Christian, alienation of, from Paul, 233
  appreciation of *Didache* by, 248
  outlook of, 235
Humour of Jesus, 130
Hunger, Jesus and, 144
Hyksos, invaders of Egypt, 6

Iberians, 40
Ida, mount, 55
Ignatian Letters, 220, 260 *et seq.*
Ignatius, 182, 185, 220, 260 *et seq.*
  cult of his relics, 261
  letter to *Ephesians,* 262
    Philadelphians, 182, 263
    Polycarp, 262, 263
    Romans, 185, 262, 264
    Smyrneans, 262, 263
    Trallians, 264
Ikhnaton (Akhenaten), 9, 18, 20
Ikon, imperial, 308
Ilium, 312
Illyricum, 50, 240
Immanuel, 70
Indo-Europeans, 14, 43
Indus, river, 25
Infant baptism, 277

Ionia, 22, 64
Ionian philosophers, 23
  science, 23
Iranians, 14
Irenaeus, 264
Iron beads, in ancient Egypt, 4
  military use of, 10, 21
Iron-oxide, burial with red, 2
Isaiah, book of, 14, 16, 268, 270, 321
  mistaken reference to, 156
  mistranslation in Septuagint, 70
Iscariot, meaning of, 156
Isis, 56, 57, 58, 314
Israel, kingdom of, 12, 16, 20
Israelites, 10
"Italian band," 333
Italy, 24, 56, 260, 299
Ituraea, 76, 77, 112

Jairus, daughter of, 83
James, the Lord's brother, 37, 114, 173, 179, 181, 203
  death of, 305
Jehovah, 65, 66
  provenance of the name, 17
Jeremiah, book of, 70
Jericho, 73
Jerome, 81, 163, 173, 217
Jerusalem, destruction of, 164
  Jesus in, chap. ix
  Paul's final visit to, 211 *et seq.*
  the new, 93
Jesus, *see* especially chapters v, vi and viii
  age when Galilean ministry began, 76, 77, 78
  birthday of, 79, 80
  brothers and sisters of, 86
  meagre information as to, 117
  no myth, 126
  son of God, chapter vi
  year of birth, 74
Jewish Antiquities of Flavius Josephus, 35, 75, 77, 89, 99, 112, 113, 271, 304, 305
  possible interpolations in, 304, 305
Jewish nationalism, 297
  sects, 34 *et seq.*
Jewish War, of Flavius Josephus, 75
Jews, controversial hostility to, 257
  absence of, in Aristides, 319
  number of, in ancient world, 212
John, Epistles General of, 119
  First Epistle of, 163, 279
  Gospel according to, 32, 33, 118 *et seq.,* 142, 143, 180, 267, 277, 282, 283
    absence of story of Last Supper in, 289
    age of Jesus during his ministry in, 78
    author an eye-witness?, 122

John, Gospel according to—contd.
  author not an apostle, 123
  baptism of Jesus in, 269, 272
  eucharistic theology of, 291, 292
  information as to Passion Week, 151,
    153, 155, 157, 159, 161, 162, 167,
    170, 176, 177
  Jesus as *Logos,* or Word of God, 94,
    95, 96, 97
  last chapter an appendix, 121, 170, 172
  miracles in, 95, 96, 120, 121
  symbolism of, 120, 121
  the three passovers in, 145, 146
John of Ephesus, author of fourth gos-
    pel, 119, 121
John the apostle, 107, 123, 124, 179, 261
  death of, 123, 124
John the Baptist, 37, 76, 80, 110, 267
    et seq.
  Josephus and, 271
John the Presbyter, 105, 106, 107
Jonathan, high priest, 214
Joseph, called Caiaphas, 77; *see also*
    Caiaphas
Joseph, husband of Mary, 69, 71, 72,
    80, 83, 87, 88
  not mentioned by *Mark,* 86
Joseph, prime minister in Egypt, 11, 78
Joseph of Arimathaea, 167
Josephus, Flavius, 26, 35, 36, 75, 77, 81,
    89, 99, 112, 113, 214, 271
  dubious mention of Jesus and James,
    304, 305
Judaea, 11
  return of Jews to, 13
Judah, kingdom of, 12, 13, 20
Judaism, Alexandrian, 94
  and Hellenic culture, 29
  and Law of Moses, 232
  heretical, 257
  in time of Christ, 34
  liberal, 29, 30
  preservation of, 27
Judas Iscariot, 155, 156, 175, 181, 288
  treachery forgotten in 1 *Cor.* xv, 228
Judas Maccabaeus, 27
Judas of Galilee, rebel, 113
Jude, Epistle of, 190
Julian "the apostate," emperor, 60, 335
  house, divine origin of, 88
Julio-Claudians, 46, 63
Julius Africanus, 72
Julius Caesar, 45, 48, 49, 88, 121, 312
Jupiter, 163
Justin Martyr, 177, 206, 207, 221, 282,
    284, 290, 315, 319 *et seq.,* 331
  his end, 329
  First Apology of, 221, 276, 281, 283,
    319 *et seq.*
  Second Apology, of 319 *et seq.*

Dialogue with Trypho the Jew, 319, 320,
    321, 323
Martyrdom of, 320, 329

Kassites, 6, 13
Kerioth, 156
Khafre, 5
Khufu, 5
Kidron valley, 150
King, Greek term for emperor, 189, 303
Kingdom of God, 134 *et seq.,* 325
Kings, valley of the, 9
Kiss, greeting with a holy, 331

Labyrinth, Crete, 21
Lactantius, 43
Lamarckian, 239
Lamb of God, 56, 151, 153
Laodicea, 241
Laodiceans, Epistle to the, 218, 220
  probably *to the Ephesians,* 218, 222
Lares and Penates, 48
Large-scale uniformity of nature, 66
Last Supper, 108, 118, 119, 226, 227,
    247, 251, 252, 281 *et seq.,* 290, 327
  presence of Judas, 288
  was it the passover?, 160 *et seq.*
  of Mithra, 59, 248, 327
Latin words in *Mark,* 109, 110
Laureion, silver mines at, 25
Law, Jewish, students of, 197
Law of Moses, Paul and, 233 *et seq.*
Laws of nature, 66
Lawyers, use of term in New Testa-
    ment, 35
Lazarus, 95, 119, 120, 150
  Rich Man and, parable of, 140
Legion, Roman, constitution of, 85
Leo, writer of *Didache,* 247
Letters between Pliny and Trajan, 307,
    308, 309
Levant, 10, 21, 28, 84, 86, 197, 200
Levantine sovereigns, 133
Levi, son of Alphaeus, 118
Levi, sons of, 35
Lictors, Roman, origin of, 39
Life of Apollonius of Tyana, Philostratus,
    126, 198
Life of Constantine, Eusebius, 163
Life of Flavius Josephus, 75
Lives of eminent philosophers, Diogenes
    Laertius, 87
Lives of the Caesars, Suetonius, 87, 311,
    312
Lives, Plutarch, 197
"Living water," baptism in, 277
Logos (Word), 30, 32, 33, 58, 90, 93, 94
    et seq., 121, 243, 317, 327, 331, 332
  doctrine of Heracleitus, 32 *et seq.,* 94
  prologue to fourth gospel, 32

Lord's Prayer, the, 144
Supper, the, 109, 281, 294, 310; *see also* Eucharist
Lost end of *Mark*, 168, 169
Loyalty to the emperor, expression of, 291, 300
Lucan, stoic poet, 208
Lucian of Samosata, 230
Luke the physician, 114, 205, 243, 245
Luke, the gospel and its author, 110 *et seq.*
Luke, 31, 32, 34, 47, 147, 161, 162, 167, 168, 172, 174, 181, 207, 209, 218, 273, 274, 282, 283, 298, 301, 302; *see also* Q
and baptism of Jesus, 267 *et seq.*
and beginning of ministry of Jesus, 76, 77
and birthday of Jesus, 79
and divorce, 110, 258
and Josephus, 77, 112, 113
and the ascension, 175 *et seq.*
and the Last Supper, 152, 286 *et seq.*, 287, 288
and the life to come, 140, 141
and the resurrection, 169, 170, 282
and the synoptic problem, 98 *et seq.*
and the trial of Jesus, 159
and year of birth of Jesus, 74 *et seq.*
authorship of, and of *Acts,* 113 *et seq.*
birth stories in, 68, 69, 71, 86, 88
date of writing, 99
genealogy of Jesus in, 72
in Justin's *First Apology,* 321
knowledge of Nazareth, 82
quality as an historian, 116
the Emmaus story in, 166, 171
use of the Septuagint, 104
Western Text of, 287
Lydia, convert at Philippi, 205, 277
Lydia, in western Asia Minor, 22, 38
Lyons, persecution at, 315
Lysanias, tetrarch, 76, 77, 112
Lystra, in southern Galatia, 200, 231

Maccabaeus, Judas, 27
Maccabees, books of, 26, 27
Macedon, 25, 26
Macedonia, 114, 204, 205, 210, 226, 231
Machaerus, 271
Magic, sympathetic, 52, 278
Magical change, in baptism, in Hermas, 259
in Justin, 326
in Paul, 234
not Christian, 275
in Justin's eucharistic theology, 327
in pseudo-Pauline eucharistic theology, 293
repudiated in Johannine theology, 292

Magical texts, Egyptian, 8
Magicians, Jewish and Samaritan, 3;
magnificat, 71
Malachi, book of, 79
Malaria, 24, 44
Malta, 114, 214
Mammon, personification of har wealth, 301
Man, antiquity of, 1
neolithic, 2
palaeolithic, 1
Manichaean heresy, 19
Maran atha, 250, 253
Marcellus, 194
Marcion, heretic, 116, 191, 218, 21 222, 266, 284, 321, 322
criticism of, by Justin, 322
Marcus Aurelius, emperor, 46, 64, 26 313, 314, 315, 319, 329, 330, 33 333
epidemic under, 332
financial crisis under, 332
Meditations of, 314
Marius, Roman general, 45
Mark, the gospel and its author, 31, 1 *et seq.*
and Pauline redemption theolog 288
and the Last Supper, 285, 286
its date, 109
lost end of, 168, 169
nature of, 107
Papias, testimony as to, 106
personality of, 108
priority among synoptists, 101
transliterated Latin words in, 10 110
Mark, "interpreter of Peter," 106, 1
the cousin of Barnabas, 243, 245
Marriage, "spiritual," in second ce tury, 229
Martinus, 329
Martyrdom of Polycarp, 265, 319
Martyrdom of the Holy Martyrs, 320, 32
Mary Magdalene, 171
Mary, mother of Jesus, 69, 71, 73, 7 96
at the foot of the cross, 119, 162
calumny against, 89
Mass, Black, 295
the, 252, 287
Matthew, the customs officer, 118
Matthew, the gospel and its author, 3 38, 83, 85, 99, 107, 117, 118, 11 159, 180, 221, 249, 250, 254, 28 297, 299, 300; *see also* Q
ancient regard for, 98, 165
and baptism, 267, 268, 269
and the arrest of Jesus, 155, 156
and the ascension, 175, 177

atthew, and the burial of Jesus, 167,168
and the crucifixion, 160, 161, 163
and the eucharist, 152, 286
and the primacy of Peter, 183, 184
and the resurrection, 169, 173
and the synoptic problem, 99 *et seq.*
birth stories in, 68, 69, 86, 87, 88
contrasts with *Luke*, 71
date of birth of Jesus, 74
genealogy of Jesus, 72
midrash in, 103, 104
testimony of Papias, 106
use of doublets, 103
use of Old Testament, 70
use of term Nazarene, 80
edes, 13, 14
edicine, deterioration of, in antiquity,
    64, 313
Hippocratic, 23, 64
edieval paintings and frescoes, 39
editations of Marcus Aurelius, 314
elchizedek, 91
eleager at Gadara, 82
enander, poet, 32, 228
endelian inheritance, 89
enkaure, 6
esopotamia, 4, 5
astrology and divination in, 9
cuneiform inscriptions of, 7
irrigation in, 5
essiah, the, 37
essianic hopes, 135
etaphysics, Greek, 23
icah, prophecy of, 70
teaching of, 18
drash, in Matthew, 103, 104
iletus, in Ionia, 23, 211
ilitary service of Christians, earliest
    records of, 333
inistry of Jesus, length of, 144
success or failure?, 146
inos, of Crete, 21
inos, poem of Epimenides, 207
inotaur, the, 21
inucius Fundanus, Hadrian's letter to,
    329
iracle of Cana, and coming of *Logos*,
    96, 121
of Christianity, the supreme, 174
iracles, chapter iv, 116, 164
ishnah, the, 35
ithra, Persian god, 50, 52, 58 *et seq.*,
    79, 85, 93, 197, 199, 248, 290, 310,
    323, 327
altar-piece of, 59
Phrygian dress of, 59
ithraic fraternities, 51
legend, the, 59
ithraism, overthrow of, 60
rivalry with Christianity, 290

Mithraists, persecution of, 335
Moab, Hebrew tribe, 10, 17
Moabite stone, 17
Monism, stoic, 33, 94, 241
Monotheism, ethical, 16, 18, 125, 336
    of Akhenaten, 9, 18
    opportunist, 337
    pagan, 317
    solar, 18
Montanist heresy, 187
Morality, early Christian, 237, 259, 317,
    319, 324, 330, 331
Mosaic food laws, *Barnabas* and, 257
    Law, 233
    and pharisees, 35
    redivision of land under, 212
Moses, 6, 9, 10, 16, 20, 193
    and invasion of Palestine, 11
"Mother of tenderness," Isis, 57
Mother, the Great, of Ida, Cybele, 55,
    56
Mount of Olives, 149, 150, 192
Mount Olympus, gods of, 24, 318, 331
Mycenaean, civilization, 21
Mycenaeans, 10
Mysteries, Egyptian, 331
Mystery-cults and Graeco-Roman civi-
    lization, 54
Mystery-religions, chapter iii, 295, 296
    and Justin Martyr, 322, 323
    and Paul, 199, 238, 243
    nature of, 50
Muratorian Canon, 260

Nablous (Flavia Neapolis), in Samaria,
    319
Nazarene, Jesus called a, 70, 80
    Jesus the, 80, 81, 168, 180
Nazareth, 69 *et seq.*, 80, 81, 82
    economic conditions of, 132
    population of, 82
    water supply of, 81
Nebuchadrezzar, 12, 13
Nehemiah, book of, 15
Neo-Babylonian empire, 13
Neolithic civilization, 2, 3
Nero, emperor, 92, 208, 214, 305, 306
    murder of, 46
    penal measures in time of, 312
    persecution under, 47, 111, 112, 185,
        194, 215, 306
Nero, Life by Suetonius, 312
New Testament, 47, 62, 64, 192, 247,
    258, 260, 262, 264, 266, 289, 314,
    317
    earliest fragment of, 123
    earliest manuscripts of, 258
    early strata of, 184
    miracles in, 67
Nicaea, Council of, 152

Nicodemus, 119, 167
Nile, the river, 1, 4, 5
Nineveh, 9, 13
Nisan, month, 150 *et seq.*
Noah, in the days of, 190
Numbers, book of, 78, 91
numen, 48
numina, 47

Octavian, *see* Augustus
Oedipodean incests, 315, 330
Oedipus, 330
Old Testament, formation of, 15, 16
  immortality in, 20
  hints of religious evils in, 42
  use by Justin, 320
  used for prophetic texts, 69, 70, 84, 117
Olives, mount of, 149, 150, 192
Olympic festival, Herod and the, 28
Olympus in Cilicia, 197
  mount, deities of, 24, 318, 331
Onesimus, slave, 245
"Oracles," or "Sayings," 106, 107
  Sibylline, 55
Orientalized Judaism, 241
Origen, 318, 331, 332, 333, 334
Origen, *Against Celsus*, 89, 318, 331 *et seq.*, 334
Origin of species, Darwin, 219
"Original sin," 240, 275, 276
Orpheus, 53
Orphic theology and Orphism, 53, 54
Osiris, lord of the dead, 7, 52, 57, 58
Ostian way, 187
Oxyrhynchus, Egypt, 138

Pacifism, Christian, 237, 297, 299, 300, 330, 333, 334
Pacifists, Christian, before a modern tribunal, 311
Painting, Greek, 2, 22
Palaeolithic civilization, 2
Palestine in early times, 9, 10, 11
Pallas, freedman, 213, 214
Palm Sunday, 146
Pantheism, of stoics, 94
  solar, 60
Panthera, transformation of *parthenos*, 89
Papias, 105, 106, 107, 123, 144, 145, 192, 220
Papyri, Aramaic, 29
Papyrus-fragments, 122, 138
Paradise, 202
Passing of Peregrinus, Lucian, 230
Passover, ritual at the, 152
  was the Last Supper a—?, 151 *et seq.*, 288
Passovers, number in fourth gospel, 145, 146
Pastoral epistles, 217

Patmos, isle of, 92
Patricians and plebeians at Rome, 4
Paul, 38, 43, 47, 84, 87, 90, 94, 98, 1
  142, 179, chap. xii, 333
  a married man, 182, 183
  a Roman citizen, 196, 199, 205, 2
    et seq.
  and humanism, 235
  and Judaism, 232 *et seq.*
  apostasy of, 199
  conversion of, 201 *et seq.*
  end of, 111, 112, 215, 216
  "kinsmen" of, 197
  revelation of the Lord to, 201, 202, 2
  weak eyesight of, 200
Pauline literature and Justin, 321
Paulus, Sergius, *see* Sergius Paulus
Pentateuch, 16
Pentecost, 175, 181, 274
Peraea, ruled by Archelaus, 81
Peregrinus, religious adventurer, 23
Pergamon, 59
Persecution of early Christians, 92, 1
    123, 194, 265, 298
  as described by Pliny, 307 *et seq.*
  as described by Tacitus, 306
  under Domitian, 303
  under Marcus Aurelius, 315
  under Nero, 306
  under Trajan, 261
Perseus, 325
Persia, 6, 37
Persian beliefs among the Jews, 65
  empire, 14, 15, 19, 197
    destruction of, 25
  religion, Mithra in, 58, 59, 60
  scriptures, 19
Pessinus, 55
Pestilence, under Marcus Aurelius, 3
petalon of the high priest, 123
Peter, *see* chapters x and xi
  a married man, 182, 183
  and Paul conjoined, 184 *et seq.*, 19
  and Pentecost, 274
  and the resurrection, 168, 171, 17
    175, 176
  books ascribed to, *see* chapter xi
  end of, 181, 182
  Galilean accent of, 180
  in Rome?, 185 *et seq.*, 243
  Mark interpreter of, 106, 144, 145
  primacy of, in the church, 183, 18
Peter, Acts of, 194
  Apocalypse of, 184, 192, 193
  First Epistle of, 184, 185, 303
    date of, 190
  Gospel of, 176, 184, 193
  Second Epistle of, 184, 190
    reference to Paul in, 116, 191
    the transfiguration in, 191, 192

Pharisee and Publican, parable of, 104
  Paul a, 233, 244
Pharisees, 34 *et seq.*, 212, 233
  Jesus and the, 36
Philadelphians, letter of Ignatius to the, 182, 263
Philemon, 245
Philemon, Epistle of Paul to, 241, 244, 245
Philip of Macedon, 25
Philip, the apostle, 105, 106, 183
Philip, the tetrarch, 77
Philippi, in Macedonia, 114, 205, 333
Philippians, Epistle of Paul to the, 183, 199, 241, 243, 244
  Letter of Polycarp to the, 264
Philistines, 10, 12
Philo, 34, 94, 198
Philostratus, early third-century writer, 126, 198
Phoenicia, 12, 18, 42, 53, 94, 146
Phoenicians, culture of, 20, 22
  trading stations of, 38
Phoenix, Clement's story of the, 255
Phrygia, 55, 204
Phrygian dress of Mithra, 59
Phrygian-Lycaonian population, 231
Physics, ancient, 23
  foundations of modern, 23
Pilgrim's Progress, Bunyan, 119, 258
Pilate, Pontius, procurator, 77, 150, 158, 159, 160, 306
Pilate's wife, dream of, 104, 159
Pius, bishop of Rome, 260
Plato and Platonism, 23, 31, 87, 207, 317, 320
Platonic teaching, 175
Plea (or *Embassy*) *of Athenagoras*, 330
"Pleroma," fullness of God's being, 242
Pliny, the elder, 307
Pliny, the younger, 210, 253, 261, 304, 306, 307 *et seq.*, 310, 311
Pliny and Trajan, *Letters* between, 307, 308, 309
Plutarch, 24, 197
  Lives, 197
Polycarp, 220, 221, 261, 264, 265
Polycarp, letter of Ignatius to, 262, 263
Polycarp, Martyrdom of, 265, 319
Polycarp to the Philippians, Letter of, 221, 264
Polycrates, bishop of Ephesus, 123
Polytheism, Syrian, 17
Pompey, Roman general, 45, 197
Pontius Pilate, *see* Pilate
  "Acts" of, 322
Pontus, in Asia Minor, 208, 322
Population of Roman empire, 299
"Praise of Love," 226, 230, 255
Pre-existent Lord, Jesus as, 243, 244

Priest and victim, 91
  the, as butcher, 291
Priority of *Mark* among the synoptists, 101
Priscilla, 208
Prodigal Son, parable of, 31, 104
Prophets of Israel, eighth-century, 16, 20
  Hebrew, originality of, 19
Proverbs, book of, 29, 30
Psalms, 16, 90, 91, 321
  dates of certain, 16
Ptolemies, Egyptian rulers, 26
Ptolemy, and Serapis, 57
Ptolemy, son of Mennaeus, 77
Punic, or Carthaginian, religion, 42
  speech, 43
  stock, the, 43
Puteoli, Italian port, 214
Pythagoras, mystic and mathematician, 53, 54, 198

Q, the second source, 99 *et seq.*, 117, 126 *et seq.*, 184, 193, 250, 268, 269, 270, 273, 275, 299, 300, 301
Quadratus, second-century apologist, 317
Quarto-decimans, 151
Quirinius, legate of Syria, census of, 74, 75, 76, 77, 113
  Justin's error, 322
  personality of, 76

Rachel, 70
Ramah, 70
Red Sea, crossing of, 11
Relics, cult of, 261
Religion, ancient Egyptian, 7, 8
  nature of primitive, 51
  Roman, 47
  Sumerian-Semitic, 8, 9
Resurrection of Jesus, 164, 168 *et seq.*
  cautious attitude of Aristides, 319
  in 1 *Corinthians* xv, 172, 173
  nature of, 164, 165
  second-century defence of, 317, 325
Resurrection, doctrine of, in Old Testament, 20
  of the body, 139
  teaching of Jesus as to, 140
Revelation of St. John the Divine, see Apocalypse
Rhodes, 114
Rich Man and Lazarus, parable of, 140, 302
Ritual murders and anti-Semitism, 42
"Rod of iron," 93
Roman character, 44
  citizen, Paul a, 196, 228
  citizens, remitted to Rome for trial, 199, 308, 309

Roman—*contd.*
  empire, estimated population of, 299
  financial administration, 46
  names changed by adoption, 318
  religion and Christianity, 48
  republic, disintegration of, 45
  virtues, 48
Romans, 15, 43 *et seq.*
  influence of Etruscans upon, 38
Romans, Epistle of Paul to the, 73, 185,
    197, 210, 215, 233 *et seq.*, 278, 302,
    303
  final salutations in, 240, 241
Romans, letter of Ignatius to the, 185,
    262, 264
Rome, 62, 114, 195, 236, 260, 261, 304
  Etruscan kings of, 38
  fire of, 111, 185, 194, 215, 237, 303,
    306
  foundation of, 38
  genius of, 48, 85
  Mark written at—?, 109, 110
  Paul at, 214, 215, 216, 305
  sacked by Gauls, 45
Rosetta stone, 7
"Rudiments" or "elementals," 241
Russian steppes, 297
Rusticus, prefect of Rome, 329
Rylands library, Manchester, 122

Sacrifice, human, among Semites, 17,
    18, 42
Sacrificial animals, market for, 308
Sadducees, 34, 36, 139, 212
"St. John, Apostle and Evangelist," 124
Salammbô, 42
Salonica, in ancient times Thessalonica,
    114, 206, 243
Samaria, woman of, 119
Samaritan, Justin a, 319
Samaritan magicians, 37
Samnites, 45
Samos, Ionian island, 23
Samuel, second book of, 78
Samuel, time of, 16
Sanhedrin, 112, 153, 157, 158, 167, 212,
    305
Satan, 37
Satrapies, Persian, 15
Saul, 115, 181, 196, 200; *see* Paul
saulos, waddling, 196
Saviour-God, 52, 289
Scipio, 41, 55
Scribes, Jewish, 34
Scythians, 297, 298
Second coming of Christ, 192, 224, 225,
    236, 249, 255, 259, 276
Second source, or Q, 99 *et seq.*; *see
    also* Q
Seleucid kings, 15, 26 *et seq.*

Seleucus, 26
Semites and Sumerians, 4, 5
Semites, north African, 43
Semitic uses, in *Apocalypse,* 92
  in *Luke,* 104, 110
Semo Sancus, Sabine deity, 322
Senate, Roman, 45, 46, 48, 57, 321, 329
Seneca, stoic teacher and statesman, 94,
    208, 304
Septimius Severus, emperor, 43
Septuagint, the, 30, 69, 70, 90, 104, 198,
    236, 238, 270
Serapeum, at Alexandria, 57
Serapis, cult of, 57
Sergius Paulus, proconsul of Cyprus,
    196, 333
Sermon on the Mount, 99, 117, 250
"Severe" letter to the Corinthians, 225,
    231
Sheol, 20
Shepherd of Hermas, see Hermas
Shiloh, 323
Shishak, 12
Sibylline oracles, 55
Sicily, 24
Sidon, in Phoenicia, 12, 145, 146
Silas, or Silvanus, companion of Paul,
    205, 206
Silvanus, or Silas, companion of Paul,
    223
Simon Bar-Jonah, 183
Simon Magus, 322
Simon Peter, 155, 179, 180; *see* Peter
Simon the leper, 150
Sin after baptism, 259, 260, 279, 280
Sinaiticus, Codex, 256, 258
Sinope, 191
"Slaughter of the innocents," 70, 71
Slavery, Roman, 49, 301
  and Christianity, 245
Smyrna, 261
Smyrnaeans, letter of Ignatius to the, 262,
    263
Social conditions of early Christians, 63
Socialist sympathies of early Christians,
    297, 301, 302
Socrates, 23, 24, 207
Sodom, 92
  and Gomorrah, 190
Solar pantheism and Mithraism, 60
Soli, in Cilicia, 207
Solomon, king, 6, 12, 16, 41, 129
Solomon's porch, in the temple, 80, 181
Son of man, 37
Soviet government, 256
Spain, 2, 24, 215, 240
Spaniards, 26
  Romanized, 208
speculator, 110
Spiritual marriage, 229

Star-goddess in the *Apocalypse*, 93
Star out of Judah, 91
Stephen, 37, 181, 195, 238
    date of martyrdom of, 201
Stoic monists, 33, 94, 241
Stoics and stoicism, 33 *et seq.*, 125, 208
Strabo, geographer, 77, 197
"Substance," 129
Suetonius, historian, 87, 116, 121, 208,
    311, 312
Suez, isthmus of, 6
Sulla, Roman general, 39, 45
Sumerians, 4, 20
    pictographic writing of, 4
Sumerian-Semitic religion, 8
Sunday, the Lord's day, 93, 253, 310
    worship on, according to Justin, 321,
    328
Superstitious world, a, in antiquity, 65
Susa, 6
Sympathetic magic, 52
Synoptic gospels, definition of, 98
    problem, 99 *et seq.*
Syracuse, 214
Syria, 9, 10, 76, 79, 86, 147, 203, 204
Syriac version of Ignatian *Letters*, 262
Syrian calendar, ancient, 124
    gospel, *Matthew* a—?, 117
    paganism, 20
Syro-phoenician woman, 145

Taboo in Roman religion, 47
Tacitus, 94, 116, 237, 304, 305 *et seq.*
    Annals, 306
    Histories, 57, 120, 312
Talmud, 35, 128
Tanit, Carthaginian goddess, 42
Tarsus, in Cilicia, 196, 197, 198, 199,
    200
taurobolium, 52
Tell el-Amarna, Egypt, 9
Temple, the, at Jerusalem, 28, 35, 80,
    146, 181
Temptation of Jesus, 143, 300
Tertullian, 42, 43, 191, 333
    Against Marcion, 218
Text, Western, of *Luke*, 287
Thebes, Egypt, 9
Theism, ethical, of Akhenaten, 9
Thessalonians, Epistles to the, 208, 223,
    224, 225
Theudas, pseudo-Messiah, 113
Thomas, apostle, 121, 175, 176, 263
Thrace, 53
Thucydides, 31
Thyestean banquets, 315, 330
Thyestes, 330
Tiber, the river, 322
Tiberias of Galilee, 81, 82, 83
    and Jesus, 81, 83

Tiberius, emperor, 47, 76, 81, 112, 306
Tiberius Alexander, procurator, 113
Tiglath-pileser, 83
Tigris, the river, 1, 4, 5
Timiotinian bath, 329
Timothy, 218, 223, 224
Timothy, First Epistle to, 217, 218, 219
    Second Epistle to, 215, 216, 217
Titan-born world, 54
Titans, the, 53
Titus, emperor, 75, 164, 257
Titus, companion of Paul, 203, 226
Titus, Epistle to, 207, 217
Tomb, the empty, 168 *et seq.*
Totemistic religion, in ancient Egypt, 7
Trachonitis, 76, 77, 112
Trajan, emperor, 120, 253, 261, 306,
    307, 309, 313, 315, 316
Trallians, letter of Ignatius to the, 264
Transfiguration of Jesus, 143, 145, 191,
    192, 193
Travel-diary of Luke, 113, 114
Trial of Jesus, the Jewish, 157
    by Herod, 159
    by Pilate, 158, 159
Tribute to Caesar, 298, 302, 325
Troas, 114, 210, 226
Trojan war, 10
Troy, 204
Tutankhamen, 9
Two Ways, The, 248, 250, 258, 318
Tyana, in Cappadocia, 126
Tyre, in Phoenicia, 12, 25, 40, 114, 145,
    146

"Uniform repetition of likenesses," 66
Uniformity of nature, 66, 108
"Unknown god," 207
Ur of the Chaldees, 20

Valley of the Kings, Thebes, 9
Vatican, 187
Vaticanus, Codex, 258
Venice, 40
Venus, 164
Vespasian, emperor, 120, 121, 213
Vesta and the Vestal Virgins, 48
Vesuvius, eruption of, 307
viculus, applied to Nazareth, 81
Village life of Jesus, 126
"Vine of David," *see* "Holy vine of
    David"
Virgil, 208
Virgin birth, among insects, 88
    biological possibility of a, 88
Virgin birth of Jesus, the, 67, 70, 72, 87,
    96, 317, 319, 324, 325
    and *Logos* doctrine, 97
    bizarre equivalent of, 93
    cautious statement of Aristides, 319

Virgin birth of Jesus, the—*contd.*
    defence of, by Justin, 325
    source of calumny, 89
Virgin "daughter," 229

Water and blood, symbolism of, 163
Way, the (Christian), 200, 202, 213, 224, 242
Ways, The Two, 248, 250, 258, 318
Wealth, and its abuses during rise of Christianity, 301
Weaving, discovery of, 3
"We-passages," in *Acts,* 113, 114, 115
Western churches and synods, 151
Western Text of *Luke,* 287
Whitsunday, 178
Wine at eucharist, mixed with water, 326
    replaced by fish, 109, 172
    replaced by water, 172, 194, 283
Wisdom literature, of the Jews, 16
Wisdom of Solomon, 16, 30, 140, 270, 285
Witch, test of a suspected, 293
Woman of Samaria, 119
Women at worship in church, in 1 *Corinthians,* 229, 230

not admitted to Mithraic fraternities, 51, 59
Word, translation of *Logos,* 32, 94, 95, 327; *see Logos*
World-control, winning of, by Rome, 44 *et seq.*
Worship, Christian, according to Justin, 325 *et seq.*
    according to Pliny, 310
    according to the *Didache,* 247 *et seq.*
Writing, discovery of, 3, 5

Yahweh (Jehovah), 17, 42
"Year of the four emperors," 46
Yokefellow, synonym for wife, 183

Zacharias, father of John the Baptist, 71, 76
Zama, battle of, 41
Zebedee, 179
    sons of, 123, 124
Zechariah, book of, 156
Zeno, founder of stoicism, 33, 94
Zeus, 27, 53, 200
Zoroaster, Persian sage, 18, 19, 37, 60